BUSINESS
COMBINATIONS &
INTERNATIONAL
ACCOUNTING

Hartwell C. Herring III
Professor of Accounting, Utica College

THOMSON
SOUTH-WESTERN

Australia · Canada · Mexico · Singapore · Spain · United Kingdom · United States

THOMSON

SOUTH-WESTERN

Business Combinations & International Accounting, 1e
Hartwell C. Herring III

Editor-in-Chief:
Jack W. Calhoun

Vice President/Team Director:
Melissa S. Acuña

Publisher:
Bill Schoof

Senior Developmental Editor:
Sara E. Wilson

Senior Marketing Manager:
Julie Lindsay

Production Editor:
Salvatore N. Versetto

Manufacturing Coordinator:
Doug Wilke

Compositor:
Navta Associates, Inc.

Printer:
West Group
Eagan, Minnesota

Design Project Manager:
Michelle Kunkler

Cover and Internal Designer:
Ellen Pettengell Design
Chicago, Illinois

Cover Painting:
©2001 Frank Stella/Artists Rights
Society (ARS)
New York, New York

Media Developmental Editor:
Sally Nieman

Media Production Editor:
Lora I. Craver

**Library of Congress Cataloging-in-
Publication Data**
Herring, Hartwell, C.
   Business combinations and interna-
tional accounting / Hartwell C.
Herring, III.
      p. cm.
   Includes bibliographical references
and index.
    ISBN 0-538-87893-2 (alk. paper)
    1. Consolidation and merger of
corporations—Accounting. 2.
Corporations—Accounting. I. Title.

HF 5686.C7 H429 2003
657'.96—dc21

                    2001047397

PREFACE

Accounting educators are being challenged to revolutionize curriculum structure, curriculum goals, and the relative emphasis placed on student skills as compared with student knowledge. *Business Combinations and International Accounting* provides the professor with a resource that can be used to teach a class in different ways. As key components of a course that places greater emphasis on skills development, this text covers the essential issues in business combinations and international accounting. In such an environment, this book would not be the driver of the course in the way that traditional Advanced Accounting books are written. The set of nine chapters would be used as a springboard resource in a course that includes research projects, student presentations, case studies, and role playing exercises.

Alternatively, the Advanced Accounting course can be taught using different modules to cover only those topics needed to meet the course goals. *Business Combinations and International Accounting* is one in a series of modules from which to choose. This series allows instructors the flexibility of selecting specific topics for coverage in their course. As of January, 2002, the additional modules available include *Today's Essentials of Governmental and Not-For-Profit Accounting and Reporting* by Martin and West (0-324-11164-9) and *Accounting for Partnerships* by Stokes (0-324-12098-2). Contact the publisher for information about the availability of other modules.

Key Features

Focus on Core Content: This innovative module by Hartwell Herring covers the basic principles of business combinations and international accounting in a straightforward manner. Core topics are presented step-by-step so readers can easily understand the concepts and procedures involved in business mergers and consolidations and in accounting for foreign exchange transactions and reporting.

Current Coverage: The most recent GAAP is applied to the content in this module. The FASB Statements No. 141 and 142 are clearly presented. The coverage of pooling of interests is presented in its own chapter to allow course content flexibility.

Topical Approach: Using the topical approach allows readers to develop and build upon their understanding and accounting skills as they proceed through the module.

Interpretive Exercises: Strategically placed within the body of the chapters, these exercises direct readers to apply what they have learned to a variety of situations. New data or other assumptions are provided along with specific questions to be answered. These exercises assist readers as they gradually increase their understanding of the chapter content.

Conceptual Questions and Reflection: To enhance reader understanding of the basic reasoning behind the process, the author has included questions that focus on how different accounting choices and approaches impact reported information.

Ties to the Real World: Information gleaned from business publications and from actual financial reports is used to illustrate chapter concepts and the role of accounting in the business community.

Objective-based Learning: Each chapter begins with a series of clearly-stated, measurable learning objectives that help readers focus on specific learning goals. These objectives are repeated at the beginning of the content summary.

Supporting Materials

The printed **Instructor's Resource Manual** (0-324-02383-9) presents solutions to the assignments and the complete test bank.

The **Instructor's Resource CD** (0-324-02381-2) contains the electronic files for the solutions to the assignments, the test bank, and the PowerPoint® slides for display in the classroom.

Several of these resources and other supporting content are available on the Advanced Accounting Modular Series Web site (http://advanced.swcollege.com).

Acknowledgments

Helpful feedback on the content of this text was received from several individuals throughout the development of the chapters. I extend a special thank you to all who have assisted me. In particular, I wish to acknowledge the following individuals who shared their detailed comments and suggestions:

James Chiu, California State University—Northridge
Lola Dudley, Eastern Illinois University
Donald Edwards, University of Arkansas at Little Rock
Jack Ethridge, Stephen F. Austin State University
Robert Needham, Bucknell University
James Reburn, Samford University
Charles Tritschler, Purdue University
Donald Wallin, The Ohio State University

Hartwell C. Herring, III

ABOUT THE AUTHOR

Hartwell C. Herring III is Professor of Accounting at Utica College in Utica, New York. A CPA, Dr. Herring received BBA and MS degrees from The University of Mississippi and his Ph.D. from The University of Alabama. He was also an accounting faculty member at The University of Tennessee for twenty-seven years, where he rose to the rank of Professor of Accounting. During his career, Professor Herring has published extensively, particularly on subjects related to accounting education, including articles in *Issues in Accounting Education*, *Management Accounting*, and *Journal of Accounting Education*. He has also written professionally-published continuing education materials and was co-author of the monograph, *A Framework for the Development of Accounting Education Research*, published by the American Accounting Association. His research support includes funding from the AICPA, The Haskins & Sells Foundation, The American Accounting Association, and The Coopers & Lybrand Foundation. He currently serves as an associate editor of *Accounting Education*, an international journal and has served on the editorial boards of both *Issues in Accounting Education* and *Journal of Accounting Education*.

Dr. Herring has taught all areas of financial accounting, including principles, intermediate, advanced, international, governmental accounting, and accounting for not-for-profit organizations. He is a member of the American Accounting Association, the Institute of Management Accountants, and the American Association of University Professors. During summer vacations and holidays, Dr. Herring enjoys hiking and camping with his wife Polly. He also enjoys the study of French language and culture and has traveled extensively in France.

TABLE OF CONTENTS

This book is dedicated to my wife: Paulette

And to my children: Joseph, Catherine, and Christina

BUSINESS COMBINATIONS

A business combination occurs when two or more companies come under common ownership. This combining can occur in two ways: (1) one company can acquire all of the assets and assume all of the liabilities of another company or (2) one company can acquire a controlling interest in the outstanding common stock of another company, creating a parent-subsidiary relationship. Chapter 1 of this book explains the theory and illustrates the procedures for the first type of combination following the currently accepted **purchase method** of accounting. Accounting for the second type of business combination, the parent-subsidiary relationship, is more complex. The basic theory and practice of accounting for subsidiaries is covered in Chapters 2 through 7. Since subsidiary ownership involves an investment in common stock, Chapter 2 reviews accounting for common stock investments, particularly the procedures for applying the equity method of accounting. Chapters 3 through 6 explain the theory and practice of preparing consolidated financial statements for a parent company and its subsidiaries where the subsidiary was also acquired using the purchase method of accounting. In July 2001, the Financial Accounting Standards Board finalized rules that make the purchase method of accounting the only acceptable method for all business combinations. However, a second method of accounting for business combinations, called the **pooling of interest method,** was used for many business combinations until very recently. Chapter 7 explains how this method affects the balance sheet and results of operations of both types of business combinations. While not permitted under current accounting rules, the pooling of interest method of accounting will continue to affect financial reporting as long as subsidiaries acquired using this accounting method are owned.

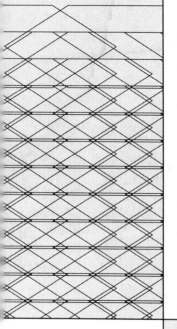

CHAPTER 1

BUSINESS COMBINATIONS INVOLVING THE MERGER OR CONSOLIDATION OF NET ASSETS

LEARNING OBJECTIVES

- Explain the business and economic incentives for business combination transactions
- Describe the two basic types of business combinations
- Account for mergers/consolidations using the purchase method
- State the financial statement disclosures required for purchase method mergers/consolidations

THE BUSINESS AND ECONOMIC INCENTIVES FOR BUSINESS COMBINATIONS

On December 16, 1996, the headlines in *USA Today* announced, "Aerospace Giants to Merge." The related articles went on to describe how The Boeing Company and McDonnell Douglas Corporation planned to form a single company in an arrangement whereby Boeing would acquire $13.3 billion of McDonnell Douglas stock. The plan called for McDonnell Douglas shareholders to receive .65[1] shares of Boeing common stock in exchange for each share of McDonnell Douglas common stock. This merger agreement, which was completed in July 1997, created a major corporation in the defense industry, rivaling Lockheed-Martin in size. It left only two companies in the world in the business of manufacturing large commercial jetliners. The remaining competitor is Airbus Industrie, a consortium of companies in Great Britain, France, Germany, and Spain. During the decade of the 1990s, the combined Boeing-McDonnell Douglas had an average market share of about two-thirds of the total worldwide market for large commercial jetliners. The addition of McDonnell Douglas defense contracts also greatly increased Boeing's penetration into that segment of the aerospace industry.

The decision to proceed with a business combination is affected by both positive and negative events. Both types of events were apparent in the Boeing-McDonnell Douglas plan. After a defense department review of initial proposals, Boeing and Lockheed-Martin were the two remaining companies competing for the U.S. Military $350 billion joint strike fighter contract. Boeing will benefit from McDonnell Douglas's expertise in competing for this contract. McDonnell Douglas, on the other hand, was no longer in a strong position to remain independent in a shrinking defense market, having been eliminated by the defense department as a potential contractor for a large military contract. Moreover, its share of the large commercial jetliner market was less than 5% of the total worldwide market. By combining, these companies hoped to reduce the risks associated with doing business because the new combined entity would be more diverse than either company was separately.

This example demonstrates that business combinations are undertaken for a variety of legitimate business reasons and that several reasons usually exist for any particular situation. In a business environment where competitive forces are constantly changing, the ability to form new companies from existing ones is an efficient way for companies to adjust to these forces, allowing all stakeholders to ultimately benefit. Following is a summary of some of the important motivations for forming business combinations, including those apparent in the above example.

- Horizontal and vertical integration—Horizontal integration involves combining with companies in the same line of business. Recent examples include combinations in the communications industry such as the Bell Atlantic-NYNEX[2] combination in 1996. The core business of these two companies is telephone communications. As the communications industry becomes more deregulated, industry analysts expect further consolidation of telephone services throughout the United States. Vertical integration involves acquisition of companies that serve as suppliers to or customers of the acquiring company. Vertical integration is common in many industries. An excellent example is the petroleum industry, where all the major companies have operations in three vertically related segments—exploration and production, refining, and marketing.

---

[1] This exchange ratio was later revised to 1.3 shares of Boeing for each share of McDonnell Douglas when Boeing stock was split two for one prior to the date the acquisition became final.

[2] Bell Atlantic changed its name to Verizon Corporation in 2000.

- Diversification to manage business risks—A diversified business organization engages in several different kinds of businesses in order to minimize the effects of risk on the combined entity. Business risks associated with the business cycle, product liability, and changing markets may sometimes be reduced through diversification. An excellent example of a diversified company is the General Electric Company, which had sales revenue in 1999 of $60.9 billion.[3] Its largest segment, industrial products and systems, accounts for only 19% of this total. Its other businesses include such diverse segments as aircraft engines, broadcasting, home appliances, and locomotives.

- Avoid a hostile takeover—Sometimes management may agree to combine with another company in order to avoid being acquired by a company that is viewed as being an undesirable partner. While rarely admitting so, the management of a company that is the target of a hostile takeover may fear that the acquisition will result in the termination of their employment. However, managements usually posture their opposition to hostile takeover bids in terms of the adverse affects on existing shareholders. A case in point is the merger of Pennzoil and Quaker State in the aftermath of Pennzoil's rejection of a hostile takeover bid by Union Pacific Resources Group in 1997.

- Retirement of key shareholder/managers—Smaller, closely held companies are sometimes offered for sale because key shareholder/managers plan to retire and wish to diversify their assets. The retiring management may also need to raise cash in anticipation of the need to pay estate taxes.

TYPES OF BUSINESS COMBINATIONS

There are essentially two types of business combinations—**merger/consolidation and stock acquisition.** In a merger, one or more companies are **merged** into an existing company or into a new company organized to facilitate the combination. When a new company is formed from the merger of two or more companies, the combination is usually called a **consolidation.** However, both a **merger** and a **consolidation** are essentially the same type of combination: one in which the assets and liabilities of two or more companies are combined into a single company. The other type of business combination is called an **acquisition of stock.** In an **acquisition of stock,** one company (the **parent company**) acquires more than 50% of the outstanding voting common stock of another company (the **subsidiary company**). Subsequent to acquisition both companies remain separate entities, but their financial statements are combined for purposes of external reporting. The combined financial statements of a parent company and its subsidiaries are called **consolidated financial statements.**[4]

---

[3] This total is General Electric's revenue from all businesses except financial services. General Electric Capital Services, Inc., a financial services subsidiary, had an additional $55.7 billion of revenue.

[4] When reading news articles, proxy statements, corporate annual reports, and other documents where business combinations are reported, one invariably encounters a substantial amount of confusion regarding the terms used in the paragraph. For example, in proxy statements and other legal documents, as well as in the business press, the term **merger** is often used in a very general sense to indicate that a business combination has occurred. In particular, the term **merger** is frequently used to refer to what is actually an **acquisition of stock** in a technical accounting sense. In this textbook as well as in all cases where technical accounting issues are discussed, it is imperative that we use the terms **merger, consolidation,** and **acquisition of stock** to describe specific types of business combinations, as has been done in this paragraph.

Merger/Consolidation

As the term **merger** implies, only a single company survives after the combination. A company acquired in a **merger** transfers its assets and liabilities to the books of the acquiring company and is then liquidated. Normally this transfer is accomplished by having the shareholders of the acquired company exchange all of their shares for cash and/or securities of the acquiring company. The acquired company is then liquidated, and the surviving company records its assets and liabilities. A **consolidation** of two companies involves creating a new company into which the two companies are merged rather than having one of the two original companies merged into the other. Both **mergers** and **consolidations** are characterized by a combination of the participating companies' assets and liabilities. In both arrangements, only one company remains after the combination. Because the acquired companies are dissolved, both **mergers** and **consolidations** can only be accomplished if 100% of the companies are combined. Figure 1-1 illustrates the features of a merger and a consolidation.

FIGURE 1-1 Merger of Company B into Company A

Phase 1: Acquisition of Common Stock

Company A → Cash or other Consideration → Company B Shareholders
Company B Shareholders → 100% of Company B common stock (Investment in Company B recorded) → Company A

Then, Phase 2: Dissolution of Common B

Company A → Company B common stock retired (Investment in Company B removed)
100% of net assets of Company B recorded by Company A
Company B is dissolved

Consolidation of Companies A and B into Company C
Phase 1:

Company C (new company) → Cash or other Consideration → Company A Shareholders and Company B Shareholders
100% of Company A and B common stock (Investment in Companies A and B recorded)

Phase 2: Acquisition of Common Stock

Company C → Company A and B common stock retired (Investments in Companies A and B removed)
100% of net assets of Companies A & B recorded by Company C
Companies A & B are dissolved

Acquisitions of stock

In an **acquisition of stock** business combination, both companies involved in the combination continue to exist as separate entities. To effect this type of combination, the acquiring company exchanges its cash or securities for a **controlling interest** in the voting common stock of the acquired company. Historically, a **controlling interest** was defined as ownership of more than 50% of another company's outstanding voting common stock. In 1995, the FASB issued an exposure draft that would redefine control in a more conceptual way, opening the door to the possibility that control might exist in cases where less than 50% of the voting common stock of a subsidiary company is owned. However, the essential elements of a business combination classified as an acquisition of stock are that both companies involved in the combination remain separate entities after the combination and that one of the companies owns a **controlling interest** in the voting common stock of the other. Figure 1-2 illustrates the features of an acquisition of stock.

FIGURE 1-2 Acquisition of Stock Business Combination

Phase 1: Acquisition of Company B Common Stock

Company A

Cash or other consideration →

← Company B common stock
(Investment in Company B recorded)

Company B Shareholders

Then, Phase 2: Separate operation of each company

Company A*
(Parent Company)

Company A owns a controlling interest in Company B common stock

Company B
(Subsidiary Company)

*Company A shows its investment in Company B on its balance sheet.

Consolidated financial statements

In a business combination accounted for as a merger/consolidation, where only one company survives, financial statements prepared after the combination are created from the books and records of the surviving company. While the accounting change itself must be reported in the year of the acquisition, no continuing accounting problems are created when an asset combination occurs. However, in the case of an acquisition of stock, all parties to the combination remain separate entities. GAAP requires the financial statements of parent and subsidiary companies to be combined together in what are called **consolidated financial statements.**[5] It is important to understand the difference between the accounting technique **consolidated financial statements,** used to combine financial statements in stock acquisition combinations, and the exchange transaction **consolidation,** which describes a business combination where the net assets of two companies are **merged** into a newly organized company.

ACCOUNTING FOR BUSINESS COMBINATIONS

Approximately 90% of recent business combinations were characterized by a transaction where the acquiring company **purchased** (for cash, debt, or equity securities) a controlling interest in another company. The other 10% of business combinations were characterized by a transaction where a company exchanged 90% or more of its voting common stock for the voting common stock of the acquiring company (i.e., stock for stock) in a specialized transaction called a **pooling of interests.**[6] Prohibited after 2001, the pooling of interests method requires that twelve separate criteria be satisfied. The most notable of these is that *only common stock* may be exchanged for at least 90% of the acquired company's common stock or 100% of its net assets. If any of the twelve criteria for pooling is not met, the **purchase** method must be used. Therefore, four possibilities exist as illustrated by the following matrix:

Merger/Consolidation— Purchase Method	Acquisition of Stock— Purchase Method
Merger/Consolidation— Pooling of Interests Method	Acquisition of Stock— Pooling of Interests Method

The pooling of interests method has been subjected to criticism because it ignores the fair market values underlying the transaction. The FASB has recently moved to abolish the pooling method.[7] As noted above, the pooling method has been used for only a minority of business combinations. However, it is more common in large-size acquisitions. For example, pooling accounting was planned for the

---

[5] Statement of Financial Accounting Standards No. 94, *Consolidation of all Majority-Owned Subsidiaries* (Norwalk, CT: FASB, 1987) requires that all majority owned subsidiaries, except those for which control does not rest with the parent company or for which control is deemed temporary, be consolidated.

[6] American Institute of Certified Public Accountants, *Accounting Trends & Techniques: 1999 Fifty-Third Edition* (New York: American Institute of Certified Public Accountants, 1999). *Accounting Trends'* annual survey of 600 companies reports 344 business combinations in the year 1998, of which 27 (7.8%) were accounted for as poolings. The percentage of poolings to total combinations averaged less than 12% in the three previous years.

[7] "Merger-Accounting Method Under Fire," *The Wall Street Journal,* Tuesday, April 15, 1997. On July 1, 1997, *The Wall Street Journal* reported that the FASB was considering an amendment to goodwill amortization rules as an alternative to abolishing pooling. According to the article, the FASB stated, "that it may retain poolings but make purchase accounting less onerous by eliminating amortization of goodwill." Companies would also be able to test goodwill for "impairment" as an alternative to mandatory amortization. On April 21, 1999, the FASB announced that it would eliminate pooling accounting in a final standard to be issued in late 2000. In June, 2001 the FASB issued Statement of Financial Accounting Standards No. 141, *Business Combinations* (Norwalk, CT: FASB, 2001) requiring all business combinations initiated after June 30, 2001 to use the purchase method.

Boeing-McDonnell Douglas combination described previously and for a $23 billion combination of two telecommunications companies: Bell Atlantic Corporation and NYNEX Corporation.[8]

Because of the specialized nature of pooling and its controversial status, pooling is covered in a separate chapter in this textbook. The first four chapters illustrate and explain business combinations using the purchase method of accounting. This chapter explains and illustrates accounting for merger/consolidations using the purchase method of accounting. Chapters 2 through 4 cover the subject of acquisitions of stock using the purchase method. Chapter 7 is devoted to accounting for both types of combinations using the pooling of interests method. Chapters 5 and 6 cover additional business combinations issues that relate to stock acquisitions accounted for by either the purchase or pooling methods.

The conceptual differences between pooling and purchase

Figure 1-3 contains two footnote disclosures of recent acquisitions. The Harmon Industries footnote excerpt discloses three acquisitions, one of which is described as a stock acquisition and the others as asset acquisitions. All are accounted for under the purchase method. The other footnote is from the Boeing Company annual report for 1996 describing the planned acquisition of McDonnell Douglas by Boeing to be accounted for by the pooling of interests method. The footnotes focus on disclosing the method of accounting for the transaction (purchase or pooling of interests) rather than on the technical method of combining the accounts (merger vs. consolidated financial statements). The significance of this focus is due to the fact that **the combined financial statements of the acquiring company and the acquired company at the date of acquisition are not affected by whether the combination is a merger or a stock acquisition with consolidated financial statements.** However, the financial statements **are affected by the method of accounting** used for the combination. It is noteworthy that the Boeing acquisition of McDonnell Douglas is described as a merger, accounted for as a pooling of interests. It is a matter of fact, however, that the Boeing combination was actually an acquisition of stock with McDonnell Douglas "continuing as a wholly-owned subsidiary of Boeing."[9]

As is illustrated in this and later chapters, the purchase method is essentially an accounting method whereby an acquisition is recorded at *fair market value* on the date of acquisition. Any excess of the cost of an acquired entity over the fair market value of the net identifiable assets of the acquired company is recognized as goodwill.[10] The conceptual basis of a purchase method acquisition is that an arm's-length transaction between the parties to the combination has resulted in what is essentially a purchase of one company by the other. A pooling of interests, by contrast, was not considered to be a sale, but only an agreement whereby the two companies agree to pool their resources and operate as a combined economic entity. Accordingly, a pooling did not involve, in theory, an exchange. Instead, the book

---

[8] *Ibid*, April 15, 1997.

[9] The Boeing Company and McDonnell Douglas Corporation, *Joint Proxy Statement*, July 20, 1997.

[10] Statement of Financial Accounting Standards No. 141, *Business Combinations*, (Norwalk, CT: FASB, 2001) par. 43.

FIGURE 1·3 Footnote from Annual Report of Harmon Industries, Inc. for 1999

Note 12—On February 28, 1999, the Company acquired the stock of Syseca, Inc. for a purchase price of $9,500,000 in cash. This acquisition has been accounted for by the purchase method of accounting and accordingly, the operating results have been included in the Company's consolidated results of operations from the date of acquisition. The excess of the consideration given over the fair value of net assets acquired has been recorded as goodwill of $9,684,000.

On March 18, 1999, the Company acquired certain assets and assumed certain liabilities of DJR, Inc. This acquisition was made with the issuance of 94,409 shares of unregistered common stock valued at $12.71 per share and $1,681,000 in cash. In addition to the initial purchase price, the purchase agreement provides for a contingent payment. This payment is based upon the average earnings before taxes for the period from October 1, 1998 through December 31, 2001. This acquisition has been accounted for by the purchase method of accounting and accordingly, the operating results have been included in the Company's consolidated results of operations from the date of acquisition. The excess of the consideration given over the fair value of net assets acquired has been recorded as goodwill of $479,000. Any additional consideration will also be recorded as goodwill.

On March 25, 1999, the Company acquired certain assets and assumed certain liabilities related to Golden Gate Switchgear, Inc. This acquisition was made with the issuance of 28,846 shares of unregistered common stock valued at $20.80 per share and $680,000 in cash. This acquisition has been accounted for by the purchase method of accounting and accordingly, the operating results have been included in the Company's consolidated results of operations from the date of acquisition. The excess of consideration given over the fair value of net assets acquired has been recorded as goodwill of $2,007,000.

Footnote from the Annual Report of the Boeing Company for 1996

Note 20—On December 15, 1996, the Company and McDonnell Douglas Corporation jointly announced the signing of a merger agreement. Pending government and shareholder approvals, McDonnell Douglas shareholders will receive 0.65 of a share of Boeing common stock for each share of McDonnell Douglas common stock pursuant to which McDonnell Douglas will merge with Boeing in a stock-for-stock transaction. The merger is intended to be accounted for as a pooling of interests. The merger would result in the issuance of approximately 138 million additional shares of the Company. The transaction, which is subject to approval by the McDonnell Douglas shareholders, the authorization of additional shares by Company shareholders and approvals by certain regulatory agencies, is expected to be completed in the third quarter of 1997. The merged companies will operate under the name of the Boeing Company. Combined sales for the companies would have been approximately $36,500 (million) in 1996 before consideration of intercompany transactions and conforming accounting methods.

values of the two entities were used to record all transactions associated with the combination. The problem that arose was that two very similar transactions were accounted for in fundamentally different ways—either at fair market value or book value, depending upon technical circumstances. Accounting theoreticians have struggled with this problem for decades. APB 16[11] was only a partial solution. While

---

[11] Accounting Principles Board Opinion No. 16, *Business Combinations* (New York: American Institute of Certified Public Accountants, 1970).

APB 16 ended pooling accounting as a full alternative to purchase accounting, it allowed pooling accounting for business combinations that were dominated by one of the companies involved as long as the technical provisions of the Opinion were met. As with purchases, business combinations accounted for as poolings were the result of arm's-length negotiations based on the fair values of the assets of the companies involved in the combination. However, pooling accounting ignored these market values when the transaction was recorded. As noted in footnote 7, FASB Statement 141 bans pooling for combinations initiated after June 30, 2001.

■ CONCEPT QUESTION AND REFLECTION

> If a business combination is accounted for as a purchase, the assets and liabilities of the acquired company will be reported in the consolidated financial statements at fair market value. Additional goodwill may also result if the consideration given for the acquired company is greater than the fair market value of its net assets. In contrast, pooling accounting results in the acquired company assets being reported at historical book values in the consolidated financial statements. What impact might these differences have on the reported earnings of the combined entity under purchase accounting vs. pooling accounting? Are the managers and shareholders likely to be concerned about the method of accounting used in the combination? Why or why not?

The purchase method of accounting for a merger—book and fair market value equal

The initial transaction (phase 1) of a business combination accounted for by the purchase method is recorded in the same manner for both merger/consolidations and for acquisitions of stock. This initial transaction requires the acquiring company to record an investment in the acquired company equal to the fair market value of the investment or the amount of the consideration given, whichever is more objective. For example, let us assume Acquisition Company and Target Company have the following financial statements immediately prior to the purchase by Acquisition of all of Target's outstanding common stock in the open market from Target's shareholders.

Acquisition Company		**Target Company**	
Cash	$ 50,000	Cash	$ 5,000
Other assets	50,000	Other assets	35,000
Total assets	100,000	Total assets	40,000
Liabilities	20,000	Liabilities	10,000
Common stock, $1 par	20,000	Common stock, $1 par	10,000
Retained earnings	60,000	Retained earnings	20,000
Total liabilities and equity	$100,000	Total liabilities and equity	$40,000

ILLUSTRATION OF A CASH ACQUISITION Note first, the book value of Target's net assets is $30,000 ($40,000 of assets less $10,000 in liabilities). Second, assume the fair market value of Target's net assets is equal to its book value and Acquisition purchases all of the outstanding common stock of Target in the open market. The entry to record the acquisition of Target Company on Acquisition Company's books is as follows:

(1) Investment in Target Company *Asset*   30,000
         Cash   30,000
            To record the purchase of common stock Target's shareholders—phase 1

In addition, if the combination is a merger, Acquisition Company makes the following entry to record the assets and liabilities of Target Company on its books. This entry brings the balance in the investment account to zero.

(2) Cash   5,000
     Other Assets   35,000
         Liabilities   10,000
         Investment in Target Company   30,000
            To record phase 2 of the merger

After this entry, Target Company ceases to exist as a separate entity. Had the business combination been an acquisition of stock, Acquisition Company would make only the first entry and would prepare consolidated financial statements. Note how the second entry eliminates the investment account "Investment in Target" and replaces it with the individual asset and liability balances of Target Company. The effects of the two entries on the financial statements of Acquisition Company can be determined by preparing a brief worksheet analysis showing the above two entries being posted to Acquisition Company's balance sheet:

Acquisition Company		**Debit**		**Credit**		**Combined**
Cash	$ 50,000	(2) 5,000	(1)	30,000		$ 25,000
Other assets	50,000	(2) 35,000				85,000
Investment in Target		(1) 30,000	(2)	30,000		
Total assets	100,000					110,000
Liabilities	20,000		(2)	10,000		30,000
Common stock, $1 par	20,000					20,000
Retained earnings	60,000					60,000
Total liabilities						
and equity	$100,000					$110,000

ILLUSTRATION OF A NON-CASH ACQUISITION The accounting procedures to be followed in the case of non-cash consideration are essentially the same case. If debt securities are exchanged for Target Company common stock, liability accounts are credited. If equity securities are issued in exchange for Target Company common stock, these are recorded at fair market value on the date of issue. For example, instead of paying cash, assume Acquisition Company acquires 100% of Target Company's common stock in exchange for its own $1 par common stock on a date when the fair market value of Acquisition stock was $5 per share. The number of unissued shares of Acquisition required is 6,000 shares ($30,000 fair market value of Target net assets ÷ $5 per share). The journal entry on Acquisition's books to record the acquisition is as follows:

(1)	Investment in Target Company	30,000	
	Common stock, $1 par		6,000
	Additional paid-in capital		24,000
	To record phase 1 of the merger		

As in the previous case, assuming the acquisition is a merger with dissolution of Target Company, an additional entry to record the assets and liabilities of Target on Acquisition's books is required. This entry is identical to the case of the cash purchase:

(2)	Cash	5,000	
	Other Assets	35,000	
	Liabilities		10,000
	Investment in Target		30,000
	To record phase 2 of the merger		

A worksheet to show the financial statement effects of this acquisition is as follows:

Acquisition Company		Debit		Credit		Combined
Cash	$ 50,000	(2) 5,000				$ 55,000
Other assets	50,000	(2) 35,000				85,000
Investment in Target		(1) 30,000	(2)	30,000		
Total assets	100,000					140,000
Liabilities	20,000		(2)	10,000		30,000
Common stock, $1 par	20,000		(1)	6,000		26,000
Additional paid-in capital			(1)	24,000		24,000
Retained earnings	60,000					60,000
Total liabilities and equity	$100,000					$140,000

Notice that the combined assets in the cash acquisition total $110,000, whereas they total $140,000 in the stock acquisition. This difference arises because Acquisition Company cash was reduced by the $30,000 used to purchase Target Company stock in the first illustration. However, unissued stock was exchanged for the Target Company net assets in the second illustration.

◢ CONCEPT QUESTION AND REFLECTION

1. How likely is it an acquisition would be recorded for exactly the book value of an acquired company's net assets, as shown in the two illustrations on pages 11 and 12? Why or why not?
2. Could the market value of Acquisition Company common stock be affected by either of the above two acquisitions? Which type of transaction is more likely to affect Acquisition Company's common stock market price? Explain.

Incidental costs associated with purchase method acquisitions

Three categories of incidental costs may arise in connection with investments in the common stock of other companies. These are:

- Direct acquisition costs—Costs paid to outside consultants, including attorneys and CPAs, for services rendered in connection with the acquisition.
- Issue costs—Costs incurred in connection with the issuance of securities used as consideration in the business combination.
- Internal costs—Additional general and administrative costs of the acquiring company related to the business combination.

In purchase method acquisitions, direct acquisition costs are treated as consideration and are debited to the investment account. These costs are essentially additional costs of the investment itself because they are necessary and essential costs to complete the acquisition. Issue costs are accounted for in the same way as any other issue costs incurred in connection with the sale or issuance of securities. When common stock is issued for cash, issue costs reduce the net proceeds received from the stock issue. Thus, these costs are reflected in financial statements by reducing additional paid-in capital. Internal general and administrative costs should be charged to expense. While this treatment is not necessarily consistent with the accounting treatment of other costs associated with an acquisition, it is often difficult or impossible to determine precisely which internal expenses are merger or acquisition related and which are simple ordinary business expenses. Consequently, expensing these costs is appropriate. To summarize, the three types of incidental costs in *purchase* method combinations are accounted for as follows:

Type of Cost	Accounting Treatment
Direct acquisition costs	Capitalize (debit) as investment
Issue costs	Debit to additional paid-in capital
Internal costs of the merger	Debit to expenses

The purchase method of accounting for a merger—purchase price exceeds fair value of net assets acquired

A significant number of business combinations involve a payment by the acquiring company of amounts in excess of the fair market value of the identifiable net assets of the acquired company on the date of acquisition. An existing business with a successful operating history normally has infrastructure in the form of a customer base, technical expertise, managerial expertise, and many other intangible factors that create value over and above the amortized historical costs of its identifiable net assets. Hence, it is not uncommon for a business combination transaction to give rise to goodwill, which must be recorded at the time of the merger. A business combination transaction is required in order for goodwill to be reported in the financial statements of a business enterprise. Furthermore, **the only circumstance under which goodwill is actually recorded in the ledger of a company is a business combination accounted for as a purchase and involving either a merger or a consolidation of net assets.**[12]

To illustrate this type of transaction, assume Principal Company purchases all of the outstanding voting common stock of Sentinel Company for $200,000 cash on January 1, 20x1 and that Sentinel is immediately liquidated and merged into Principal. On the acquisition date, each company has the following book and fair values for its assets and liabilities:

---

[12] As you will see in Chapter 3, an *acquisition of stock* business combination may result in goodwill in the consolidated financial statements of the parent and subsidiary companies, but such goodwill is not recorded in the ledger of the parent company.

	Principal Company		Sentinel Company	
	Book Value	**Fair Value**	**Book Value**	**Fair Value**
Cash	$240,000	$240,000	$ 15,000	$ 15,000
Other current assets	50,000	60,000	25,000	25,000
Land	100,000	125,000	50,000	50,000
Buildings (net)	260,000	350,000	100,000	120,000
Total assets	650,000		190,000	
Current liabilities	25,000	25,000	10,000	10,000
Long-term liabilities	100,000	105,000	40,000	30,000
Common stock, $1 par	250,000		50,000	
Retained earnings	275,000		90,000	
Total liabilities and equity	$650,000		$190,000	

The following entry records Principal's purchase of the common stock of Sentinel:

(1)	Investment in Sentinel Company	200,000	
	Cash		200,000
	To record phase 1 of the merger		

An additional entry is required to record the merger. It records the assets and liabilities of Sentinel on the books of Principal, allowing Sentinel to be subsequently dissolved. Before this entry is made, we must determine the values to be assigned to the assets and liabilities of the acquired company, and whether any additional goodwill will also be recorded. Because the price paid for the investment exceeds both the book value and the fair value of the identifiable net assets of Sentinel, a method of analysis is needed to determine what values should be assigned to those assets. The most efficient way of making this determination is to prepare an **allocation schedule** assigning the difference between the cost of the investment in Sentinel ($200,000) and the underlying book value of Sentinel's net assets ($140,000) to the net assets acquired in the merger. This allocation schedule will serve as a basis for the entry that liquidates the account "Investment in Sentinel Company" and replaces it with the individual asset and liability accounts.

Price of Sentinel Stock			$200,000
Stockholders' equity of Sentinel:			
Common stock		$50,000	
Retained earnings		90,000	140,000
Excess of cost over book value			60,000
Allocation:			
Buildings undervalued			20,000
Long-term liabilities overvalued			10,000
Goodwill (residual amount) Plug figure			30,000
Excess of cost over book value			$ 60,000

The schedule indicates that the buildings account of Sentinel will be increased by $20,000 and long-term liabilities decreased by $10,000 when the merger is recorded. In addition, goodwill in the amount of $30,000 will be recorded at the time of the merger. A purchase method business combination where the price of the investment exceeds the fair market value of the net assets of the acquired company will result in all of its assets and liabilities being recorded in the merger at fair market value. In addition, goodwill equal to the excess of the purchase price over the **fair market value** of the identifiable net assets will be recorded in the merger. Only the assets and liabilities purchased are adjusted to fair market value. As the schedule comparing book and fair values indicates, Principal Company also has assets and liabilities whose book and fair values are different. These assets are **not** adjusted because they were not being purchased.

Principal's entry to record the merger of the net assets of Sentinel and eliminate the investment account from entry (1) is as follows:

		Debit	Credit
(2)	Cash	15,000	
	Other Current Assets	25,000	
	Land	50,000	
	Buildings (net)	120,000	
	Goodwill	30,000	
	Current liabilities		10,000
	Long-term liabilities		30,000
	Investment in Sentinel		200,000

A worksheet can then be prepared to show the financial position of the two companies immediately after the acquisition. This worksheet is prepared by posting the above two journal entries to the beginning asset and liability balances of Principal Company:

Principal Company	Book Value		Debit		Credit	Combined
Cash	$240,000	(2)	15,000	(1)	200,000	$ 55,000
Other current assets	50,000	(2)	25,000			75,000
Land	100,000	(2)	50,000			150,000
Buildings (net)	260,000	(2)	120,000			380,000
Goodwill		(2)	30,000			30,000
Investment in Sentinel		(1)	200,000	(2)	200,000	–
Total assets	650,000					690,000
Current liabilities	25,000			(2)	10,000	35,000
Long-term liabilities	100,000			(2)	30,000	130,000
Common stock, $1 par	250,000					250,000
Retained earnings	275,000					275,000
Total liabilities and equity	$650,000					$690,000

● INTERPRETIVE EXERCISE

Prepare the acquisition journal entries for the Principal-Sentinel Acquisition, assuming the price given for the Sentinel common stock was $220,000. How would this increased price affect the combined balances in the balance sheet?

FINANCIAL STATEMENTS IN PURCHASE COMBINATIONS

The financial statements subsequent to a merger report combined income only for periods after the combination. Financial statements for comparative prior years are not restated. However, footnotes must show combined pro-forma operating results for the current year and comparative prior year, if the combined entity is a public enterprise. Other footnotes describe the details of the transaction, including information about intangible assets, combined operating results, and balance sheet effects.[13]

Figure 1-4 gives two examples of footnotes describing acquisitions. Because of recent and ongoing changes in accounting standards for business combinations, these examples can only serve to illustrate the general nature of supplemental disclosures. The reader should refer to the authoritative literature for specific guidance. The footnote taken from the 1999 Annual Report of General Mills, Inc. discloses information related to three acquisitions accounted for under the purchase method. The footnote from the 1999 Annual Report of the ExxonMobil Corporation discloses information related to the merger of the two companies that was accounted for as a pooling of interests, an accounting method that cannot be used after 2001.

FIGURE 1-4: Footnote from the 1999 Annual Report of General Mills, Inc.

2. ACQUISITIONS

On January 15, 1999, we acquired Lloyd's Barbeque Company, St. Paul, Minnesota, a producer of refrigerated entrees. On February 10, 1999, we acquired Farmhouse Foods Company, Union City, California, a West Coast marketer of rice and pasta side-dish mixes. The aggregate purchase price of these acquisitions, both of which were accounted for using the purchase method, totaled approximately $130 million. Goodwill of $113 million associated with these acquisitions is being amortized on a straight-line basis over 40 years. The results of the acquired businesses have been included in the consolidated financial statements since their respective acquisition dates. Our fiscal 1999 financial results would not have been materially different if we had made these acquisitions at the beginning of the fiscal year.

On January 31, 1997, we acquired the branded ready-to-eat cereal and snack mix businesses of Ralcorp Holdings, Inc., including the CHEX and COOKIE CRISP brands. This acquisition included a Cincinnati, Ohio, manufacturing facility, and trademark and technology rights for the branded products in the Americas. The purchase price of $570 million involved the issuance of about $355 million in General Mills common stock (approximately 5.4 million shares) to Ralcorp shareholders and the assumption of about $215 million of Ralcorp public debt and accrued interest. This acquisition was accounted for using the purchase method of accounting. Goodwill of approximately $550 million is being amortized on a straight-line basis over 40 years. The results of the acquired businesses have been included in the consolidated financial statements since the acquisition date.

[13] Statement of Financial Accounting Standards No. 141, *Business Combinations*, (Norwalk, CT: FASB, 2001), pars. 51–58.

Footnote from the 1999 Annual Report of Exxon Mobil Corporation

3. Merger of Exxon Corporation and Mobil Corporation

On November 30, 1999, a wholly-owned subsidiary of Exxon Corporation (Exxon) merged with Mobil Corporation (Mobil) so that Mobil became a wholly-owned subsidiary of Exxon (the "Merger"). At the same time, Exxon changed its name to Exxon Mobil Corporation (ExxonMobil). Under the terms of the agreement, approximately 1.0 billion shares of ExxonMobil common stock were issued in exchange for all the outstanding shares of Mobil common stock based upon an exchange ratio of 1.32015. Following the exchange, former shareholders of Exxon owned approximately 70 percent of the corporation, while former Mobil shareholders owned approximately 30 percent of the corporation. Each outstanding share of Mobil preferred stock was converted into one share of a new class of ExxonMobil preferred stock.

As a result of the Merger, the accounts of certain refining, marketing and chemicals operations jointly controlled by the combining companies have been included in the consolidated financial statements. These operations were previously accounted for by Exxon and Mobil as separate companies using the equity method of accounting.

The Merger was accounted for as a pooling of interests. Accordingly, the consolidated financial statements give retroactive effect to the Merger, with all periods presented as if Exxon and Mobil had always been combined. Certain reclassifications have been made to conform the presentation of Exxon and Mobil.

The following table sets forth summary data for the separate companies and the combined amounts for periods prior to the Merger.

| (millions of dollars) | Nine Months Ended September 30 | | Year Ended December 31 |
	1999	1998	1997
Revenues			
Exxon	$ 89,378	$117,772	$ 137,242
Mobil	42,782	53,531	65,906
Adjustments (1)	6,033	7,987	9,925
Eliminations	(7,248)	(9,648)	(11,327)
Exxon Mobil	$130,945	$169,642	$ 201,746
Net Income			
Exxon	$ 3,725	$ 6,370	$ 8,460
Mobil	1,901	1,704	3,272
Exxon Mobil	$ 5,626	$ 8,074	$ 11,732

(1) Consolidation of activities previously accounted for using the equity method of accounting.

In association with the Merger, $625 million pre-tax ($469 million after-tax) of costs were recorded as merger related expenses. Charges included separation expenses of approximately $350 million related to workforce reductions (approximately 1,750 employees at year-end 1999), plus implementation and merger closing costs. The reserve balance, primarily related to severance, at year-end 1999 of approximately $330 million, is expected to be expended in 2000.

Certain property—primarily refining, marketing, pipeline and natural gas distribution assets—must be divested as a condition of the regulatory approval of the Merger by the U.S. Federal Trade Commission and the European Commission. These assets, with a carrying value of approximately $3 billion, are expected to be sold Merger by the U.S. Federal Trade Commission and the European Commission in the year 2000. The properties have historically earned approximately $200 million per year.

● **INTERPRETIVE EXERCISE**

What additional information, if any, would General Mills have disclosed if FASB Statement 141 had been effective in 1999?

Companies reporting business combinations accounted for under the new mandatory purchase accounting rules (effective in the year 2001) are also required to disclose a substantial amount of information about intangible assets acquired. They must distinguish between those intangible assets subject to amortization and those not being amortized. For assets being amortized, these disclosures include the amount of amortization expense recorded, the gross carrying amount, and accumulated amortization as of the balance sheet date. Those amounts are also disclosed by major class of intangible asset. For assets not being amortized, the gross carrying amount and amounts by major asset class must be disclosed. Goodwill must be shown in a separate line in the balance sheet. Additional disclosures are also required when and if intangible assets that are subject to review for impairment are determined to be impaired. (See Appendix 1 later in this chapter for a discussion of intangible asset impairment.)

COMPREHENSIVE ILLUSTRATION

Assume Public Company purchases all of the outstanding voting common stock of Local Company for $900,000 cash on January 1, 20x1, in a merger transaction whereby Local is dissolved. In addition, Public pays $25,000 to a management consulting firm for services related to the acquisition. Immediately prior to the acquisition, Public and Local have the following book and fair values:

	Public Company		Local Company	
	Book Value	**Fair Value**	**Book Value**	**Fair Value**
Cash	$ 950,000	$950,000	$ 25,000	$ 25,000
Other current assets	75,000	75,000	125,000	125,000
Land	125,000	100,000	100,000	200,000
Buildings	350,000	400,000	125,000	325,000
Equipment	750,000	900,000	500,000	400,000
Total assets	2,250,000		875,000	
Current liabilities	75,000	70,000	50,000	50,000
Bonds payable	200,000	190,000	200,000	180,000
Common stock, $1 par value	500,000		100,000	
Retained earnings	1,475,000		525,000	
Total liabilities and equity	$2,250,000		$875,000	

The following entry records the purchase of the Local common stock by Public Company:

(1) Investment in Local Company Common Stock   925,000
      Cash   925,000
              To record phase 1 of the merger

Note that the payment of $925,000 consists of $900,000 given in exchange for Local Company common stock as well as $25,000 of direct acquisition costs paid to the consulting firm. An additional entry is needed to record the merger. However, it is first necessary to analyze the differences between the book and fair values of Local Company. This analysis determines the disposition of any excess of cost over book value at the date of the acquisition. The following illustration allocates the excess of the cost of the investment ($925,000) over the book value of Local's common stock ($625,000) at the date of acquisition.

Cost of Local common stock		$925,000
Stockholders' equity of Local		
Common stock	$100,000	
Retained earnings	525,000	625,000
Excess of cost over book value		**300,000**
Allocation:		
Land undervalued		100,000
Building undervalued		200,000
Equipment overvalued		(100,000)
Bonds payable overvalued		20,000
Goodwill		**80,000**
Excess of cost over book value		**$300,000**

In the analysis, the **excess of cost over book value** of $300,000 represents the amount by which the investment cost of $925,000 exceeds the net book value of the investee assets of $625,000. When the merger is recorded, the net assets of Local must be increased by $300,000 if the merger entry is to balance. The second part of the schedule shows the amounts by which the book values of the individual assets and liabilities of Local will be increased or decreased in the merger entry. The positive numbers represent increases in debit balance accounts or decreases in credit balance accounts, and the negative number represents a decrease in a debit balance account. For example, the book value of the land on the books of Local is $100,000 and its fair market value on the date of acquisition is $200,000. Thus, the allocation schedule indicates the land carrying value will be increased by the difference between these two amounts, $100,000, in the merger entry.

The situation regarding the building is similar. The building has a book value of $125,000 and a fair value of $325,000 on the date of the acquisition. Therefore, this asset is undervalued by the difference between these two amounts, $200,000, on this date. In the merger, the buildings account will be increased by the amount of this excess and recorded at $325,000. The situation regarding the equipment is different. Local Company's equipment has a book value of $500,000 and a fair value of $400,000 on the date of the acquisition. Since the book value is **greater** than the fair value, this difference is deducted in the allocation schedule. Stated another way, this difference is deducted because the $300,000 difference between the cost of Local common stock and its book value would have been larger had the equipment not been overvalued on the books of Local. In recording the equipment in the merger, its book value would be reduced by the amount of the $100,000 overvaluation, resulting in the equipment being recorded at $400,000 on the books of Public Company.

The final element with a book-fair value differential on the Local Company balance sheet is bonds payable, a liability. As shown in the schedule of book and fair value differences, the bonds payable are overvalued by $20,000. When the merger is recorded, this overvaluation will be reflected in Public Company's ledger by recording $20,000 of discount on the bonds payable. Such an overvaluation might arise because of increases in prevailing market interest rates since the date these bonds were originally issued by Local. In the allocation schedule, **overvaluation** of the bonds is added just as the **undervaluation** of the land and buildings was added because bonds payable has a credit balance. Thus, undervaluation of assets and overvaluation of liabilities have the same effect on allocation of the excess of cost over book value in a business merger.

The following table summarizes the relationship between overvalued and undervalued assets and liabilities on the excess of cost over book value:

Effect on Excess of Cost Over Book Value

	Increase	Decrease
Undervalued assets		will X differential
Overvalued assets	X	
Undervalued liabilities	X	
Overvalued liabilities		X

(handwritten note at left: Company valuing)

The goodwill in the allocation schedule is the residual amount needed in order that the column total $300,000. In effect, the result of Public Company purchasing the Investment in Local Company common stock for $300,000 more than its underlying book value is that goodwill in the amount of $80,000 will be recorded in the merger. If the book values and fair market values of Local were equal on the date of the merger, the new goodwill would be $300,000. Thus, the difference between the $300,000 excess of cost over book value and the $80,000 of goodwill is the amount by which the identifiable assets and liabilities of Local are adjusted when the merger is recorded on Public Company's books.

Based on the above analysis, the entry required to record the merger and eliminate the account Investment in Local Company common stock would be as follows:

(2)	Cash	25,000	
	Other current assets	125,000	
	Land	200,000	
	Buildings	325,000	
	Equipment	400,000	
	Goodwill	80,000	
	Discount on bonds payable	20,000	
	Current liabilities		50,000
	Bonds payable		200,000
	Investment in Local Company common stock		925,000
	To record phase 2 of the merger		

The following worksheet shows the financial position of the two companies immediately after the acquisition:

Public Company	Book Value	Debit		Credit		Combined
Cash	$ 950,000	(2)	25,000	(1)	925,000	$ 50,000
Other current						
assets	75,000	(2)	125,000			200,000
Land	125,000	(2)	200,000			325,000
Buildings	350,000	(2)	325,000			675,000
Equipment	750,000	(2)	400,000			1,150,000
Goodwill		(2)	80,000			80,000
Investment in						
Local		(1)	925,000	(2)	925,000	-
Total assets	2,250,000					2,480,000
Current liabilities	75,000			(2)	50,000	125,000
Bonds payable	200,000			(2)	200,000	400,000
Discount on						
bonds payable		(2)	20,000			(20,000)
Common stock,						
$1 par value	500,000					500,000
Retained earnings	1,475,000					1,475,000
Total liabilities						
and equity	$2,250,000					$2,480,000

SUMMARY

The following learning objectives were stated at the beginning of the chapter:

- Explain the business and economic incentives for business combination transactions
- Describe the two basic types of business combinations
- Account for mergers/consolidations using the purchase method
- State the financial statement disclosures required for purchase method mergers/consolidations

Business combinations are undertaken for a variety of sound business reasons. While these types of transactions appear to come in cycles, with certain periods of time having more intense activity, business combinations are a very common event. Essentially two types of business combinations exist. Both **mergers** and **consolidations** are business combinations where the assets and liabilities of one or more companies are combined together to form a single company. The acquired company or companies in mergers/consolidations are usually liquidated. An **acquisition of stock** is a combination where a **parent company** obtains a controlling interest in the outstanding common stock of another company called the **subsidiary.** Instead of being merged into the parent company, the subsidiary continues to operate as a separate entity. An acquisition of stock combination requires only that the financial statements of the parent and its subsidiaries be combined together in what are called **consolidated financial statements.** Techniques for preparation of these statements are covered in later chapters of this textbook. Mergers and consolidations in which the acquired company is dissolved require a purchase of 100% of the outstanding common stock of the acquired company, recording this acquisition in an investment account. A second entry is then made to dissolve the acquired company, recording its assets and liabilities on the books of the acquiring company, and eliminating the investment account recorded in the first entry. If the price paid for the investment is greater than the book values of the acquired company's net assets, the difference is assigned to the identifiable assets and liabilities or to goodwill. This analysis is performed by preparing a schedule that allocates the cost-book value differential to the appropriate assets (including goodwill) and to liabilities.

APPENDIX 1: ## Accounting for Goodwill

LEARNING OBJECTIVE

■ State the fundamentals of accounting for goodwill

Intangible assets can be classified as either identifiable or unidentifiable. Identifiable intangible assets include such assets as patents, copyrights, and others that have been purchased or developed internally. Purchased identifiable intangible assets are recorded at cost, amortized over their estimated useful lives, and periodically tested for impairment in accordance with FASB Statement 121.[1] Except for the legal costs of registering trademarks and patents, the costs associated with internally developed identifiable intangible assets are normally charged to expense as incurred.

Goodwill represents those assets that cannot be identified specifically. As in the case of internally developed identifiable intangible assets, the costs associated with internally developed goodwill are charged to expense on a current basis. It is likely that many companies have unrecorded goodwill associated with the reputation of their products, service, and managerial expertise. However, this goodwill is not reported as an asset. **In order for goodwill to appear in the financial statements of a company, it must have been purchased in a business combination.** As illustrated in this chapter, goodwill is measured as the excess of the fair value given in a business combination over the fair market value of the underlying identifiable net assets.

Several accounting methods are potentially applicable to purchased goodwill. There are good arguments for and against the use of all of these. Essentially, two issues are involved. First is the question of whether goodwill is *capitalized* as an intangible asset *or written off* against additional paid-in-capital immediately after the business combination is recorded. If goodwill is capitalized as an asset the second question is whether it is *amortized* periodically or considered to have an *indefinite life* subject to periodic review for impairment. For more than 30 years, the accepted accounting method for purchased goodwill was to capitalize and amortize it over its useful life. A further provision in the authoritative literature was that goodwill for which no definite life could be determined would have a maximum amortization period for 40 years. Goodwill and other intangible assets were required to be written down if later evidence or events indicated that the asset was impaired.[2]

In June 2001, the FASB reaffirmed that it would require purchased goodwill to be recognized as an asset and measured as the excess of the cost of an acquired entity over its identifiable net assets. The FASB also concluded that goodwill should *not* be amortized but should be tested for impairment at the **reporting unit level.** "A reporting unit is an

---

[1] Statement of Financial Accounting Standards No. 121, *Accounting for the Impairment of Long-lived Assets to be Disposed of* (Norwalk, CT: FASB, 1995).

[2] Accounting Principles Board Opinion No. 17, *Intangible Assets* (New York: American Institute of Certified Public Accounts, 1970).

operating segment or one level below an operating segment (referred to as a component). A component of an operating segment is a reporting unit if the component constitutes a business for which discrete financial information is available . . ."[3] Thus, goodwill might be tested for impairment at the entity level if it has only one operating segment or at a lower level depending on the organizational structure and the number of operating segments in the entity.

FASB 142 further requires that goodwill be tested for impairment annually and on an interim basis (if an event occurs that suggests that goodwill is impaired) by comparing the fair value of the reporting unit with its carrying amount. If carrying amount exceeds fair value, goodwill is considered to be impaired. The **impairment test** is done by calculating implied goodwill as of the financial statement date in the same manner that goodwill was originally determined—as the difference between the fair value of the reporting unit and the fair value of all its identifiable net assets. If implied goodwill is less than the carrying amount of goodwill an impairment loss is recognized. The fair value of the entity for impairment test purposes is based on market values (if available) or the use of an appropriate analytical model (present value models, option pricing models, and others).[4]

SUMMARY

The following learning objective was stated at the beginning of this appendix:

- State the fundamentals for accounting for goodwill.

Goodwill comes into existence only through the purchase of a business entity. It is the excess of the fair value given (the price paid) over the fair market value of the underlying identifiable net assets acquired in the business combination. Historically, goodwill has been capitalized as an asset and amortized over its estimated useful life. With the new FASB directive, amortization of goodwill is no longer allowed.

Goodwill must be tested for impairment at the reporting level as of the financial statement date. This testing must be done at least annually and sooner if something has happened that may have caused impairment.

APPENDIX 2: Bargain Purchase Acquisitions

LEARNING OBJECTIVE

- Account for bargain purchase mergers/consolidations using the purchase method

The purchase method of accounting for a merger—purchase price falls between book value and fair market value of net assets acquired

Sometimes, because of measurement error in determining fair market value or adverse economic conditions, an acquiring company may purchase control of another company for a price that is *less than the fair market value* of its identifiable net assets. When this type of acquisition occurs, a so-called **bargain purchase** situation results.

---

[3] Statement of Financial Accounting Standards No. 142, *Goodwill and Other Intangible Assets* (Norwalk, CT: FASB, 2001), par. 30.

[4] *Ibid.*, pars. 19–25.

If the price paid for the acquisition falls between the book and fair market value of the identifiable net assets, the residual figure in the allocation analysis will be negative, giving rise to what is usually called **negative goodwill.** The FASB has proposed that negative goodwill be allocated to **all of the acquired assets of the entity other than cash and cash equivalents, trade receivables, inventory, financial instruments carried at fair value, assets held for sale, and deferred tax assets. Any negative goodwill remaining after all assets to which it can be assigned are reduced to zero should be reported as an extraordinary gain.**[1]

To illustrate these procedures, assume the Principal-Sentinel acquisition on January 1, 20x1, at a price of $152,000 when Sentinel Company had the following book and fair values in its balance sheet:

Sentinel Company

Assets	Book Value	Fair Value
Cash	$ 15,000	$ 15,000
Other current assets	25,000	25,000
Land	50,000	50,000
Buildings (net)	100,000	130,000
Total assets	190,000	

Liabilities and Equities		
Current liabilities	10,000	10,000
Long-term liabilities	40,000	40,000
Common stock, $1 par value	50,000	
Retained earnings	90,000	
Total liabilities and equity	$190,000	

An allocation schedule for this acquisition would appear as follows:

Price of Sentinel common stock		$152,000
Stockholders equity of Sentinel:		
Common stock	$50,000	
Retained earnings	90,000	140,000
Excess of cost over book value		$ 12,000

Allocation:		Allocate Negative Goodwill	Final Allocation
Land	$	$ (5,000)	$ 5,000
Buildings undervalued	30,000	(13,000)	43,000
Negative goodwill (residual amount)	(18,000)	18,000	-
Excess of cost over book value	$12,000		$48,000

Allocation of the negative goodwill:

	Relative Market Values		Negative Goodwill		Allocation
Land	$ 50,000/$180,000*	×	$18,000	=	$ (5,000)
Building	$130,000/$180,000	×	$18,000	=	(13,000)

* *$180,000 equals the sum of the fair market values of the assets to which goodwill may be allocated.*

---

[1] *Ibid.*, pars. 6–8.

In the above case, the excess of cost over book value is less than the amount necessary for the buildings to be recorded in the merger at their fair market value of $130,000. The negative residual that results from increasing the carrying value of the buildings to fair market value is the **negative goodwill** of $18,000. This negative goodwill is assigned to the long-term assets in accordance with the relative fair market value of those long-term assets, as shown in the illustration. Note that negative goodwill is assigned to both the land and the buildings even though the book and fair market value of the land are equal. Thus, journal entries to record the acquisition and merger are as follows:

(1)	Investment in Sentinel Company	152,000	
	Cash		152,000
(2)	Cash	15,000	
	Other current assets	25,000	
	Land	50,000	
	Buildings (net)	130,000	
	Goodwill		18,000
	Current liabilities		10,000
	Long-term liabilities		40,000
	Investment in Sentinel Company		152,000
(3)	Goodwill	18,000	
	Land		5,000
	Buildings (net)		13,000

As an alternative, entries (2) and (3) may be combined. The negative goodwill may first be allocated to the identifiable assets before the entry is recorded:

(2)	Cash	15,000	
	Other Current Assets	25,000	
	Land ($50,000 − $5,000)	45,000	
	Buildings (net) ($130,000 − $13,000)	117,000	
	Current liabilities		10,000
	Long-term liabilities		40,000
	Investment in Sentinel Company		152,000

Assuming Principal Company had a balance sheet as shown in the following schedule, a worksheet (using the first set of entries) can then be prepared to show the financial position of the two companies immediately after the acquisition:

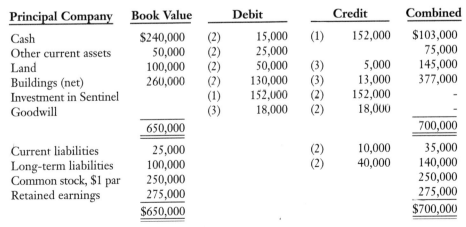

Principal Company	Book Value		Debit		Credit	Combined
Cash	$240,000	(2)	15,000	(1)	152,000	$103,000
Other current assets	50,000	(2)	25,000			75,000
Land	100,000	(2)	50,000	(3)	5,000	145,000
Buildings (net)	260,000	(2)	130,000	(3)	13,000	377,000
Investment in Sentinel		(1)	152,000	(2)	152,000	–
Goodwill		(3)	18,000	(2)	18,000	–
	650,000					700,000
Current liabilities	25,000			(2)	10,000	35,000
Long-term liabilities	100,000			(2)	40,000	140,000
Common stock, $1 par	250,000					250,000
Retained earnings	275,000					275,000
	$650,000					$700,000

reflects journal entries

The purchase method of accounting for a merger—purchase price is less than the book value of net assets acquired

The most extreme case of a **bargain purchase** situation is where the price paid for the common stock of the acquired company is *less than the book value* of its net assets. In this case, there is no excess of **cost over book value** to be assigned to the net assets acquired in the merger. Rather, there is an **excess of book value over cost.** The analysis to be constructed, however, is very similar to that for the bargain purchase situation where the price falls between the book value and fair market value of the acquired company's net assets. To illustrate this situation, assume that Principal Company acquired Sentinel Company on January 1, 20x1 at a price of $116,000 when Sentinel Company had the following book and fair values in its balance sheet:

Sentinel Company

Assets	Book Value	Fair Value
Cash	$ 15,000	$ 15,000
Other current assets	25,000	25,000
Land	50,000	50,000
Buildings (net)	100,000	130,000
Total assets	190,000	

Liabilities and Equities		
Current liabilities	10,000	10,000
Long-term liabilities	40,000	40,000
Common stock, $1 par value	50,000	
Retained earnings	90,000	
Total liabilities and equity	$190,000	

The allocation schedule for the acquisition would appear as follows:

Price of Sentinel common stock		$116,000
Stockholders equity of Sentinel:		
Common stock	$50,000	
Retained earnings	90,000	140,000
Excess of cost over book value		$(24,000)

		Allocate Negative Goodwill	Final Allocation
Allocation			
Land	$	$(15,000)	$(15,000)
Buildings undervalued	30,000	(39,000)	(9,000)
Negative goodwill (residual amount)	(54,000)	54,000	-
Excess of cost over book value	$(24,000)		$(24,000)

Allocation of the negative goodwill:

	Relative Market Values		Negative Goodwill		Allocation
Land	$ 50,000/$180,000*	×	$ 54,000	=	($15,000)
Building	$ 130,000/$180,000	×	$ 54,000	=	($39,000)

* *$180,000 equals the sum of the fair values of the assets to which goodwill may be allocated.*

In this case, the price paid for the investment is below the underlying book value of the acquired company's net assets, even though one of these assets (Buildings) has a fair market value in excess of book value. Note that the amount of negative goodwill ($54,000) is measured as the difference between the price paid for Sentinel of $116,000 and the fair market values of the net assets of Sentinel of $170,000. Also note that the negative goodwill is assigned to both the land and building even though the building is the only asset that has a book-fair market value difference at the acquisition date. A series of journal entries for both the acquisition and the merger is as follows:

(1)	Investment in Sentinel	116,000	
	Cash		116,000
(2)	Cash	15,000	
	Other current assets	25,000	
	Land	50,000	
	Buildings (net)	130,000	
	Goodwill		54,000
	Current liabilities		10,000
	Long-term liabilities		40,000
	Investment in Sentinel		116,000
(3)	Goodwill	54,000	
	Land		15,000
	Buildings (net)		39,000

As an alternative, entries (2) and (3) may be done in one step, by allocating the negative goodwill prior to recording the merger.

(2)	Cash	15,000	
	Other current assets	25,000	
	Land ($50,000 − $15,000)	35,000	
	Buildings (net) ($130,000 − $39,000)	91,000	
	Current liabilities		10,000
	Long-term liabilities		40,000
	Investment in Sentinel		116,000

Assuming Principal Company had a balance sheet as shown in the following schedule, a worksheet (using the first set of entries) can then be prepared to show the financial position of the two companies immediately after the acquisition:

Principal Company	Book Value	Debit			Credit	Combined
Cash	$240,000	(2)	15,000	(1)	116,000	$139,000
Other current assets	50,000	(2)	25,000			75,000
Land	100,000	(2)	50,000	(3)	15,000	135,000
Buildings (net)	260,000	(2)	130,000	(3)	39,000	351,000
Investment in Sentinel		(1)	116,000	(2)	116,000	—
Goodwill		(3)	54,000	(2)	54,000	—
	650,000					700,000
Current liabilities	25,000			(2)	10,000	35,000
Long-term liabilities	100,000			(2)	40,000	140,000
Common stock, $1 par	250,000					250,000
Retained earnings	275,000					275,000
	$650,000					$700,000

⬤ **INTERPRETIVE EXERCISE**

> Prepare an allocation schedule and worksheet for the merger of Principal and Sentinel if the purchase price was $107,000 for the above acquisition.

SUMMARY

The following learning objective was stated at the beginning of this appendix:

- Account for bargain purchase mergers/consolidations using the purchase method

Mergers or consolidations may sometimes involve a payment of less than the fair market value for the identifiable net assets of the acquired company. This type of event is called a **bargain purchase,** and the allocation schedule will show a **negative goodwill** residual. Negative goodwill that should be allocated to non-current assets other than financial assets, assets held for sale, and deferred taxes. When there is more than one class of such long-term assets, a relative market value allocation procedure is needed to compute the amount by which each long-term asset is reduced. In the unlikely event that negative goodwill remains after non-current assets other than marketable securities are reduced to zero, this residual is reported as an extraordinary gain.

QUESTIONS

1. Explain why the management of a company may wish to acquire control of another company.
2. Contrast the structure of a business combination characterized as a merger with a business combination characterized as a consolidation.
3. When one company is merged into another company, it may be liquidated. Describe two ways that a business combination might be structured whereby the company acquired is liquidated.
4. Explain how an acquisition of stock business combination allows the companies involved to remain separate entities after the combination.
5. Differentiate between a consolidation and consolidated financial statements.
6. In an acquisition of stock type business combination, the two parties to the combination are called the parent company and the subsidiary company. Why are these terms useful in describing this type of combination?
7. What value is assigned to the investment account in a purchase method business combination? If the investment account is closed out in a merger transaction, what value is assigned to the assets and liabilities of the acquired company when they are recorded on the books of the acquiring company?
8. Are the assets and the liabilities of an acquiring company revalued when it acquires another company in a purchase method business combination? Explain.
9. When an acquiring company issues its own common stock in a business combination, is the stock recorded at book value or fair market value? Explain.
10. Under what condition is goodwill reported in the balance sheet of a company? How is it measured?
11. How are direct acquisition costs, issue costs, and internal expenses associated with a business combination transaction reported in the financial statements of an acquiring company? Explain the reasons for your answer.

12. For what period are combined results of operations shown in the financial statements of companies involved in a purchase method business combination?

13. Describe the pro-forma disclosures required in footnotes of companies involved in a purchase method business combination.

14. (Appendix 1) Describe how goodwill originates and when impairment testing is to be done. What information is needed to determine if goodwill is impaired?

15. (Appendix 2) Under what conditions can "negative goodwill" arise in connection with a business combination? What disposition is made of negative goodwill in the combined financial statements?

EXERCISES

Exercise 1-1   **(Multiple choice: select the best answer for each item.)**

1. Which of the following types of business combinations is least similar to the others?
   a. Merger
   b. Consolidation
   c. Acquisition of stock
   d. All of the above are equally similar.

2. In a business combination in which one company is merged into another, the company acquired
   a. remains a subsidiary of the acquiring company.
   b. is normally liquidated and its net assets are recorded by the acquiring company.
   c. can never be liquidated, but its net assets are always recorded by the acquiring company.
   d. must be purchased for cash.

3. In a business combination characterized as an acquisition of stock, the parent company
   a. must acquire at least 90% of the subsidiary's voting common stock.
   b. must acquire a controlling interest in the subsidiary's voting common stock.
   c. must acquire 100% of the subsidiary's voting common stock.
   d. may acquire less than 100% of the subsidiary's voting common stock only if the combination is accounted for by the purchase method.

4. In a business combination accounted for by the purchase method, the initial investment in the common stock of the acquired company is recorded at
   a. fair market value on the date of acquisition.
   b. book value of the subsidiary's net assets on the date of acquisition.
   c. the lower of a or b above.
   d. at fair market value only if fair market value is higher than book value.

5. Which of the following statements is true for a business combination where the fair market values of the net assets acquired are greater than their book values?
   a. Goodwill will be recorded equal to the difference between the fair market value and book value of the net assets acquired.
   b. Goodwill will be recorded equal to the excess of price paid over the fair market value of the net assets acquired.
   c. Goodwill will be recorded equal to the excess of price paid over the book value of the net assets acquired.
   d. None of the above is true.

6. If a company is acquired in a purchase method business combination in exchange for common stock of the acquiring company, the issue costs associated with the stock
   a. are charged to additional paid-in-capital.
   b. are recorded as goodwill.
   c. are charged to expense.
   d. are capitalized as part of the investment in the stock of the acquired company.

7. In all business combination transactions, footnotes must contain
   a. the method of accounting for the combination.
   b. a description of the company acquired.
   c. a description of the consideration given in exchange for the net assets and/or stock of the acquired company.
   d. All of the above are required disclosures.
8. The existence of overvalued assets (when comparing book and market value) on the books of a company acquired in a purchase method business combination
   a. increases the excess of cost over book value applicable to unrecorded goodwill.
   b. decreases the excess of cost over book value applicable to unrecorded goodwill.
   c. has the same effect as overvalued liabilities on the excess of cost over book value applicable to unrecorded goodwill.
   d. means that there will never be goodwill recorded in the business combination.
9. Direct acquisition costs associated with a purchase method business combination are
   a. accounted for in the same manner as issue costs.
   b. accounted for in the same manner as consideration given to the selling shareholders.
   c. must always be expensed.
   d. capitalized as a deferred charge and amortized over a period of not more than five years.
10. Which of the following statements is true when the liabilities of an acquired company are overvalued (when comparing book and market value) on the books of a company acquired in a purchase method business combination?
   a. The excess of book value over fair value of the liabilities will decrease residual goodwill.
   b. The excess of book value over fair value of the liabilities will increase residual goodwill.
   c. Goodwill cannot result in the allocation analysis.
   d. Goodwill will always result in the allocation analysis.
   e. None of the above is correct.

Exercise 1-2　　　**(Merger with a cash payment)**

April Company acquires a 100% interest in November Company by purchasing all of its outstanding common stock for $170,000 cash. There were no additional direct acquisition costs incurred in connection with the acquisition. Immediately prior to the acquisition, November had the following balance sheet. All assets and liabilities had book values approximately equal to the fair market values.

Assets		Liabilities and Equity	
Cash	$ 10,000	Current liabilities	$ 5,000
Other current assets	35,000	Long-term debt	50,000
Plant and equipment	145,000	Common stock, no par value	25,000
Intangible assets	15,000	Retained earnings	125,000
Total assets	$205,000	Total liabilities and equity	$205,000

Immediately after the acquisition of the stock, November Company was merged into April Company and dissolved.

Required:

(1) Record the journal entries for the acquisition of the common stock of November Company by April Company.
(2) Record the journal entry for the merger of November into April on April's books.

Exercise 1-3	**(Merger with a stock issue)**

Using the balance sheet data in exercise 1–2, assume that April Company acquired 100% of the outstanding common stock of November Company in exchange for 6,000 shares of its own $10 par common stock with a market value of $30 per share on the date of the acquisition. Also assume that the expenses of issue were $5,000.

Required:

(1) Record the journal entries for the acquisition of the common stock of November and the issue costs on the books of April Company.
(2) Record the journal entry for the merger of November into April on April's books.

Exercise 1-4	**(Business and economic incentives for business combinations)**

Go to your library and obtain a recent copy of the business periodical *Mergers and Acquisitions* or a similar periodical that frequently reports news about business combinations. Read an article about a recent business combination. Write a one-page report that summarizes the article and discuss the potential impact of this combination on the customers and shareholders of the company.

Exercise 1-5	**(Structuring a business combination)**

The Nancy Wagner Golf Club Company is a 10-year old company that manufactures golf clubs, specializing in providing high-end products for women golfers. The company's flagship line is a set of graphite shaft titanium clubs sold under the trademark "Nancy." The company's annual sales grew at a rate of 20% to 25% per year for the first eight years, but for the two most recent years, sales growth has slowed to only 8% to 10% per year. Company president Rebecca Jamieson and the board of directors have outlined two possible strategies to get the company back on a more aggressive growth pattern. These are as follows:

a. Maintain the manufacturing focus on products for women players, but expand the product line to include clothing, bags, shoes, and accessories. The company will outsource production of these items to other companies and will market them exclusively through golf shops.
b. Aggressively move into specialty retailing by opening retail outlets in key markets where golf is a significant recreational activity. This strategy will be pursued by acquiring a 60% interest in Eagle Discount Golf, a publicly traded company that operates 65 stores throughout the United States.

Required:

Alone or in a discussion group

(1) Evaluate the above strategies in terms of the business opportunities that each offers, the costs likely to be incurred in pursuing them, and any potential business risks that are apparent.
(2) Assume that the board elects to pursue both strategies. Outline the ways that the transaction described in part (b) could be structured. Which of these seems to be the best choice? Explain why you support this alternative.

Exercise 1-6	**(Journal entries for a merger)**

On January 1, 20x4, Pascal Company and Shoreline Company agree to a business combination whereby Pascal acquires all of the outstanding common stock of Shoreline for $300,000. Pascal also incurs $25,000 in direct acquisition costs paid to a management consulting firm. Shoreline Company is to be liquidated and merged into Pascal Company on April 1, 20x4, the effective date of the merger.

On April 1, 20x4, immediately prior to the merger, Shoreline had the following book and fair market values:

Assets	Book Value	Fair Value
Cash	$ 25,000	$ 25,000
Other current assets	40,000	40,000
Plant and equipment	250,000	275,000
Total assets	315,000	

Liabilities and Equity		
Current liabilities	10,000	10,000
Long-term liabilities	50,000	50,000
Common stock	50,000	
Retained earnings	205,000	
Total liabilities and equity	$315,000	

Required:

Record all the journal entries on the books of Pascal Company to record the acquisition and merger of Shoreline Company.

Exercise 1-7

(Journal entries for a merger; Appendix 1)

Refer to the data in exercise 1–6. Prepare the journal entries for the acquisition of Shoreline Company by Pascal, assuming that the consideration given was $250,000 cash plus $15,000 direct acquisition cost.

Exercise 1-8

(Journal entries for a merger)

On July 1, 20x1, Power Corporation and Sundown Drilling Company agree to a business combination whereby Power acquires all of the outstanding common stock of Sundown Drilling for $75,000 in cash and 100,000 shares of Power common. Sundown Drilling is to be liquidated and merged into Power on October 1, 20x1, the effective date of the merger. On October 1, 20x1, Power common has a par value of $1.00 per share and a market value of $3.00 per share. Power also pays $30,000 to a consulting firm in connection with the merger. The internal costs of the Power acquisitions department are estimated to be $15,000 for this acquisition.

On October 1, 20x1, immediately prior to the merger, Sundown Drilling had the following book and fair market values:

	Book Value	Fair Market Value
Cash	$ 75,000	$ 75,000
Other current assets	140,000	140,000
Plant and equipment	225,000	250,000
Patents	65,000	40,000
Total assets	505,000	
Current liabilities	45,000	45,000
Bonds payable	200,000	200,000
Common stock, no par value	50,000	
Retained earnings	210,000	
Total liabilities and equity	$505,000	

Required:

Record all the journal entries on the books of Power to record the acquisition and merger of Sundown Drilling.

Exercise 1-9

(Journal entries for a merger with negative goodwill; Appendix 1)

Assume the same facts as in exercise 1–8 except that Power acquires Sundown Drilling for a cash price of $252,750 and that there were no internal expenses and no common stock was issued.

Required:

Record all the journal entries on the books of Power to record the acquisition and merger of Sundown Drilling.

Exercise 1-10

(Bargain purchase; Appendix 2)

Pacific Feed Company acquired the Pet Food businesses of Standard Mills, Inc. on January 1, 20x1 for $60,000. In addition, Pacific incurred $5,000 in consulting fees in connection with this acquisition. On this date, the Standard Mills, Inc. net assets of the pet food businesses had the following book and fair market values:

Assets	Book Value	Fair Market Value
Cash	$ 10,000	$ 10,000
Other current assets	30,000	30,000
Plant and equipment - net	100,000	130,000
Total assets	140,000	170,000

Liabilities		
Current liabilities	20,000	20,000
Long-term debt	70,000	70,000
Total liabilities	$ 90,000	$ 90,000

Required:

Record Pacific Feed Company's journal entries required for the acquisition of the net assets of Standard Mills, Inc. following the purchase method of accounting.

Exercise 1-11

(Bargain purchase; Appendix 2)

Peripheral Systems Company acquired Sunspot Micro Company in a purchase business combination for $50,000 cash on January 1, 20x4. Additional direct acquisition costs totaled $10,000. The acquisition was accomplished by a purchase of 100% of the outstanding common stock of Sunspot, followed by a dissolution of Sunspot. Sunspot Micro Company's assets were then recorded on the books of Peripheral, and Sunspot's common stock was retired.

Immediately prior to the acquisition, Sunspot Micro had the following net assets:

Assets	Book Value	Fair Market Value
Cash	$ 20,000	$ 20,000
Other current assets	40,000	30,000
Land	50,000	80,000
Building - net	80,000	100,000
Machinery and equipment - net	65,000	120,000
Total assets	255,000	350,000

Liabilities

Current liabilities	30,000	30,000
Long-term debt	125,000	140,000
Total liabilities	$155,000	$170,000

Required:

Give the journal entries to record both the acquisition and the merger of Sunspot into Peripheral.

PROBLEMS

Problem 1-1

(Financial disclosures of acquisitions)

Find a Web site for a large corporation and locate or download its most recent annual financial report. You can do this by using a search command or experiment by simply looking for an address in the format of http://www.companyname.com. Search until you find a company that has reported an acquisition within the last year. For all such acquisitions, the company should have a footnote detailing the disclosure requirements required by par. 51 of FASB Statement 141.

Required:

(1) Determine if the disclosure requirements are in compliance with FASB 141.
(2) Write a one-page report describing the acquisition and explaining the business reasons for it.

Problem 1-2

(Combined balance sheet after a merger, cash acquisition)

On January 1, 20x3, Tower Company acquired 100% of the outstanding common stock of Arthur Company in exchange for $160,000 cash. Tower Company also incurred $10,000 of direct acquisition costs in the form of consulting fees in connection with this acquisition. Immediately after the stock acquisition, Arthur Company was merged into Tower Company and dissolved. The balance sheets of the two companies immediately prior to the merger were as follows:

	Tower Company	Arthur Company
Cash	$200,000	$ 35,000
Other current assets	155,000	65,000
Plant assets	250,000	250,000
Total assets	605,000	350,000
Current liabilities	140,000	50,000
Long-term debt	200,000	130,000
Capital stock	100,000	25,000
Retained earnings	165,000	145,000
Total liabilities and equity	$605,000	$350,000

At the date of acquisition, the book values and fair market values of the net assets of both companies were approximately equal.

Required:

Prepare a combined balance sheet for the merged companies immediately after the acquisition and dissolution of Arthur Company.

Problem 1-3

(Combined balance sheet after a merger, stock acquisition)

Refer to the data in problem 1–2. Assume that Tower Company issued 10,000 shares of $10 par common stock with a market value of $170,000. There were no issue costs or direct acquisition costs.

Required:

Prepare a combined balance sheet for the merged companies immediately after the acquisition and dissolution of Arthur Company.

Problem 1-4

(Journal entries for a merger)

On January 1, 20x2, Boston Company acquired all of the common stock of Hartford Company in a business combination accounted for as a purchase for $300,000 cash. Immediately thereafter, Hartford's net assets were merged into Boston and Hartford was dissolved. Additional direct acquisition costs totaled $15,000. Immediately prior to the purchase, Hartford Company had the following balance sheet:

Hartford Company
Balance Sheet
December 31, 20x1

Assets		Liabilities and Equity	
Current Assets	$ 50,000	Liabilities	$ 125,000
Land	100,000	Common stock, $5 par	50,000
Building	300,000	Additional paid-in capital	175,000
Accumulated depreciation,		Retained earnings	25,000
Building	(75,000)		
Total assets	$ 375,000	Total liabilities and equity	$ 375,000

On December 31, 20x1, Hartford's assets and liabilities had fair market values equal to the following:

Current assets	$ 40,000
Land	110,000
Building	250,000
Liabilities	110,000

Required:

(1) Prepare an allocation schedule for the acquisition of Hartford by Boston.
(2) Record the acquisition of the investment in the common stock of Hartford and the subsequent merger on the books of Boston.

✓ **Problem 1-5**

(Journal entries and worksheet for a merger)

Tinker Company acquired all of the common stock of Toy Company in a business combination accounted for as a purchase for $100,000 cash and 40,000 shares of its own $1 par common stock. At the time of the purchase, Tinker Company common stock had a market value of

$8 per share. Issue costs were $10,000. In addition, Tinker Company paid a finders fee to a management consulting firm of $20,000, and the internal expenses of its own legal department for activities related to the merger totaled $15,000. Immediately prior to the acquisition, the book and fair market values of the assets and liabilities of the two companies were as follows:

	Tinker Company		Toy Company	
	Book Value	Fair Value	Book Value	Fair Value
Cash	$ 200,000	$ 200,000	$ 30,000	$ 30,000
Other current assets	30,000	30,000	25,000	25,000
Land	75,000	90,000	60,000	125,000
Buildings (net)	250,000	225,000	125,000	175,000
Equipment (net)	175,000	190,000	175,000	200,000
Total assets	730,000		415,000	
Current liabilities	60,000	65,000	55,000	55,000
Long-term liabilities	260,000	250,000	150,000	175,000
Common stock, $1 par	100,000		50,000	
Retained earnings	310,000		160,000	
Total liabilities and equity	$ 730,000		$ 415,000	

Required:

(1) Prepare an allocation schedule for the acquisition of Toy by Tinker.
(2) Record the acquisition of the investment in the common stock of Toy and the subsequent merger on the books of Tinker.
(3) Prepare a worksheet to combine the balance sheets of the two companies.

✓ **Problem 1-6**

(Journal entries and worksheet for a merger; Appendix 2)

Assume the same facts as in problem 1–5 except that the Tinker Company common stock has a market value of $2⅝ ($2.625) on the day of the merger.

Required:

(1) Prepare an allocation schedule for the acquisition of Toy by Tinker.
(2) Record the acquisition of the investment in the common stock of Toy and the subsequent merger on the books of Tinker.
(3) Prepare a worksheet to combine the balance sheets of the two companies.

Problem 1-7

(Financial statement after a consolidation)

On October 1, 20x0, River Rouge Cosmetics Company and Herbal Plant Farms, Inc. reach an agreement whereby the two companies agree to consolidate into a newly formed company, Rouge-Herbal, Inc. Rouge-Herbal, Inc. will issue 10,000 shares of no par common stock for all of the outstanding common stock of River Rouge and 12,000 shares of no par common stock for all of the outstanding common stock of Herbal Plant Farms. No cash will be involved in the transactions. The acquisitions are to be accounted for by the purchase method.

On October 1, 20x0, immediately prior to the consolidation, the two companies had the following book and fair values:

	River Rouge		Herbal Plant Farms	
	Book Value	Fair Value	Book Value	Fair Value
Current assets	$ 20,000	$ 20,000	$ 35,000	$ 35,000
Accounts receivable	40,000	35,000	50,000	48,000
Buildings	150,000	175,000	150,000	160,000
Plant and equipment	200,000	190,000	275,000	300,000
Total assets	410,000		510,000	
Current liabilities	35,000	35,000	50,000	50,000
Notes payable	100,000	95,000	75,000	78,000
Common stock	50,000		65,000	
Retained earnings	225,000		320,000	
Total liabilities and equity	$410,000		$510,000	

Required:

Prepare a balance sheet for Rouge-Herbal, Inc. immediately after the consolidation of River Rouge and Herbal Plant Farms.

Problem 1-8

(Bargain purchase; Appendix 2)

On January 1, 20x2, Presidium Company acquired 100% of the outstanding voting common stock of Standoff Company and immediately merged Standoff's net assets into Presidium. Presidium Company was then dissolved. The consideration given for Standoff's common stock was 10,000 shares of Presidium common with a par value of $1 and a market value of $18.50 per share. In addition, Presidium incurred $20,000 in issue costs. Immediately prior to the acquisition, the following data are available for the two companies:

Assets	Presidium Book Value	Standoff Book Value	Standoff Fair Market Value
Cash	$ 50,000	$ 45,000	$ 45,000
Other current assets	40,000	25,000	25,000
Land	100,000	25,000	45,000
Buildings—net	150,000	100,000	90,000
Machinery and equipment—net	200,000	30,000	45,000
Total assets	540,000	225,000	250,000
Liabilities and Equity			
Current liabilities	50,000	20,000	20,000
Long-term debt	300,000	25,000	20,000
Common stock	100,000	40,000	
Retained earnings	90,000	140,000	
Total liabilities	$540,000	$225,000	$ 40,000

Required:

Prepare a balance sheet for Presidium subsequent to the acquisition.

Problem 1-9

(Planning a business combination)

National Cookie Company was a food processing company that was formed in 1901 in Pittsburgh by Antonio Aguilar, a Spanish immigrant. By 1930, it was manufacturing and distributing its products nationwide. Shortly after the end of World War II, the company undertook an aggressive expansion program into European markets and changed its name to International Cookie Company. By 1995, International Cookie was operating worldwide and had changed its name again to INCC, Inc. International Cookie is widely held, and the Aguilar family is no longer active in the management of the company. Institutional investors own 27% of its common stock.

La Banane, Inc. is a banana and coffee importer headquartered in New Orleans and was formed in 1926 by two brothers from Honduras, Emilio and Arturo Sanchez. La Banane, Inc. is a holding company with two subsidiaries, Sanchez Brothers Fruit Company and Columbian Aromatic Coffee Company. The parent company is controlled by the Sanchez family, who own 70% of the common stock. The current president of the company is Isabel Perez, a granddaughter of Arturo Sanchez.

The current president of INCC, Inc., Robert Anderssen, upon authorization by the INCC board of directors, had approached La Banane, Inc. management with a proposal that the two companies combine. The management of both companies have agreed in principle that the combination may be a positive step, however, they are unsure of what alternatives are available to structure the transaction.

Required:

You have been engaged as a consultant and have been asked to answer the following questions:
(1) What alternatives could the two companies use to structure a combination? State the advantages and disadvantages of each.
(2) What arguments can the management of INCC present to its shareholders in favor of the combination?
(3) What problems can you foresee in structuring the combination and in subsequent management of the combined organization that you would discuss with the directors of the two companies in connection with your engagement?

Problem 1-10

(Research case: disposing of a product line)

Rover Feed Company is a leading manufacturer of pet foods and has a full line of products for dogs and cats, as well as products for other domestic animals such as horses. It also has a 4% market share in the ready-to-eat cereal business, an industry that is dominated by three other companies. Rover's management has decided, with board of director approval, to dispose of its ready-to-eat cereal business. Currently that business is operated as a division rather than as a separate subsidiary. It has two factories. One is located in Des Moines, Iowa, and the other is in Dayton, Ohio. Products are shipped by rail and truck lines to customers throughout the United States. Eighty percent of its business is done with 20 large supermarket companies.

Summarized financial data (in millions of dollars) for the ready-to-eat cereal division of Rover Feed Company for the two most recent fiscal years ended December 31 are as follows:

	Year 2	Year 1
Sales	$3,561	$3,775
Operating income	(122)	120
Net assets	240	265

Debate and discussion among management and the directors has centered on what to do with this division. Three suggestions have been proposed. Alternative one calls for selling the two factories and related equipment outright. Alternative two involves creating a subsidiary company to which the assets and liabilities of the ready-to-eat cereal division are transferred, followed by a sale of the subsidiary. Alternative three involves transferring the assets and liabilities to a newly organized subsidiary followed by a spin-off of the subsidiary. While the division was historically profitable, the division has not done well recently because of increasingly aggressive marketing by its competitors and changes in dietary preferences of heath-conscious consumers. Management believes that the division can be sold, but it is not sure whether it can be sold at a profit. Preliminary indications are that at least two competitors are interested in discussing a possible sale.

Required:

Evaluate the three alternatives suggested for the divestiture. In your evaluation, discuss what additional information you would like to have, as well as how that information would affect your recommendation about the best course of action.

Problem 1-11

(Research case: accounting for an acquisition)

Five States Gas Company is a gas utility company that has been aggressively moving into distribution of propane gas in the areas where it has traditionally sold natural gas. Natural gas is distributed to residential and commercial customers through pipelines. Propane gas, however, is delivered using tanker trucks. Its principal users are residential customers and small businesses in rural areas and towns where natural gas is not available. One of the ways that Five States Gas has been expanding is by purchasing existing businesses. Many of these businesses are small, family-owned propane distribution companies having fewer than 2,500 customers. Five States acquires these businesses for cash, acquiring all the depot and storage assets, as well as the distribution equipment. Hourly paid employees of the newly acquired businesses are normally offered employment with Five States. Administrative functions, such as purchasing, billing, and accounting, are centralized at Five States Headquarters. Virtually all of these acquisitions are accounted for as asset mergers, being merged into a subsidiary, Five States Propane Company. The typical acquisition also includes a non-compete agreement for a period of 10 years, in which the seller agrees not to compete with Five States Propane Company in the sale and distribution of propane gas or competing products. These non-compete agreements are obtained in exchange for amounts ranging from $100,000 to $500,000 cash, in addition to amounts paid for the net assets acquired.

Five States is currently negotiating with Arland LP Gas, Inc., a family-owned propane distribution and service company located in a three-county area. The following data from Arland's audited financial statements for the last four years is available.

Fiscal Years ending *12/31*

	Year 4 (Current Year)	Year 3	Year 2	Year 1
Average number of customers	3,100	2,950	2,833	2,715
Average revenue per customer	$ 480	$ 465	$ 466	$ 447
Total revenue	1,488,000	1,371,750	1,320,178	1,213,605
Net income	44,640	37,723	59,408	51,578
Appraised value of identifiable net assets	425,000	433,000	414,000	398,000

Required:

Answer the following questions.
(1) Discuss the issues that Five States should consider in estimating a fair market value for Arland. Calculate at least two estimates of fair market value assuming that a normal return on identifiable net assets is 9% after taxes.

(2) How would you recommend accounting for any goodwill paid upon acquisition?

(3) Assuming Five States pays $250,000 over 10 years for a non-compete agreement, how would you account for this payment?

Problem 1-12

(Research case: planning and implementing an acquisition)

Western Lumber and Paper Company is a multinational forest products company headquartered in Portland, Oregon. It reached an agreement in principle to acquire a small lumber company, the McIntosh Lumber Company, which operates a lumber and plywood factory in Mississippi. McIntosh also owns 110,000 acres of timberland in Mississippi and Alabama. Yet to be determined is the precise purchase price for the acquisition. McIntosh Lumber Company has 24 shareholders, all of whom are either company employees or descendants of the original founding partners who organized the company in 1901.

The balance sheet for the most recent year before the acquisition is shown below along with the net income for the last five years. The average rate of return for companies in the lumber industry during this five-year period was 16% on common equity, after taxes.

McIntosh Lumber Company
Balance Sheet
December 31, 20x1

Assets		Liabilities and Equity	
Cash	$ 435,000	Accounts payable	$ 135,000
Accounts receivable (net)	125,000	Notes payable to officers	500,000
Inventories	3,340,000	Notes payable to banks	2,500,000
Other assets	14,000	Total current liabilities	3,135,000
Total current assets	3,914,000		
		Long-term portion of	
Timberland	25,475,000	notes payable to banks	18,000,000
Plant site	350,000	Total liabilities	21,135,000
Buildings	5,234,000		
Equipment	17,347,000	Stockholders' equity	
Less Accumulated depreciation	(12,345,000)	Common stock, no par	
Total property, plant,		value, 10,000 shares	
and equipment		issued and	
	36,061,000	outstanding	5,000,000
		Retained earnings	13,840,000
Total assets	$39,975,000	Total liabilities and equity	$39,975,000

Net income for the previous five years:

Current year	$21,507,200
Year 4	11,435,988
Year 3	(233,000)
Year 2	32,400,000
Year 1	33,500,988

Additional information:

a. The timberland assets of McIntosh Lumber Company have been appraised by an independent consultant at $2,500 per acre.

b. Western Lumber engineers have evaluated the plant and equipment and have estimated that it will take $40 million to upgrade and modernize the plywood plant and the sawmill.

This modernization will enable the company to double production capacity with no additional increase in operating expenses other than depreciation.

Required:

(1) Discuss the major factors that Western Lumber must take into account in deciding how much to offer for this acquisition. Calculate a target price or a range of prices that you believe represents a realistic final price and show how you estimated these amounts.
(2) Assuming the price paid by Western Lumber exceeds the underlying book values of McIntosh's net assets, how will this excess be accounted for in a merger? What will be the impact on the net income of future years?
(3) Suppose the price ultimately agreed upon is $300 million. What are the ramifications of a purchase for cash as opposed to a purchase in which the consideration given is common stock of Western Lumber?

Problem 1-13

(Group or individual Internet project)

Identify a company involved in a hostile takeover dispute. Find the company's Web site. Gather information from press releases, news articles, and other sources and prepare a 15-minute computer presentation on the facts of the case, the issues giving rise to the dispute, and its final resolution.

CHAPTER 2

ACCOUNTING FOR INVESTMENTS IN THE COMMON STOCK OF AFFILIATES

LEARNING OBJECTIVES

■ Describe the methods of accounting required for different types of common stock investments

■ Compare accounting for common stock investments using the cost method and the equity method

■ Apply the equity method where investment cost exceeds the fair market value of identifiable investee net assets

ACCOUNTING FOR ACQUISITIONS OF COMMON STOCK

As Figure 2-1 illustrates, there are three possible classifications for common stock investments: passive investments, substantial influence investments, and controlled investments. This chapter provides an overview of each of these followed by illustration and discussion of issues related to parent company accounting for controlled investments to be consolidated. Chapter 1 described two types of business combinations. **Mergers and consolidations** result in a single entity that owns all of the assets and liabilities of the entities that were merged into it. As was illustrated in Chapter 1, these combinations require the surviving company to record the acquisition of these assets and liabilities on its books. When the purchase method is used, these transactions may require adjustment of the carrying values of target company assets and liabilities and/or the recording of purchased goodwill at the time of the acquisition. After the merger or consolidation is completed, no particularly unique accounting problems remain. The surviving entity merely prepares its financial statements in the same manner as any other business entity.

By contrast, an **acquisition of stock** business combination requires relatively little accounting on the part of the acquiring company on the acquisition date. It is only necessary that the acquiring company record an investment in the stock of the investee (target) company on the acquisition date. When the purchase method is used, the investment is recorded at *fair market value on the acquisition date*. An acquisition of stock creates an investment account that remains on the books of the acquiring company. The existence of this investment account requires the recording of journal entries for the resulting investment income. Furthermore, ownership of a controlling interest in the voting common stock of another company requires, with only limited exceptions, preparation of consolidated financial statements for the parent and subsidiary companies. The sequence of events for a stock acquisition business combination is: (1) acquisition of the common stock investment by the parent company; (2) accounting for the resulting investment account on the books of the parent company; and (3) preparation of consolidated financial statements at the end of the year. This sequence is depicted in the middle column of Figure 2-1, which illustrates the decision process and actions in accounting for controlled and noncontrolled common stock investments. The remainder of this chapter will focus on step (2), accounting for common stock investments. Procedures for preparation of consolidated financial statements will be covered in later chapters of this textbook.

Passive investments in common stock

Passive investments in common stock are those investments where the investor does not own sufficient shares to exercise substantial influence* on the policy decisions of the target company's board of directors or to control the election of those directors. According to FASB Statement No. 115[1], passive investments in common stock are initially recorded at **cost,** with **mark-to-market** adjustments made on the financial statement date to increase or decrease the carrying value of the investments to fair market value. Under the **cost** method, dividends received on common stock investments are recorded as dividend income by the investor. The unrealized gains or losses resulting from the adjustment to fair market value are either included in income or deferred as an element of stockholders' equity depending upon whether the investments are classified as "trading

---

* See next section for explanation of substantial influence.

[1] Statement of Financial Accounting Standards No. 115, *Accounting for Certain Investments in Debt and Equity Securities* (Norwalk, CT: Financial Accounting Standards Board, 1993).

securities" or "securities available for sale." In general, unrealized gains and losses on the "trading securities" portfolio are included in income, whereas gains and losses on the "securities available for sale" portfolio are deferred as an element of stockholders' equity. For a more comprehensive discussion and illustration of these adjustments, please refer to the investments chapter of an intermediate accounting textbook.

FIGURE 2·1: Passive, Substantial Influence and Controlled Investments in Common Stock

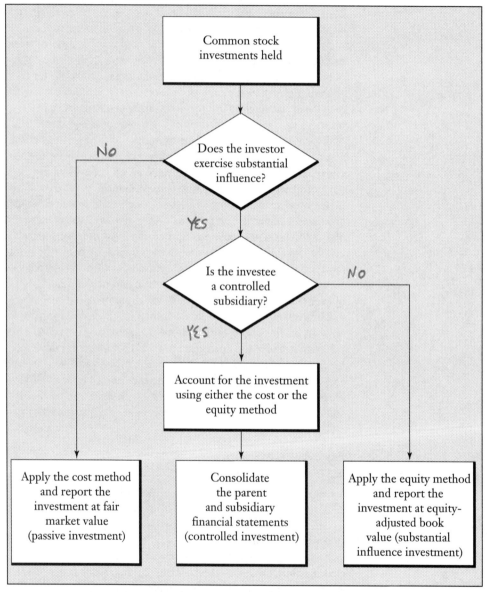

Substantial influence investments in common stock

APB Opinion No. 18[2] requires the equity method of accounting for unconsolidated investments in common stock if the investor exercises a *substantial influence* on the

[2] Accounting Principles Board Opinion No. 18, *The Equity Method of Accounting for Investments in Common Stock* (New York: American Institute of Certified Public Accountants, 1971).

investee. Under the equity method, an investment in the common stock of another company is recorded at cost when purchased, just as for passive investments. Income from an investment accounted for under the equity method is based upon the underlying income earned by the investee, resulting in a rather unusual journal entry that debits the investment account and credits an income account:

Investment in Common Stock   XX
      Equity in Investee Earnings (Income from Invest)   XX
(To record the investor's equity share of the investee's earnings under the
        equity method)

Dividends from an investment accounted for under the equity method are reported as a return of capital. Accordingly, any dividend received is credited to the investment account:

Cash   XX
      Investment in Common Stock   XX
(To record the receipt of dividends from the investee under the equity method)

The theory underlying the equity method is that income from the investment in common stock should be calculated using the same accounting principles the investee uses to measure its income. The most difficult question to answer in deciding whether to use the equity method of accounting for an investment in common stock is deciding whether substantial influence exists. *APB Opinion No. 18* contains a provision, which allows, in absence of evidence to the contrary, the **presumption of substantial influence** when the investment equals or exceeds 20% of the outstanding voting common stock of the investee.[3] Interpretation of this provision proved troublesome for many companies because it was not completely clear what constituted "evidence to the contrary." There have been occasional instances of the use of the equity method for less than 20%-owned investees.[4]

Some critics argued that the equity method was misleading because it required recognition of income that had not been realized in the form of cash dividends received. In 1981, the FASB issued Interpretation No. 35, which provided criteria under which the presumption of substantial influence could be overcome.[5] This Interpretation specifies the presumption of substantial influence may be overcome by "substantial evidence to the contrary." Several examples are given:

a. Opposition by the investee, such as litigation or complaints to a regulatory agency.
b. Execution of an agreement whereby the investor surrenders substantial rights as a shareholder.

---

[3] Accounting Principles Board Opinion No. 18, par. 17.

[4] Use of the equity method for less than 20% owned would seem to be permitted if the investor has the ability to exercise substantial influence. APB 18 does not specifically discuss the less than 20%-owned case. Factors indicative of the ability to exercise substantial influence include representation on the board of directors or other factors indicating the ability to influence corporate policy. However, in the opinion of the author, the adoption of the equity method for a less than 20%-owned investment should be done only after careful analysis of the substantial influence issue.

[5] Statement of Financial Accounting Standards Interpretation No. 35, *Criteria for Applying the Equity Method of Accounting for Investments in Common Stock* (Norwalk, CT: Financial Accounting Standards Board, 1981).

    c. Existence of another individual or group exercising majority ownership.

    d. The investor tries and fails to obtain information that would enable it to apply the equity method.

    e. The investor tries and fails to obtain representation on the board of directors of the investee.

Because the equity method of accounting recognizes unrealized income, the financial media has sometimes questioned its use (see box: "Is the Equity Method Misleading"). In defense of the equity method, however, it should be observed that this approach to disclosure has been used for more than 30 years and has not been recently questioned. Recent FASB standards (notably those on investments and the reporting of comprehensive income) have increased the practice of reporting unrealized income.

IS THE EQUITY METHOD MISLEADING?

The equity method of accounting is an unusual method of measuring income because it reports income during the period that the investee realizes it rather than when the investor receives it. An investor using the equity method will report income on its investment even if no dividends are declared. The financial press has criticized this process of reporting income in absence of a cash inflow.

The authoritative literature has either skirted the issue of the non-cash nature of equity method income or ignored it completely. APB Opinion No. 18 uses rather vague arguments to defend the equity method, describing it as "an appropriate means of recognizing increases or decreases measured by generally accepted accounting principles in the economic resources underlying the investments."[6] The theoretical merit of the equity method is not discussed at all in the Opinion. The FASB has discussed the equity method only once, in FASB Interpretation No. 35.[7] This pronouncement only deals with the issue of when the presumption of substantial influence might be overcome.

Rarely are equity earnings material in relation to total net income. If they are, care must be taken to assure that the financial statement reader understands that equity earnings are non-cash. Standard practice accomplishes this disclosure in the cash flow statement, particularly when the indirect method for cash flow presentation is used. Using this approach, the non-cash portion of equity earnings is subtracted from net income in arriving at cash provided by operations. It is clear that only sophisticated financial statement users can easily interpret these somewhat complex and very abstract disclosures. Thus, the ultimate question of whether the equity method of accounting is appropriate when equity earnings are a material portion of net income, or whether the equity method should be used at all, is essentially unresolved.

Controlled investments in common stock

FASB Statement No. 94[8] requires that financial statements of majority-owned subsidiaries be included in the consolidated financial statements of the parent company unless control of the subsidiary does not rest with the parent company or control is deemed to be temporary. These two conditions occur infrequently. For example, control

---

[6] Accounting Principles Board Opinion No. 18, par. 10.

[7] FASB Interpretation No. 35, *Criteria for Applying the Equity Method of Accounting for Investments in Common Stock* (Norwalk, CT: Financial Accounting Standards Board, 1987).

[8] Statement of Financial Accounting Standards No. 94, *Consolidation of All Majority Owned Subsidiaries* (Norwalk, CT: Financial Accounting Standards Board, 1987).

more than 58%
→ Bankrupcy
← foreign
   country
  prohibits

of a subsidiary in bankruptcy would rest with the bankruptcy trustee and not with the parent company. Also, a subsidiary headquartered in a foreign country where the foreign government significantly restricts the transfer of capital to the parent company's country would not be controlled by the parent company. Prior to the issuance of *FASB Statement No. 94*, subsidiaries had to have operations that were economically similar to that of the parent company in order to be consolidated. This requirement meant subsidiaries in financial industries, such as insurance and finance, were generally not consolidated with a parent company whose principal business was in a different industry. These unconsolidated subsidiaries would have been accounted for by the equity method. For example, General Motors Corporation did not consolidate its financial subsidiary, GMAC, prior to the effective date of *FASB Statement No. 94*. After this effective date, all subsidiaries must be consolidated without regard to industry classification unless the subsidiary is not controlled by the parent company. Often companies will have passive, substantial influence, and controlled investments. Footnotes to the financial statement will describe the accounting policies and procedures followed by the company. Figure 2-2 provides two examples of such disclosures. The example from the ExxonMobil Corporation for 1999 is very straightforward. The other footnote, from the annual report of General Motors Corporation for 1994, is more extensive because the company has material investments of a passive nature that must be reported in accordance with FASB Statement No.115.

A COMPARISON OF THE COST METHOD AND THE EQUITY METHOD

The requirement to consolidate a subsidiary makes the parent's method of accounting for the investment irrelevant to the financial statements of the consolidated entity. As will be illustrated in Chapter 3, preparation of consolidated financial statements is a worksheet process. In the worksheet, the investment in common stock account for each subsidiary is eliminated and replaced by the assets, liabilities, revenues, expenses, and stockholders' equity of the subsidiary. Since the investment account does not appear in the consolidated financial statements, it may be accounted for by either the cost method or the equity method. The following footnote section from the 1996 annual report of the International Paper Company illustrates the contrast between the equity method and consolidation:

> "In late April of 1995, the Company acquired approximately 26% of Carter Holt Harvey, a New Zealand-based forest and paper products company for $1.1 billion. The acquisition increased International Paper's ownership to just over 50%. As a result, Carter Holt Harvey was consolidated into International Paper's financial statements beginning on May 1, 1995. Prior to this date, the equity accounting method was utilized."

If the cost method is used, the investment is initially recorded in the same manner as any other asset. An investment acquired for cash is recorded at cost. An investment acquired for non-cash consideration is recorded at either the fair market value of the consideration given or the fair market value of the asset received, whichever is more objective. Any cash dividends received by the investor are credited to dividend income.[9] The **basic** procedures for investments accounted for under the equity method are only slightly different. The initial investment under the equity amount is recorded in the same manner as for the cost method. Income under the equity method

---

[9] Note that the FASB 115 requirement to adjust cost method investments to fair market value on the financial statement date does not apply to common stock investments to be consolidated because the investment account is eliminated in the consolidated statements worksheet.

FIGURE 2-2: Disclosure of Common Stock Investments

Exxon Corporation
Principles of Consolidation. The consolidated financial statements include the accounts of those significant subsidiaries owned directly or indirectly more than 50 percent of the voting rights held by the corporation, and for which other shareholders do not possess the right to participate in significant management decisions. Amounts representing the corporation's percentage interest in the underlying net assets of other significant subsidiaries and less than majority owned companies in which a significant equity ownership interest is held, are included in "Investments and advances"; the corporation's share of the net income of these companies is included in the consolidated statement of income caption "Earnings from equity interests and other revenue."

Investments in other companies, none of which is significant, are generally included in "Investments and advances" at cost or less. Dividends from these companies are included in income as received.

(Source: Annual report of ExxonMobil Corporation for 2000)

General Motors Corporation
Principles of Consolidation. The consolidated financial statements include the accounts of General Motors Corporation (General Motors, GM, or the Corporation) and domestic and foreign subsidiaries, which are more than 50% owned. During 1992, the Corporation obtained a majority interest in National Car Rental System, Inc. (NCRS). The accounts of NCRS were consolidated effective December 31, 1992. General Motors share of earnings or losses of associates in which at least 20% of the voting securities is owned is included in consolidated operating results under the equity method of accounting (see note 2).
Accounting changes. . . . Also effective January 1, 1994, the Corporation adopted FASB No. 115, Accounting for Certain Investments in Debt and Equity Securities, which resulted in a $241.0 million after-tax increase in Stockholders' Equity. This Standard requires the recording at fair value of debt securities which are not expected to be held to maturity and equity securities which have a readily determinable fair value. Unrealized gains and losses resulting from changes in fair value are included as a separate component of Stockholders' Equity. . . . The ongoing 1994 effect was a $121.2 million decrease in Stockholders' Equity. Marketable securities, other than certain securities held by GMAC, and its subsidiaries (and described in Note 11), are considered available for sale; $869.4 million mature within one year, $248.2 million mature in two to five years, and a substantial amount of the remaining $227.4 million matures after 10 years.

(Source: Annual report of General Motors Corporation for 1994)

is calculated as the investor's share of the net income of the investee as described above. Cash dividends are accounted for as a return of capital and credited to the investment account. These two methods are compared in the following illustration:

On January 1, 20x1 Major Company purchases a 90% interest in the common stock of Minor Company for $40,000, an amount equal to 90% of the book value of Minor's common stock on the date of acquisition. During 20x1 Minor Company earns $20,000. On November 1, 20x1 Minor declares $5,000 in cash dividends, payable to stockholders of record on November 15, 20x1.

The journal entries for the cost and equity methods are as follows:

To record		Cost Method		Equity Method	
1/1/x1	Initial investment	Investment in Minor	40,000	Investment in Minor	40,000
		Cash	40,000	Cash	40,000
11/15/x1	Dividend received	Cash	4,500	**Cash**	**4,500**
		Dividend Income	**4,500**	**Investment in Minor**	**4,500**
		($5,000 × 90% = $4,500)		($5,000 × 90% = $4,500)	
12/31/x1	Equity income	No entry		**Investment in Minor**	**18,000**
				Equity in Minor Income	**18,000**
				($20,000 × 90% = $18,000)	

No entry is made under the cost method for Minor's net income. As the illustrations show, the equity method reports the income from the investment using the same measurement principles the investee uses and reports the dividends as a return of investment. The cost method simply reports dividends received as income. Under the cost method, the investor would not report any income in absence of a dividend.

● INTERPRETIVE EXERCISE

Record the entries for the year 20x2 for Major's investment in Minor if Minor earns $30,000 during the year 20x2, declares $5,000 in dividends on May 1, payable May 15 and declares $10,000 in dividends on November 1, payable November 15.

EQUITY METHOD INVESTMENTS WHERE COST EXCEEDS FAIR MARKET VALUE OF INVESTEE'S IDENTIFIABLE NET ASSETS

X   If an investment in common stock accounted for by the equity method is acquired for a price that is greater than or less than the underlying book value of the investee's net assets, the equity method entries are somewhat more complex than the basic procedures illustrated above. Specifically, the existence of such a *differential* means the income reported by the investor would not equal the income of the investee multiplied by the investor's percentage of ownership. Assuming the fair market value of the investee's net assets does not equal the book value, three possible scenarios exist:

1. Price paid exceeds fair market value of identifiable investee net assets.
2. Price paid falls between book and fair market value of underlying identifiable investee net assets.
3. Price paid is less than book value of identifiable investee net assets.

Cases (2) and (3) above are so-called bargain purchase scenarios because the price paid is less than the fair market value of identifiable investee net assets. These two cases are covered in the Appendix to this chapter. For case (1) above, the income reported under the equity method will be *lower* than the underlying income if the differential is due to undervalued net assets with a limited life. To compute equity income under these circumstances, an allocation schedule is required. The purpose of the schedule is to determine which investee assets and liabilities are the underlying cause of the differential. These allocated amounts are then amortized to determine the annual adjustments to equity in investee income, a result accomplished by comparing the book and fair values of the investee's assets and liabilities *at the date the investment is acquired*. The differences in these amounts are assumed to be the reason for the difference between the cost of the stock investment and the underlying book value. Any differential not explained by the book-fair market value differences in the investee's identifiable assets and liabilities is assumed to be unrecorded goodwill. Following is an example of this process:

> Johnson Company acquires an 80% interest in Woodside Company for $30,000 on January 1, 20x0. On this date, Woodside Company has common stock of $20,000 and retained earnings of $10,000. The book values and fair market values of Woodside Company's net assets are equal, except for equipment with a 5-year life, a fair market value of $25,000, and a book value of $20,000. Any unrecorded goodwill underlying the acquisition is assumed to have an indefinite life. During the year ended December 31, 20x0, Woodside reports net income of $3,000 and pays dividends of $1,500.

An allocation schedule for the above acquisition is shown below:

Cost of Woodside common stock		$ 30,000
Stockholders' equity of Woodside		
Common stock	$ 20,000	
Retained earnings	10,000	
	$ 30,000	
Percentage of ownership	80%	24,000
Excess of cost over book value		6,000
Allocation:		
Equipment undervalued ($5,000 × 80%)		4,000
Goodwill (remainder of excess)		2,000
Excess of cost over book value		6,000
Amortization:		
Equipment amortization ($4,000/5 years)		$ 800

Johnson Company's journal entries to recognize its investment and equity in Woodside income and dividends from Woodside would be as follows:

January 1, 20x1	Investment in Woodside	30,000	
	Cash		30,000
	To record the acquisition of the investment on January 1, 20x0		
December 31, 20x0	Investment in Woodside	2,400	
	Equity in Woodside Income		2,400
	To record equity income: $3,000 × 80% = $2,400		
December 31, 20x0	Equity in Woodside Income	800	
	Investment in Woodside		800
	To record amortization of excess of *cost over book value* attributable to equipment		
December 31, 20x0	Cash	1,200	
	Investment in Woodside		1,200
	To record the dividends received by Johnson: $1,500 × 80% = $1,200		

The above entries result in a year-end balance in Johnson Company's account, Investment in Woodside, of $30,400 ($30,000 + $2,400 − 800 − $1,200).

Changes in ownership percentage of common stock investments

Circumstances may arise that cause an investor to either increase or decrease the size of an investment in the common stock of another company. If the change in ownership percentage causes the investor to lose substantial influence or to gain substantial influence, an accounting change occurs. For example, should the percentage interest in an investment in the common stock accounted for by the equity method change so that the investor's percentage falls below 20%, it is reasonable to argue that the investor no longer exercises substantial influence. If the facts in the case confirm that the equity method is no longer appropriate, the investor should discontinue use of the equity method and account for the investment in accordance with FASB Statement 115. This particular change in accounting methods should be applied prospectively, and the effects of prior year's use of the equity method should not be adjusted or corrected.[10] However, when an investor increases its ownership in an investee so that a change from the cost method to the equity method is required, such change should be accounted for by the retroactive restatement method. The Investment account, the retained earnings of the investor, and the investment income of the current year should all be adjusted retroactively.[11]

A corporate investor might also increase its percentage ownership in an investee from a noncontrolling interest holding to a controlling interest holding. The acquisition of a subsidiary in this manner is called a **step-by-step acquisition.** Its key feature is the acquisition of a controlling interest in the subsidiary in two or more separate transactions. Accounting for step-by-step acquisitions does not require any new or unique procedures. If the initial noncontrolling interest acquisition in the investee was large enough to be accounted for by the equity method, the investor has two alternative courses of action. It may discontinue use of the equity method and adopt the cost method prospectively. Alternatively, the investor may continue using the equity method for the additional shares purchased. In this case, acquisition of a controlling interest simply requires an additional allocation schedule for the second purchase, or block, of stock. The equity method calculations are performed by constructing a separate allocation schedule for each block of stock acquired. *At no time are the separate stock acquisitions combined for purposes of applying the equity method.* The following example illustrates a step-by-step acquisition involving use of the equity method.

> Assume that Parent Company purchases a 25% interest in the common stock of Target Company on January 1, 20x0 for $15,000 at a time when Target Company has Common Stock of $10,000 and Retained earnings of $30,000. Exactly one year later Parent Company increases its ownership percentage in Target Company to 75% by purchasing an additional 50% block of Target stock for $40,000. All assets and liabilities of Target have book values approximately equal to fair market values on both January 1, 20x0 and 20x1. Thus, any excess of cost over book value is attributable to unrecorded goodwill. During the two years, Target Company has income and dividends as follows:
>
> | | 20x0 | 20x1 |
> |---|---|---|
> | Net income | $ 15,000 | $ 20,000 |
> | Dividends | 5,000 | 10,000 |

For purposes of applying the equity method, each block of stock requires a separate allocation schedule as of the date of purchase. Thus, as illustrated by the following:

---

[10] Accounting Principles Board Opinion No. 18, par. 19.

[11] *Ibid.*

		25% block	50% block
Date acquired		1/1/x0	1/1/x1
Purchase price		$ 15,000	$ 40,000
Stockholders' equity of Target Co. 1/1/x0			
Common stock	$ 10,000		
Retained earnings	30,000		
Total	40,000		
	25%	10,000	
Stockholders' equity of Target Co. 1/1/x1			
Common stock	10,000		
Retained earnings*	40,000		
Total	$ 50,000		
	50%		25,000
Goodwill		$ 5,000	$ 15,000

*Retained earnings 1/1/x0 + net income for the year − dividends for the year = $30,000 + $15,000 − $5,000

The equity method entries to be made by Parent Company for the two years are as follows:

Journal entries for the year 20x0

1/1/x0	Investment in Target	15,000	
	Cash		15,000
	To record purchase of 25% of Target common stock for $15,000		

12/31/x0	Investment in Target	3,750	
	Equity in Target Income		3,750
	To record 25% of Target income of $15,000		

12/31/x0	Cash	1,250	
	Investment in Target		1,250
	To record 25% of Target's 20x0 dividends of $5,000		

Journal entries for the year 20x1

1/1/x1	Investment in Target	40,000	
	Cash		40,000
	To record the purchase of an additional 50% of Target common stock		

12/31/x1	Investment in Target	15,000	
	Equity in Target Income		15,000
	To record 75% of Target income of $20,000		

12/31/x1	Cash	7,500	
	Investment in Target		7,500
	To record 75% of Target's dividends of $10,000		

Interim acquisitions

If an investment in the common stock of a subsidiary is acquired on a date other than the first or last day of the subsidiary's fiscal year, the subsidiary's books will probably not be closed. In this case, the retained earnings balance in the subsidiary's ledger will not reflect the actual retained earnings on the date of acquisition. In order to prepare an allocation schedule, it is necessary to determine subsidiary income and dividends from the date of the last closing up to the date of acquisition. This interim operating information is then incorporated into the allocation schedule for purposes of applying the equity method of accounting. The following example illustrates these procedures:

Calder Company acquires an 80% interest in Bryan Company for $60,000 on April 1, 20x0. On January 1, 20x0 Bryan had common stock with a par value of $10,000 and retained earnings of $30,000. For the first three months of 20x0, Bryan earned $20,000. On February 15, 20x0, Bryan directors declared a cash dividend of $10,000 payable to stockholders of record on March 1, 20x0. The book values and fair market values of Bryan Company's net assets were approximately equal on April 1, 20x0, and any excess of cost over book value is assumed to be attributable to unrecorded goodwill. For the remainder of the fiscal year ended December 31, 20x0, Bryan had net income of $30,000 and paid an additional $15,000 in dividends.

Assuming goodwill has an indefinite life, an allocation schedule for the acquisition of Bryan by Calder would be as follows:

Cost of Bryan common stock, April 1, 20x0		$ 60,000
Stockholders' equity of Bryan Company		
Common stock, January 1, 20x0	$ 10,000	
Retained earnings, January 1, 20x0	30,000	
Bryan income, January 1–April 1, 20x0	**20,000**	
Dividends paid March 1, 20x0	**(10,000)**	
	$ 50,000	
Percentage of ownership	80%	40,000
Excess of cost over book value		20,000
Allocation:		
Goodwill		$ 20,000

Since the ledger balance of Bryan's retained earnings does not reflect the actual retained earnings on the date of acquisition, both the interim income and the interim dividend must be incorporated into the allocation schedule. In effect, these adjustments allow the calculation of the stockholders' equity of Bryan as if Bryan had closed its books on April 1, 20x0. Based on the above data, Calder Company's entries to apply the equity method of accounting can be made in the normal manner. The equity income in the second entry is Calder's share of the income Bryan earned from April 1 through December 31. The equity adjustments for the year 20x0 on Calder's books are as follows:

April 1, 20x0	Investment in Bryan	60,000	
	Cash		60,000
	To record the acquisition of the investment on April 1, 20x0		
December 31, 20x0	Investment in Bryan	24,000	
	Equity in Bryan Income		24,000
	To record equity income: $30,000 \times 80\% = \$24,000$		
December 31, 20x0	Cash	12,000	
	Investment in Bryan		12,000
	To record the dividends received by Calder: $15,000 \times 80\% = \$12,000$		

AVOIDING A HOSTILE TAKEOVER

A so-called poison pill or shareholder rights plan is a provision adopted by a corporation's board of directors. The provision allows the target of a hostile takeover attempt to issue new common stock to its shareholders at substantial discount off market value. These provisions normally are adopted without shareholder approval. Some companies have also made hostile takeovers more difficult through the use of staggered election of directors. Such an arrangement makes it more difficult for outsiders to gain control of the board of directors in a proxy fight. Another tactic is a provision that requires the acquiring company to pay all shareholders the highest price offered to any single shareholder during a specific period. This provision would prevent a takeover by paying a premium price to only selected large shareholders during a takeover attempt.

Critics of these provisions argue that they allow the management of underperforming companies to retain their tenure indefinitely. Proponents suggest poison pills give the existing management time to develop alternative strategies to enhance shareholder value or to negotiate more favorable terms, perhaps by searching out alternative buyers.

A case in point involves a hostile attempt by Union Pacific Resources to takeover Pennzoil by offering $84 a share for Pennzoil stock. Pennzoil management rejected the offer stating that it had an alternative (undisclosed) plan for creating shareholder value. It is unclear whether poison pills are ultimately in the best interests of the shareholders of a target company. In the Pennzoil case, its stock was selling for only $77 three months after Union Pacific Resources filed suit in an attempt to force Pennzoil directors to lift anti-takeover defenses.

(Source: *USA Today*, September 15, 1997)

◤ CONCEPTUAL QUESTION AND REFLECTION

Why might an acquisition be done using a step-by-step approach rather than by obtaining a controlling interest with the first acquisition?

SUMMARY

The following learning objectives were stated at the beginning of this chapter:

- Describe the methods of accounting required for different types of common stock investments
- Compare accounting for common stock investments using the cost method and the equity method
- Apply the equity method where investment cost exceeds the fair market value of identifiable investee net assets

Common stock investments create investment accounts in the financial statements. The methods of accounting for these investments vary according to whether they are passive investments, substantial influence investments, or controlled investments. Generally, passive investments are required to be accounted for by the cost method, with additional entries made at the financial statement date to adjust the carrying value of these investments to market value. The unrealized gains and losses resulting from these adjustments will either be included in income or as an element of stockholders' equity, depending on management's intentions regarding the length of time the investments will be owned. Substantial influence investments are required to be accounted for by the equity method.

Investments in unconsolidated subsidiaries are also required to be accounted for by the equity method. However, investments in subsidiaries to be consolidated may be accounted for by either the cost method or the equity method because the investment account is eliminated in consolidated financial statements.

Applying the equity method to an acquisition accounted for by the purchase method requires preparation of an allocation schedule. This schedule determines the appropriate amount of cost-book value differential and amortization for purposes of computing equity method income. The income to be recognized under the equity method is equal to the investee's book net income multiplied by the ownership percentage plus or minus the amortization of cost-book value differential as determined by the allocation schedule. The equity method requires that cash dividends be recorded as a return of capital credited to the investment account. Additional adjustments and procedures may be required in situations where the percentage of ownership in an investee changes, particularly where the percentage change is large enough to result in a change in the method of accounting for the investment.

APPENDIX : Bargain Purchase Situations

LEARNING OBJECTIVES

- Apply the equity method where investment cost falls between book and fair market value of underlying identifiable investee net assets
- Apply the equity method where investment cost is less than book value of underlying identifiable investee net assets

Case 1: Investment cost falls between book and fair market value of underlying investee net assets

As explained in Appendix 2 in Chapter 1, in cases where the cost of an investment in common stock falls between the fair value and the underlying book value of the investee's net assets, a bargain purchase situation results. This situation might arise because the investee's assets are overvalued on its books due to changes in business conditions, the marketability of its products, excess capacity in the industry, increased competition from new entrants into the market, or other reasons. In this case, the excess of **cost over book value** is analyzed using an allocation schedule in the same manner as previously illustrated. Because the price paid for the investment is less than fair market value of identifiable net assets, the residual number in the analysis is likely to be negative. This result is called negative goodwill. Negative goodwill should be allocated to non-financial, long-term assets other than equity-method investments and some deferred items. This allocation should be done unless there are no remaining balances in these long-term assets to which it may be assigned. Allocation of negative goodwill is done using a relative market value allocation process whereby the negative goodwill is assigned to the appropriate assets. Long-term assets are included in the allocation schedule even if there is no difference between their book value and fair market values at the date the investor acquires its interest in the target company common stock.

To illustrate this case, assume the same facts as the example for Exhibit 2-1, except that the price paid by Johnson Company for the Woodside common stock is only $25,600:

Johnson Company acquires an 80% interest in Woodside Company for $25,600 on January 1, 20x0. On this date, Woodside Company has common stock of $20,000 and retained earnings of $10,000. The book values and fair market values of Woodside Company's net assets are equal, except as noted in the schedule of land, building, and equipment below.

	Book Value	Fair Market Value
Land	$ 25,000	$ 25,000
Building	100,000	100,000
Equipment	20,000	25,000
	$145,000	$150,000

Any unrecorded goodwill underlying the acquisition is assumed to have an indefinite life. During the year ended December 31, 20x0, Woodside reports net income of $3,000 and pays dividends of $1,500. Buildings had a remaining useful life of 10 years, and equipment had a remaining useful life of 5 years. Assume straight-line depreciation.

An allocation schedule for the above example is shown in Exhibit 2-2.

EXHIBIT 2-2

Cost of Woodside common stock		$ 25,600
Stockholders' equity of Woodside		
Common stock	$ 20,000	
Retained earnings	10,000	
	$ 30,000	
Percentage of ownership	80%	24,000
Excess of cost over book value		1,600
Allocation:		
Equipment undervalued ($5,000 × 80%)		4,000
Negative goodwill (remaining differential)		(2,400)
		$ 1,600

Final allocation:	Initial Allocation	Allocate Negative Goodwill*	Final Allocation
Land	$ –	$ (400)	$ (400)
Building	–	(1,600)	(1,600)
Equipment	4,000	(400)	3,600
Negative goodwill	(2,400)	2,400	–

Amortization of excess of book value over cost:	
Building	$(1,600)/10 = $(160)
Equipment	$3,600/ 5 = 720
Net decrease in equity income	$ 560

*Land $25,000/$150,000 × $2,400 = $400
Building $100,000/$150,000 × $2,400 = $1,600
Equipment $25,000/$150,000 × $2,400 = $400

In the above example, the excess of cost over book value is $1,600, however, the investor has an ownership interest in underlying equipment assets that are undervalued by $5,000. Allocating cost-book value differential to equipment equal to 80% of $5,000 results in $2,400 of negative goodwill as shown in the allocation schedule. The existence of $2,400 of negative goodwill triggers the relative market value allocation procedures, which assign this negative goodwill to all three categories of long-term assets—land, building, and equipment. The negative goodwill must be allocated to all plant assets even though only the equipment was undervalued. The final allocation to the building results in negative amortization of $160 per year, and the final allocation to the equipment results in positive amortization of $720 per year. Any differential allocated to land is not amortized because land is assumed to have an indefinite life. Thus, the equity method income will be reduced by a net of $560 ($720 − $160) for the first five years after acquisition of the investee. This schedule results in the following equity method adjustments on Johnson's books:

January 1, 20x0	Investment in Woodside	25,600	
	Cash		25,600
	(To record the acquisition of the investment on January 1, 20x0)		
December 31, 20x0	Investment in Woodside	2,400	
	Equity in Woodside Income		2,400
	(To record equity income of $3,000 × 80%)		
December 31, 20x0	Equity in Woodside Income	560	
	Investment in Woodside		560
	(To record amortization of excess of *book value over cost* based on the allocation schedule)		
December 31, 20x0	Cash	1,200	
	Investment in Woodside		1,200
	(To record the dividend received by Johnson: $1,500 × 80% = $1,200)		

Case 2: Investment cost is less than underlying book value

A bargain purchase can also occur when the purchase price of an investment in common stock is less than underlying book value of the net assets of the investee. In this case, the allocation schedule will show an **excess of book value over cost** and will likely result in negative goodwill. To illustrate, assume the same facts as in Case 1 except that the price paid by Johnson Company is only $22,000 and that the book and fair market values of Woodside are as shown below. Further assume the buildings have a remaining life of 10 years, the plant and equipment has a remaining life of 5 years, and that straight-line depreciation is applicable.

	Book Value	Fair Market Value
Land	$ 25,000	$ 25,000
Building	100,000	100,000
Equipment	20,000	25,000
Total	$ 145,000	$ 150,000

The allocation schedule appears in Exhibit 2-3.

EXHIBIT 2-3

Cost of Woodside common stock		$ 22,000	
Stockholders' equity of Woodside			
Common stock	$ 20,000		
Retained earnings	10,000		
	$ 30,000		
Percentage of ownership	80%	24,000	
Excess of cost over book value		(2,000)	
Allocation:			
Equipment undervalued ($5,000 × 80%)		4,000	
Negative goodwill (remaining differential)		(6,000)	
		$ (2,000)	

Final allocation:	**Initial Allocation**	**Allocate Negative Goodwill***	**Final Allocation**
Land	$ –	$ (1,000)	$ (1,000)
Building	–	(4,000)	(4,000)
Equipment	4,000	(1,000)	3,000
Negative goodwill	(6,000)	6,000	–

Amortization of excess of book value over cost:	
Building	$(4,000)/10 = $(400)
Equipment	$3,000/ 5 = 600
Net decrease in equity income	$200

*Land	$25,000/$150,000 × $6,000 = $1,000
Building	$100,000/$150,000 × $6,000 = $4,000
Equipment	$25,000/$150,000 × $6,000 = $1,000

In the above illustration, the negative goodwill is allocated to the Land, Building, and Equipment using the relative market values of each. Thus, the amount of the negative goodwill assigned to the Land account is the ratio of the market value of the land ($25,000) to the total market value of all three assets ($150,000). The Building and Equipment allocations are done in the same manner using their individual market values in the numerator of the ratios. In the final allocation, the differential assigned to the Land is not amortized because land is assumed to have an indefinite life. The final allocation to the building results in negative amortization of $400 per year for 10 years, and the final allocation to the equipment results in positive amortization of $600 per year for 5 years. Thus, the equity method income will be reduced by a net of $200 per year for the first 5 years after acquisition of the investee and increased by $400 per year during years 6 through 10. The equity method adjustments required of Johnson Company include entries for the earnings of the investee company, the amortization of cost-book value differential per the allocation schedule, and the dividends declared by the investee. These entries are as follows:

January 1, 20x0	Investment in Woodside	22,000	
	Cash		22,000
	To record the acquisition of the investment on January 1, 20x0		

December 31, 20x0 Investment in Woodside 2,400
        Equity in Woodside Income 2,400
    To record equity income of $3,000 \times 80\%$

December 31, 20x0 Equity in Woodside Income 200
        Investment in Woodside 200
    To record amortization of excess of *book value over cost*
    based on the allocation schedule

December 31, 20x0 Cash 1,200
        Investment in Woodside 1,200
    To record the dividend received by Johnson:
    $1,500 \times 80\% = \$1,200$

SUMMARY

The following learning objectives were stated at the beginning of this Appendix:

- Apply the equity method where investment cost falls between book and fair market value of underlying identifiable investee net assets
- Apply the equity method where investment cost is less than book value of underlying identifiable investee net assets

Bargain purchase acquisitions may occur because the assets of an acquisition company are overvalued on its books due to changing business conditions, the current market for its products, specific industry factors, and other reasons. When an allocation schedule is prepared in a bargain purchase situation, the residual number in the analysis will be less than the amount needed to adjust the subsidiary long-term assets to full fair market value on the acquisition date. The resulting deficiency in the analysis is called negative goodwill. Negative goodwill must be further assigned to certain non-financial, long-term assets in order to complete the allocation schedule. The general approach shown in the illustrations is to allocate the negative goodwill to those assets using the ratios of their market values. After this procedure is accomplished, the equity method adjustments are calculated in the same manner as for other acquisitions, except that amortization of cost-book value differential may sometimes result in additions rather than deductions from equity in investee earnings.

QUESTIONS

1. Describe the differences between business combinations classified as *mergers, consolidations,* and *acquisitions of stock.*
2. What is meant by substantial influence in the context of common stock investments?
3. *FASB Statement 115* requires that certain common stock investments be accounted for by the so-called "mark to market" approach. Briefly describe how one might go about applying the "mark to market" approach to a common stock investment.
4. *APB Opinion 18* requires that investments in unconsolidated investees in which a substantial influence is exercised be accounted for by the *equity method.* Discuss the equity method from a conceptual viewpoint. What conceptual arguments can be made in favor of the equity method? What is the principal criticism of this approach?
5. What is *cost-book value differential* in the context of the equity method? How does the existence of cost-book value differential affect the amount of equity method income reported during a given accounting period?

6. How will the existence of an *excess of cost over book value* attributable to unrecorded goodwill affect the calculation of equity in investee earnings under the equity method?
7. How does an investor using the equity method account for dividends received from an investee?
8. According to *APB Opinion 18*, the ownership of 20% or more of the voting common stock of an investee constitutes a *presumption of substantial influence* for purposes of determining whether the equity method should be employed. Under what condition may the presumption of substantial influence be overcome?
9. Did FASB Interpretation 35 address the issue of whether substantial influence could be assumed when a less than 20% ownership is held in the common stock of an investee? What is your opinion about the use of the equity method under these circumstances?
10. Is the equity method of accounting required for a common stock investment that must be consolidated in accordance with *FASB Statement No. 94?*
11. How is *cost-book value differential* attributable to undervalued tangible assets accounted for under the equity method of accounting?
12. What type of accounting change occurs when an investor sells common stock in an equity method investment sufficient to lose the ability to exercise substantial influence? How is accounting change reported in the financial statements of the investor?
13. What type of accounting change occurs when the ownership percentage in common stock is increased so that the required method of accounting changes from the cost method to the equity method? How is this change reported in the financial statements of the investor?
14. Explain how the equity accounts of an investee affect the calculation of cost-book value differential in an interim acquisition where the books of the investee have not been closed on the date of acquisition.
15. (Appendix) What is *negative goodwill?* How does the existence of *negative goodwill* affect the application of the equity method of accounting to an investment in common stock?
16. (Appendix) A proposed FASB standard would treat residual unallocated negative goodwill as an extraordinary gain. Evaluate the merit of this proposal.

EXERCISES

Exercise 2-1   **(Multiple choice: select the best answer for each item.)**

1. An *acquisition of stock* business combination is a transaction characterized by
   a. one company acquiring more than 50% of the voting common stock of another company.
   b. one company acquiring the net assets of another company.
   c. one company acquiring at least 20% of the voting common stock of another company.
   d. two companies combining to form a single company.
2. Passive investments in common stock
   a. are reported in the financial statements of the investor at historical cost.
   b. are required to be accounted for by the equity method in accordance with *APB Opinion 18.*
   c. are adjusted to fair market value at the financial statement date with all unrealized gains and losses included in income.
   d. are recorded at cost initially and adjusted to fair market value at the financial statement date.
3. An investment in common stock is considered to be a "substantial influence" investment if
   a. the investor owns at least 10% of the common stock of the investee.
   b. the investor has the ability to influence the policy decisions of the investee.
   c. there is no evidence that indicates that the investor cannot influence the policy decisions of the investee.
   d. the investor uses the equity method of accounting for the investment.

4. According to *FASB Statement 94*, a majority-owned subsidiary would normally be
   a. accounted for by the cost method.
   b. accounted for by the equity method.
   c. consolidated.
   d. both b and c.

5. If an investment is accounted for by the cost method, dividends received from the investee are
   a. accounted for as a return of capital.
   b. accounted for as income.
   c. accounted for as income only if the earnings of the investee exceed dividends declared subsequent to the date of acquisition of the investment.
   d. accounted for as a reduction in the investment account.

6. Which of the following is true regarding the conditions under which the presumption of substantial influence for a 20% or more owned investee may be overcome?
   a. when the investee actively opposes the investor's ownership of the common stock
   b. when there is another shareholder or shareholder group that exercises majority ownership
   c. when the investor is unable to elect a director of its choice
   d. when any of the above events occur

7. The existence of an excess of cost over book value in connection with a common stock investment accounted for by the equity method means that the investor
   a. will probably report income greater than its proportionate share of the investee's income.
   b. will probably report income equal to its proportionate share of the investee's income.
   c. will probably report income less than its proportionate share of the investee's income.
   d. will never report income equal to its proportionate share of the investee's income.

8. Negative goodwill arises when
   a. the price of an investment in the common stock of another company is greater than the fair market value of the investee's net assets.
   b. the price of an investment in the common stock of another company is less than the fair market value of the investee's net assets.
   c. the price of an investment in the common stock of another company is greater than the book value of the investee's net assets.
   d. the price of an investment in the common stock of another company is less than the book value of the investee's net assets.

9. A change from the equity method to the cost method of accounting for an investment in the common stock of another company
   a. is accounted for by the retroactive restatement method.
   b. is accounted for by the cumulative effect method.
   c. is accounted for by the prospective method.
   d. is required if percentage of ownership falls below 50%.

10. A change from the cost method to the equity method of accounting for an investment in the common stock of another company
    a. is accounted for by the retroactive restatement method.
    b. is accounted for by the cumulative effect method.
    c. is accounted for by the prospective method.
    d. is required if the percentage of ownership increases above 20%.

Exercise 2-2	**(Cost and equity methods)**

Wilson Company acquired a 90% interest in Alexander Company on January 1, 20x3 by purchasing 9,000 shares of Alexander's common stock at a price of $25,000. The purchase price approximately equaled the book value of Alexander's net assets on the date of acquisition. During 20x3, Alexander has net income of $5,000 and paid a $1,000 cash dividend.

Required:

(1) Prepare the journal entries to account for Wilson's investment in Alexander during 20x3 using both the cost method and the equity method.
(2) Compute the balance in the account "Investment in Alexander Company" as of December 31, 20x3 under both the cost method and the equity method.

Exercise 2-3   (Cost and equity methods)

Moore Company acquired a 30% interest in Lesser Company on January 1, 20x7 by purchasing 3,000 shares of Lesser's $1 par value common stock at a price of $40,000 in the open market. On the date of acquisition, Lesser's net assets had a book value approximately equal to fair value. During 20x7, Lesser had net income of $4,000 and paid $2,000 in cash dividends.

Required:

(1) Prepare the journal entries to account for Moore Company's investment in Lesser Company during 20x7 using both the cost method and the equity method.
(2) Compute the balance in the account "Investment in Lesser" as of December 31, 20x7 under both the cost method and the equity method.

Exercise 2-4   (Cost and equity methods)

Rayburn Company acquired a 40% interest in Greene Company by purchasing 4,000 shares of Greene's $1 par value common stock in the open market for $60,000. On the date of acquisition, January 1, 20x1, Green had common stock with a par value of $10,000 outstanding, no additional paid-in capital, and retained earnings of $20,000. Any cost-book value differential is assumed to be applicable to undervalued copyrights with a 10-year life. During 20x2, Greene company had net income of $20,000 and paid $6,000 in cash dividends.

Required:

(1) Prepare the journal entries to account for Rayburn Company's investment in Greene Company during 20x1 using both the cost method and the equity method.
(2) Compute the balance in the account "Investment in Greene Company" as of December 31, 20x1 under both the cost method and the equity method.

Exercise 2-5   (Step-by-step acquisition)

Generous Company purchased a 10% interest in Leaner Company for $40,000 on January 1, 20x1. During 20x1, Leaner reported net income of $12,000 and paid $5,000 in dividends. On January 1, 20x2, Generous purchased an additional 30% interest in Leaner Company for $150,000. During 20x2, Leaner had net income of $15,000 and paid $6,000 in dividends. The stockholder's equity of Leaner on January 1, 20x1 is shown below:

Common stock, $1 par	$100,000
Retained earnings	250,000
	$350,000

Required:

For Generous Company books:
(1) Record the journal entries for the acquisition of the 10% interest and the income/dividends from the investment for 20x1.

(2) Record any adjusting entry required for the 10% holding as a result of an increase in the total percentage ownership to 40% on January 1, 20x2. Assume the 40% holding is a substantial influence investment. Any differential is assumed to be applicable to undervalued patents with a 10-year life.
(3) Record the appropriate entries for income/dividends on investment for 20x2.

Exercise 2-6　　　　**(Discontinuing use of the equity method)**

On January 1, 20x2, Passport Company purchased a 25% interest in World Trade Company at a cost of $400,000. On this date, World Trade Company had common stock in the amount of $400,000 (no par value) outstanding and retained earnings of $1,200,000. The book and fair market values of World Trade Company identifiable net assets were approximately equal on this date. During 20x2 and 20x3, World Trade Company had net income of $150,000 and $180,000, respectively, and paid dividends of $30,000 each year. On December 31, 20x2, Passport Company sold 80% of its holding in World Trade Company for $410,000, leaving it with only a 5% interest. The 25% interest was a substantial influence investment, but the 5% holding held after December 31, 20x2 is considered to be a passive investment.

Required:

(1) Record the acquisition of the investment on January 1, 20x2 and the equity entries needed for 20x2 and 20x3.
(2) Compute the gain or loss on the sale of 80% of the original investment and record an entry for the sale on December 31, 20x3.
(3) Are any adjusting entries required to restate the 5% interest remaining on December 31, 20x3 to the cost method? Explain.

Exercise 2-7　　　　**(Interim acquisition)**

Peach State Company acquired a 60% interest in Sandstone Company on May 1, 20x3 at a price of $267,000. On the date of its previous closing, January 1, 20x3, Sandstone company had stockholders' equity as follows:

Common stock, $1 par	$ 50,000
Additional paid-in capital	150,000
Retained earnings	200,000
Total	$400,000

Sandstone's net income for 20x3 was $60,000 and was earned evenly over the year. Sandstone also paid four $5,000 cash dividends to stockholders of record on March 31, June 30, September 30, and December 31. Any differential is assumed to be goodwill with an indefinite life.

Required:

Prepare an allocation schedule for the acquisition of the Sandstone common stock by Peach State Company and give the equity method entries for 20x3.

Exercise 2-8　　　　**(Bargain purchase—Appendix)**

NVEST Company acquired a 100% interest in Sunset Company on January 1, 20x6 at a price of $75,000. On this date, Sunset Company had the following book and fair values for its balance sheet:

Assets

Cash	$ 25,000	$ 25,000
Other current assets	10,000	10,000
Plant and equipment	100,000	110,000
Goodwill	30,000	*
	165,000	

Liabilities and equity

Current liabilities	15,000	$ 15,000
Long-term debt	50,000	50,000
Capital stock, $1 par value	40,000	
Retained earnings	60,000	
	$165,000	

* Note: The value of goodwill should be determined by the purchase analysis.

Sunset's equipment has an estimated remaining life of 10 years. During 20x6, Sunset Company earned $30,000 and paid $10,000 in dividends.

Required:

Prepare an allocation schedule for the NVEST acquisition of Sunset and record the equity entries for 20x6.

Exercise 2-9

(Bargain purchase—Appendix)

Pearson Company acquired a 90% interest in Starship Company for a price of $80,000 on January 1, 20x4. On this date, Starship had the following book and fair market values in its balance sheet:

Assets

Cash	$ 10,000	$ 10,000
Other current assets	25,000	29,000
Land	30,000	30,000
Buildings	50,000	40,000
Equipment	30,000	50,000
	145,000	

Liabilities

Current liabilities	45,000	45,000
Capital stock, $1 par value	40,000	
Retained earnings	60,000	
	$145,000	

Starship's buildings have an estimated remaining useful life of 12 years, and the equipment has an estimated remaining life of 10 years. The other current assets were all fully amortized by the end of 20x4. During 20x4, Starship had a net income of $15,000 and paid dividends of $8,000.

Required

Prepare an allocation schedule and record Pearson Company's equity method entries for the investment for 20x4. Also compute the balance in Pearson's investment in Starship account as of December 31, 20x4.

PROBLEMS

Problem 2-1   **(Cost and equity methods)**

On January 1, 20x2, Mallard Company purchased in the open market 3,000 shares of the $1 par value common stock of Pintail Company for $30,000. On this date, Pintail Company had 10,000 shares of common stock issued and outstanding, no additional paid-in capital, and a retained earnings balance of $90,000. The assets and liabilities of Pintail Company in its December 31, 20x1 balance sheet had book values that were approximately equal to their market values. During the year ended December 31, 20x2, Pintail Company had net income of $20,000 and paid dividends of $5,000. *could have said Recieun the would be that Amount not 30%*

Required:

(1) Assume that Mallard Company is unable to exercise substantial influence on the policy and operational decisions of Pintail because the president of Pintail Company, Dee Coy, owns 55% of the remaining common stock. Prepare all the entries that Mallard should make during 20x2 to account for its investment in Pintail Company.
(2) Assume that Mallard Company does exercise substantial influence on the policy and operational decisions of Pintail Company. Prepare all the entries that Mallard should make during 20x2 to account for its investment in Pintail Company.

Problem 2-2   **(Cost and equity methods)**

The American Car Company builds railroad tank cars. On January 1, 20x3, it purchases in the open market a 40% interest in the common stock of Superior Air Systems, a company that manufactures the air brake systems that American installs in the freight cars it builds. The price of the 40% interest is $650,000. On the date of acquisition, Superior Air Systems has 100,000 shares of no par value common stock with a stated value of $1 per share outstanding and a retained earnings balance of $900,000. The cost-book value differential is assumed to be due to goodwill with an indefinite life. During the years ended December 31, 20x3 and 20x4, Superior reports net income and dividends as follows:

Assume No AddPic

	20x3	20x4
Net income	$ 10,000	$ 200,000
Dividends	40,000	40,000

Required:

(1) Prepare all the journal entries that American Car Company would make during 20x3 and 20x4 related to the investment in the common stock of Superior Air Systems, assuming that it uses the cost method to account for the investment.
(2) Assume instead that American Car Company uses the equity method for its investment in Superior. Prepare all the required journal entries for 20x3 and 20x4 that American would make relative to its investment in Superior.

Problem 2-3   **(Equity method)**

Alpha Company acquired a 60% interest in the common stock of Bravo Company on July 1, 20x5 for $72,000 by purchasing 3,000 shares of Bravo Company $10 par common stock in the open market. On this date, Bravo had stockholders' equity consisting of 5,000 shares of $10 par common stock and $40,000 of retained earnings. All of Bravo's assets and liabilities had book values approximately equal to market values except for equipment with a book value of $50,000 and a fair market value of $70,000. The equipment has a remaining life of four years and any unrecorded goodwill associated with the investment is assumed to have an indefinite life.

During the six months ended December 31, 20x5 Bravo reported net income of $10,000 and paid a $3,000 dividend on November 15 to stockholders of record on October 21.

Required:

(1) Prepare an allocation schedule for the purchase of the investment in Bravo Company by Alpha Company.
(2) Prepare Alpha Company's journal entries to account for the acquisition of the investment and the income and dividends of Bravo, using the equity method of accounting.
(3) Prepare a schedule showing the account balance in the account, "Investment in Bravo Company" for the period from July 1 to December 31, 20x5.

Problem 2-4   **(Equity method, interim acquisition)**

On April 1, 20x3, Coastal States Paper Company purchased a 25% interest in Moss Point Lumber Company for $191,250. This purchase represented 10,000 shares of Moss Point Lumber Company $10 par common stock. As of December 31, 20x2, the Moss Point Lumber Statement of Financial Position showed the following balances:

Assets		Liabilities and Stockholders' Equity	
Cash	$ 10,000	Accounts payable	$ 15,000
Accounts receivable	25,000	Bonds payable	60,000
Inventories	75,000	Common stock	400,000
Land	50,000	Additional paid-in capital	100,000
Buildings (net)	400,000	Retained earnings	185,000
Equipment (net)	200,000		
	$ 760,000		$ 760,000

All of Moss Point Lumber's assets and liabilities had a book value approximately equal to fair market value except for the land, which had a fair market value of $82,000 on April 1, 20x3. Any remaining cost-book value differential is assumed to be applicable to patents with a remaining life of five years. Between January 1, 20x3 and April 1, 20x3, Moss Point Lumber Company earned $48,000 and paid $12,000 in dividends. It did not close its books on April 1, 20x3, the date that Coastal States acquired its 25% common stock interest. For the remainder of the year, Moss Point earned $52,000 and paid $14,000 in dividends.

Required:

(1) Prepare an allocation schedule for the Coastal States acquisition of the 25% interest in Moss Point Lumber Company.
(2) Give all the entries required on the books of Coastal States to account for the Investment in Moss Point common stock under the equity method of accounting.
(3) Prepare a schedule showing Coastal States' balance in the account Investment in Moss Point Lumber Company as of December 31, 20x3.

Problem 2-5   (Equity method)

Handy Corporation purchased a 75% interest in BackPack, Inc. on January 1, 20x3 for $512,500, acquiring 15,000 shares of BackPack's $10 par common stock. On December 31, 20x2, BackPack had the following balance sheet:

Assets		Liabilities and Stockholders' Equity	
Cash	$ 20,000	Accounts payable	$ 15,000
Accounts receivable	45,000	Notes payable	45,000
Inventories	75,000	Bonds payable	100,000
Land	65,000	Common stock	200,000
Buildings (net)	280,000	Additional paid-in capital	170,000
Equipment (net)	225,000	Retained earnings	180,000
	$ 710,000		$ 710,000

On the date of acquisition, all of the assets and liabilities of BackPack had book and fair values approximately equal except as shown in the following schedule. Any cost-book value differential not attributable to the following items is assumed to be goodwill with an indefinite life.

	Book Value	Fair Market Value	Estimated Life
Inventories	$ 75,000	$ 95,000	1 year*
Building (net)	280,000	240,000	15 years
Equipment (net)	225,000	325,000	5 years
Total	$ 580,000	$ 660,000	

*All inventories are expected to be sold within the following 12 months.

During 20x3 and 20x4, Backpack had book net income of $40,000 and $50,000, respectively. It paid cash dividends of $25,000 each year.

Required:

(1) Prepare an allocation schedule for the acquisition by Handy Corporation of the 75% interest in BackPack, Inc. common stock.
(2) Prepare all entries required for the investment for 20x3 and 20x4, using the equity method of accounting.
(3) Construct a schedule showing the balance in the account Investment in Backpack Common at December 31, 20x4.

Problem 2-6   (Acquisition in exchange for common stock)

On January 1, 20x8, Jarvis Company acquired 60% of the $1 par value common stock of Brown Company by issuing 10,000 shares of its own $10 par common stock. On the date of acquisition, Jarvis Company common stock had a market value of $50 per share. Jarvis also paid $10,000 in cash to its investment bankers for expenses related to the issue of the common stock. Relevant data for Brown Company on January 1, 20x8 are as follows:

	Book Value	Fair Market Value
Cash	$ 75,000	$ 75,000
Other current assets	125,000	125,000
Land	50,000	50,000
Building	300,000	250,000
Equipment	250,000	350,000
	800,000	
Accounts payable	40,000	40,000
Long-term debt	160,000	120,000
Common stock, $1 par value	200,000	
Retained earnings	400,000	
	$ 800,000	

The building and equipment have estimated remaining useful lives of 10 years and 5 years, respectively. The long-term debt matures 4 years from the date of the acquisition by Jarvis. Any unrecorded goodwill related to the stock acquisition is estimated to have an indefinite life. During the year ended December 31, 20x8, Brown Company had a net loss of $30,000 and did not declare any dividends. During the year ended December 31, 20x9 Brown Company had net income of $160,000 and paid $20,000 in dividends.

Required:

(1) Prepare an allocation schedule for the acquisition by Jarvis of a 60% interest in the common stock of Brown.
(2) Record the journal entries for the acquisition of the common stock, the payment of the issue costs, and all equity method adjustments for the two years 20x8 and 20x9.
(3) Construct a schedule showing the balance in the account Investment in Brown Common Stock as of December 31, 20x9.

Problem 2-7

(Step-by-step acquisition)

On January 1, 20x7, Tower Company acquired a 10% interest in Horizon Company for $25,000 cash, acquiring 10,000 shares of Tower $1 par value common stock. During 20x7, Horizon earned $5,000 and paid a $2,000 dividend. Tower accounted for this investment by the cost method. The following year, 20x8, Horizon earned $10,000 and paid a $3,000 dividend. On January 1, 20x9, Tower increased its interest in Horizon by acquiring an additional 20,000 shares of Horizon $1 par value common stock at a price of $60,000, enabling it to exercise a substantial influence over the operations of Horizon. The assets and liabilities of Horizon had book and fair market values that were approximately equal on both January 1, 20x7 and January 1, 20x9. Any cost-book value differential is assumed to be applicable to copyrights with a 20-year life. For the year ended December 31, 20x9, Horizon had a book net income of $15,000 and paid $5,000 in dividends.

The stockholders' equity of Horizon on January 1, 20x7 and 20x9 was as follows:

	1/1/x7	1/1/x9
Common stock	$ 100,000	$ 100,000
Additional paid-in capital	25,000	25,000
Retained earnings	75,000	85,000
Total	$ 200,000	$ 210,000

Required:

(1) Record the acquisition of the 10% interest on January 1, 20x7 and the 20x7 and 20x8 entries to account for the investment, using the cost method.
(2) Record the acquisition of the additional 20% interest on January 1, 20x9.
(3) Prepare any required schedules and entries necessary for the accounting change from the cost method to the equity method as of January 1, 20x9.
(4) Record the entries needed to account for the investment under the equity method for 20x9.

Problem 2-8

(Equity method and negative goodwill—Appendix)

Orange Company acquired 100% of the outstanding common stock of White Company on September 1, 20x1, the first day of its fiscal year, for $200,000 cash. Relevant data from White's balance sheet on this date is shown below:

	Book Value	Fair Market Value
Cash	$ 5,000	$ 5,000
Accounts receivable	15,000	15,000
Inventories	35,000	35,000
Land	50,000	60,000
Building (net)	250,000	300,000
Equipment (net)	200,000	240,000
	555,000	
Accounts payable	60,000	60,000
Long-term debt	340,000	340,000
Common stock, $1 par value	50,000	
Retained earnings	105,000	
	$ 555,000	

The Building has a remaining life of 5 years and the Equipment has a remaining life of 3 years. Any underlying goodwill is estimated to have an indefinite life. During the fiscal years ended August 31, 20x2 and 20x3, White Company reported net income of $25,000 and $35,000, respectively. During each of these two years, White also paid $20,000 in cash dividends.

Required:

(1) Prepare an allocation schedule for the acquisition of White Company by Orange Company.
(2) Give the entries required to account for the acquisition of the common stock of White and all equity method entries for the two fiscal years ended August 31, 20x2 and 20x3.
(3) Prepare a schedule showing the balance in the account Investment in White Company for the two years ended August 31, 20x2 and 20x3.

Problem 2-9

(Equity method with negative goodwill—Appendix)

Refer to problem 2-6 above. Assume that the Jarvis Company common stock had a market value of $34 per share on the date of issue and that Jarvis also incurred $9,000 of direct acquisition costs in connection with the acquisition. Issue costs remain at $10,000.

Required:

(1) Prepare an allocation schedule for the acquisition by Jarvis of a 60% interest in the common stock of Brown, allocating the negative goodwill to the remaining long-term assets.
(2) Record the journal entries for the acquisition of the common stock, the payment of the issue costs, and all equity method adjustments for the two years 20x8 and 20x9.

(3) Construct a schedule showing the balance in the account Investment in Brown Common Stock as of December 31, 20x9.

Problem 2-10   **(Research case: criteria for applying the equity method)**

Jeanne LeBlanc is a CPA employed with the firm of Moreau & Associates. During her audit of the financial statements of Orleans Equipment Company, Jeanne finds an account, Investment in the Common Stock of Southland Equipment, Inc. The account has a balance of $123,500 and is being accounted for by the equity method. According to records on hand at Orleans Equipment Company, Southland has the same fiscal year as Orleans. Orleans based its equity method adjustments on unaudited financial statements of Southland. Jeanne's review of these financial statements shows that the Orleans holding is a 16% interest in the outstanding common stock of Southland. According to Warren Wiley, controller of Orleans Equipment, they are using the equity method because they are able to exercise a substantial influence over the operations of Southland. During the year under audit, Orleans Equipment had a net income of $75,000 of which $40,000 constituted "Equity in the earnings of Southland Equipment, Inc." Southland did not pay any dividends during the year in question.

Required:

Discuss the evidence that Jeanne should obtain and the factors that she should consider in deciding whether Orleans Equipment Company has properly accounted for its investment in Southland Equipment, Inc. Include in your answer a conclusion about whether the equity method may ever be used for a 16%-owned investee.

Problem 2-11   **(Research case: criteria for applying the equity method)**

You are the auditor in charge of the December 31, 20x9 audit of Tennessee Transport Company, a trucking company headquartered in Memphis, Tennessee. Tennessee Transport has a 35% interest in Hazardous Trucking Company, a company that specializes in hauling low-level radioactive waste and medical waste. This investment was acquired on July 1, 20x9 at a cost to Tennessee of $4,000,000. You have obtained an audited financial statement of Hazardous Trucking and other purchase investigation data as of the date of acquisition and find that the book value of the identifiable assets of the investee were approximately $1,000,000. Further investigation reveals that there is no reason to believe that the fair market values of these assets are different from book values. In your discussions with the vice president for operations of Tennessee Trucking, Clyde Koski, you learn that Hazardous has some really solid and profitable contracts and that there is very little competition for several jobs that Hazardous will be bidding on.

Tennessee Transport is accounting for its investment in Hazardous by the cost method. Your audit assistant questioned Koski about that method of accounting and was rebuffed. According to Koski, Tennessee Trucking has no intention of recording any non-cash income from this investment and believes that it would be inappropriate to do so. This position was also expressed by the controller, Laura Jackson, a CPA and five-year employee of the company.

Required:

Evaluate Tennessee Transport's decision to use the cost method for this investment. Make a note of any assumptions that you are making in your evaluation.

Problem 2-12   **(Research case: accounting for common stock investments)**

The following footnote excerpt is taken from the 1996 Annual Report of United Cities Gas Company.

"During the first quarter of 1995, UCG Energy (a wholly owned subsidiary of United Cities Gas Company) purchased a 45% interest in certain contracts related to the gas marketing business of Woodward Marketing, Inc. (WMI), a Texas Corporation. In exchange for the acquired interest, the shareholders of WMI received $5,000,000 in the Company's common stock (320,512 shares) and $832,000 in cash in May 1995, and may, if certain earnings targets are met receive up to $1,000,000 in cash to be paid over a five-year period. In exchange for its own gas marketing contracts and the acquired 45% interest in the WMI gas marketing contracts, UCG Energy received a 45% interest in a newly formed limited liability company, Woodward Marketing, LLC. (WMLLC). WMI received a 55% interest in WMLLC in exchange for its remaining 55% interest in the WMI gas marketing contracts. WMLLC provides gas marketing services to industrial customers, municipalities and local distribution companies, including "United" Cities "Gas Company."

The ownership structure of the parent, United Cities Gas Company, the two investees, and Woodward Marketing after the above transaction was as follows:

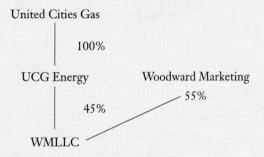

Required:

(1) How should United Cities Gas account for its investments in UCG Energy and WMLLC?
(2) How should Woodward Marketing account for its investment in WMLLC?
(3) Assume that the value of the tangible identifiable assets of WMLLC equaled $432,000. How should UCG Energy account for the $5,400,000 excess of the cost of the investment in WMLLC over value of these identifiable net assets?

Problem 2-13

(Internet case: hostile takeovers)

Search the Internet and identify a recent hostile takeover case and research the facts and actions taken by each company. Prepare a written (and/or oral) presentation on the history and circumstances of the case and its current or final status. You may use periodicals to identify potential takeover cases to research.

CHAPTER 3

CONSOLIDATED BALANCE SHEET ON THE DATE OF ACQUISITION

LEARNING OBJECTIVES

- Explain the logic underlying the consolidation process
- State the criteria for consolidation of a subsidiary
- Explain the parent company approach and the economic unit approach of consolidation
- Prepare a worksheet for a consolidated balance sheet for affiliated companies immediately after acquisition

THE CONCEPT OF CONSOLIDATION

A consolidated financial statement for a parent company and its subsidiaries is a financial statement prepared by combining the individual statements of the affiliated companies. As you will see, a number of adjustments, called **elimination entries,** are required immediately prior to combining the accounts. The need to make adjustments to the accounts before consolidating means that the most efficient way to prepare consolidated financial statements is with the use of a consolidated statements worksheet. In this chapter, you will learn how to prepare a worksheet for a consolidated balance sheet immediately after acquisition of a subsidiary company by a parent company. In subsequent chapters, you will learn how to prepare a full set of statements (Income Statement, Statement of Retained Earnings, Balance Sheet, and Statement of Cash Flows) in the years subsequent to the acquisition.

Consolidated statements worksheets are **off the books** in the sense that none of the accounting work involved in their preparation, **including the elimination entries,** is entered into the journals and ledger of either the parent company or the subsidiary companies. Recall from Chapter 2, however, that the parent company **does record** entries to account for its investment in the subsidiary using either the cost method or the equity method. In order to contrast the difference between cost or equity method adjustments (on the parent company books) with elimination entries (on the consolidated worksheet only), this book shows all elimination entries in a shaded format.

The purpose of consolidated financial statements is to show the financial position and results of operations of separate but affiliated companies as if they were a single company. This approach is in accordance with the **economic entity concept.** Under the economic entity concept, GAAP requires a single set of financial statements be prepared for each **economic entity.** When an **entity** consists of more than one corporation, consolidated financial statements are required. Consolidated financial statements present the financial position and results of operations of the economic entity that consists of two or more legal entities. These legal entities—the parent company and the subsidiaries—continue to exist separately. Therefore, it would not be appropriate for the financial activities of the parent and subsidiaries to be actually combined into a single set of accounting records. Figure 3-1 illustrates the relationship between a parent company and its subsidiaries.

FIGURE 3-1 Diagram of a Consolidated Group of Three Companies

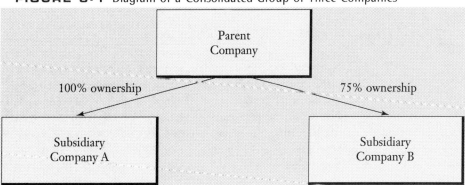

Historically, a consolidated statements worksheet was done by hand on one or more accountant's worksheets. Depending on the particular approach used, a worksheet to consolidate one parent company and one subsidiary requires a worksheet of six or more columns, resulting in the need to use a foldout worksheet, usually called 12 column or 14 column working paper. With the advent of the personal computer (PC), it is more efficient to prepare these worksheets using a PC spreadsheet. While the mathematics of consolidated statements worksheets are not complex, the need to post elimination entries makes the PC spreadsheet a very efficient way of preparing consolidated financial statements.

Learning the theory and practice of consolidated financial statements is a very important subject in financial accounting because the practice is so common. The vast majority of publicly traded companies, as well as many closely held companies, have subsidiaries. As was observed in Chapter 1, there are several reasons for these affiliations. Business corporations with international operations often will form separate subsidiary companies for each country or geographic region in which they have substantial operations. This approach to organizing the business is dictated by legal considerations, taxation, and the natural effect of cultural diversity on business practices, production and distribution, and product mix. For example, the pharmaceutical manufacturer Johnson & Johnson has more than 190 operating companies worldwide.[1] Subsidiaries will also often be established for diversified companies or for lines of business, which form an essential component of corporate activity but are functionally unrelated to the core business. A common example of this type of situation is the existence of finance type subsidiaries. Many manufacturers of durable goods (automobiles, appliances, and farm equipment) have finance subsidiaries that provide financial services to consumers or dealers. Another example is the ownership by retailing companies of affiliates in the insurance business. These subsidiaries are frequently very profitable entities. Their operations may complement those of the parent company, which will often be in another industry. *FASB Statement 94* requires that all majority-owned subsidiaries, including those whose principal business is financial services, be consolidated.

As shown in Figure 3-2, both the automotive and the financial services segments of the General Motors Corporation (GM) significantly impact the company. The automotive section (GMA) brings in a very large portion of GM's revenues—$147,400 in 2000. The financial services section (GMAC) provides a significantly larger return, as measured by income from continuing operations as a percentage of net revenues—6.77% in 2000.

CONSOLIDATION POLICY—THE CRITERIA FOR CONSOLIDATION

As the above discussion demonstrates, there are many different reasons for corporate affiliations and many different types of affiliated companies. In addition, a subsidiary need not be 100% owned. Indeed, one of the advantages of the **stock acquisition** business combination is that control of a subsidiary can be achieved with less than 100% ownership, whereas a **merger** cannot normally be accomplished with much less than complete ownership. Prior to 1987, GAAP required a subsidiary to be **controlled** and to have **economically homogeneous** operations in order to be consolidated.

---

[1] Information based on Johnson & Johnson 2000 financial information is located on its Web site, http://www.jnj.com.

FIGURE 3-2 Comparison of Manufacturing and Financial Services Revenues and Return (in millions of dollars)

	General Motors Corporation (GM)			General Motors Automotive (GMA)			General Motors Acceptance Corporation (GMAC)		
	2000	**1999**	**1998**	**2000**	**1999**	**1998**	**2000**	**1999**	**1998**
Net Sales and Revenues (a)	$184,632	$176,558	$155,445	$147,400	$146,056	$129,054	$23,661	$20,218	$17,914
Income from Continuing Operations (b)	$4,452	$5,576	$3,049	$2,291	$4,981	$1,634	$1,602	$1,527	$1,325
Income (b) as Percentage of Net Sales and Revenues (a)	2.41%	.16%	1.96%	1.55%	3.41%	1.27%	6.77%	7.55%	7.40%

Source: Annual reports of the General Motors Corporation for 2000 and 1999

Control was generally interpreted to mean ownership of more than 50% of the voting common stock of the subsidiary unless other circumstances indicated that it was controlled by another entity, such as a bankruptcy trustee. The concept of economically homogeneous operations was generally interpreted to mean all manufacturing, retailing, and service activities except those whose principal business was financial services such as banking and insurance. These unconsolidated subsidiaries were normally accounted for by the equity method and carried as investments in the consolidated financial statements. The result of this approach was that the consolidated financial statements would not report any of the assets and liabilities of these unconsolidated subsidiaries but would simply show a single account for the investment in the common stock. The income statement of the consolidated entity would report a single line in the income statement for these subsidiaries as well—**equity in the income of unconsolidated subsidiaries.**

The problem with the above approach was that it results in less than optimal disclosure, particularly in the balance sheet. A brief discussion of the relationship between a manufacturing or retailing parent company and its financial services subsidiary is illustrative. One purpose of a financial services subsidiary is to make loans to consumers or dealers who purchase the products of the parent company. The operating profit of such a subsidiary results from its fees for servicing the loans to its customers and from the interest it charges on those loans. The subsidiary can also leverage its investment and increase profitability by borrowing. Depending on the level of risk it chooses to take, some portion of the subsidiary's debt will be long-term debt. The subsidiary's principal business is financing the parent company's sales, either by direct loans to the customer or by purchasing the receivables of the parent company in accordance with a factoring arrangement. The transactions, which finance the sales of the parent company, allow the parent company to report its sales as essentially cash sales. The parent company also avoids the need to borrow money to finance its sales because this function is done by the subsidiary. The financial reporting problem that arises is that the parent's financial statements will not show either the receivable from the lending transactions or the related long-term debt if the subsidiary is unconsolidated. As mentioned earlier, prior to 1987, GAAP did not allow consolidation of this type of subsidiary, giving rise to a reporting problem that became known as **off balance sheet financing.**

In 1987, the FASB issued *FASB Statement No. 94*, "Consolidation of All Majority-Owned Subsidiaries," which was designed to provide financial statement users with more complete information about the financial position of consolidated entities.[2] *FASB Statement No. 94* requires consolidation of all majority-owned subsidiaries unless control is deemed temporary or control does not rest with the parent company. A subsidiary in the process of being sold or spun-off is an example of a temporarily controlled subsidiary. Other conditions may result in control being transferred from the parent company to another entity. For example, the court-appointed trustee would normally control a subsidiary in bankruptcy. In addition, a subsidiary domiciled in another country may be controlled by the government of that country under certain conditions. The imposition of capital repatriation restrictions by the local government is generally grounds for nonconsolidation. Unconsolidated subsidiaries are accounted for by the equity method and reported in the consolidated financial statements as investments. However, the existence of conditions that give rise to uncertainty regarding the realization of the investment in the subsidiary require use of the cost method. Refer to Figure 2-1 in Chapter 2 for a flow chart of the decision process for accounting for passive, substantial influence, and controlled investments in common stock.

Consolidation of Finance Company Subsidiaries

The following data taken from the annual report of the General Electric Company illustrate the potential impact of finance company subsidiaries on a consolidated balance sheet:

	General Electric Company and Consolidated Affiliates*	General Electric Company Separate	GECS (General Electric Capital Services—a finance subsidiary
Total Assets (millions of US$)	**$437**	**$97**	**$371**
Total Liabilities (millions of US$)	382	37	320

*After transactions between General Electric Company and GECS have been eliminated

Source: Annual report of General Electric Company for 2000.

Ongoing work by the FASB has resulted in proposals that define control as being more of a conceptual issue than being an issue of the percentage of voting stock owned.[3] Under this approach, control is the non-shared decision-making ability of an entity to direct the policies and management that guide the activities of another entity. Thus, it is possible that we shall see less-than-50%-owned subsidiaries consolidated in the future if evidence indicates the policy-making decisions of an entity are controlled by a less-than-50% investor.

All companies must disclose consolidation policy in footnotes to financial statements if subsidiary operations materially affect the financial statements.[4] This disclosure is frequently the first of the accounting policies footnotes. Figure 3-3 shows examples from two recent corporate annual reports.

---

[2] Statement of Financial Accounting Standards No. 94, *Consolidation of All Majority-Owned Subsidiaries* (Stamford, CT: FASB 1987).

[3] Based on news releases posted on the FASB Web site.

[4] Accounting Principles Board Opinion No. 22, *Disclosure of Accounting Policies* (New York: American Institiute of Certified Accountants, 1972), par.12.

FIGURE 3-3 Disclosure of Consolidation Policy in Financial Statement Footnotes

General Electric Company —The consolidated financial statements represent the adding together of all affiliates—companies that General Electric directly or indirectly controls, either through majority ownership or otherwise. Results of associated companies—generally companies that are 20% to 50% owned and over which General Electric Company, directly or indirectly, has significant influence—are included in the financial statements on a "one-line" basis.

Source: Annual report of the General Electric Company for 2000.

Occidental Petroleum Corporation —The consolidated financial statements include the accounts of Occidental Petroleum Corporation, all entities where Occidental has majority ownership of voting interests and Occidental's proportionate interests in oil and gas exploration and production ventures. All material intercompany accounts and transactions have been eliminated. Investments in less than majority-owned enterprises, except for oil and gas exploration and production ventures, are accounted for on the equity method.

Source: Annual report of the Occidental Petroleum Corporation for 2000.

● **INTERPRETIVE EXERCISE**

Following *FASB 94* criteria, a 49%-owned finance affiliate would not be consolidated. Why might a company create a financing affiliate and retain only a minority interest in its common stock?

CONSOLIDATION THEORY

Recall that a merger transaction accounted for by the purchase method of accounting (Chapter 1) requires that the assets and liabilities of the merged company be recorded at fair market value on the books of the acquiring entity. The purchase method of accounting also requires reporting the assets and liabilities of a subsidiary in the consolidated financial statements on the date of acquisition at fair market value. When the subsidiary is less than 100% owned, a question arises regarding the values to be assigned to consolidated subsidiary assets and liabilities whose book values and fair market values differ on the acquisition date. Two alternative practices exist. Currently, the most common practice is to follow what is called the **parent company approach**. Under the parent company approach, the assets and liabilities of the subsidiary are consolidated at an amount equal to their book value plus the controlling interest share of the amount by which fair market value exceeds book value on the date of acquisition. For example, assume an 80%-owned subsidiary had buildings with a book value of $100,000 and a fair market value of $200,000 on the acquisition date. The consolidated balance sheet as of the date of acquisition would report these buildings at $180,000 (historical book value plus 80% of the fair value-book value differential = $100,000 + (($200,000 − $100,000) × 80%), following the parent company approach. The argument in favor of this approach is that the acquisition transaction by the parent company involves only the controlling interest share of the fair market value-book value differential. While this argument may be valid on strict technical grounds, it is not consistent with economic reality.

Under the **economic unit approach,** subsidiary assets and liabilities would be consolidated at the same values for both wholly owned and less than 100%-owned subsidiaries. Under this approach, all subsidiary assets and liabilities would be consolidated at fair market value on the date of acquisition. In the above example, subsidiary buildings with a book value of $100,000 and a fair market value of $200,000 on the acquisition date would be consolidated at $200,000. The existence of a noncontrolling interest would not affect asset valuation.

Under current GAAP, either the parent company approach or the economic unit approach may be used. The economic unit approach is, however, more consistent with the move toward fair market value recognition that permeates all recent FASB Standards, notably those concerned with investments (*FASB Statements 115 & 124*) and contributions (*FASB Statement 116*).[5] The illustrations that follow in this and later chapters follow the economic unit approach.

The following illustration summarizes the differences between consolidated net assets under the parent company approach as compared with the economic unit approach.

Conservative

Parent company approach   Consolidated net assets =   Historical cost of parent company net assets   +   Historical cost of subsidiary net assets   +   *controlling interest* **CI%** × Excess of FMV over BV of subsidiary net assets

more crazy

Economic unit approach   Consolidated net assets =   Historical cost of parent company net assets   +   Historical cost of subsidiary net assets   +   **100%** of Excess of FMV over BV of subsidiary net assets

Where: CI% = controlling interest percent
FMV = fair market value
BV = book value

Proportional consolidation—a hybrid approach to investment reporting

A third alternative approach is theoretically possible and sometimes used in unusual circumstances, particularly where companies wish to adopt a compromise approach that falls between the equity method and consolidation. This approach, called **proportional consolidation,** consolidates only the controlling interest share of the investee's assets and liabilities. Proportional consolidation is a generally accepted practice in the petroleum industry for exploration and production ventures. In order to diversify risks, exploration efforts are often conducted as joint ventures where no company owns a majority interest in the venture. For example, assume a 40%-owned investee had buildings with a book value of $100,000 and a fair market value of $200,000 on the acquisition date. Proportional consolidation would report these

[5] Statement of Financial Accounting Standards No. 115, *Accounting for Certain Investments in Debt and Equity Securities.* Statement of Financial Accounting Standards No. 124, *Accounting for Certain Investments Held by Not-for-Profit Organizations.* Statement of Financial Accounting Standards No. 116, *Accounting for Contributions Received and Made* (Stamford, CT: Financial Accounting Standards Board, 1995–1996).

assets at a value of $80,000 ($200,000 × 40%) in the consolidated financial statements. Figure 3-3, on page 77, shows a footnote from the 2000 annual report of the Occidental Petroleum Corporation describing its use of proportional consolidation. Proportional consolidation may seem intuitively appealing at first glance, but this approach should not be used for controlled subsidiaries. Both the parent company approach and the economic unit approach to consolidation provide more complete information for the statement user. These approaches show subsidiary assets and liabilities at approximately full value on the date of acquisition and also present an equity account for the noncontrolling interest in the consolidated balance sheet.

■ CONCEPT QUESTION AND REFLECTION

> What are some of the ways that the fair market value of business assets can be determined?

CONSOLIDATED BALANCE SHEET AT THE DATE OF ACQUISITION

Consolidation procedures are affected by the parent company's ownership percentage and by the existence of a differential between the price paid for the investment and its underlying book value. Accordingly, four illustrations are given for the following cases:

1. 100%-owned subsidiaries—cost and book value are equal
2. Less-than-100%-owned subsidiaries—cost and book value are equal
3. 100%-owned subsidiaries—cost is greater than book value
4. Less-than-100%-owned subsidiaries—cost is greater than book value

100%-owned subsidiaries—cost and book value are equal

The procedures for consolidation of purchase method subsidiaries begins with an allocation schedule. This schedule is identical to the schedule used for applying the equity method of accounting as illustrated in Chapter 2. The allocation schedule is prepared as of the date of acquisition and supports the consolidation procedures used in all future years. Next, a worksheet for consolidated financial statements is prepared. In simple illustrations, the consolidated statements worksheet may seem unnecessary because of the small number of adjustments required. However, we will see that more complex consolidation situations are much easier to analyze by using a worksheet than would be the case in attempting to prepare the statements in a less formal way.

As an illustration, assume that on January 1, 20x0, Logan Company acquires 100% of Kelly Company common stock for a cash price of $100,000 in a business combination accounted for by the purchase method. On the date of acquisition, Kelly Company capital consists of 50,000 shares of $1 par value common stock outstanding and a retained earnings balance of $50,000. There are no direct acquisition costs, and Kelly' assets have book values approximately equal to fair market values on the date of acquisition. The following journal entry records this acquisition on the books of Logan:

1/1/x0	Investment in Kelly Company	100,000	
	Cash		100,000

An allocation schedule for the acquisition of Kelly by Logan is as follows:

Cost of Kelly stock		$100,000
Stockholders' equity of Kelly		
Common stock, $1 par value	$ 50,000	
Retained earnings	50,000	
	$100,000	
Percentage of ownership	100%	100,000
Excess of cost over book value		$ 0

In this simple example, a consolidated balance sheet for Kelly and Logan on January 1, 20x0 is prepared by combining the accounts of the two companies after making one worksheet elimination entry. This entry requires that we eliminate both the Investment in Kelly account and the stockholders' equity accounts of Kelly. To illustrate how this elimination entry is made, refer to Exhibit 3-1, which shows the worksheet for the Consolidated Balance Sheet. Assume that the assets, liabilities, and stockholders' equity of Logan and Kelly immediately after the acquisition of the Kelly common stock by Logan on January 1, 20x0 are as illustrated in the first two columns of the worksheet shown in Exhibit 3-1. A consolidated balance sheet is prepared by posting a single elimination entry on this worksheet and extending the balances of the assets and liabilities across the worksheet to the consolidated column. In general journal form entry (1) is as follows:

1/1/x1	Common stock, Kelly	50,000	
	Retained earnings, Kelly	50,000	
	Investment in Kelly		100,000

EXHIBIT 3-1   100% owned acquisition—book and fair value are equal
Logan and Kelly Worksheet for Consolidated Balance Sheet, January 1, 20x0

			Elimination Entries		
Assets	Logan	Kelly	Debit	Credit	Consolidated
Cash	$ 250,000	$ 15,500			$ 265,500
Accounts receivable	300,000	65,000			365,000
Inventories	525,000	75,500			600,500
Land	325,000	25,000			350,000
Building	400,000	35,000			435,000
Equipment	275,000	22,500			297,500
Investment in Kelly	100,000			(1) 100,000	–
	2,175,000	238,500			2,313,500
Liabilities and Equity					
Current liabilities	575,000	63,000			638,000
Long-term debt	1,060,000	75,500			1,135,500
Common stock, Logan $5 par	250,000				250,000
Retained earnings, Logan	290,000				290,000
Common stock, Kelly $1 par		50,000	(1) 50,000		–
Retained earnings, Kelly		50,000	(1) 50,000		–
	$2,175,000	$238,500	$100,000	$100,000	$2,313,500

Exhibit 3-1 shows how the consolidated statements worksheet transforms two separate financial statements into a single financial statement. Entry (1) accomplishes two objectives. First, it eliminates the account "Investment in Kelly," which is replaced by the individual assets and liabilities of Kelly in the consolidated statement. Second, the entry eliminates the stockholders' equity accounts of Kelly. Since Logan owns all of Kelly Company common, from a consolidated viewpoint, Kelly Company common stock is essentially treasury stock. Since GAAP requires reporting treasury stock as temporarily retired, subsidiary stock is eliminated in a consolidation. **The concept that drives all consolidation procedures is that consolidated financial statements should show only the results of transactions with outsiders.** The effects on the accounts of transactions between the parent company and its subsidiaries or between subsidiaries should always be eliminated.

Less-than-100%-owned subsidiaries—cost and book value are equal

Assume that Logan acquired only an 80% interest in the common stock of Kelly. If the price paid for Kelly common is equal to the book value of the net assets of Kelly, the price paid by Logan would be $80,000.

In order to prepare a consolidated balance sheet, an allocation schedule is first prepared:

Cost of Kelly stock		$ 80,000
Stockholders' equity of Kelly		
Common stock, $1 par value	$ 50,000	
Retained earnings	50,000	
	$ 100,000	
Percentage of ownership	80%	80,000
Excess of cost over book value		$ 0

If the subsidiary is less than 100% owned, a **noncontrolling interest** in the equity of the consolidated companies exists. In order to show this noncontrolling interest in the consolidated balance sheet, the entry to eliminate the Investment in Kelly and Kelly's equity accounts is altered slightly:

1/1/x0	Common stock, Kelly	50,000	
	Retained earnings, Kelly	50,000	
	Investment in Kelly		80,000
	Noncontrolling interest		**20,000**

The entry eliminates 100% of the stockholders' equity of Kelly and the account "Investment in Kelly." The noncontrolling interest equity account is equal to the noncontrolling interest percentage (20%) times the Kelly stockholders' equity ($100,000). The noncontrolling interest account is a new account, created by this entry. Therefore, the noncontrolling interest is shown in the consolidated statements but does not appear in separate statements of either the parent company or its subsidiaries. The worksheet for the consolidated balance sheet is shown in Exhibit 3-2.

EXHIBIT 3-2   80% owned acquisition—book and fair value are equal
Logan and Kelly Worksheet for Consolidated Balance Sheet, January 1, 20x0

Assets	Logan	Kelly	Elimination Entries Debit	Elimination Entries Credit	Consolidated
Cash	$ 270,000	$ 15,500			$ 285,500
Accounts receivable	300,000	65,000			365,000
Inventories	525,000	75,500			600,500
Land	325,000	25,000			350,000
Building	400,000	35,000			435,000
Equipment	275,000	22,500			297,500
Investment in Kelly	80,000			(1) 80,000	–
	2,175,000	238,500			2,333,500
Liabilities and Equity					
Current liabilities	575,000	63,000			638,000
Long-term debt	1,060,000	75,500			1,135,500
Common stock, Logan $5 par	250,000				250,000
Retained earnings, Logan	290,000				290,000
Common stock, Kelly $1 par		50,000	(1) 50,000		–
Retained earnings, Kelly		50,000	(1) 50,000		–
Noncontrolling interest				(1) 20,000	20,000
	$2,175,000	$238,500	$100,000	$100,000	$2,333,500

100%-owned subsidiaries—cost is greater than book value

When the cost of a subsidiary investment exceeds the underlying book value of the subsidiary's net assets as of the date of acquisition, additional elimination entries are required. The purchase method of accounting for business combinations requires that a consolidated balance sheet show the assets of the subsidiary in the financial statements at the fair market value as of the date of acquisition. Subsidiary assets should not be consolidated at book value if fair market value and book value are different on the acquisition date. As in the previous illustrations, the first step in preparing a worksheet for consolidated financial statements is to construct an allocation schedule based on the acquisition data. As an example, assume that Picardi Company acquires Sanchez Company on January 1, 20x0, in a purchase method business combination, whereby Picardi pays $150,000 for all of the outstanding common stock of Sanchez Company. In addition, Picardi incurs $10,000 in direct acquisition costs in the form of consulting fees. Immediately prior to the acquisition, Sanchez had assets and liabilities with book and fair market values on January 1, 20x0, as shown in Exhibit 3-3.

When the cost of an investment in a subsidiary company is not equal to the underlying book value of the subsidiary's net assets, the assets and liabilities of the subsidiary must be adjusted in the consolidated statements to fair market value. Accordingly, an allocation schedule is required. This schedule is prepared in the same manner as for an investee to be merged as for an investee accounted for by the equity method. The allocation schedule for the acquisition of the Sanchez Investment by Picardi is shown in Exhibit 3-4. This schedule also provides all the necessary data needed for the elimination entries in the worksheet for a consolidated balance sheet.

EXHIBIT 3-3 Sanchez Company
Schedule of Book and Fair Values, January 1, 20x0

Assets	Book Value	Fair Value
Cash	$ 15,000	$15,000
Accounts receivable	25,000	25,000
Inventories	30,000	30,000
Land	14,250	14,250
Building	45,750	50,750
Equipment	27,500	37,500
	157,500	
Liabilities and Equity		
Current liabilities	12,500	12,500
Long-term debt	25,000	25,000
Common stock, Sanchez $5 par	50,000	
Additional paid-in capital	20,000	
Retained earnings, Sanchez	50,000	
	$157,500	

EXHIBIT 3-4

Cost of Sanchez stock		$160,000*
Stockholders' equity of Sanchez		
Common stock, $1 par value	$ 50,000	
Additional paid-in capital	20,000	
Retained earnings	50,000	
	$120,000	
Percentage of ownership	100%	120,000
Excess of cost over book value		40,000
Allocation:		
Building undervalued		5,000
Equipment undervalued		10,000
Goodwill		25,000
Excess of cost over book value		$ 40,000

* $150,000 + $10,000 direct acquisition fees

Using the data in the allocation schedule, the following elimination entries are required for the consolidation of Picardi and Sanchez as of January 1, 20x0. The first entry eliminates the stockholders' equity accounts of the subsidiary and Picardi's account, "Investment in Sanchez." The difference between these two accounts is the **excess of cost over book value** that must be assigned to other subsidiary accounts in the consolidation. The excess of cost over book value in the allocation schedule represents the total amount of additional net upward valuations that must be made in the subsidiary's net assets upon consolidation. For purposes of convenience and illustration, this allocation is made in a second entry. You will see that the two entries may be easily combined into a single compound entry. However, we will continue to illustrate this process in separate entries for clarity. The second entry eliminates the excess of cost over book value[6] and adjusts the remaining assets and liabilities of the subsidiary in accordance with the schedule of book and fair values in Exhibit 3-4.

1/1/x0		
Common stock, Sanchez	50,000	
Additional paid-in capital, Sanchez	20,000	
Retained earnings, Sanchez	50,000	
Excess of cost over book value	**40,000**	
Investment in Sanchez		160,000

1/1/x0		
Buildings	**5,000**	
Equipment	**10,000**	
Goodwill	**25,000**	
Excess of cost over book value		**40,000**

The separate financial statements of the two companies, the elimination entries, and the consolidated totals for the balance sheet on January 1, 20x0, are shown in Exhibit 3-5.

EXHIBIT 3-5 Picardi and Sanchez
Worksheet for Consolidated Balance Sheet, January 1, 20x0

			Elimination Entries				
Assets	Picardi	Sanchez		Debit		Credit	Consolidated
Cash	$ 250,000	$ 15,000					$ 265,000
Accounts receivable	275,000	25,000					300,000
Inventories	367,500	30,000					397,500
Land	200,000	14,250					214,250
Building	500,000	45,750	(2)	5,000			550,750
Equipment	590,000	27,500	(2)	10,000			627,500
Investment in Sanchez	160,000				(1)	160,000	–
Goodwill			(2)	25,000			25,000
Excess of cost over book value			(1)	**40,000**	(2)	**40,000**	–
	2,342,500	157,500					2,380,000
Liabilities and Equity							
Current liabilities	225,500	12,500					238,000
Long-term debt	450,000	25,000					475,000
Common stock, Picardi, $1 par	775,000						775,000
Additional paid-in capital, Picardi	347,500						347,500
Retained earnings, Picardi	544,500						544,500
Common stock, Sanchez $5 par		50,000	(1)	50,000			–
Additional paid-in capital, Sanchez		20,000	(1)	20,000			–
Retained earnings, Sanchez		50,000	(1)	50,000			–
	$2,342,500	$157,500		$200,000		$ 200,000	$2,380,000

[6] "Excess of cost over book value" is just a temporary "holding" account. It appears only as part of the elimination process on the worksheet and will never appear as an account on any financial statement.

Less-than-100%-owned subsidiaries—cost is greater than book value

When a subsidiary with undervalued net assets is acquired in a transaction where less than 100% of its outstanding voting common stock is acquired, the noncontrolling interest is affected.[7] Exhibit 3-6 shows an allocation schedule for the Picardi-Sanchez consolidation assuming that Picardi pays the same price as in Exhibit 3-4, but acquires only a 90% interest in the voting common stock of Sanchez. Because Picardi acquires only a 90% interest, the excess of cost over book value increases to $52,000. The allocation section of the schedule is also affected by the existence of a 10% noncontrolling interest in the subsidiary. Any adjustment in the identifiable net assets of the subsidiary will now change the amount of the noncontrolling interest. In this example, the building is undervalued by $5,000 and the equipment is undervalued by $10,000. When these are adjusted upward on the consolidated statements worksheet, the noncontrolling interest must be increased by 10% of the total of these two adjustments, or $1,500 ($15,000 × 10%). **The remaining amount of the excess of cost over book value of $38,500 is assumed to be applicable to unidentifiable assets—goodwill. Furthermore, this goodwill is deemed to be solely applicable to the controlling interest,** since it is the parent company, not the noncontrolling interest, that reflects the existence of goodwill through its payment of a premium price. Thus, no further adjustment is needed to the noncontrolling interest account.[8]

EXHIBIT 3-6 90% Acquisition with an Excess of Cost Over Book Value
Picardi and Sanchez Allocation Schedule

Cost of Sanchez stock		$160,000
Stockholders' equity of Sanchez		
Common stock, $1 par value	$ 50,000	
Additional paid-in capital	20,000	
Retained earnings	50,000	
	$120,000	
Percentage of ownership	90%	108,000
Excess of cost over book value		52,000
Allocation:		
Building undervalued		5,000
Equipment undervalued		10,000
Increase in noncontrolling interest		(1,500)*
Goodwill		38,500
Excess of cost over book value		$ 52,000

* ($5,000 + $10,000) × 10%

---

[7] There are several ways this scenario may be handled in the consolidated statements worksheet. According to the parent company approach, only that portion of cost-book value differentials applicable to the controlling interest should be reflected in the consolidated statements. However, the action required by the economic unit approach is to adjust subsidiary identifiable net assets to 100% of fair market value as of the date of acquisition. All illustrations in this book follow the economic unit approach.

[8] It would be technically possible to record an amount of goodwill applicable to both controlling and noncontrolling interest, however, the currently prevailing position is that goodwill in a less-than-100% acquisition should be only that amount applicable to the controlling interest.

Using the data in the allocation schedule, the following elimination entries are required for the consolidation of Picardi and Sanchez as of January 1, 20x0. The first entry eliminates the stockholders' equity accounts of the subsidiary, the parent's account "Investment in Sanchez," and establishes a noncontrolling interest equal to the subsidiary stockholders' equity multiplied by the noncontrolling interest (10%). The difference between these three amounts is the excess of cost over book value, which will be a debit amount when the price paid for the investment exceeds the fair value of the subsidiary net assets on the date of acquisition. The second entry assigns the excess of cost over book value to the appropriate accounts in accordance with the allocation schedule. Thus, the buildings account and the equipment account are increased by $5,000 and $10,000, respectively, resulting in these items being reported at fair market value on the date of acquisition. The noncontrolling interest account initially set up in the first entry is increased by $1,500 to reflect the increased carrying values of the identifiable assets. The remaining amount of the excess of cost over book value is recorded as goodwill (applicable to the controlling interest).

1/1/x0	Common stock, Sanchez	50,000	
	Additional paid-in capital, Sanchez	20,000	
	Retained earnings, Sanchez	50,000	
	Excess of cost over book value	**52,000**	
	Investment in Sanchez		160,000
	Noncontrolling interest		12,000*

*(Sanchez equity of $120,000 × 10%)

1/1/x0	Buildings	5,000	
	Equipment	10,000	
	Goodwill	**38,500**	
	Excess of cost over book value		**52,000**
	Noncontrolling interest		**1,500**

The separate financial statements of Picardi and Sanchez, the elimination entries, and the consolidated totals for the balance sheet on January 1, 20x0, are shown in Exhibit 3-7.

Financial statement disclosure of noncontrolling interest

When a noncontrolling interest exists as a result of a less-than-100%-owned subsidiary, a question arises regarding the appropriate classification of the noncontrolling interest account in the consolidated balance sheet. Three potential classifications exist. The noncontrolling interest could potentially be shown as a liability, as an element of stockholders' equity, or in a separate section between liabilities and stockholders' equity. Reporting of noncontrolling interest as an element of stockholders' equity is the preferred approach. Noncontrolling interest does not meet the definition of a liability in *FASB Concepts Statement No. 6*; thus, it seems clear that this alternative is not appropriate.[9] The other alternative, showing the noncontrolling

---

[9] Statement of Financial Accounting Concepts No. 6, *Elements of Financial Statements* (Stamford, CT: Financial Accounting Standards Board, 1985).

EXHIBIT 3-7 90% Acquisition with an Excess of Cost Over Book Value
Picardi and Sanchez Worksheet for Consolidated Balance Sheet, January 1, 20x0

			Elimination Entries			
Assets	Picardi	Sanchez	Debit		Credit	Consolidated
Cash	$ 250,000	$ 15,000				$ 265,000
Accounts receivable	275,000	25,000				300,000
Inventories	367,500	30,000				397,500
Land	200,000	14,250				214,250
Building	500,000	45,750	(2)	5,000		550,750
Equipment	590,000	27,500	(2)	10,000		627,500
Investment in Sanchez	160,000				(1) 160,000	–
Goodwill			(2)	**38,500**		38,500
Excess of cost over book value			(1)	**52,000**	(2) 52,000	–
	2,342,500	157,500				2,393,500
Liabilities and Equity						
Current liabilities	225,500	12,500				238,000
Long-term debt	450,000	25,000				475,000
Common stock, Picardi, $1 par	775,000					775,000
Additional paid-in capital, Picardi	347,500					347,500
Retained earnings, Picardi	544,500					544,500
Common stock, Sanchez $5 par		50,000	(1)	50,000		–
Additional paid-in capital, Sanchez		20,000	(1)	20,000		–
Retained earnings, Sanchez		50,000	(1)	50,000		–
Noncontrolling interest					(1) **12,000**	
					(2) **1,500**	13,500
	$2,342,500	$157,500		$225,500	$ 225,500	$2,393,500

between the liability and the stockholders' equity section, is the most common disclosure under current practice. However, the definition of stockholders' equity is broad enough to include noncontrolling interests even though, from a strict technical standpoint, the subsidiary shareholders that make up the noncontrolling interest are not shareholders of the parent company. There is also no reason why there should be a separate section in the consolidated balance sheet for noncontrolling interests. Thus, the appropriate disclosure of noncontrolling interests from a conceptual perspective is to include this account as a separate element of stockholders' equity.

Comprehensive illustration

Assume that Prospect Company acquires 90% of the voting common stock of Sunshine Company for $290,000 on January 1, 20x0, and also incurs an additional $10,000 of direct acquisition costs. The balance sheet of Sunshine Company and the fair market values of its assets and liabilities as of January 1, 20x0, is shown in Exhibit 3-8. Based on this information, an allocation schedule necessary to prepare a consolidated balance sheet for both Prospect Company and its subsidiary, Sunshine Company, is shown in Exhibit 3-9.

EXHIBIT 3·8 Sunshine Company
Schedule of Book and Fair Values, January 1, 20x0

Assets	Book Value	Fair Value
Cash	$ 45,000	$ 45,000
Accounts receivable	30,000	30,000
Inventories	55,000	60,000
Land	30,000	35,000
Building	75,000	100,000
Equipment	100,000	85,000
	335,000	355,000
Liabilities and Equity		
Current liabilities	40,000	40,000
Long-term debt	100,000	90,000
Common stock, $1 par	100,000	
Additional paid-in capital	25,000	
Retained earnings	70,000	
	$335,000	130,000
Net asset fair market value		$225,000

EXHIBIT 3·9 Prospect and Sunshine
Allocation Schedule

Cost of Sunshine stock		$300,000
Stockholders' equity Sunshine		
Common stock, $1 par value	100,000	
Additional paid-in capital	25,000	
Retained earnings	70,000	
	$195,000	
Percentage of ownership	90%	175,500
Excess of cost over book value		124,500
Allocation:		
Inventory undervalued		5,000
Land undervalued		5,000
Building undervalued		25,000
Equipment overvalued		(15,000)
Long-term debt overvalued		10,000
Increase in noncontrolling interest		(3,000)*
Goodwill		97,500
Excess of cost over book value		$124,500

* ($5,000 + $5,000 + 25,000 − 15,000 + 10,000) × 10%

The allocation schedule shows an excess of cost over book value of $124,500. This is the amount by which the net assets of Sunshine must be increased in **total** in the consolidation elimination entries. The allocation section of the schedule provides the necessary detail to make these entries. Note that the inventory, land, and building accounts are all undervalued. Thus, these accounts will be **debited** in the elimination entries. The equipment, however, is **overvalued by $15,000** and will have to be decreased in value by an elimination entry. Since a decrease in an asset account must be accomplished with a **credit,** this overvaluation is shown in the allocation schedule as a negative number. Note also that the long-term debt is **overvalued by $10,000.** In the consolidations worksheet, an elimination entry will be needed that includes a **debit** to this account for $10,000 in order to reduce the long-term debt account because it has a credit balance. Accordingly, the allocation schedule shows the overvaluation of long-term debt as a positive number. **In effect, the allocation schedule shows the elimination entry debits as positive amounts and the elimination entry credits as negative amounts.**

In addition to the investment in subsidiary account and the subsidiary stockholders' equity, other accounts may require elimination as well. An important category of these is intercompany debts. If any of the companies involved in a consolidation has obligations to any of the other companies, intercompany debt exists. For example, assume Sunshine Company owes Prospect Company $7,000. This intercompany debt would be shown on the books of Sunshine as an account payable and on the books of Prospect as an account receivable. Neither of these amounts may be included in the financial statements because, from a consolidated perspective, neither the payable nor the receivable involves an external entity.

As in the previous illustrations, the noncontrolling interest must be increased by the net increase in the identifiable assets of the subsidiary multiplied by the noncontrolling interest percent. The residual number in the allocation schedule is the goodwill, which is only applicable to the controlling interest shareholders. The required elimination entries for this consolidation, including the entries based on the allocation schedule in Exhibit 3-9 and the intercompany account payable, are as follows:

1/1/x0	Common stock, Sunshine	100,000	
	Additional paid-in capital, Sunshine	25,000	
	Retained earnings, Sunshine	70,000	
	Excess of cost over book value	124,500	
	Investment in Sunshine		300,000
	Noncontrolling interest		19,500*

*(100,000 + 25,000 + 70,000) × 10% = 19,500)

1/1/x0	Inventory	5,000	
	Land	5,000	
	Building	25,000	
	Long-term debt	10,000	
	Goodwill	97,500	
	Equipment		15,000
	Noncontrolling interest		3,000
	Excess of cost over book value		124,500

1/1/x0	Accounts payable	7,000	
	Accounts receivable		7,000

The first entry eliminates the stockholders' equity of Sunshine and the parent company's account, investment in Sunshine. This entry also establishes a $19,500 noncontrolling interest account equal to the noncontrolling interest percent (10%) of

Sunshine Company stockholders' equity. The debit difference between these three amounts is equal to the excess of cost over book value in the allocation schedule (Exhibit 3-9). The second entry eliminates the unallocated differential by assigning it to the assets and liabilities of the subsidiary based upon the allocation schedule. The third entry eliminates the intercompany account receivable and account payable. The separate financial statements of the two companies, the elimination entries, and the consolidated totals are shown in Exhibit 3-10. Note that the debit in entry (3) is posted to the "current liabilities" account because no separate account for accounts payable appears in the consolidated balance sheet.

EXHIBIT 3-10   Prospect and Sunshine
Worksheet for Consolidated Balance Sheet, January 1, 20x0

Assets	Prospect	Sunshine		Debit		Credit	Consolidated
Cash	$ 500,000	$ 45,000					$ 545,000
Accounts receivable	245,000	30,000			(3)	7,000	268,000
Inventories	350,000	55,000	(2)	5,000			410,000
Land	180,000	30,000	(2)	5,000			215,000
Building	490,000	75,000	(2)	25,000			590,000
Equipment	740,000	100,000			(2)	15,000	825,000
Investment in Sunshine	300,000				(1)	300,000	–
Goodwill			(2)	97,500			97,500
Excess of cost over book value			(1)	124,500	(2)	124,500	–
	2,805,000	335,000					2,950,500
Liabilities and Equity							
Current liabilities	350,000	40,000	(3)	7,000			383,000
Long-term debt	700,000	100,000	(2)	10,000			790,000
Common stock, Prospect,							
$1 par	500,000						500,000
Additional paid-in capital,							
Prospect	347,500						347,500
Retained earnings, Prospect	907,500						907,500
Common stock, Sunshine							
$1 par		100,000	(1)	100,000			–
Additional paid-in capital,							
Sunshine		25,000	(1)	25,000			–
Retained earnings, Sunshine		70,000	(1)	70,000			–
Noncontrolling interest					(1)	19,500	22,500
					(2)	3,000	
	$2,805,000	$335,000		$469,000		$469,000	$2,950,500

(Column group header: **Elimination Entries**)

SUMMARY

The following learning objectives were stated at the beginning of the chapter:

- Explain the logic underlying the consolidation process
- State the criteria for consolidation of a subsidiary

- Explain the parent company approach and the economic unit approach of consolidation
- Prepare a worksheet for a consolidated balance sheet for affiliated companies immediately after acquisition

Consolidated financial statements are based on the theory that the primary focus of financial reporting is the **economic entity.** Acquisitions-of-stock business combinations create economic entities composed of more than one business corporation. Accordingly the financial statements of the parent company and its subsidiaries are consolidated for reporting purposes. Immediately after acquisition of a subsidiary by a parent company, a consolidated balance sheet may be prepared. This chapter illustrates that the most efficient way of preparing this financial statement is with the use of a worksheet where the separate financial statements of the companies to be consolidated are combined. This worksheet allows the elimination entries to be posted to the financial statement elements prior to their final consolidation. The worksheet is easily prepared with the use of computerized spreadsheet software, although it also may be done manually. The worksheet for consolidated financial statements is **off the books** because the elimination entries and the subsidiary accounts are never entered in the parent company's ledger.

Current FASB standards require that all majority-owned subsidiary companies be consolidated, unless control does not rest with the parent company. Proposals have been made, however, that would require consolidation of a subsidiary that was deemed controlled, even where the parent company does not own a majority interest in the subsidiary's common stock. For example, control might be achieved if the parent company owns more than 50% of the shares voted at the annual meeting.

Two alternative theories may serve as a basis for determining the reported value of subsidiary company assets in consolidated financial statements. Under the **parent company approach,** the assets and liabilities of the subsidiary are consolidated at an amount equal to their book value plus or minus the controlling interest share of the difference between book value and fair market value. Under the **economic unit approach,** subsidiary assets and liabilities are consolidated at fair market value for both 100%-owned subsidiaries and less-than-100%-owned subsidiaries. The **parent company approach** is currently the prevalent practice. However, the **economic unit approach** better reflects the fair market values of the net assets exchanged. There is no difference between the economic unit approach and the parent company approach for 100%-owned subsidiaries.

A consolidated balance sheet is based upon an allocation schedule that assigns the excess of cost over book value (or book value over cost) to the assets and liabilities of the subsidiary. This schedule also serves as the basis for the elimination entries that eliminate the reciprocal accounts in the consolidated financial statements. At the date of acquisition, the principle reciprocal accounts are the investment in the subsidiary on the books of the parent company and the stockholders' equity accounts of the subsidiary. In situations where there is an excess of cost over book value, goodwill may be recorded in the consolidation process.

In years subsequent to the date of acquisition, consolidated financial statements must also be prepared. In these later years, a full set of statements—an income statement, a retained earnings statement, a balance sheet, and a cash flow statement—must all be prepared. The allocation schedule prepared as of the date of acquisition serves as a basis for these financial statements as well. In addition, the method of accounting used to account for the investment in the subsidiary common stock will affect the consolidation procedures. These procedures will be illustrated and discussed in Chapter 4.

A P P E N D I X

LEARNING OBJECTIVE

■ Prepare a consolidation worksheet as of the date of acquisition for a bargain purchase situation

Bargain purchase acquisitions of a 100% interest

As was illustrated in Chapter 1, a business combination may occur under bargain purchase conditions, whereby the price paid for the investment in the subsidiary is less than the fair market value of the net identifiable assets of the investee. A bargain purchase may occur because the subsidiary has not exhibited a record of past operating performance sufficient to justify an acquisition price equal to or greater than the appraised value of its identifiable net assets. In a bargain purchase, an allocation schedule is prepared to determine the amount of the differential (either an excess of cost over book value or an excess of book value over cost). The allocation section of the schedule is prepared in the same manner as previous illustrations, except that the residual figure for goodwill will be a negative number—indicating negative goodwill. As was illustrated for the asset acquisition scenarios in the appendix to Chapter 1, negative goodwill must be further allocated to certain long-term nonfinancial assets of the subsidiary.[11] For subsidiaries to be consolidated, this allocation is done on the worksheet for consolidated statements.

As an example, assume that the Picardi-Sanchez consolidation (Exhibits 3-3 and 3-4) involves the payment of $100,000 (including direct acquisition cost) for a 100% interest in the voting common stock of Sanchez. Based on the book/fair market data in Exhibit 3-3, this price is $20,000 less than the book value of Sanchez net assets and $35,000 less than the fair market value of those assets. Exhibit 3-11 presents an allocation schedule suitable for developing a consolidated balance sheet for Picardi and Sanchez under these conditions. Since the price paid for the subsidiary is less than the book value of the subsidiary's net assets, the differential is an **excess of book value over cost** and is shown in Exhibit 3-11 as a **negative** number. The allocation section increases the carrying value of the buildings by $5,000 and the equipment by $10,000, which are undervalued by these amounts, respectively. These allocations are the same as the previous scenarios. In this case, however, the residual amount of goodwill is a negative $35,000, the amount necessary for the total of the goodwill (a negative $35,000) and the undervaluations of the buildings and equipment (a positive $15,000) to equal $20,000. According to FASB Statement 141[12], negative goodwill must be assigned to certain long-term nonfinancial assets in accordance with their relative market values. The last portion of the schedule uses the fair market values of Sanchez long-term assets to allocate the negative goodwill to all of the long-term assets including the land, which did not have a book/fair market value differential.

---

[11] Statement of Financial Accounting Standards No. 141, *Business Combinations* (Norwalk, CT: FASB, 2001) par. 43–45. Non-financial assets to which goodwill is not allocated include assets held for sale, deferred tax assets, prepaid pension plan assets, and investments accounted for by the equity method.

[12] *Ibid.*, par. 44. If any negative goodwill remains after appropriate non-financial assets are reduced to zero, it is recognized as an extraordinary gain. par. 45.

EXHIBIT 3-11 100% Acquisition with an Excess of Book Value Over Cost
Picardi and Sanchez Allocation Schedule

Cost of Sanchez stock		$ 100,000	
Stockholders' equity of Sanchez			
Common stock, $1 par value	$ 50,000		
Additional paid-in capital	20,000		
Retained earnings	50,000		
	$ 120,000		
Percentage of ownership	100%	120,000	
Excess of book value over cost		(20,000)	
Allocation:			
Building undervalued		5,000	
Equipment undervalued		10,000	
Negative goodwill		(35,000)	
Excess of book value over cost		$ (20,000)	

Allocation of negative goodwill	Initial Allocation	Allocate Negative Goodwill*	Final Allocation
Land	$ –	$ (4,866)	$ (4,866)
Building	5,000	(17,329)	(12,329)
Equipment	10,000	(12,805)	(2,805)
Negative goodwill	(35,000)	35,000	–

	Fair Value/Total of Fair Values × Negative Goodwill*
Land	$14,250/$102,500 × $(35,000) = $(4,866)
Building	$50,750/$102,500 × $(35,000) = $(17,329)
Equipment	$37,500/$102,500 × $(35,000) = $(12,805)

Negative goodwill is allocated to all nonfinancial assets, including those with book value equal to fair value.

Exhibit 3-11 provides the information necessary to make three elimination entries that are posted on the consolidated statements worksheet. These entries are shown below:

1/1/x0	Common stock, Sanchez	50,000	
	Additional paid-in capital, Sanchez	20,000	
	Retained earnings, Sanchez	50,000	
	Excess of book value over cost		20,000
	Investment in Sanchez		100,000
1/1/x0	Excess of book value over cost	20,000	
	Buildings	5,000	
	Equipment	10,000	
	Negative goodwill		35,000
1/1/x0	Negative goodwill	35,000	
	Land		4,866
	Buildings		17,329
	Equipment		12,805

The first entry eliminates the stockholders' equity accounts of Sanchez, the Investment in Sanchez account, and establishes an excess of book value over cost account equal to the difference between the Sanchez stockholders' equity and the investment account. In this case, this amount is a credit of $20,000. The second entry eliminates this excess of book value over cost and adjusts the undervalued assets and liabilities of the subsidiary in accordance with the allocation schedule. The residual figure in this second entry is always goodwill. If the goodwill is positive, as in previous illustrations, no other entries are required. If the goodwill is negative (indicated by a credit balance), as in this case, it is eliminated in a third entry using the relative market value allocation shown in Exhibit 3-11.[13] The separate statements of the two companies, the elimination entries, and the consolidated totals for this scenario are shown in Exhibit 3-12.

Bargain purchase acquisitions of less than a 100% interest

A final series of illustrations shows a bargain purchase scenario where a noncontrolling interest exists. Assume, for example, that Picardi acquires 90% of the

EXHIBIT 3-12 Picardi and Sanchez
Worksheet for Consolidated Balance Sheet, January 1, 20x0

Assets	Picardi	Sanchez	Elimination Entries Debit		Elimination Entries Credit		Consolidated
Cash	$ 310,000	$ 15,000					$ 325,000
Accounts receivable	275,000	25,000					300,000
Inventories	367,500	30,000					397,500
Land	200,000	14,250			(3)	4,866	209,384
Building	500,000	45,750	(2)	5,000	(3)	17,329	533,421
Equipment	590,000	27,500	(2)	10,000	(3)	12,805	614,695
Investment in Sanchez	100,000				(1)	100,000	–
Negative goodwill			(3)	35,000	(2)	35,000	
Excess of book value over cost			(2)	20,000	(1)	20,000	–
	2,342,500	157,500					2,380,000
Liabilities and Equity							
Current liabilities	225,500	12,500					238,000
Long-term debt	450,000	25,000					475,000
Common stock, Picardi,							
$1 par	775,000						775,000
Additional paid-in							
capital, Picardi	347,500						347,500
Retained earnings, Picardi	544,500						544,500
Common stock, Sanchez,							
$5 par		50,000	(1)	50,000			–
Additional paid-in							
capital, Sanchez		20,000	(1)	20,000			–
Retained earnings, Sanchez		50,000	(1)	50,000			–
	$2,342,500	$157,500		$190,000		$190,000	$2,380,000

[13] This allocation eliminates the negative goodwill balance of $35,000 by debiting it and crediting the plant assets for a total of $35,000. the allocation to land, building, and equipment is based on their fair market values.

outstanding voting common stock of Sanchez for a price of $100,000, including direct acquisition costs. Book and fair market value of Sanchez net assets are the same as in the previous illustrations. The allocation schedule for a consolidated balance sheet is shown in Exhibit 3-13. In this case, the $100,000 purchase price is $8,000 less than 90% of the underlying book value of Sanchez net assets. This $8,000 of excess of book value over cost represents the net amount of required write-downs in Sanchez net assets in the consolidated balance sheet. The allocation section of the Exhibit 3-13 increases the building by its $5,000 undervaluation, the undervalued equipment by $10,000, **and increases the noncontrolling interest by $1,500 to reflect the increased carrying values of these two identifiable assets.** These revaluations result in negative goodwill in the amount of $21,500 (applicable to the controlling interest). Finally, this negative goodwill is allocated to the long-term assets of the subsidiary in the same manner as the previous illustration.

EXHIBIT 3-13 90% Acquisition with an Excess of Book Value Over Cost
Picardi and Sanchez Allocation Schedule

Cost of Sanchez stock		$ 100,000
Stockholders' equity of Sanchez		
Common stock, $1 par value	$ 50,000	
Additional paid-in capital	20,000	
Retained earnings	50,000	
	$ 120,000	
Percentage of ownership	90%	108,000
Excess of book value over cost		(8,000)
Allocation:		
Building undervalued		5,000
Equipment undervalued		10,000
Increase in noncontrolling interest		(1,500)*
Negative goodwill		(21,000)
Excess of book value over cost		$ (8,000)

  * ($5,000 + $10,000) × 10% noncontrolling interest

Allocation of negative goodwill	Initial Allocation	Allocate Negative Goodwill**	Final Allocation
Land	$ –	(2,989)	(2,989)
Building	5,000	(10,645)	(5,645)
Equipment	10,000	(7,866)	2,134
Negative goodwill	(21,500)	21,500	–

	Fair Value/Total of Fair Values × Negative Goodwill**
Land	$14,250/$102,500 × $(21,500) = $(2,989)
Building	$50,750/$102,500 × $(21,500) = $(10,645)
Equipment	$37,500/$102,500 × $(21,500) = $(7,866)

**Negative goodwill is allocated to all nonfinancial assets, including those with book value equal to fair value.

The required elimination entries based on Exhibit 3-13 are shown below:

1/1/x0			
	Common stock, Sanchez	50,000	
	Additional paid-in capital, Sanchez	20,000	
	Retained earnings, Sanchez	50,000	
	Excess of book value over cost		8,000
	Investment in Sanchez		100,000
	Noncontrolling interest		12,000

1/1/x0			
	Buildings	5,000	
	Equipment	10,000	
	Excess of book value over cost	8,000	
	Negative goodwill		21,500
	Noncontrolling interest		1,500

1/1/x0			
	Negative goodwill	21,500	
	Land		2,989
	Buildings		10,645
	Equipment		7,866

The first entry eliminates the stockholders' equity accounts of Sanchez, establishes a noncontrolling interest account equal to the noncontrolling interest percentage (10%) multiplied by total subsidiary equity, and eliminates the Investment in Sanchez account. The residual figure in this entry is the excess of book value over cost, an $8,000 credit. The second entry adjusts the buildings and equipment to fair market value on the acquisition date, eliminates the excess of book value over cost from the first entry, and increases the noncontrolling interest by the noncontrolling interest percentage (10%) multiplied times the $15,000 undervaluation in the subsidiary net assets. The residual figure in this entry is the negative goodwill of $21,500. Because the goodwill is negative, a third entry is required to allocate this goodwill to the long-term nonfinancial assets (land, buildings, and equipment). The relative market value allocation calculations are shown in Exhibit 3-13. A worksheet for a consolidated balance sheet, showing beginning unconsolidated balances for the two companies, consolidation elimination entries, and consolidated totals in shown in Exhibit 3-14.

EXHIBIT 3·14 90% Acquisition with an Excess of Book Value Over Cost
Picardi and Sanchez Worksheet for Consolidated Balance Sheet, January 1, 20x0

Assets	Picardi	Sanchez	Debit		Credit		Consolidated
				Elimination Entries			
Cash	$ 310,000	$ 15,000					$ 325,000
Accounts receivable	275,000	25,000					300,000
Inventories	367,500	30,000					397,500
Land	200,000	14,250			(3)	2,989	211,261
Building	500,000	45,750	(2)	5,000	(3)	10,645	540,105
Equipment	590,000	27,500	(2)	10,000	(3)	7,866	619,634
Investment in Sanchez	100,000				(1)	100,000	–
Negative goodwill*			(3)	**21,500**	(2)	**21,500**	–
Excess of book value over cost			(2)	**8,000**	(1)	**8,000**	–
	2,342,500	157,500					2,393,500
Liabilities and Equity							
Current liabilities	225,500	12,500					238,000
Long-term debt	450,000	25,000					475,000
Common stock, Picardi,							
$1 par	775,000						775,000
Additional paid-in							
capital, Picardi	347,500						347,500
Retained earnings, Picardi	544,500						544,500
Common stock,							
Sanchez, $5 par		50,000	(1)	50,000			–
Additional paid-in							
capital, Sanchez		20,000	(1)	20,000			–
Retained earnings, Sanchez		50,000	(1)	50,000			–
Noncontrolling interest					(1)	12,000	
					(2)	1,500	13,500
	$2,342,500	$157,500		$164,500		$164,500	$2,393,500

* As long as the subsidiary's long-term nonfinancial assets are greater than zero after the adjustment of the elimination entries, negative goodwill's consolidated balance will be zero. In the rare case where negative goodwill remains after non-financial assets are reduced to zero, it is reported in the income statement as an extraordinary gain.

SUMMARY

The following learning objective was stated at the beginning of this appendix.

■ Prepare a consolidation worksheet as of the date of acquisition for a bargain purchase situation

In a bargain purchase, an allocation schedule is prepared to determine the amount of the differential (either an excess of cost over book value or an excess of book value over cost). The allocation section of the schedule is prepared in the same manner as in the case of an excess of cost over book value, except that the residual figure for goodwill will be a negative number—indicating negative goodwill. As was illustrated for the asset acquisition scenarios in the appendix to Chapter 1, negative goodwill must be further allocated to certain long-term nonfinancial assets of the subsidiary.

This allocation is done using the relative market values of the assets to which it is allocated. A relative market value ratio (RMV ratio) is first computed for each applicable long-term asset by dividing the individual market values by the total market value of all applicable long-term assets. The amount of negative goodwill assigned to each long-term asset is determined by multiplying negative goodwill by the RMV ratios. Finally, a worksheet entry is made eliminating the negative goodwill and reducing the applicable long-term assets by the results of the allocation. Essentially this process adds one elimination entry to the consolidation analysis—elimination of the negative goodwill.

QUESTIONS

1. Discuss the concept of control as it applied to subsidiary companies that may be consolidated.
2. Why is it important that all subsidiaries be consolidated?
3. Explain why consolidation is a better method of reporting than preparing separate financial statements for each subsidiary.
4. Under what condition might control of a subsidiary company rest with an entity other than the parent company?
5. Contrast the parent company theory and the entity theory as they pertain to consolidated financial statements.
6. Explain what is meant by proportional consolidation and why it may or may not be appropriate as a means of accounting for a controlled subsidiary.
7. Discuss the alternative financial statement disclosure options for a noncontrolling interest in a consolidated subsidiary. Which approach has the strongest conceptual support?
8. What disposition is made of the excess of cost over book value in an allocation schedule for a controlled subsidiary?
9. Explain how the noncontrolling interest is affected by the existence of an excess of cost over book value in the consolidation of a controlled subsidiary.
10. How is negative goodwill assigned to subsidiary assets in an allocation schedule for a controlled subsidiary?
11. Does goodwill pertain to controlling and noncontrolling interest alike or only to the controlling interest?
12. How are reciprocal payable and receivable accounts between affiliates reported in consolidated financial statements?

EXERCISES

Exercise 3-1

(Multiple choice: select the best answer for each item.)

1. Elimination entries for consolidated financial statements
   a. are posted to the general ledger of the parent company.
   b. are posted to the general ledger of the subsidiary company.
   c. are posted to the general ledger of both the parent and subsidiary company.
   d. are not entered into the books of original entry of the companies being consolidated.
2. When subsidiary financial statements are consolidated,
   a. its financial records are merged with those of the parent company.
   b. its financial statements are combined with those of the parent company on a worksheet.
   c. the subsidiary is liquidated.
   d. all of the above are true.

3. Which of the following sentences best describes the term "control" as it relates to an investment in a subsidiary?
   a. The parent company owns 100% of the subsidiary's outstanding voting common stock.
   b. The parent company owns 50% or more of the subsidiary's outstanding voting common stock.
   c. The parent company can exercise substantial influence over the subsidiary's corporate policy.
   d. The parent company exercises effective control over the subsidiary's corporate policy, the election of a majority of directors, dividend policy, and other important corporate decisions.

4. FASB 94, *Consolidation of All Majority-Owned Subsidiaries*, requires
   a. consolidation of all majority-owned subsidiaries under all conditions.
   b. consolidation of all subsidiaries whose operations are economically homogeneous with those of the parent company.
   c. consolidation of all majority-owned subsidiaries unless control does not rest with the parent company.
   d. consolidation of all wholly owned subsidiaries.

5. In absence of bargain purchase conditions, a purchase method consolidation prepared under the entity theory consolidates subsidiary assets and liabilities at
   a. full fair market value.
   b. book value plus the controlling interest share of the difference between book value and fair market value.
   c. subsidiary book value.
   d. at full fair market value only if the parent company assets are adjusted to fair market value.

6. In an allocation schedule prepared for a purchase method stock acquisition to be consolidated, any direct acquisition costs
   a. are included in the price paid for the acquisition.
   b. are accounted for as acquisition expense by the parent company.
   c. are deducted from parent company additional paid-in capital.
   d. are debited to a goodwill account.

7. According to the entity theory, in an allocation schedule prepared for a purchase method stock acquisition to be consolidated, any undervalued subsidiary assets are
   a. consolidated at fair market value.
   b. consolidated at fair market value only if the price paid for the investment is greater than the fair market value of the subsidiary's net identifiable assets.
   c. consolidated at fair market value only if the price paid for the investment is greater than the book value of the subsidiary's net identifiable assets.
   d. consolidated at book value plus the controlling interest share of the excess of fair value over book value.

8. In absence of bargain purchase conditions, according to the parent company theory, an allocation schedule prepared for a purchase method stock acquisition values subsidiary assets at
   a. fair market value.
   b. fair market value only if the price paid for the investment is greater than the fair market value of the subsidiary's net identifiable assets.
   c. fair market value only if the price paid for the investment is greater than the book value of the subsidiary's net identifiable assets.
   d. book value plus the controlling interest share of the excess of fair value over book value.

9. The noncontrolling interest account
   a. must be shown in the consolidated balance sheet as a liability.
   b. should be shown in the consolidated balance sheet as an element of stockholders' equity.
   c. must be shown in the consolidated balance sheet as an element of stockholders' equity.
   d. should be shown in the consolidated balance sheet in a separate section between liabilities and equity.

10. (Appendix) In a bargain purchase situation, any negative goodwill
    a. is allocated to all of the subsidiary's identifiable assets and liabilities.
    b. is allocated only to subsidiary long-term assets other than marketable securities.
    c. is allocated only to subsidiary land, building, and equipment.
    d. is allocated first to subsidiary long-term assets other than marketable securities. After these are reduced to zero, any remaining negative goodwill is carried to the consolidated financial statements.

Exercise 3-2

(Consolidation concepts)

Obtain a corporate annual report that contains consolidated financial statements. (A good place to access such reports is the Internet or a library.) Review this annual report and carefully read the footnotes describing the consolidation policy and procedures.

Required:

a. Based on your review, describe the types of businesses that the parent and subsidiaries are engaged in.
b. What reasons are apparent for the parent-subsidiary relationship as opposed to the companies being combined through either a merger or consolidations within a single corporation?
c. Review the way the noncontrolling interest (sometimes called the minority interest) is reported in the balance sheet and the income statement. What approach is the company using to report this information? Explain your reasoning.

Exercise 3-3

(Criteria for consolidation)

Go to the textbook's Web site or to http://www.pathfinder.com and download the most recent annual report of Time Warner, Inc. or locate another annual report with both consolidated and unconsolidated investees. Review the accounting policies for the consolidated and unconsolidated investees.

Required:

Explain the concept of control as it relates to a parent and its subsidiaries. Had the company you reviewed complied with generally accepted accounting principles in regard to consolidation? In your view, could control be achieved with less than 50% ownership of an investee? Explain your reasoning.

Exercise 3-4

(Parent company and economic unit approaches)

Go to the textbook's Web site for links to assist you in finding the annual report of a company with noncontrolling interests (e.g., Sears, Roebuck, and Co.). Download the annual report and review the financial statement disclosures related to Investments in Subsidiaries.
a. Determine whether the company is using the economic unit approach or the parent company approach with respect to the reporting of noncontrolling interests (sometimes called minority interests).
b. Explain how these disclosures would change if the alternative approach was used.

Exercise 3-5

(Consolidated balance sheet)

Wilson Company acquired 100% of the outstanding voting common stock of Johnson Company at a price of $100,000 on January 1, 20x1. The purchase price included $5,000 of direct acquisition costs. On this date, the book and fair values of Johnson Company's net assets were approximately equal. Immediately prior to the acquisition, the two companies had the following balance sheets:

Assets	Wilson	Johnson
Cash	$ 225,000	$ 18,000
Accounts receivable	125,000	49,500
Inventories	410,000	80,000
Land	235,000	10,000
Building	75,000	42,500
Equipment	135,000	25,000
	1,205,000	225,000

Liabilities and Equity		
Current liabilities	37,500	75,000
Long-term debt	250,000	50,000
Common stock, Wilson $5 par	500,000	
Retained earnings, Wilson	417,500	
Common stock, Johnson $1 par		50,000
Retained earnings, Johnson		50,000
	$1,205,000	$225,000

Required:

Prepare a consolidated balance sheet for Wilson and Johnson immediately after the acquisition of Johnson Company common stock by Wilson Company.

Exercise 3-6

(Consolidated balance sheet with goodwill)

Refer to the information in exercise 3-5 above. Assume that Wilson paid $110,000 for the common stock of Johnson, including $5,000 of direct acquisition costs and that the book and market values of Johnson Company identifiable assets are approximately equal. Prepare a consolidated balance sheet for the two companies immediately after acquisition.

Exercise 3-7

(Consolidated balance sheet)

Perrine Company acquired 80% of the outstanding voting common stock of Simplicity Company for cash of $80,000 on January 1, 20x1, in a purchase method business combination. Immediately prior the the acquisition, the two companies had the following balance sheets:

Assets	Perrine	Simplicity
Cash	$125,000	$ 10,000
Accounts receivable	30,000	20,000
Inventories	50,000	50,000
Land	40,000	
Building—net	60,000	40,000
Equipment—net	55,000	60,000
	360,000	180,000

Liabilities and Equity		
Current liabilities	40,000	30,000
Long-term debt	100,000	50,000
Common stock	150,000	10,000
Retained earnings	70,000	90,000
	$360,000	$180,000

Required:

Prepare a worksheet for a consolidated balance sheet immediately after the acquisition. Assume that Simplicity's assets and liabilities had a book value approximately equal to fair value on the acquisition date.

Exercise 3-8   **(Consolidated balance sheet)**

Porter Company acquired 100% of the outstanding voting common stock of Sercy Company for cash of $150,000 on January 1, 20x1, in a purchase method business combination. Immediately prior the the acquisition, the two companies had the following balance sheets:

Assets	Porter	Sercy
Cash	$250,000	$ 25,000
Accounts receivable	55,000	40,000
Inventories	35,000	35,000
Land	50,000	65,000
Building—net	75,000	30,000
Equipment—net	120,000	75,000
	585,000	270,000

Liabilities and Equity		
Current liabilities	95,000	10,000
Long-term debt	250,000	130,000
Common stock	100,000	20,000
Retained earnings	140,000	110,000
	$585,000	$270,000

Required:

Prepare a worksheet for a consolidated balance sheet immediately after the acquisition. Assume that Sercy's assets and liabilities had a book value approximately equal to fair value on the acquisition date.

Exercise 3-9   **(Allocation schedule with negative goodwill; appendix)**

Utica Company acquired 100% of the outstanding common stock of Rome Company on July 1, 20x2, for a price of $ 90,000. Utica Company also paid $5,000 to external consultants in connection with the acquisition. On this date, Rome Company had the following balance sheet:

Assets	Book Value	Fair Value
Cash	$ 30,000	$ 30,000
Accounts receivable	25,000	25,000
Inventory	40,000	50,000
Land	20,000	50,000
Building—net	35,000	60,000
Equipment—net	40,000	90,000
	190,000	

Liabilities and equity		
Current liabilities	30,000	
Long-term debt	100,000	
Common stock, $1 par	10,000	
Retained earnings	50,000	
	$190,000	

Required:

a. Record the acquisition of Rome Company on Utica Company's books as of July 1, 20x2.
b. Prepare an allocation schedule for the acquisition, including calculations needed to eliminate the negative goodwill.
c. Record the consolidated balance sheet elimination entries. A worksheet is not required.

Exercise 3-10 **(Acquisition and elimination entries)**

Pacific Company acquired 70% of the outstanding common stock of Simpkins Company in a purchase method acquisition on January 1, 20x3. Pacific issued 10,000 shares of its own $1 par common stock as consideration. On this date, Pacific common had a market value of $12 per share. Issue costs paid in cash were $5,000. Simpkins Company had the following balance sheet on the date of acquisition:

Assets

Cash	$ 20,000
Accounts receivable	80,000
Land	10,000
Building—net	100,000
Equipment—net	50,000
	260,000

Liabilities and equity

Current liabilities	25,000
Bonds payable	35,000
Common stock, no par value	60,000
Retained earnings	140,000
	$260,000

On the acquisition date, all of the Simpkins Company's assets and liabilities had a book value approximately equal to fair market value.

Required:

a. Record the entry on Pacific Company's books to record the acquisition.
b. Record the elimination entries for a consolidated balance sheet immediately after acquisition.

PROBLEMS

Problem 3-1 **(Acquisition and elimination entries)**

Barczek Company acquired an 80% interest in the common stock of Sargent Company on January 1, 20x3, and prepared the following allocation schedule:

Cost of Sargent Stock		$ 90,000
Stockholders' equity of Sargent		
Common stock, $1 par value	$ 50,000	
Retained earnings	30,000	
	$ 80,000	
Percentage of ownership	80%	64,000
Excess of cost over book value		26,000
Allocation:		
Building undervalued		15,000
Increase in noncontrolling interest		(3,000)*
Goodwill		13,000
Excess of cost over book value		$ 25,000
* $15,000 × 20%		

Required:

a. Prepare Barczek Company's journal entry to record the stock acquisition.
b. Give the elimination entries in general journal form that Barczek would prepare in connection with a worksheet for a consolidated balance sheet for Barczek and Sargent.

Problem 3-2 **(100% acquisition of subsidiary and elimination entries)**

Skywriter acquired 100% of the outstanding common stock of Whitecloud Company for a price of $130,000 at a time when Whitecloud had book and fair market values as shown below. Skywriter also paid $2,500 of direct acquisition costs in the form of legal fees to outside consultants.

Whitecloud Company
Schedule of Book and Fair Values
January 1, 20x0

Assets	Book Value	Fair Value
Cash	$ 24,500	$ 24,500
Accounts receivable	37,500	37,500
Inventories	25,000	25,000
Land	14,000	14,000
Building	39,000	44,000
Plant and equipment	45,000	55,000
	185,000	200,000
Liabilities and Equity		
Current liabilities	27,500	27,500
Long-term debt	50,000	50,000
Common stock, Whitecloud $5 par	10,000	
Additional paid-in capital	40,000	
Retained earnings, Whitecloud	57,500	
	$185,000	77,500
Net asset fair market value		$122,500

Required:

a. Prepare an allocation schedule for the acquisition of Whitecloud by Skywriter.
b. Prepare the required elimination entries in general journal form that are needed for a worksheet for a consolidated balance sheet for the two companies.

Problem 3-3 **(80% acquisition of subsidiary and elimination entries)**

Refer to the data in problem 3-2. Assume that Skywriter acquired an 80% interest in Whitecloud common stock at a cost of $108,000, plus $3,000 of direct acquisition costs.

Required:

a. Prepare an allocation schedule for the acquisition of Whitecloud by Skywriter.
b. Prepare the required elimination entries in general journal form that are needed for a worksheet for a consolidated balance sheet for the two companies.

Problem 3-4   **(100% acquisition for cash; worksheet)**

Balance sheets for Target Company and Bullseye Company as of December 31, 20x3, are shown below.

Assets	Target	Bullseye
Cash	$ 375,000	$ 27,500
Accounts receivable	525,000	32,500
Inventories	350,000	35,000
Land	175,000	20,000
Building	400,000	48,000
Equipment	600,000	33,500
Investment in Bullseye	128,000	
	2,553,000	196,500
Liabilities and Equity		
Current liabilities	250,000	33,500
Long-term debt	975,000	50,000
Common stock, Target, $1 par	500,000	
Additional paid-in capital, Target	250,000	
Retained earnings, Target	578,000	
Common stock, Bullseye, $5 par		25,000
Additional paid-in capital, Bullseye		15,000
Retained earnings, Bullseye		73,000
	$2,553,000	$196,500

On this date, Target acquired 100% of the outstanding voting common stock of Bullseye in a purchase method acquisition for $123,000. Target also paid $5,000 to a consulting firm for a finder's fee. All of Bullseye Company's assets and liabilities had book values approximately equal to fair market values except for land, which had a fair market value of $25,000.

Required:

a. Prepare a journal entry to record the investment by Target in the common stock of Bullseye.
b. Prepare an allocation schedule for the acquisition.
c. Prepare a worksheet for a consolidated balance sheet for the two companies.

Problem 3-5   **(80% acquisition for stock; worksheet)**

On January 1, 20x5, Heavy Company acquired an 80% interest in the common stock of Light Company in exchange for 10,000 shares of Heavy common stock. On the date of the acquisition, Heavy common had a market value of $15 per share. Heavy also incurred $5,000 in issue costs in connection with the acquisition. All of Light Company's assets and liabilities had book values approximately equal to market values except for buildings, which had a market value of $20,000 in excess of book value and equipment, which had a market value of $25,000 less than book value. The two companies had the following balance sheets immediately after the acquisition:

Assets	Heavy	Light
Cash	$ 150,000	$ 12,000
Accounts receivable	235,500	22,000
Inventories	75,000	33,400
Land	10,000	10,000
Building	340,000	40,000
Equipment	165,000	75,000
Investment in Light	150,000	
	1,125,500	192,400

Liabilities and Equity		
Current liabilities	75,500	12,400
Long-term debt	345,000	65,000
Common stock, $1 par	400,000	40,000
Additional paid-in capital	125,000	20,000
Retained earnings	180,000	55,000
	$1,125,500	$192,400

Required:

a. Prepare a journal entry to record the investment by Heavy in the common stock of Light.
b. Prepare an allocation schedule for the acquisition.
c. Prepare a worksheet for a consolidated balance sheet for the two companies.

Problem 3-6   **(90% acquisition for cash—multiple book and fair value differences; worksheet)**

Anchor Company acquired 90% of the outstanding common stock of Chain Company for $380,000 cash on January 1, 20x6. Anchor also paid $3,000 in direct acquisition costs for a consulting firm. Immediately after the acquisition, the balance sheets of the two companies were as follows:

Assets	Anchor	Chain
Cash	$ 267,500	$ 15,000
Accounts receivable	125,000	58,600
Inventories	100,000	44,400
Land	150,000	25,000
Building	750,000	230,500
Equipment	800,000	165,000
Investment in Chain	383,000	
	2,575,500	538,500

Liabilities and Equity		
Current liabilities	155,500	75,500
Bonds payable	450,000	120,000
Common stock, $1 par	400,000	
Additional paid-in capital	800,000	
Retained earnings	770,000	
Common stock, $5 par		50,000
Additional paid-in capital		150,000
Retained earnings		143,000
	$2,575,500	$538,500

All of Chain Company's assets and liabilities had book values approximately equal to market values except for the following:

Land undervalued	$ 20,000
Building undervalued	40,000
Equipment overvalued	20,000
Bonds payable overvalued	15,000

Required:

a. Record the entry on Anchor Company's books for the acquisition of the Chain Company stock.
b. Prepare an allocation schedule for the acquisition.
c. Prepare a worksheet for a consolidated balance sheet for the two companies.

Problem 3-7

(Consolidated balance sheet; worksheet)

Polk Company acquired a 100% interest in Stern Company's for a price of $80,000 cash, including a $10,000 fee paid to a consulting firm. On this date, immediately after the acquisition, Polk and Stern had the following balance sheets:

Assets	Polk	Stern
Cash	$ 15,000	$ 5,000
Accounts receivable	60,000	20,000
Inventories	120,000	30,000
Land	100,000	40,000
Building—net	200,000	60,000
Equipment—net	250,000	100,000
Patents	0	40,000
Investment in Scoreless Company	80,000	
	825,000	295,000

Liabilities and Equity		
Current liabilities	75,500	100,000
Long-term debt	225,000	100,000
Common stock, no par value	200,000	140,000
Retained earnings	325,000	(45,000)
	$825,000	$295,000

All of Stern Company's assets and liabilities have a book value approximately equal to fair value except for the patents, which are considered to be worthless.

Required:

Prepare a worksheet for a consolidated balance sheet immediately after acquisition.

Problem 3-8

(Consolidated balance sheet; worksheet)

Prairie Company acquired 100% of the voting common stock of Seashore Company in a purchase method business combination on October 1, 20x4. The purchase price consisted of $100,000 cash and a $150,000 five-year 8% note. Immediately after the acquisition, the two companies had the following balance sheets:

Assets	Prairie	Seashore
Cash	$ 40,000	$ 10,000
Accounts receivable	60,000	25,000
Inventories	95,000	55,000
Land	200,000	100,000
Building—net	150,000	150,000
Equipment—net	425,000	75,000
Patents	50,000	–
Investment in Seashore Company	250,000	
	1,270,000	415,000
Liabilities and Equity		
Current liabilities	70,000	35,000
Long-term debt	650,000	140,000
Common stock, no par value	200,000	50,000
Retained earnings	350,000	190,000
	$1,270,000	$415,000

All of Seashore's assets and liabilities have a book value equal to market value except for equipment that was undervalued by $10,000 and long-term debt that was undervalued by $20,000.

Required:

Prepare a worksheet for a consolidated balance sheet immediately after acquisition.

Problem 3-9 **(90% acquisition for stock with negative goodwill; worksheet; appendix)**

On January 1, 20x2, Perlstein Company purchased a 90% interest in the outstanding common stock of Park Company by issuing 10,000 shares of its $10 par common stock. On the date of issue, Perlstein common had a market value of $28 per share. Expenses of issue were $5,000. The balance sheets of the two companies immediately prior to the combination were as follows:

Assets	Perlstein	Park
Cash	$ 125,000	$ 25,000
Accounts receivable	95,000	43,000
Inventories	65,000	32,000
Land	100,000	25,000
Building	134,000	175,000
Equipment	660,000	200,000
Investment in Park	280,000	
	1,459,000	500,000
Liabilities and Equity		
Current liabilities	155,500	80,000
Bonds payable	125,000	120,000
Common stock, $10 par	250,000	
Additional paid-in capital	350,000	
Retained earnings	578,500	
Common stock, $5 par		50,000
Additional paid-in capital		45,000
Retained earnings		205,000
	$1,459,000	$500,000

All of Park's assets and liabilities had book and fair market values approximately equal except for the equipment that had a fair market value of $220,000 on the acquisition date.

Required:

a. Record the entry on Perlstein's books for the acquisition of Park Company stock.
b. Prepare an allocation schedule for the acquisition.
c. Prepare a worksheet for a consolidated balance sheet for the two companies.

Problem 3-10   **(100% acquisition for cash; worksheet)**

Peerless Company acquired a 100% interest in Sycamore Company on January 1, 20x4, for $300,000 cash. Peerless also paid $20,000 to a consulting firm for appraisal services in connection with the acquisition. On the acquisition date, Sycamore Company assets and liabilities were approximately equal except for buildings that were undervalued by $50,000 and long-term debt that was overvalued by $10,000. Immediately after the acquisition, the two companies had the following balance sheets:

Assets	Peerless	Sycamore
Cash	$75,000	$15,000
Accounts receivable	85,000	25,000
Inventories	35,000	40,000
Land	50,000	80,000
Building	80,000	120,000
Equipment	300,000	190,000
Investment in Sycamore	320,000	
	945,000	470,000
Liabilities and Equity		
Current liabilities	75,000	20,000
Bonds payable	125,000	120,000
Common stock, $1 par	110,000	100,000
Retained earnings	635,000	230,000
	$945,000	$470,000

On the date of acquisition, Sycamore owed Peerless $25,000 in accounts payable. The Marketable securities account on the books of Peerless included $50,000 of Sycamore bonds, which had been purchased at par.

Required:

a. Prepare the elimination entries in general journal form for a worksheet for a consolidated balance sheet for Peerless and Sycamore.
h. Prepare a worksheet for a consolidated balance sheet as of January 1, 20x4.

Problem 3-11   **(Consolidated balance sheet; worksheet; appendix)**

Passive Company acquired 100% of the voting common stock of Stoic Company in a purchase method business combination on January 1 20x3, for $200,000 cash. Immediately after the acquisition, the two companies had the following balance sheets:

Assets	Passive	Stoic
Cash	$ 30,000	$ 15,000
Accounts receivable	75,000	45,000
Inventories	98,000	75,000
Land	100,000	60,000
Building—net	47,500	135,000
Equipment—net	432,500	90,000
Goodwill	50,000	–
Investment in Stoic Company	200,000	
	1,033,000	420,000
Liabilities and Equity		
Current liabilities	35,000	40,000
Long-term debt	475,000	180,000
Common stock, no par value	100,000	10,000
Retained earnings	423,000	190,000
	$1,033,000	$420,000

All of Stoic's assets and liabilities had a book value equal to market value except for land undervalued by $40,000, building by $15,000, and equipment undervalued by $60,000.

Required:

a. Prepare a worksheet for a consolidated balance sheet immediately after acquisition.
b. Explain how Passive Company came to have goodwill in its separate financial statements.

Problem 3-12   **(Consolidated balance sheet; worksheet; appendix)**

Pinto Company acquired 80% of the voting common stock of Silo Company in a purchase method business combination on January 1 20x1, for $40,000 cash. Immediately after the acquisition, the two companies had the following balance sheets:

Assets	Pinto	Silo
Cash	$ 35,000	$ 5,000
Accounts receivable	41,000	70,000
Inventories	109,000	40,000
Land	90,000	10,000
Building—net	65,000	45,000
Equipment—net	234,500	50,000
Goodwill	50,000	–
Investment in Stoic Company	40,000	
	664,000	220,000
Liabilities and Equity		
Current liabilities	65,000	75,000
Long-term debt	235,000	85,000
Common stock, no par value	30,000	10,000
Retained earnings	334,000	50,000
	$664,000	$220,000

All of Silo's assets and liabilities had a book value equal to market value except for land undervalued by $20,000, building by $45,000, and equipment undervalued by $30,000.

Required:

a. Prepare an allocation schedule for the acquisition.
b. Prepare a consolidated balance sheet worksheet for the two companies.

Problem 3-13   **(Consolidation policy)**

You are the auditor for Landmark Company, an electronics company specializing in industrial controls, headquartered in Chicago. In addition to manufacturing facilities in Chicago, Landmark has investments in three companies—Low-Budget Finance, Auto-Matic Monitor, and Sterling Arms, Inc. Other audit firms with whom your firm has a long-standing associate relationship audit all the investees. Low-Budget Finance is an insurance and finance company specializing in second mortgages and home equity loans. Landmark owns 65% of Low-Budget. Low-Budget was acquired on July 1 of the current fiscal year. Auto-Matic Monitor was a California competitor until Landmark acquired 100% of its common stock two years ago. Auto-Matic was profitable for the first two years after acquisition, but sustained heavy losses due to a slowdown in the defense industry in California and a strike by the machinists union in the most recent year. Auto-Matic is currently operating with replacement workers at 50% of capacity. You have information that indicates that Auto-Matic may have to declare bankruptcy if business conditions do not improve within six months. Sterling Arms is a manufacturer of military rifles located in Indonesia. Landmark owns 45% of its common stock. Sterling has been very profitable in recent years.

Lawson Cassidy, controller of Landmark, has proposed that only Sterling Arms be consolidated. According to Cassidy, Low-Budget should not be consolidated because it is in the finance business and including its results in the consolidated statements would make the "numbers meaningless to our institutional investors" who want to compare results with other companies in the industry. He says that Auto-Matic should not be consolidated because it is highly likely that it will be placed into involuntary bankruptcy during the coming year. His argument for consolidating Sterling Arms is that Landmark effectively controls the company because there are no other shareholders who own more than 3% of Sterling's stock.

Required:

a. What are your recommendations about how each of the three investees should be accounted for?
b. What other information would you like to have and how would this information affect your decision?

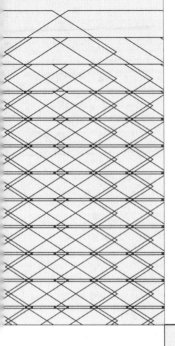

CHAPTER 4

CONSOLIDATED FINANCIAL STATEMENTS SUBSEQUENT TO ACQUISITION

LEARNING OBJECTIVES

- Analyze the effects of accounting method on the investment in subsidiary account

- Prepare a worksheet for consolidated financial statements (income statement, retained earnings statement, and statement of financial position) when the investment in subsidiary is accounted for by the equity method.

- Prepare a worksheet for consolidated financial statements (income statement, retained earnings statement, and statement of financial position) when the investment in subsidiary is accounted for by the cost method.

EFFECTS OF METHOD OF ACCOUNTING ON THE INVESTMENT IN SUBSIDIARY ACCOUNT

Chapter 3 showed that consolidated financial statements are prepared by combining the accounts of the parent company and its subsidiaries after **eliminating** the reciprocal accounts. The purpose of these elimination entries is to produce consolidated financial statements that only show the results of transactions with outsiders. At the date of acquisition, the reciprocal accounts consist of the parent company's investment in subsidiary account and the stockholders' equity accounts of the subsidiary. In the year immediately following the acquisition and in all subsequent years, the parent company will account for its investment in subsidiary using either the equity method or the cost method. These transactions and others create additional reciprocal account balances, which also must be eliminated. An important goal of this chapter is to illustrate why these elimination entries are needed and to show how to prepare and incorporate them into the worksheet for consolidated financial statements.

Choice of accounting method for subsidiary investments

Recall from Chapter 2 that GAAP requires different methods of accounting for investments in common stock depending upon the level of control or influence exercised by the investor over the operations of the investee. Passive investments in common stock are generally accounted for using the **cost method,** with mark-to-market adjustments at year-end as described *in FASB Statement 115.* Substantial influence investments are accounted for by the **equity method** in accordance with *APB Opinion No. 18. FASB Statements 94 and 141* require that controlled subsidiaries be consolidated. On first glance, it would appear that these three sets of principles represent mutually exclusive alternatives. However, consolidation is actually an additional procedure, which follows choice of accounting method for the investment in the subsidiary.[1] *FASB Statement 115* and *APB Opinion No. 18* provide guidance about how financial statements must present investments in common stock in financial statements. *FASB Statements 94 and 141* provide guidance about procedures to prepare consolidated financial statements. In the process of preparing the consolidated financial statements, the investment in common stock account is eliminated. Consolidation, however, is only a worksheet procedure used to prepare consolidated financial statements. **The ledger account for the investment in common stock remains on the parent company's books and must be accounted for through the year using either the cost method or the equity method.**

To summarize, a stock acquisition business combination occurs when a parent company acquires a controlling interest investment in the common stock of another company. The parent company then records journal entries **on its books** to account for this investment and prepares a consolidated financial statements worksheet at the end of the year. In the process of preparing the consolidated financial statements worksheet, the **worksheet account** for the investment in the common stock of the subsidiary is eliminated. The consolidated financial statements worksheet is **off the books** in that the elimination entries and the consolidated account balances are not recorded in the journals and ledger of either the parent company or its subsidiaries. Because there is no account for the common stock investment in the consolidated financial statements, it does not matter what method of accounting is used for this

---

[1] See Figure 2-1 in Chapter 2 for a flowchart of the investment accounting decision process.

investment on the books of the parent company. As a result, the parent company may account for an investment in the common stock of a subsidiary to be consolidated by either the **cost method** or the **equity method.** The method of accounting selected does affect the specific elimination entries necessary on the worksheet for consolidated financial statements because the investment in subsidiary account balance is affected by the choice of equity method or cost method.

Relationship between the investment account and the subsidiary stockholders' equity under the equity method

Consolidation of financial statements is a dynamic process whereby the accounts for investment in subsidiary and subsidiary stockholders' equity may have different balances each year. If the equity method is used, the **difference** between these accounts forms the basis for the amount to be assigned to goodwill or to other accounts such as inventories or plant assets each year in the consolidation worksheet. To illustrate, assume that Park Corporation acquired a 90% interest in Standard Corporation on January 1, 20x1, for $272,000, at which time Standard's capital stock and retained earnings were $180,000 and $100,000, respectively. The $20,000 cost/book value differential was determined to be goodwill with an indefinite life. An allocation schedule for this acquisition would appear as follows:

EXHIBIT 4-1

Investment in Standard 1/1/x1		$272,000
Stockholders' equity of Standard		
Common stock	$180,000	
Retained earnings	100,000	
	280,000	
Ownership percentage	90%	252,000
Goodwill		$ 20,000

Also assume that Standard had net income of $50,000 and paid $20,000 in dividends during the year ended 12/31/x1. If Park used the equity method of accounting, the relationship between the investment account on the books of the parent and the stockholders' equity of the subsidiary at the date of acquisition and at the end of the year 20x1 would be as follows:

	1/1/x1	12/31/x1
Investment in Standard	$272,000	$299,000
Common stock—Standard	180,000	180,000
Retained earnings—Standard	100,000	130,000
Total stockholders' equity	280,000	310,000
90% of total stockholders' equity	252,000	279,000
Unamortized goodwill*	$ 20,000	$ 20,000

* Goodwill is not amortized and remains at $20,000 unless written down as the result of an impairment loss.

The change in the investment in Standard account is the result of two equity method entries:

12/31/x1	Investment in Standard	45,000	
	Equity in Standard income		45,000
	(To record equity in Standard income = $50,000 × 90%)		
	Cash	18,000	
	Investment in Standard		18,000
	(To record dividends received from Standard 5 $20,000 3 90%)		

Posting the acquisition entry and the two equity entries to the investment account gives the following balances:

Investment in Standard

1/1/x1	272,000	
12/31/x1	45,000	18,000
12/31/x1	299,000	

By applying the equity method, the investment in Standard account increased $27,000. This increase is equal to the increase in Standard's retained earnings during the year multiplied by the controlling interest percent.* Thus, the use of the equity method causes the change in the investment in subsidiary for the year 20x1 to equal the change in the subsidiary retained earnings multiplied by the controlling interest percentage less the amortization of cost-book value differential, which in this case is zero because goodwill is not amortized. If the cost method is used, the account for the investment is subsidiary does not change and would remain at $272,000 in our example. Since the investment account and the subsidiary equity accounts are eliminated in the consolidated statements worksheet, it is apparent that the elimination entries will be different when the cost method is used as compared with the equity method. This chapter will illustrate consolidation procedures for both the equity method and the cost method. The worksheet for equity method investment accounts will be illustrated first.

---

*The general case of the relationship between the **change** in Investment in Subsidiary and the **change** in Subsidiary Equity over time is given by the following expression:

(1) $\Delta I_{t...t+n} = [\Delta SRE_{t...t+n} \times CI\%] - CBVA_{t...t+n}$

Where: ΔI = Change in Investment in Subsidiary

ΔSRE = Change in Subsidiary Retained Earnings

$CI\%$ = Controlling interest percentage

CBVA = Cost-Book Value Amortization

$_{t...t+n}$ = time period from t to t+n

Applying formula (1) to the data in the illustration gives a change in the investment account balance of $27,000:

$27,000 = (\$30,000 \times 90\%) - \$0$

And adding this result to the beginning of year investment in subsidiary account balance gives the ending balance:

$299,000 = \$272,000 + \$27,000$

FORMATS FOR CONSOLIDATED FINANCIAL STATEMENTS WORKSHEETS

Worksheets for consolidated financial statements are used to combine the financial statements for a parent company and its subsidiaries. These worksheets may be set up in several different ways. No particular approach seems to be superior to another, and it is somewhat redundant to learn more than one approach. The so-called **vertical worksheet** consolidates the **financial statements** of the affiliates, while the **horizontal worksheet** consolidates the **trial balances** of the affiliates. If the horizontal approach is used, the accountant must prepare the financial statements of the consolidated entity after the worksheet is completed, whereas the vertical approach results in an essentially completed set of financial statements. Once either of these approaches is learned, it is relatively easy to learn the alternative approach if desired. All the illustrations in this textbook use the vertical approach as depicted in Exhibit 4-2.

PURCHASE METHOD SUBSIDIARIES ACCOUNTED FOR BY THE EQUITY METHOD—YEAR 1

A consolidated statements worksheet for the Park-Standard consolidation is shown in Exhibit 4-2. Following vertical worksheet format, Exhibit 4-2 begins with an income statement, followed by the statement of retained earnings, and the statement of financial position. Eliminating all of the reciprocal accounts that represent transactions between the parent company and its subsidiary completes the worksheet. For reference purposes, these eliminations may be classified into the categories shown in Figure 4-1.

FIGURE 4-1: Categories of Elimination Entries

a. Adjustments for omissions and errors
b. Elimination of intercompany profit on transactions between affiliates and elimination of reciprocal assets and liabilities
c. Elimination of current year equity earnings and intercompany dividends
d. Establishment of noncontrolling interest share of subsidiary income
e. Elimination of beginning of year balances of subsidiary stockholders' equity and the investment in subsidiary
f. Allocation and amortization of excess of cost over book value (or book value over cost)

Adjustments for errors and omissions

The principal errors or omissions (item a in Figure 4-1) that routinely occur in consolidated statements worksheets relate to use of the cost method when accounting for the investment account. As previously noted, it is not technically incorrect to account for a subsidiary investment to be consolidated using the cost method. However, as demonstrated later in the chapter, adjustments are required in all years after the initial year to convert the cost method balance in the investment in subsidiary to the equity method in order to complete the worksheet. Because Park used the equity method to account for its investment in Standard and there are no errors or omissions, no entries are needed in Exhibit 4-2 for errors and omissions.

EXHIBIT 4.2 Park Corporation and Subsidiary
(Equity Method) Worksheet for Consolidated Financial Statements

Statement of Income	Park	Standard	Eliminations				Consolidated	
For the Year ended 12/31/x1								
Sales	$ 470,000	$ 210,000					$ 68,000	
Equity in Standard income	45,000		(2)	45,000			-	
Cost of sales	(160,000)	(115,000)					(275,000)	
Operating expenses	(168,000)	(45,000)					(213,000)	
Net Income	187,000	50,000					192,000	
Controlling interest income*							187,000	A
Noncontrolling interest income**			(3)	5,000			5,000	
Retained earnings Jan. 1	166,000	100,000	(4)	100,000			166,000	
Add net income	187,000	50,000					187,000	A
Less: Dividends	(175,000)	(20,000)			(2)	18,000	(175,000)	
					(3)	2,000		
Retained earnings, Dec. 31	178,000	130,000					178,000	B
Balance sheet 12/31/x1								
Cash	180,500	26,000					206,500	
Accounts receivable	210,000	58,000					268,000	
Dividends receivable	4,500				(1)	4,500	-	
Inventories	40,000	31,000					71,000	
Land	75,000	40,000					115,000	
Buildings - net	250,000	90,000					340,000	
Machinery - net	350,000	125,000					475,000	
Investment in Standard	299,000				(2)	27,000	-	
					(4)	272,000		
Excess of cost over book value			(4)	20,000	(5)	20,000	-	
Goodwill			(5)	20,000			20,000	
	1,409,000	370,000					1,495,500	
Accounts payable	215,000	30,000					245,000	
Dividends payable	40,000	5,000	(1)	4,500			40,500	
Other liabilities	351,000	25,000					376,000	
Common stock	625,000	180,000	(4)	180,000			625,000	
Retained earnings	178,000	130,000					178,000	B
Noncontrolling interest					(3)	3,000		
					(4)	28,000	31,000	
	$ 1,409,000	$ 370,000		$ 374,500		$ 374,500	$ 1,495,500	

* $192,000 − $5,000 = $187,000   ** $50,000 × 10% = $5,000

Elimination of intercompany profit and elimination of reciprocal assets and liabilities

This item refers to a broad group of intercompany transactions that commonly occur between affiliated companies. Most types of elimination entries for this category of items will be covered in chapters 6 and 7. Exhibit 4-2 does show, however, that Park and Standard have reciprocal assets and liabilities. These result from the fact that Standard declared dividends during the year 20x1, but has not yet paid all of these dividends. Accordingly, the first elimination entry needed is to eliminate the $4,500 dividends receivable on the books of Park and the same amount of dividends payable on the books of Standard. From a consolidated perspective, all but $500 (10%) of the dividends payable are a reciprocal. Thus, the $4,500 dividends receivable account should be eliminated against $4,500 of the dividends payable. The remaining $500 of the dividends payable represents the liability for dividends due to the noncontrolling interest shareholders and is shown in the consolidated financial statements. In general journal form, this entry is as follows:

(1)	Dividends payable	4,500	
	Dividends receivable		4,500

Elimination of current year equity earnings and intercompany dividends

Recall from the previous illustrations that Standard Corporation had net income of $50,000 during the year 20x1 and declared dividends of $20,000. Accordingly, we eliminate the $45,000 balance in the Equity in Standard income account and $18,000 (the controlling interest share) of Standard's dividends. The difference between the $45,000 debit and the $18,000 credit is a $27,000 credit to the account investment in Standard. This credit restates the investment in Standard account to its balance at the beginning of the year. This entry, in general journal form, is as follows:

(2)	Equity in Standard income	45,000	
	Dividends—Standard		18,000
	Investment in Standard		27,000

Establishment of the noncontrolling interest share of consolidated net income

The noncontrolling interest share of consolidated net income in situations without intercompany profit transactions is calculated as follows.

NISCNI = Subsidiary net income × NCI% – NCIA
Where: NISCNI—Noncontrolling interest share of consolidated net income
NCI%—Noncontrolling interest percentage
NCIA—Amortization of excess applicable to the noncon-
trolling interest

For the Park-Standard consolidation in the year 20x1, this calculation is: $50,000 × 10% = $5,000 – $0. Since the excess of cost over book value in the allocation schedule is allocated 100% to goodwill, there is no amortization of excess attributable to the NCI. Also eliminated is the remaining $2,000 balance in the subsidiary dividend account. The difference between these two accounts (noncontrolling interest income and noncontrolling interest dividends) represents the amount by which the noncontrolling interest equity account increased during 20x1. We credit noncontrolling interest for this difference in order that all changes in the noncontrolling interest during the year are reflected in a single account in the statement of financial position. This entry in general journal form is as follows:

(3)	Noncontrolling interest income	5,000	
	Dividends—Standard		2,000
	Noncontrolling interest		3,000

Elimination of beginning of year balances of subsidiary stockholders' equity and investment in subsidiary

Entry (2), which restates Investment in Standard to its beginning of year balance, allows the remaining balance of Investment in Standard to be eliminated against the beginning of year balances of the stockholders' equity of the subsidiary. This approach is necessary in order that we may eliminate the beginning retained earnings balance of the subsidiary. As we shall see, making this entry as of the beginning of the year facilitates completion of the worksheet. Accordingly, we eliminate the opening balances of the subsidiary's common stock (which did not change during the year), subsidiary retained earnings, and the parent's investment in Standard account. At this time, the beginning **noncontrolling** interest is established by multiplying the beginning balance of the subsidiary stockholders' equity by the noncontrolling interest percentage ($280,000 × 10%). GAAP requires that the noncontrolling interest in stockholders' equity be shown as a single amount in the consolidated statement of financial position. Thus, 100% of the subsidiary equity is eliminated even when there is a noncontrolling interest, with the amount applicable to the noncontrolling interest being shown in a new equity account. When the equity method of accounting is used, the difference between the beginning balances of subsidiary stockholders' equity ($280,000) and the sum of noncontrolling interest and investment in subsidiary ($28,000 + $272,000) will equal the **excess of cost over book value** as of the beginning of the year. In this example, this **excess** as of 1/1/x1 is $20,000. The entry, using the data from the Park-Standard illustration, is as follows:

(4)	Common stock—Standard	180,000	
	Retained earnings—Standard	100,000	
	Excess of cost over book value	20,000	
	Noncontrolling interest		28,000
	Investment in Standard		272,000

Allocation and amortization of unamortized differential

It is now necessary to allocate the excess of cost over book value (category f in Figure 4-1). Note that in entry (4) we assigned the excess of cost over book value to a temporary account by that name. According to our original allocation schedule as shown in Exhibit 4-1, this amount is attributable to goodwill. Thus, we must eliminate the excess of cost over book value recorded in entry (4) and then record the appropriate amount of goodwill. Since all the differential is attributable to goodwill, there is no entry for differential amortization.* The entry to record goodwill is given below:

(5)	Goodwill	20,000	
	Excess of cost over book value		20,000

---

* If some portion of the cost-book value deferential were appreciable to an identifiable asset, it would have to be amortized. An example is shown in the comprehensive illustration later in this chapter.

Entries (1) through (5) are posted to the consolidated financial statements worksheet in Exhibit 4-2.

COMPLETION OF THE CONSOLIDATED STATEMENTS WORKSHEET

After all of the elimination entries are posted to the worksheet (see Exhibit 4-2), the worksheet is simply extended across by adding the balances of all parent and subsidiary accounts, adjusted for the entries in the elimination columns, except for beginning and ending retained earnings. The retained earnings accounts are extended as follows: First, the consolidated net income ($192,000) must be allocated to the controlling interest and the noncontrolling interest. The controlling interest share of consolidated net income is equal to the net income less the noncontrolling interest share of consolidated net income (see entry 3) and is carried down to the retained earnings statement as indicated by the letter (A) in at the extreme right of the worksheet. The noncontrolling interest share of consolidated net income is transferred, net of dividends received by noncontrolling shareholders, to the noncontrolling interest account in the statement of financial position by elimination entry (3). Next, the ending consolidated retained earnings account is carried down to the statement of financial position as indicated by the letter (B). After completing the extensions and footings, four additional accuracy checks can be made:

1. The account, equity in subsidiary income, will always be zero in the consolidated statement of income unless there are other unconsolidated subsidiaries.
2. Controlling interest net income will equal parent company net income when the equity method of accounting has been used. (In cases where there are intercompany profits, this identity will only exist if equity method adjustments are made for intercompany profits. See discussion in Chapter 6.)
3. The account for investment in subsidiary will always be zero unless there are other unconsolidated subsidiaries.
4. The temporary account, excess of cost over book value, will always be zero.

You will quickly find that a most efficient way of preparing this worksheet is through the use of a computer spreadsheet. Cell formulas may be entered for all data except primary account balances, and the spreadsheet program will extend and foot the remaining amounts, completing the worksheet.

PURCHASE METHOD SUBSIDIARIES ACCOUNTED FOR BY THE EQUITY METHOD—SUBSEQUENT YEARS

In the year following the initial year, the worksheet for consolidated financial statements is prepared in essentially the same manner as in the previous year. Since many of the account balances of the two companies will have changed, it is helpful to illustrate the elimination entries and worksheet procedures for the second year. Any future year's worksheet would be completed using the same procedures as for the second year. Assume that the account balances prior to consolidation for Park and Subsidiary are as shown in the first two columns of Exhibit 4-3. Note that there are several account balances in Exhibit 4-3 that can be referenced to Exhibit 4-2. The ending balances of retained earnings for the year 20x1 are shown in Exhibit 4-3 as the beginning retained earnings for 19x2. Also note that the balance for the investment in Standard is the ending balance (per books) for the year 20x1 adjusted to reflect the book entries as required by the equity method of accounting for the year 19x2. The changes, based on a subsidiary net income of $70,000 and subsidiary dividends of $30,000 in this account on Park books for the year 19x2 are as follows:

		Investment in Standard	
balance	1/1/x2	299,000	
income	12/31/x2	63,000	27,000 dividends
balance	12/31/x2	335,000	

The equity method entries in the above account on Park books, in general journal form, are:

12/31/x1	Investment in Standard	63,000	
	Equity in Standard income		63,000
	($70,000 × 90%)		
	Cash	27,000	
	Investment in Standard		27,000
	($30,000 × 90%)		

Refer again to the six types of elimination entries listed in Figure 4-1. As in the previous year, there are no errors or omissions in the account balances of the two companies. Also, as in the previous year, the subsidiary has not yet written checks for all of its declared dividends. Exhibit 4-3 shows that Standard has declared $30,000 in dividends during the year 20x2, with $7,500 of these unpaid as of 12/31/x2. Likewise, Park has a balance of $6,750 in dividends receivable on its books representing 90% of these dividends. Two factors indicate that these dividends are intercompany. First, Park has no other investments in common stock other than the investment in the subsidiary. Second, the dividend receivable account has a balance of exactly 90% of the subsidiary dividends payable account. Accordingly, the appropriate elimination entry is:

(1)	Dividends payable	6,750	
	Dividends receivable		6,750

The second entry eliminates the equity method income for the year and restates the investment in Standard account to its balance as of January 1, 20x2. Note that the equity income is only eliminated for the current year. **It is not necessary to eliminate the equity income for the previous year.** In all consolidation worksheets, the investment in the subsidiary is eliminated against the beginning of year balance in the subsidiary stockholders' equity accounts. In our illustrations, the only stockholders' equity account that has changed is the retained earnings account. This account, at 1/1/x2, reflects the subsidiary income for the previous year; thus, the account for investment in Standard should also reflect previous years' subsidiary income. Accordingly, we eliminate equity income and dividends of the parent company as follows:

(2)	Equity in Standard income	63,000	
	Dividends—Standard		27,000
	Investment in Standard		36,000

($70,000 × 90% = $63,000)
($30,000 × 90% = $27,000)

EXHIBIT 4-3 Park Corporation and Subsidiary
(Equity Method) Worksheet for Consolidated Financial Statements

Statement of Income	Park	Standard	Eliminations			Consolidated	
For the Year ended 12/31/x2							
Sales	$ 545,000	$ 325,000				$ 870,000	
Equity in Standard income	63,000		(2)	63,000		-	
Cost of sales	(245,000)	(185,000)				(430,000)	
Operating expenses	(133,000)	(70,000)				(203,000)	
Net Income	230,000	70,000				237,000	
Controlling interest income*						230,000	A
Noncontrolling interest income**			(3)	7,000		7,000	
Retained earnings Jan. 1	178,000	130,000	(4)	130,000		178,000	
Add net income	230,000	70,000				230,000	A
Less: Dividends	(155,000)	(30,000)			(2) 27,000	(155,000)	
					(3) 3,000		
Retained earnings, Dec. 31	253,000	170,000				253,000	B
Balance sheet 12/31/x2							
Cash	165,000	18,500				183,500	
Accounts receivable	197,000	67,400				264,400	
Dividends receivable	6,750				(1) 6,750	-	
Inventories	63,475	33,200				96,675	
Land	75,000	50,000				125,000	
Buildings - net	290,000	105,000				395,000	
Machinery - net	310,000	145,000				455,000	
Investment in Standard	335,000				(2) 36,000	-	
					(4) 299,000		
Excess of cost over book value			(4)	20,000	(5) 20,000	-	
Goodwill			(5)	20,000		20,000	
	1,442,225	419,100				1,539,575	
Accounts payable	155,750	46,600				202,350	
Dividends payable	25,000	7,500	(1)	6,750		25,750	
Other liabilities	408,475	15,000				423,475	
Common stock	600,000	180,000	(4)	180,000		600,000	
Retained earnings	253,000	170,000				253,000	B
Noncontrolling interest					(3) 4,000		
					(4) 31,000	35,000	
	$ 1,442,225	$ 442,100		$ 422,750	$ 422,750	$ 1,539,575	

*($237,000 − $7,000 = $230,000)   **($70,000 × 10% = $7,000)

Entry (3) establishes the noncontrolling interest share of consolidated net income and eliminates the dividends paid to noncontrolling shareholders, assigning the difference directly to the noncontrolling interest account in the statement of financial position:

(3)	Noncontrolling interest income	7,000	
	Dividends—Standard		3,000
	Noncontrolling interest		4,000

($70,000 × 10% = $7,000)
($30,000 × 10% = $3,000)

Entry (4) eliminates the beginning of year balance of Investment in Subsidiary and the beginning of year balances Subsidiary stockholders' equity, assigning the difference to excess of cost over book value. Since goodwill is not amortized, this amount is the same as for the previous year, or $20,000. In addition, the opening balance of the noncontrolling interest, established in this entry, is equal to 10% of the beginning subsidiary equity [($180,000 + $130,000) × 10% = $31,000].

(4)	Common stock—Standard	180,000	
	Retained earnings—Standard	130,000	
	Excess of cost over book value	20,000	
	Noncontrolling interest		31,000
	Investment in Standard		299,000

Finally, the unamortized excess of cost over book value is allocated in the following entry:

(5)	Goodwill	20,000	
	Excess of cost over book value		20,000

Refer again to Exhibit 4-3 for an illustration of the posting of the above entries and completion of the remaining elements of the worksheet.

■ CONCEPT QUESTION AND REFLECTION

Why is goodwill recorded on the worksheet instead of the Parent Company books?

PURCHASE METHOD SUBSIDIARIES ACCOUNTED FOR BY THE COST METHOD—YEAR 1

Exhibit 4-4 shows the consolidated statements worksheet for the Park-Standard consolidation, assuming that the parent company follows the cost method. This is the approach most commonly used in practice. The equity-adjusted approach was illustrated first because an understanding of the equity method is necessary before learning to make the elimination entries to consolidate a cost method investment. There are two differences between the cost method consolidation (Exhibit 4-4) and the equity method consolidation (Exhibit 4-2) for the year 20x1. First, the account investment in Standard does not change when the cost method is used. Accordingly, its balance at 12/31/x1 is $272,000, the same balance as at the date of acquisition. Second, in place of **Equity in Standard Income,** Park has only **Dividend Income.** These differences require only minor changes in the procedures needed to prepare the consolidated statements worksheet.

In the first year after acquisition, the elimination entries required under the cost method are exactly the same as for the equity method, **except that entry (2), which eliminates the parent company's equity in subsidiary income, is replaced by an entry that eliminates its dividend income.** This entry, which is posted in Exhibit 4-4, is as follows:

(2)	Dividend income	18,000	
	Dividends—Standard		18,000

All of the other entries for the worksheet are exactly the same as for the equity-adjusted worksheet in Exhibit 4-2. Exhibit 4-4 shows all of the entries and the completed worksheet for the cost method for the year 20x1.

Recall that an equity method entry (see entry (2) in Exhibit 4-2) eliminated the Equity in Standard Income, the controlling interest in Standard's dividends, and credited the Investment in Standard for the difference between these two accounts. This credit to Investment in Standard restated the equity-adjusted investment balance to its 1/1/x1 balance, a condition necessary before eliminating the Subsidiary stockholders' equity balances. When the cost method is followed, the investment balance is unchanged from 1/1/x1 to 12/31/x; therefore, it is not necessary to make any adjustments that restate the investment account to its beginning of year balance.

PURCHASE METHOD SUBSIDIARIES ACCOUNTED FOR BY THE COST METHOD—SUBSEQUENT YEARS

Exhibit 4-5 shows the consolidated statements worksheet for the Park-Standard consolidation in the year 20x2 when the investment in Standard is accounted for by the cost method. In this case, there are two differences between this consolidation and the equity method case for the year 20x2 as shown in Exhibit 4-3. First, an entry is required to adjust the investment in Standard account to the balance that would have existed at the beginning of the year 20x1 had the equity method been followed. For the year 19x2 in the Park-Standard consolidation, this amount is calculated as follows:

Retained earnings, Standard, 1/1/x2	$130,000
Retained earnings, Standard, 1/1/x1	100,000
Increase in retained earnings during the year 19x1	30,000
Controlling interest percentage	90%
Gross increase in Investment in Standard	27,000
Amortization of cost-book value differential (goodwill)*	0
Net increase in Investment in Standard	$ 27,000

The equity adjustment (EA) is thus recorded in the worksheet as shown below:**

(EA)	Investment in Standard	27,000	
	Retained earnings—Park		27,000

---

*Goodwill is not amortized. Differential applicable to tangible assets and identifiable intangible assets would be amortized as shown in the examples in Chapter 2:

**The generalized form of this adjustment is given by the following expression:

(2) $EA = [SRE_{1/1/n} - SRE_{1/1/x1}] \times CI\% - CBVA_{1/1x1 \ldots 1/1/n}$

Where: EA = Required adjustment to the investment in subsidiary account

$SRE_{1/1/n}$ = Subsidiary retained earnings at the beginning of year n

$SRE_{1/1/x1}$ = Subsidiary retained earnings at the date of acquisition

$CI\%$ = Controlling interest percentage

$CBVA_{1/1x1 \ldots 1/1/n}$ = Cost-book value amortization from the date of acquisition to 1/1 of year n

EXHIBIT 4-4 Park Corporation and Subsidiary
(Cost Method) Worksheet for Consolidated Financial Statements

Statement of Income	Park	Standard	Eliminations				Consolidated	
For the Year ended 12/31/x1								
Sales	$ 470,000	$ 210,000					$ 680,000	
Dividend income	18,000		(2)	18,000			-	
Cost of sales	(160,000)	(115,000)					(275,000)	
Operating expenses	(168,000)	(45,000)					(213,000)	
Net Income	160,000	50,000					192,000	
Controlling interest income*							187,000	A
Noncontrolling interest income**			(3)	5,000			5,000	
Retained earnings Jan. 1	166,000	100,000	(4)	100,000			166,000	
Add controlling net income	160,000	50,000					187,000	A
Less: Dividends	(175,000)	(20,000)			(2)	18,000	(175,000)	
					(3)	2,000		
Retained earnings, Dec. 31	151,000	130,000					178,000	B
Balance sheet 12/31/x1								
Cash	180,500	26,000					206,500	
Accounts receivable	210,000	58,000					268,000	
Dividends receivable	4,500				(1)	4,500	-	
Inventories	40,000	31,000					71,000	
Land	75,000	40,000					115,000	
Buildings - net	250,000	90,000					340,000	
Machinery - net	350,000	125,000					475,000	
Investment in Standard	272,000				(4)	272,000	-	
Excess of cost over book value			(4)	20,000	(5)	20,000	-	
Goodwill			(5)	20,000			20,000	
	1,382,000	370,000					1,495,500	
Accounts payable	215,000	30,000					245,000	
Dividends payable	40,000	5,000	(1)	4,500			40,500	
Other liabilities	351,000	25,000					376,000	
Common stock	625,000	180,000	(4)	180,000			625,000	
Retained earnings	151,000	130,000					178,000	B
Noncontrolling interest					(3)	3,000		
					(4)	28,000	31,000	
	$ 1,382,000	$ 370,000		$ 349,500		$ 349,500	$ 1,495,500	

* ($192,000 − $5,000 = $187,000)   ** ($50,000 × 10% = $5,000)

Exhibit 4-1 shows Standard's retained earnings on the date the parent company acquired its controlling interest as $100,000. Furthermore, Standard's retained earnings on 1/1/x2 (see Exhibit 4-5) was $130,000. Thus, the equity adjustment (EA) using formula (2) above is:

$$EA = [\$130,000 - \$100,000] \times 90\% - \$0 = \$27,000$$

● INTERPRETIVE EXERCISE

Assuming Standard's retained earnings was $200,000 on 12/31x4, how much would the conversion entry be in the worksheet for the year ended 12/31/x5?

The equity adjustment is necessary to reestablish the functional relationship between Investment in Standard and Standard's stockholders' equity. To explain this necessity, reexamine the relationship between the Parent's investment account and the Subsidiary stockholders' equity when the equity method is used. Recall that, at the date of acquisition:

Excess of cost over book value = **Investment cost** − [Subsidiary Equity × CI%]

Where: CI%—Controlling interest percentage
In the Park-Standard consolidation, this amount was:

On 1/1/x1: $20,000 = $272,000 − ($280,000 × 90%)

The unamortized excess of cost over book value is reduced each year by the amount of amortization recorded under the equity method, resulting in the following relationship:

Unamortized excess of cost over book value = **Investment balance** − [Subsidiary Equity × CI%]

Again, for the Park-Standard consolidation, this amount was:

On 1/1/x2: $20,000 = $299,000 − ($310,000 × 90%)

When the stockholders' equity accounts of the subsidiary are eliminated, the difference between total subsidiary equity and Investment in Subsidiary, after establishing the opening balance of the minority interest, must equal the unamortized cost-book value differential as of the beginning of the year.

In order for this result to occur, the parent company must use the equity method of accounting! Subsidiary stockholders' equity increases by the amount of its **undistributed income** as its books are closed. Therefore, a reciprocal relationship is maintained between subsidiary retained earnings and the investment account only if the investment account also changes by the controlling interest share of this **undistributed subsidiary income,** adjusted for cost-book value amortization. This condition exists under the equity method but not under the cost method.[2]

The only other cost method entry that differs from the equity approach in subsequent years is the elimination of dividend income. This entry is recorded in the same manner as for the first year under the cost method. For the year 20x2 in the Park-Standard consolidation, this entry is as follows:

(2)	Dividends income	27,000	
	Dividends—Standard		27,000

---

[2] This necessity can be seen by looking at the effect of the entry (EA) on the investment balance in Exhibit 4-5. Without the $27,000 (EA) entry, entries (4) and (5) would not produce the correct ($20,000) balance for goodwill in the consolidated statement of financial position.

All of the other entries for the worksheet in Exhibit 4-5 are exactly the same as for the equity-adjusted worksheet in Exhibit 4-3.

EXHIBIT 4-5 Park Corporation and Subsidiary
(Cost Method) Worksheet for Consolidated Financial Statements

Statement of Income	Park	Standard	Eliminations				Consolidated	
For the Year ended 12/31/x2								
Sales	$ 545,000	$ 325,000					$ 870,000	
Dividend income	27,000		(2)	27,000			-	
Cost of sales	(245,000)	(185,000)					(430,000)	
Operating expenses	(133,000)	(70,000)					(203,000)	
Net Income	194,000	70,000					237,000	
Controlling interest income*							230,000	A
Noncontrolling interest income**			(3)	7,000			7,000	
Retained earnings Jan. 1	151,000	130,000	(4)	130,000	(EA)	27,000	178,000	
Add net income	194,000	70,000					230,000	A
Less: Dividends	(155,000)	(30,000)			(2)	27,000	(155,000)	
					(3)	3,000		
Retained earnings, Dec. 31	190,000	170,000					253,000	B
Balance sheet 12/31/x2								
Cash	165,000	18,500					183,500	
Accounts receivable	197,000	67,400					264,400	
Dividends receivable	6,750				(1)	6,750	-	
Inventories	63,475	33,200					96,675	
Land	75,000	50,000					125,000	
Buildings - net	290,000	105,000					395,000	
Machinery - net	310,000	145,000					455,000	
Investment in Standard	272,000		(EA)	27,000	(4)	299,000	-	
Excess of cost over book value			(4)	20,000	(5)	20,000	-	
Goodwill			(5)	20,000	(6)		20,000	
	1,379,225	419,100					1,539,575	
Accounts payable	155,750	46,600					202,350	
Dividends payable	25,000	7,500	(1)	6,750			25,750	
Other liabilities	408,475	15,000					423,475	
Common stock	600,000	180,000	(4)	180,000			600,000	
Retained earnings	190,000	170,000					253,000	B
Noncontrolling interest					(3)	4,000		
					(4)	31,000	35,000	
	$1,379,225	$ 419,100		$ 413,750		$ 413,750	$1,535,575	

*($237,000 − $7,000 = $230,000)   ** ($70,000 × 10% = $7,000)

COMPREHENSIVE ILLUSTRATION

If the identifiable assets and liabilities of an acquisition have different book and fair market values, the consolidation becomes somewhat more complex, particularly where a noncontrolling interest exists. The following comprehensive case illustration shows how to prepare a consolidation under these conditions:

Peery Corporation acquires 80% of the outstanding common stock of Simpson Corporation for a price of $400,000 at a time when Simpson has the following stockholders' equity:

Stockholders' equity of Simpson
Common stock, $5 par value	$ 100,000
Additional paid-in capital	180,000
Retained earnings	80,000
	$ 360,000

On the date of acquisition, January 1, 20x1, Simpson Corporation's assets and liabilities all had book and fair market values approximately equal except for the following items:

Inventory undervalued	$ 25,000
Building undervalued	50,000
Equipment **overvalued**	**30,000**

The inventory is assumed to be sold in the year 20x1 (the year of acquisition), while the building and equipment have estimated useful lives of 10 years and 5 years respectively. Any goodwill resulting from the acquisition is assumed to have an indefinite life.

The allocation schedule

The allocation schedule for Peery Corporation's acquisition of Simpson is shown in Exhibit 4-6. Subtracting the controlling interest percentage of Simpson stockholders' equity from the $400,000 price results in an excess of cost over book value equal to $112,000 on the date of acquisition of 1/1/x1. **The excess of cost over book value represents the total amount by which the controlling interest share in the net assets of Simpson must be increased by the elimination entries in the consolidated statements worksheet.** These allocations are accomplished by increasing the carrying amount of the inventory by $25,000, the building by $50,000, decreasing the equipment by $30,000, and increasing the noncontrolling interest by $9,000. The building and equipment are increased by the amount by which they are overvalued. However, note that the equipment is **overvalued** by $30,000. This overvaluation is reflected in the allocation schedule by subtracting the overvaluation in the analysis column. This approach may be understood by noting that the undervaluation items (inventory and building) will be increased in consolidated statements worksheet by debiting them for the amounts indicated. However, the equipment is overvalued and thus will be decreased in value by a credit $30,000 in the consolidated statements worksheet. Since these adjustments to Inventory, Building, and Equipment represent adjustments to both the controlling interest and noncontrolling interest in the net assets, the noncontrolling interest account must be increased by 20% of the total change in long-term assets as discussed later. Goodwill is the residual figure in the lower section of the allocation and is only applicable to the controlling interest shareholders.

EXHIBIT 4·6 Peery and Simpson—Allocation Schedule

			Remaining			Amortization				
Cost of Simpson Stock, 1/1/20x1		$ 400,000								
Stockholders' equity of Simpson										
Common stock, $5 par value	$ 100,000									
Additional paid-in capital	180,000									
Retained earnings	80,000									
	360,000									
Percentage of ownership	80%	288,000								
Excess of cost over book value		112,000								
			life		20x1		20x2		20x3	
Allocation:			in years	CI	NCI	CI	NCI	CI	NCI	
Inventory undervalued		25,000	1	20,000	5,000	-	-	-	-	
Building undervalued		50,000	10	4,000	1,000	4,000	1,000	4,000	1,000	
Equipment overvalued		(30,000)	5	(4,800)	(1,200)	(4,800)	(1,200)	(4,800)	(1,200)	
Increase in noncontrolling interest		(9,000)*								
Goodwill**		76,000								
Excess of cost over book value		$ 112,000		$ 19,200	$ 4,800	$ (800)	$ (200)	$ (800)	$ (200)	

* ($25,000 + $50,000 − $30,000) × 20%   **Goodwill is assumed to have an indefinite life and is not amortized.

■ CONCEPT QUESTION AND REFLECTION

> How would the overvaluation or undervaluation of a liability account, such as long-term debt, affect the amount of excess of cost over book value in an allocation schedule?

The noncontrolling interest adjustment

The existence of a noncontrolling interest complicates the allocation schedule. As discussed in Chapter 3, the **economic unit** approach to consolidation requires that the noncontrolling interest be adjusted when subsidiary identifiable assets and liabilities are overvalued or undervalued in the consolidated financial statements. This adjustment is reflected in the lower section of the allocation schedule (Exhibit 4-6) by calculating the increase in the noncontrolling interest associated with the amount of overvaluation or undervaluation of subsidiary net assets. In Exhibit 4-6, this adjustment is an increase in the noncontrolling interest of $9,000. The inventory and building are undervalued by a total of $75,000 ($25,000 + $50,000), but the equipment is overvalued by $30,000, resulting in a net undervaluation of all identifiable assets of $45,000 ($75,000 − $30,000). The noncontrolling interest is increased by its share (20%) of this amount ($45,000 × 20% = $9,000). Since noncontrolling interest is increased by a credit in the elimination entries, this $9,000 amount is also subtracted in the lower section of the allocation schedule.

The existence of overvalued or undervalued subsidiary net assets also complicates the amortization section of the allocation schedule. Refer to this section of Exhibit 4-6 where the amortization of the cost-book value differential is apportioned between the controlling interest (CI) and the noncontrolling interest (NCI) in the ratio of the 80% CI and the 20% NCI. Only the amortization applicable to the controlling interest is reflected in the parent company's equity method entries on its books. The amortization amounts for the NCI affect the calculation of noncontrolling interest income in the consolidated statements worksheet. This calculation will be illustrated shortly.

● INTERPRETIVE EXERCISE:

Assuming that Simpson Corporation had net income of $40,000 during the year 20x1 and paid dividends of $15,000, record the equity method adjustments that Peery Corporation would make on its books to account for this investment, based on the allocation schedule in Exhibit 4-6.

◆ CONCEPT QUESTION AND REFLECTION

Refer again to Exhibit 4-6. To what account would the excess of cost over book value attributable to Simpson's $25,000 undervaluation of inventory be debited in a worksheet for a consolidated statement of financial position on January 1, 20x1?

To what account would this amount be debited in the worksheet for consolidated financial statements on December 31, 20x1? Why?

Consolidated statements worksheet—equity method

Assume that Peery Company accounts for its investment in Simpson Corporation using the equity method of accounting and that the financial statements of the two companies on December 31, 20x3, are as shown in the first three columns of **Exhibit 4-7.** On this date, the balance in Investment in Simpson is now $539,200, as a result of Peery's use of the equity method of accounting. This activity is shown in the following T account:

Investment in Simpson		
January 1, 20x1	$ 400,000	
Equity effects 20x1–20x2*	77,600	
Equity income, 20x3	93,600	
Dividends received, 20x3		32,000
December 31, 20x3	539,200	

* 80% × ($200,000 – $80,000) – ($19,200 – $800)

The equity method effects for 20x1–20x2 are calculated using Formula (1) shown earlier in this chapter and represent the effect on the investment in Simpson account of Peery's use of the equity method for the two prior years. The current year's equity income is calculated as follows:

$93,600 = Standard Net income of $116,000 × 80% + differential amortization of $800

(Refer to **Exhibit 4-6** for calculation of differential amortization for the year 20x3.)

Elimination entries—equity method

The elimination entries for the Peery-Simpson consolidation for the year ended December 31, 20x3, are shown below. Entry (1) eliminates the intercompany dividend, which is reflected in the account balances for both the parent and the subsidiary. Since Peery has only one common stock investment, it is evident that all of its dividends receivable balance is an intercompany item.

| (1) | Dividends receivable | 8,000 | |
| | Dividends payable | | 8,000 |

Entry (2) eliminates Equity in Simpson income, 80% of Simpson's dividends, and credits Investment in Simpson for the difference between these two amounts. This entry also restates the balance of Investment in Simpson to its beginning of year balance on January 1, 20x3, of $477,600.

(2)	Equity in Simpson income	93,000	
	Dividends—Simpson		32,000
	Investment in Simpson		61,600

Entry (3) establishes the noncontrolling interest income account. Noncontrolling interest income is equal to Simpson's net income multiplied by the noncontrolling interest percentage less any differential amortization applicable to the noncontrolling interest. Exhibit 4-6 shows that amortization applicable to the noncontrolling interest for the year 20x3 to be $200. In this case, the amortization is **negative** because the excess attributable to overvalued equipment of $1,200 exceeds the excess attributable to undervalued buildings of $1,000. Accordingly, the noncontrolling interest income for the year 20x3 is $23,400 = $116,000 × 20% − $1,000 + $1,200.

(3)	Noncontrolling interest income	23,400	
	Dividends—Simpson		8,000
	Noncontrolling interest		15,400

Entry (4) eliminates the stockholders' equity of Simpson, the $477,600 beginning of year balance in Investment in Simpson, establishes the beginning of year balance in Noncontrolling interest of $96,000, and records the beginning of year balance in excess of cost over book value. The beginning Noncontrolling interest balance is equal to the beginning of year subsidiary equity multiplied by the noncontrolling interest percentage ($480,000 × 20% = $96,000). The beginning of year excess of cost over book value may be treated as the "plug" figure in the journal entry, but may also be calculated from the data in the allocation schedule **(Exhibit 4-6)**. The original unamortized excess of cost over book value, **which is applicable only to the controlling interest,** on 1/1/x1 was $112,000. Subtracting the amortization applicable to the controlling interest for years 20x1 and 20x2 of $18,400 from this amount leaves $93,600 ($112,000 − $18,400).

(4)	Retained earnings, 1/1/x3—Simpson	200,000	
	Common stock—Simpson	100,000	
	Additional paid-in capital—Simpson	180,000	
	Excess of cost over book value	93,600	
	Investment in Simpson		477,600
	Noncontrolling interest		6,000

EXHIBIT 4-7 Peery and Simpson
(Equity Method) Worksheet for Consolidated Financial Statements

Statement of Income	Peery	Simpson	Eliminations				Consolidated	
For the Year ended 12/31/x3								
Sales	$ 358,000	$ 225,000					$ 583,000	
Equity in Simpson income	93,600		(2)	93,600			-	
Cost of sales	(220,000)	(75,000)					(295,000)	
Operating expenses	(210,000)	(34,000)			(6)	1,000	(243,000)	
Net Income	21,600	116,000					45,000	
Controlling interest income*							21,600	A
Noncontrolling interest income**			(3)	23,400			23,400	
Retained earnings Jan. 1	362,000	200,000	(4)	200,000			362,000	
Add controlling net income	21,600	116,000					21,600	A
Less: Dividends	(5,000)	(40,000)			(2)	32,000	(5,000)	
					(3)	8,000		
Retained earnings, Dec. 31	378,600	276,000					378,600	B
Balance sheet 12/31/x3								
Cash	33,000	44,000					77,000	
Accounts receivable	120,000	88,200					208,200	
Dividends receivable	8,000				(1)	8,000	-	
Inventories	35,000	57,200					92,200	
Land	75,000	10,000					85,000	
Buildings - net	300,000	315,000	(5)	40,000	(6)	5,000	650,000	
Equipment - net	235,000	95,000	(6)	6,000	(5)	18,000	318,000	
Investment in Simpson	539,200				(2)	61,600	-	
					(4)	477,600		
Excess of cost over book value			(4)	93,600	(5)	93,600	-	
Goodwill			(5)	76,000			76,000	
	1,345,200	609,400					1,506,400	
Accounts payable	88,500	23,400					111,900	
Dividends payable	40,000	10,000	(1)	8,000			42,000	
Long-term debt	393,100	20,000					413,100	
Common stock	445,000	100,000	(4)	100,000			445,000	
Additional paid-in capital		180,000	(4)	180,000				
Retained earnings	378,600	276,000					378,600	B
Noncontrolling interest					(3)	15,400		
					(4)	96,000		
					(5)	4,400	115,800	
	$ 1,345,200	$ 609,400	$ 820,600		$ 820,600		$ 1,506,400	

* ($45,000 − $23,400 = $21,600)   ** ($116,000 × 20% + $200 = $23,400)

Entry (5) allocates the excess of cost over book value to the identifiable assets and goodwill. Following the **economic unit approach,** the buildings and equipment should be adjusted for the full amount of their book-fair market difference on January 1, 20x1, minus amortization to date. Therefore, entry (5) also requires that the noncontrolling interest be increased by $4,400 (unamortized building differential of $40,000 minus unamortized equipment differential of $18,000 = $22,000 multiplied by 20% = $4,400).*

(5)	Buildings—net	40,000	
	Goodwill	76,000	
	Equipment—net		18,000
	Excess of cost over book value		93,600
	Noncontrolling interest		4,400

Entry (6) amortizes the differential for the year 20x3. Since the differential applicable to equipment was **negative,** the equipment account is increased. The building account is decreased to adjust the consolidated balance for the increased depreciation resulting from upward adjustment of this account in the consolidated worksheet. Note that the noncontrolling interest share of consolidated net income is unaffected by this entry because the amortization applicable to the noncontrolling interest was recorded in entry (3) above.

(6)	Equipment—net	6,000	
	Buildings—net		5,000
	Operating expenses		1,000

The above entries are posted, and the consolidated statements worksheet is completed in Exhibit 4-7.

Consolidated statements worksheet—cost method

Exhibit 4-8 shows the consolidated statements worksheet for the Peery-Simpson consolidation for the year ended December 31, 20x3, assuming that Peery accounts for its investment in Simpson using the cost method. Refer to the first three columns of the worksheet for the beginning balances for both companies. Note that the only income account that Peery shows is a dividend income account equal to 80% of the dividends declared by Simpson. In addition, note that Investment in Simpson has a balance of $400,000, which is equal to the original cost of the common stock on January 1, 20x1. Unlike the equity method, the use of the cost method has no effect on the balance in the investment account. As a result, the balance in Investment in Simpson no longer reflects the proper functional relationship with the stockholders' equity of Simpson. Accordingly, an equity adjustment entry is needed to adjust Investment in Simpson to the balance that would have existed at the beginning of the year 20x3 had the equity method been used. This entry, together with all the other entries needed for a cost method consolidation at 12/31/x3, are shown below.

(EA)	Investment in Simpson	77,600	
	Retained earning—Peery		77,600

---

* Alternatively, this amount can be calculated from the original noncontrolling interest balance of $9,000 in Exhibit 4-6. From this $9,000 amount, subtract amortization for the years 20x1 and 20x2 for inventory ($5,000) and building ($2,000), and add amortization on equipment ($2,400): $4,400 − $9,000 − $5,000 − $2,000 + $2,400.

The equity adjustment (EA) as of January 1, 20x3, equals 80% of the change in the retained earnings of Simpson from the date of acquisition to January 1, 20x1, less amortization of cost-book value differential for the years 20x1 and 20x2. This calculation is $77,600 = 80\%$ of ($200,000 - $80,000) - $19,200 - $800.

Entry (1) eliminates the intercompany dividend liability and is identical to the entry in the equity method consolidation in Exhibit 4-7.

(1)	Dividends receivable	8,000	
	Dividends payable		8,000

Entry (2) eliminates the dividend income received by Peery from Simpson during the year 20x3. This entry and the EA entry above are the only entries that differ from the equity method approach.

(2)	Dividends income	32,000	
	Dividends—Simpson		32,000

The remaining entries (3) through (6) are identical to those required under the equity method:

(3)	Noncontrolling interest income	23,400	
	Dividends—Simpson		8,000
	Noncontrolling interest		15,400

(4)	Retained earnings, 1/1/x3—Simpson	200,000	
	Common stock—Simpson	100,000	
	Additional paid-in capital—Simpson	180,000	
	Unamortized differential	93,600	
	Investment in Simpson		477,600
	Noncontrolling interest		96,000

(5)	Buildings—net	40,000	
	Goodwill	76,000	
	Equipment—net		18,000
	Unamortized differential		93,600
	Noncontrolling interest		4,400

(6)	(6) Equipment	6,000	
	Buildings—net		5,000
	Operating expenses		1,000

The previous entries are posted to the consolidated statement worksheet, and the worksheet is completed as shown in Exhibit 4-8.

EXHIBIT 4-8   Peery and Simpson
(Cost Method) Worksheet for Consolidated Financial Statements

Statement of Income	Peery	Simpson	Eliminations				Consolidated	
For the Year ended 12/31/x3								
Sales	$ 358,000	$ 225,000					$ 583,000	
Dividend income	32,000		(2)	32,000			-	
Cost of sales	(220,000)	(75,000)					(295,000)	
Operating expenses	(210,000)	(34,000)			(6)	1,000	(243,000)	
Net Income	(40,000)	116,000					45,000	
Controlling interest income*							21,600	A
Noncontrolling interest income**			(3)	23,400			23,400	
Retained earnings Jan. 1	284,400	200,000	(4)	200,000	(EA)	77,600	362,000	
Add net income	(40,000)	116,000					21,600	A
Less: Dividends	(5,000)	(40,000)			(2)	32,000	(5,000)	
					(3)	8,000		
Retained earnings, Dec. 31	239,400	276,000					378,600	B
Balance sheet 12/31/x3								
Cash	33,000	44,000					77,000	
Accounts receivable	120,000	88,200					208,200	
Dividends receivable	8,000				(1)	8,000	-	
Inventories	35,000	57,200					92,200	
Land	75,000	10,000					85,000	
Buildings - net	300,000	315,000	(5)	40,000	(6)	5,000	650,000	
Equipment - net	235,000	95,000	(6)	6,000	(5)	18,000	318,000	
Investment in Simpson	400,000		(EA)	77,600	(4)	477,600	-	
Excess of cost over book value			(4)	93,600	(5)	93,600	-	
Goodwill			(5)	76,000			76,000	
	1,206,000	609,400					1,506,400	
Accounts payable	88,500	23,400					111,900	
Dividends payable	40,000	10,000	(1)	8,000			42,000	
Long-term debt	393,100	20,000					413,100	
Common stock	445,000	100,000	(4)	100,000			445,000	
Additional paid-in capital		180,000	(4)	180,000				
Retained earnings	239,400	276,000					378,600	B
Noncontrolling interest					(3)	15,400		
					(4)	96,000		
					(5)	4,400	115,800	
	$ 1,206,000	$ 609,400	$ 836,600		$ 836,600		$ 1,506,400	

* ($45,000 − $23,400 = $21,600)   **($116,000 × 20% + $200 = $23,400)

SUMMARY

The following learning objectives were stated at the beginning of the chapter:

■ Analyze the effects of accounting method on the investment in subsidiary account

- Prepare a worksheet for consolidated financial statements (income statement, retained earnings statement, and statement of financial position) when the investment in subsidiary is accounted for by the equity method.
- Prepare a worksheet for consolidated financial statements (income statement, retained earnings statement, and statement of financial position) when the investment in subsidiary is accounted for by the cost method.

Before preparing a consolidation analysis, you must determine what method of accounting the parent company uses to account for its investment in the common stock of the subsidiary. The next step is to prepare an allocation schedule as of the date of acquisition. This schedule is always prepared as of the acquisition date even though the consolidated statements worksheet is for a subsequent year. The allocation schedule serves as a basis for preparing the elimination entries, which are posted to the consolidated statements worksheet. For equity adjusted investment accounts, six classes of elimination entries are required:

a. Adjustments for omissions and errors
b. Elimination of intercompany profit on transactions between affiliates and elimination of reciprocal assets and liabilities
c. Elimination of current year equity earnings and intercompany dividends
d. Establishment of noncontrolling interest share of subsidiary income
e. Elimination of beginning of year balances of subsidiary stockholders' equity and the investment in subsidiary
f. Allocation and amortization of unamortized excess of cost over book value

In the case of cost method investment accounts, an equity adjustment entry is prepared (except in the initial year). This entry involves a debit to the investment in subsidiary and a credit to parent company Retained Earnings for the amount necessary to adjust the investment in subsidiary to the equity basis as of the beginning of the year being consolidated. This calculation conforms is shown in Formula (2):

$$(2) \qquad EA = [SRE_{1/1/n} - SRE_{1/1/x1}] \times CI\% - CBVA_{1/1x1 \ldots 1/1/n}$$

Where: EA = Required adjustment to the investment in subsidiary account
$SRE_{1/1/n}$ = Subsidiary retained earnings at the beginning of year n
$SRE_{1/1/\times1}$ = Subsidiary retained earnings at the date of acquisition
$CI\%$ = Controlling interest percentage
$CBVA_{1/1x1 \ldots 1/1/n}$ = Cost-book value amortization from the date of acquisition to 1/1 of year n

Only two of the elimination entries (a through e above) differ under the cost method as compared with the equity method. An equity adjustment entry (EA) is needed to adjust the investment in subsidiary account to the equity method in all years subsequent to the year of acquisition. In addition, entry (C) under the equity method is replaced with an entry that eliminates the dividend income the parent company recorded on its investment. The final balances in the consolidated financial statements are unaffected by the method of accounting used by the parent company for its subsidiary investment account. Only the elimination entries differ.

QUESTIONS

1. Passive investments in common stock are accounted for by the cost method with mark-to-market adjustments as required by *FASB 115*. Briefly describe this process.
2. What is the criterion for use of the equity method of accounting for investments in common stock as described in *APB Opinion 18?*
3. What methods of accounting may be used for a common stock investment to be consolidated? Why is more than one alternative acceptable?
4. How should an excess of cost over book value of a majority-owned subsidiary be allocated in the consolidated financial statements?
5. When a portion of excess of cost over book value of a majority-owned subsidiary is allocated to the subsidiary's plant and equipment, how should the noncontrolling interest be adjusted?
6. When a portion of excess of cost over book value of a majority-owned subsidiary is allocated to goodwill, how should noncontrolling interest be adjusted?
7. How does the use of the equity method of accounting affect the account balance for Investment in Subsidiary?
8. How does the use of the equity method of accounting affect the account balance for Retained Earnings of the parent company?
9. Does the use of the equity method of accounting result in consolidated balances that are different from those that would result had the cost method been used? Explain.
10. Why are reciprocal accounts for dividends receivable of the parent company eliminated against dividends payable of the subsidiary?
11. Why is the balance of the account investment in subsidiary eliminated in the consolidated financial statements?
12. How is differential attributable to subsidiary assets and liabilities treated in the consolidated financial statements?
13. Why is it only necessary to eliminate equity in subsidiary income of the current year in an equity-adjusted consolidation?
14. At what value are overvalued and undervalued assets of majority-owned subsidiaries reported in the consolidated financial statements?
15. How is the noncontrolling interest share of consolidated net income calculated when excess is attributable only to additional goodwill? When excess is attributable to subsidiary long-term assets and additional goodwill?

EXERCISES

Exercise 4-1   **(Multiple choice: select the best answer for each item.)**

1. According to *APB Opinion 18*, the equity method of accounting is required for
   a. passive investments in common stock.
   b. investments in which the investor exercises a substantial influence.
   c. all common stock investments in which 20% or more of the outstanding stock is owned.
   d. controlled subsidiaries.
2. Elimination entries for consolidated financial statements are recorded
   a. in the general ledger of the parent company.
   b. in the general ledger of the subsidiary company.
   c. in both the general ledgers of the parent company and the subsidiary company.
   d. only in the consolidated statements working paper.

3. When the parent company owns **less** than 100% of the subsidiary outstanding common stock in a purchase method acquisition, goodwill arising from the acquisition
   a. is attributable only to the controlling interest.
   b. is attributable to both the controlling interest and the noncontrolling interest.
   c. is measured as the difference between the fair market value and the book value of the subsidiary's identifiable tangible assets.
   d. is amortized only to the extent of the ownership percentage.
4. Hi Company acquired a 100% interest in the common stock of Lo Company on July 1, 20x3 for $25,000, an amount that equals the book and fair market value of Lo Company net assets. During the six months ended December 31, 20x3, Lo Company had net income of $10,000 and paid $5,000 in dividends. If Hi Company uses the equity method of accounting, what is its correct balance in Investment in Lo Company on December 31, 20x3?
   a. $25,000
   b. $35,000
   c. $30,000
   d. Cannot be determined from the information given.

Questions 5 and 6 relate to the following data:
On January 1, 20x5, Quon Company purchased 10,000 shares of the outstanding common stock of Chan Company in the open market for $25,000. This acquisition represents 100% of the outstanding common stock of Chan. On this date, Chan Company had a common stock with a par value of $10,000, no additional paid-in capital, and a retained earnings balance of $7,000. Any goodwill implicit in the acquisition is assumed to have an indefinite life. The book and fair values of its net assets were approximately equal. During the year 20x5, Chan Company had net income of $12,000 and paid $5,000 in dividends.

5. If Quon Company uses the equity method of accounting for its investment in Chan, what is the correct balance in Investment in Chan on its books on December 31, 20x5?
   a. $25,000
   b. $31,200
   c. $32,000
   d. $37,000
6. If Quon Company uses the cost method of accounting for its investment in Chan, what is the correct balance in Investment in Chan on its books on December 31, 20x5?
   a. $25,000
   b. $31,200
   c. $32,000
   d. $20,000
7. The noncontrolling interest share of consolidated net income is
   a. reported as an expense in the consolidated income statement.
   b. reported along with controlling interest share of consolidated net income as an allocation of the consolidated net income.
   c. reported only in footnote form in the consolidated financial statements.
   d. reported as a deduction from the opening balance of the noncontrolling interest equity account.
8. The ending balance of the noncontrolling interest
   a. should be reported as a liability in the consolidated financial statements.
   b. should be shown only in the footnotes for the consolidated financial statements.
   c. should be reported as an element of stockholders' equity.
   d. should be reported in a separate section of the consolidated statement of financial position between liabilities and stockholders' equity.
9. When the cost method is used for a common stock investment to be consolidated,
   a. an equity adjustment (EA) entry is required in all years beginning with the first year after acquisition.
   b. an equity adjustment (EA) entry is required in all years except the first year after acquisition.

    c. an equity adjustment (EA) entry is only required if the subsidiary is less than 100% owned.

    d. an equity adjustment (EA) entry is never required.

10. When the equity method of accounting is used for an investment in a subsidiary, the unamortized excess of cost over book value (or book value over cost) at any point in time is equal to

    a. the difference between the investment balance and the controlling interest share of subsidiary stockholders' equity.

    b. the difference between the investment balance at the beginning of the year and the investment balance at the end of the year.

    c. the difference between the investment balance at the date of acquisition and the controlling interest share of subsidiary stockholders' equity on the consolidation date.

    d. the difference between the book and fair market values of the subsidiary's net assets on the date of acquisition.

Exercise 4-2   (Acquisition of a controlling interest)

On January 1, 20x1, Williamson Company acquired 75% of the outstanding common stock of Calder Company in exchange for 100,000 shares of its own common stock. On this date, Williamson Company common stock had a par value of $1 and a market value of $5. The transaction is not expected to have a material effect on the Williamson Company market value. On this date, Calder Company had 200,000 shares of $2 par common stock outstanding. Calder Company was privately held and had no market value. Williamson Company also incurred $20,000 in issue costs and $25,000 in external legal costs in connection with this acquisition.

(a) What is the correct balance in Investment in Calder Company on the books of Williamson Company immediately after the acquisition? Explain your answer.

(b) How should the excess of cost over book value attributable to this acquisition be accounted for in the consolidated financial statements of Williamson and Calder? Explain your answer.

Exercise 4-3   (Effect of the equity method on the investment in subsidiary account balance)

On January 1, 20x1, Orange Company acquired 80% of the outstanding common stock of White Company in a business combination accounted for as a purchase. White Company is to become a subsidiary of Orange, and consolidated financial statements are to be prepared at the end of each year. The consideration given by Orange Company was $450,000 cash. On the date of acquisition, White's stockholders' equity consisted of 40,000 shares of $5 par common stock and retained earnings of $300,000. All of White's assets and liabilities had book values approximately equal to fair value except for inventories with a fair market value of $50,000 and a book value of $40,000. Any goodwill arising from the combination is assumed to have an indefinite life.

Required:

(a) Prepare an allocation schedule for the acquisition of White Company by Orange Company.

(b) Assuming that Orange Company uses the equity method of accounting, prepare the equity adjustments required for the year 20x1, assuming that White Company earns $15,000 and pays $5,000 in dividends.

(c) Calculate the balance of Investment in White Company at the end of the year 20x1.

(d) Give the elimination entries in general journal form required for the consolidated statements worksheet as of December 31, 20x1.

Exercise 4-4

(Effect of the equity method on the investment in subsidiary account balance)

George Corporation acquired 90% of the outstanding common stock of Greene Corporation for $240,000 on January 1, 20x2, at a time when Greene Corporation had the following stockholders' equity balances:

Common stock	$ 50,000
Additional paid-in capital	50,000
Retained earnings	100,000
	$200,000

On this date, all of Greene's assets and liabilities had book values approximately equal to market values except for Land, which was undervalued by $10,000 and Bonds payable, which were overvalued by $20,000. The bonds mature five years from January 1, 20x2, and any goodwill arising from the combination is assumed to have an indefinite life. During the year ended December 31, 20x2, Green Corporation reported net income of $50,000 and paid dividends of $30,000.

Required:

(a) Prepare an allocation schedule for the acquisition of Greene Corporation by George Corporation.
(b) Give the equity method entries that George would make on account of its investment in Greene for the year 20x2.
(c) Calculate the balance in George's Investment in Greene as of December 31, 20x2.
(d) Give the elimination entries as of December 31, 20x2, in general journal form for the consolidated statements worksheet for George Corporation and subsidiary.

Exercise 4-5

(Allocation schedule and elimination entries for a 100% acquisition)

Patin Company acquired a 100% interest in Spruance Company on July 1, 20x4, for $300,000 at a time when Spruance Company had the following balances in its stockholders' equity:

Common stock	$100,000
Additional paid-in capital	40,000
Retained earnings	110,000
	$250,000

All of Spruance's assets and liabilities had book values approximately equal to fair market values except for inventories that were overvalued by $15,000 and Equipment that was undervalued by $30,000. Additional cost-book value differential is attributable to goodwill with an indefinite life. The equipment had a remaining life of six years. During the six months ended December 31, 20x4, Spruance earned $40,000 and paid $15,000 in dividends. Patin uses the cost method to account for its investment in Spruance.

Required:

(a) Prepare an allocation schedule for the acquisition of Spruance by Patin.
(b) Record all the entries made by Patin for its investments in Spruance during the six months ended December 31, 20x4, assuming that Patin follows the cost method.
(c) Give the elimination entries required in the consolidated statements worksheet at December 31, 20x4.

Exercise 4-6 **(Subsequent year elimination entries under the cost method)**

Refer to the data in exercise 4-5 for the Patin-Spruance combination. Assume that in the year 20x5, Spruance earns $60,000 and pays $30,000 in dividends, and that Patin continues its use of the cost method.

Required:

(a) Record Patin's cost method entries for the year ended December 31, 20x5.
(b) Give the elimination entries required in the consolidated statements worksheet at December 31, 20x5. (Hint: Your first step is to compute Spruance's retained earnings balance at January 1, 20x5, and make an equity adjustment [EA] entry).

Exercise 4-7 **(Elimination entries for a partially owned subsidiary—equity method)**

Peer Company acquired an 80% interest in Small Company on January 1, 20x2, for $500,000 cash. Peer also paid $50,000 to a consulting firm in connection with the acquisition. On January 1, 20x2, Small Company had the following stockholders' equity:

Common stock, $1 par	$100,000
Additional paid-in capital	200,000
Retained earnings	300,000
	$600,000

All of Small's assets and liabilities had book values approximately equal to market values except for Land that was undervalued by $20,000 on the date of acquisition. Any additional cost-book value differential is assumed to be goodwill with an indefinite life.

Required:

(a) Record the equity adjustments for the year ended December 31, 20x2, on Peer Company's books, assuming that Small had net income in the year 20x2 of $100,000 and paid $40,000 in dividends.
(b) Record the elimination entries on the consolidated statements worksheet at December 31, 20x2.

Exercise 4-8 **(Elimination entries for a partially owned subsidiary—cost method)**

Refer to the data in exercise 4-7. Assume that Peer Company used the cost method to account for its investment in Small Company.

Required:

(a) Record the cost method entries on Peer Company's books for the year 20x2.
(b) Record the elimination entries on the consolidated statements worksheet at December 31, 20x2.

Exercise 4-9 **(Review of cost and equity method journal entries)**

Penny Company acquired 70% of the outstanding common stock of Spartan Company on April 1, 20x1, at a price of $100,000. On this date, Spartan Company had stockholders' equity totaling $120,000. Any cost-book value differential is assumed to be goodwill with an indefinite life. During the years ending December 31, 20x1, and 20x2, Spartan Company had net income of $20,000 and $30,000, respectively, earned evenly throughout the year. Dividends during these two years were as follows:

	Feb 1	Aug 1
Year ended December 31, 20x1	$ 6,000	$ 6,000
Year ended December 31, 20x2	8,000	8,000

Required:

(a) Record the entry for the acquisition of the 70% interest in Spartan Company by Penny Company.
(b) Record Penny Company's entries to account for its investment in Spartan Company under both the cost method and the equity method.
(c) Compute the balance in Investment in Spartan Company under both the cost method and the equity method as of December 21, 20x2.

Exercise 4-10   **(Conversion from cost to equity)**

PYC Company acquired a 100% interest in Sunset Company on January 1, 20x1, at a price of $500,000. On this date, Sunset had stockholders' equity as follows:

Common stock, $1 par	$ 50,000
Retained earnings	350,000
	$600,000

Any cost-book value differential is assumed to be goodwill with an indefinite life. PYC Company accounts for its investment in subsidiaries to be consolidated using the cost method. In connection with its consolidated statements worksheet for the year ended December 31, 20x5, the following retained earnings data for Sunset Company are available:

Retained earnings, 1/1/x5	$ 475,000
Net income, 20x5	40,000
Dividends declared in 20x5	(25,000)
Retained earnings, 12/31/x5	$ 490,000

Required:

(a) Prepare an allocation schedule for the acquisition of Sunset Company by PYC Company as of January 1, 20x1.
(b) Prepare the worksheet entry to convert the cost-based investment in Sunset account to the equity method for the December 31, 20x5, worksheet.
(c) Give the elimination entries for the consolidated statements worksheet for the year ended 12/31/x5.

Exercise 4-11   **(Conversion from cost to equity)**

Refer to the data in exercise 4-10. Assume all the same facts except that PYC acquired only a 90% interest in Sunset Company.

Required:

(a) Prepare an allocation schedule for the acquisition of Sunset Company by PYC Company as of January 1, 20x1.
(b) Prepare the worksheet entry to convert the cost-based investment in Sunset account to the equity method for the December 31, 20x5, worksheet.
(c) Give the elimination entries for the consolidated statements worksheet for the year ended 12/31/x5.

Exercise 4-12   **(Conversion from cost to equity)**

The Steinberg Company is a 90%-owned subsidiary of Peterborough Corporation. Peterborough acquired its interest on July 1, 20x2, at a cost of $560,000, and accounted for this investment using the cost method. Steinberg Company did not close its books on the acquisition date. Following is stockholders' equity data and earnings data for the year 20x2 relevant to the acquisition.

Common stock, Steinberg, January 1, 20x2	$100,000
Retained earnings, Steinberg, January 1, 20x2	220,000
Net income for the year ended December 31, 20x2	200,000
Dividends paid on March 31, 20x2	20,000
Dividends paid on September 30, 20x2	30,000

Assume that Steinberg Company earned its income evenly throughout the year. Any cost-book value differential existing at July 1, 20x2, is assumed to be goodwill with an indefinite life.

For the year ended December 31, 20x5, Steinberg Company's retained earnings account shows the following information:

Retained earnings, January 1, 20x5	$450,000
Net income for the year 20x5	175,000
Dividends declared and paid in 20x5	60,000
Retained earnings, December 31, 20x5	565,000

Required:

(a) Record the required entry to convert the cost-based investment account balance for the consolidated statements worksheet for the year ended December 31, 20x5.

(b) If Peterborough Corporation had used the equity method to account for investment in Steinberg, what would the balance in that account be as of December 31, 20x5, in Peterborough's separate financial statements?

PROBLEMS

Problem 4-1   **(Comparison of the effects of cost and equity methods on the investment account)**

Composite Company acquired 100% of Micro Company on January 1, 20x1, giving $200,000 cash and a long-term note of $300,000. On the date of acquisition, Micro Company had the following stockholders' equity balances:

Common stock, $1 par	$ 50,000
Additional paid-in capital	100,000
Retained earnings	200,000
	$350,000

On the date of acquisition, all of Micro's assets and liabilities had book values approximately equal to fair values except for Equipment that had a book value of $700,000, a market value of $800,000, and a remaining useful life of eight years. Any goodwill arising from the combination is assumed to have an indefinite life. Four years later, on December 31, 20x4, prior to closing the books, Micro's retained earnings account had a balance of $400,000.

Required:

(a) If Composite Company followed the cost method to account for its investment in Micro, what would be the book balance in that account immediately prior to preparation of the consolidated financial statements worksheet on December 31, 20x4?

(b) If Composite Company followed the equity method to account for its investment in Micro, what would be the book balance in that account immediately prior to preparation of the consolidated financial statements worksheet on December 31, 20x4?

Problem 4-2

(Allocation schedule with a noncontrolling interest; calculation of noncontrolling interest share of consolidated net income)

MegaCorp acquired MiniCorp on December 31, 20x0, in a purchase method business combination immediately after the books were closed for both companies. MegaCorp paid $100,000 for 90% of the outstanding voting common stock of MiniCorp. MiniCorp is to be operated as a separate company, but will be a consolidated subsidiary of MegaCorp. On the date of acquisition, MiniCorp had 40,000 shares of no par common stock with a stated value of $1 per share, and retained earnings of $60,000. All of MiniCorp's assets and liabilities had book values approximately equal to fair values except for a building with a 10-year remaining life that was undervalued by $10,000. Any resulting goodwill is assumed to have an indefinite life. During the year ended December 31, 20x1, MiniCorp had net income of $25,000 and paid $10,000 in dividends.

Required:

(a) Prepare an allocation schedule for the acquisition of MiniCorp as of December 31, 20x0.
(b) Compute the noncontrolling interest share of consolidated net income for the year ended December 31, 20x1.
(c) Compute the balance of the noncontrolling interest account in the consolidated statement of financial position on December 31, 20x1.
(d) In what section of the statement of financial position should the noncontrolling interest be shown? Support your answer with a brief explanation.

Problem 4-3

(Conversion from cost to equity)

Prater Company acquired a 90% interest in Sanchez Company for $100,000 on January 1, 20x0, at which time Sanchez Company had the following balances in its stockholders' equity:

Common stock, $1 par	$50,000
Retained earnings	50,000

Any cost-book value differential on this date was assumed to be goodwill with an indefinite life. Prater accounted for its investment in Sanchez, using the cost method. On December 31, 20x5, Sanchez had a retained earnings balance of $250,000. There were no changes in the common stock account over the 7-year period ending on December 31, 20x6. Sanchez net income for the year ended December 31, 20x6 was $40,000, and Sanchez paid $20,000 in dividends.

Required:

(a) Record Prater's cost method accounting entries for the year 20x6 for the above investment.
(b) Record Prater's worksheet equity adjustment entry to convert the cost method balance to the equity method for purposes of preparing consolidated financial statement working papers.

Problem 4-4

(Conversion from cost to equity)

Passpoint Corporation acquired an 80% interest in Southdown Company for a price of $500,000 on January 1, 20x3, at a time when Southdown had total stockholders' equity of $600,000. The excess of cost over book value was assumed to be goodwill with an indefinite life. During the years 20x3 and 20x4, Southdown had net income of $50,000 and $70,000, respectively, and paid dividends of $30,000 each year.

Required:

(a) Prepare the journal entries that Passpoint would make to account for this investment under the (1) cost method and (2) the equity method.
(b) Assume that Passpoint used the cost method for this investment. Prepare the elimination entry in journal form for the intercompany income for the year 20x3.
(c) Again assume that Passpoint used the cost method for this investment. Prepare the entry in journal form to convert the investment balance to the equity method as of January 1, 20x4, the 12/31/x4 consolidated statements worksheet. Also give the entry in journal form to eliminate the intercompany income for the 20x4 consolidated statements worksheet.

Problem 4-5

(Consolidation worksheet 100% acquisition)

Knox Company acquired a 100% interest in the common stock of Blount Company on January 1, 20x1, for a price of $270,000, at a time when Blount Company had common stock of $100,000 and retained earnings of $150,000. The $20,000 excess of cost over book value was assumed to be goodwill with an indefinite life. The financial statements of Knox and Blount at the end of the year 20x1 are as follows:

Statement of Income	Knox	Blount
For the Year ended 12/31/x1		
Sales	$ 655,000	$ 325,500
Equity in Blount income	33,500	
Cost of sales	(335,500)	(215,000)
Operating expenses	(114,700)	(77,000)
Net income	238,300	33,500
Retained earnings Jan. 1	123,000	150,000
Add net income	238,300	33,500
Less: Dividends	(90,000)	(12,000)
Retained earnings, Dec. 31	$ 271,300	$ 171,500
Balance sheet 12/31/x1		
Cash	210,000	33,000
Accounts receivable	75,000	32,400
Notes receivable	7,000	
Inventories	72,300	44,000
Land	100,000	25,000
Buildings - net	175,000	250,000
Machinery - net	345,000	155,000
Investment in Blount	291,500	
	$1,275,800	$ 539,400
Accounts payable	163,500	92,900
Dividends payable	22,500	
Other liabilities	388,500	175,000
Capital stock	430,000	100,000
Retained earnings, Dec. 31	271,300	171,500
	$1,275,800	$ 539,400

Required:

Prepare a worksheet for the consolidated financial statements for Knox Company and Blount Company for the year ended December 31, 20x1.

Problem 4-6 · (Consolidation worksheet with a noncontrolling interest)

Refer to the facts in problem 4-9. Assume that Knox acquired only an 80% interest in Blount on January 1, 20x1, for a price of $240,000. Any excess of cost over book value was assumed to be goodwill with an indefinite life. Based on these assumptions, the financial statements for Knox and Blount at the end of the year 20x1 are as follows:

Statement of Income	Knox	Blount
For the Year ended 12/31/x1		
Sales	$ 655,000	$ 325,500
Equity in Blount income	26,800	
Cost of sales	(335,500)	(215,000)
Operating expenses	(114,700)	(77,000)
Net income	231,600	33,500
Retained earnings, 1/1/x1	123,000	150,000
Add net income	231,600	33,500
Less: Dividends	(90,000)	(12,000)
Retained earnings, 12/31/x1	$ 264,600	$ 171,500
Balance sheet 12/31/x1		
Cash	237,600	33,000
Accounts receivable	75,000	32,400
Notes receivable	7,000	
Inventories	72,300	44,000
Land	100,000	25,000
Buildings - net	175,000	250,000
Machinery - net	345,000	155,000
Investment in Blount	257,200	
	$1,269,100	$ 539,400
Accounts payable	163,500	92,900
Dividends payable	22,500	
Other liabilities	388,500	175,000
Capital stock	430,000	100,000
Retained earnings, 12/31/x1	264,600	171,500
	$1,269,100	$539,400

Required:

(a) Prepare an allocation schedule for the acquisition of Blount by Knox.
(b) Record all required elimination entries in general journal form.
(c) Prepare a worksheet for consolidated financial statements for Knox and Blount for the year ended December 31, 20x1.

Problem 4-7 · (Consolidation worksheet with a noncontrolling interest)

On January 1, 20x4, Proctor Lumber Company acquired an 80% interest in SMP Plywood Company by issuing 10,000 shares of its own $5 par value common stock. On this date, SMP Plywood had 3,000 shares of $10 par value common stock outstanding, additional paid-in capital of $20,000, and retained earnings of $50,000. The market value of Proctor common stock was $14 per share on January 1, 20x4, and this market value is not expected to be materially affected by the acquisition. Proctor Company used the cost method to account for its investment in SMP. All of SMP's assets and liabilities had book values approximately equal to market values except for equipment with a 5-year remaining life, which was undervalued by $50,000. Any goodwill resulting from the acquisition is assumed to have an indefinite life. On December 31, 20x6, the separate financial statements of the two companies were as follows.

Statement of Income	Proctor	SMP
For the Year ended 12/31/x6		
Sales	$ 345,000	$ 175,600
Dividend income	8,000	
Cost of sales	(135,000)	(90,000)
Operating expenses	(67,500)	(55,600)
Net income	150,500	30,000
Retained earnings Jan. 1	245,000	90,000
Add net income	150,500	30,000
Less: Dividends	(40,000)	(10,000)
Retained earnings, Dec. 31	$ 355,500	$ 110,000
Balance sheet 12/31/x6		
Cash	80,000	35,000
Accounts receivable	150,000	97,500
Marketable securities	137,500	88,400
Inventories	124,500	75,000
Land	875,000	100,000
Buildings - net	345,000	500,000
Equipment - net	310,000	275,000
Investment in SMP Plywood	140,000	
	$2,162,000	$1,170,900
Accounts payable	346,000	260,900
Dividends payable	22,500	
Long-term debt	988,000	750,000
Common stock	250,000	30,000
Additional paid-in capital	200,000	20,000
Retained earnings, Dec. 31	355,500	110,000
	$2,162,000	$1,170,900

Required:

(a) Prepare an allocation schedule for the acquisition of SMP by Proctor.
(b) Prepare a consolidated statements worksheet for the year ended 12/31/x6. Note that an equity adjustment (EA) entry is required prior to entering the elimination entries.
(c) Reconcile the Proctor's separate net income to the controlling interest income.

Problem 4-8   **(Consolidation worksheet with a 100% interest)**

Patterson Company acquired 100% of St. Martin Company on January 1, 20x1, for $300,000 cash. In addition, Patterson incurred $20,000 of direct acquisition costs in connection with this acquisition. During the year 20x1, Patterson Company used the cost method to account for its investment in St. Martin. On the date of acquisition, St. Martin Company had the following balances in its stockholders' equity:

Common stock, $1 par	$100,000
Retained earnings	150,000
Total stockholders' equity	250,000

All of St. Martin's assets had book values approximately equal to fair values except for land with a book value of $20,000 and a fair value of $40,000. Any remaining excess of cost over book value is assumed to be copyrights with a 10-year life. On December 31, 20x1, the two companies had the following separate financial statements:

Statement of Income	Patterson	St. Martin
For the Year ended 12/31/x1		
Sales	$ 750,000	$ 475,000
Dividend income	25,000	
Cost of sales	(345,800)	(198,500)
Operating expenses	(125,600)	(99,500)
Net income	303,600	177,000
Retained earnings, Jan. 1	245,000	150,000
Add net income	303,600	177,000
Less: Dividends	(90,000)	(25,000)
Retained earnings, Dec. 31	$ 458,600	$ 302,000
Balance sheet 12/31/x1		
Cash	175,000	86,700
Accounts receivable	55,000	158,300
Dividends receivable	6,250	-
Inventories	83,000	239,000
Land	38,500	100,000
Buildings - net	250,000	100,000
Equipment - net	150,000	65,000
Investment in St. Martin	320,000	
	$1,077,750	$ 749,000
Accounts payable	135,150	168,750
Dividends payable	24,000	6,250
Long-term debt	210,000	172,000
Common stock	250,000	100,000
Retained earnings, Dec. 1	458,600	302,000
	$1,077,750	$ 749,000

Required:

(a) Prepare an allocation schedule for the acquisition of St. Martin Company by Patterson Company.

(b) Prepare the consolidated statements worksheet for Patterson and St. Martin for the year ended December 31, 20x1.

Problem 4-9   (Consolidation worksheet with a noncontrolling interest)

On April 1, 20x1, the Parrot Company acquired a 90% interest in the Sunshine Company for a price of $704,000 at a time when Sunshine Company had common stock consisting of 200,000 shares of $1 par common stock issued and outstanding. Sunshine's retained earnings balances on December 31, 20x0, was $400,000. Its income from the first quarter of the year 20x1 was $50,000, and its first quarter dividend of $10,000 was declared on March 15, 20x1. Sunshine Company does not have an additional paid-in capital account. On the acquisition date, all of Sunshine's assets and liabilities had book values approximately equal to fair market values except for the following:

	Book Value	Fair Value
Inventories	$ 100,000	$ 150,000
Buildings (5-year remaining life)	400,000	500,000
Equipment (4-year remaining life)	200,000	160,000
Bonds payable (mature on March 31, 20x3)	300,000	290,000
	$1,000,000	$1,100,000

The inventories were sold by Sunshine during the quarter following the acquisition. Any excess of cost over book value not explained by the above differences is assumed to be attributable to goodwill with an indefinite life. The financial statements of Parrot and Sunshine on December 31, 20x1, prior to preparation of consolidated statements were as follows:

Statement of Income	Parrot	Sunshine
For the Year ended 12/31/x1		
Sales	$ 875,000	$ 385,000
Equity in Sunshine income	34,875	
Cost of sales	(275,000)	(148,750)
Operating expenses	(321,275)	(86,250)
Pre-acquisition subsidiary income		
Net income	313,600	150,000
Retained earnings Jan. 1	340,000	400,000
Add net income	313,600	150,000
Less: Dividends	(100,000)	(40,000)
Retained earnings, Dec. 31	$ 553,600	$ 510,000
Balance sheet 12/31/x1		
Cash	240,250	59,500
Accounts receivable	88,725	138,200
Inventories	250,000	125,000
Land	20,000	125,000
Buildings - net	350,000	400,000
Equipment - net	175,000	200,000
Investment in Sunshine	711,875	
	$1,835,850	$1,047,700
Accounts payable	207,250	137,700
Bonds payable	425,000	200,000
Common stock	650,000	200,000
Retained earnings, Dec. 31	553,600	510,000
	$1,835,850	$1,047,700

Required:

(a) Prepare an allocation schedule for the acquisition of Sunshine by Parrot. Note: Your amortization should be for the nine-month period ending December 31, since the subsidiary was not owned for the full year.

(b) Prepare a worksheet for consolidated financial statements for the year ended December 31, 20x1.

Problem 4-10   **(Consolidation worksheet with a noncontrolling interest)**

On January 1, 20x3, Perno Company acquired an 80% interest in Squid Company in exchange for 50,000 shares of its $5 par common stock. Issue costs were $20,000, paid in cash. Squid Company stockholders' equity on January 1, 20x3, was as follows:

Common stock, $1 par	$100,000
Retained earnings	300,000
	400,000

On the issue date, Perno Company $5 par value common stock had a fair market value of $7 per share. Any cost-book value differential related to the acquisition was assumed to be goodwill except for Squid inventory, which was undervalued by $10,000 on the acquisition date. Perno used the cost method to account for its investment in Squid Company. On December 31, 20x6, the two companies had the following separate financial statements:

	Perno	Squid
Sales	$ 350,000	$ 200,000
Dividend income	8,000	
Cost of goods sold	(200,000)	(65,000)
Operating expenses	(100,000)	(45,000)
Net income	$ 58,000	$ 90,000
Retained earnings, January 1, 20x6	300,000	440,000
Net income	58,000	90,000
Less: Dividends	(15,000)	(10,000)
Retained earnings, December 31, 20x6	$ 343,000	$ 520,000
Cash	135,000	65,000
Accounts receivable	45,000	40,000
Inventory	75,000	75,000
Land	148,000	90,000
Buildings – net	50,000	100,000
Equipment – net	265,000	345,000
Investment in Squid Company	350,000	
	$1,068,000	$ 715,000
Current liabilities	25,000	25,000
Long-term debt	100,000	70,000
Common stock	500,000	100,000
Additional paid-in capital	100,000	-
Retained earnings	343,000	520,000
	$1,068,000	$ 715,000

Required:

Prepare a worksheet for consolidated financial statements for Perno and Squid as of December 31, 20x6.

Problem 4-11   **(Consolidation worksheet with a noncontrolling interest)**

Refer to the acquisition data for problem 4-10. If Perno had accounted for its investment in Squid Company using the equity method of accounting, the December 31, 20x6, financial statements would have the following balances:

	Perno	Squid
Sales	$ 350,000	$ 200,000
Equity in Squid Company income	72,000	
Cost of goods sold	(200,000)	(65,000)
Operating expenses	(100,000)	(45,000)
Net income	$ 122,000	$ 90,000
Retained earnings, January 1, 20x6	404,000	440,000
Net income	122,000	90,000
Less: Dividends	(15,000)	(10,000)
Retained earnings, December 31, 20x6	$ 511,000	$520,000
Cash	135,000	65,000
Accounts receivable	45,000	40,000
Inventory	75,000	75,000
Land	148,000	90,000
Buildings – net	50,000	100,000
Equipment – net	265,000	345,000
Investment in Squid Company	518,000	
	$1,236,000	$ 715,000
Current liabilities	25,000	25,000
Long-term debt	100,000	70,000
Common stock	500,000	100,000
Additional paid-in capital	100,000	–
Retained earnings	511,000	520,000
	$1,236,000	$ 715,000

Required:

(a) Prepare a worksheet for consolidated financial statements for Perno and Squid as of December 31, 20x6.
(b) Prepare a schedule reconciling Perno Company's account balance for the investment in Squid Company as of December 31, 20x6, using the cost method as compared with the account balance using the equity method.

Problem 4-12   **(International accounting standards research case)**

Go to http://www.iasb.org.uk and find the summary of IASB Standard 27 "Consolidated Financial Statements." Compare and contrast the requirements of IASB Standard 27 with United States accounting standards for the following issues:

(a) The definition of a subsidiary
(b) Requirements for consolidation of subsidiaries
(c) Allowed methods of accounting for subsidiaries on the separate books of the parent company

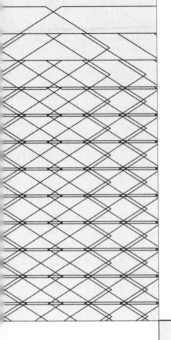

CHAPTER 5

INTERCOMPANY TRANSACTIONS IN INVENTORIES

LEARNING OBJECTIVES

- Understand the conceptual basis for elimination of intercompany accounts
- Record equity adjustments for intercompany transactions in inventory
- Record consolidated statements worksheet elimination entries for intercompany transactions in inventory
- Prepare consolidated statements worksheets that include elimination entries for intercompany transactions in inventory

CONCEPTUAL BASIS FOR ELIMINATION OF INTERCOMPANY ACCOUNTS

Intercompany transactions are transactions between affiliated companies. Because business combinations are often undertaken between companies with complementary lines of business, transactions between them are common. These transactions may involve sales of products or assets, intercompany financing arrangements, intercompany leases, purchases of affiliate debt, or similar transactions. The process of consolidating the financial statements of affiliates changes the nature of the transactions that have occurred between them. From a consolidated statements viewpoint, all transactions between affiliates are internal transactions in substance. The well-established concept of **economic entity** in financial reporting tells us that **the consolidated financial statements of a group of companies should only show the results of transactions with external entities. Therefore, the process of consolidation requires that all transactions between the parent and its subsidiaries or between subsidiaries be eliminated prior to completion of the consolidated statements worksheet.** This chapter illustrates the procedures required to make elimination entries for one type of common intercompany transaction—sale of inventory.

INTERCOMPANY TRANSACTIONS IN INVENTORY

Business combinations often involve companies within the same industry, resulting in affiliations that are either vertically or horizontally integrated. Integration allows arrangements where the products of one entity in a consolidated group are used as components in the products of other entities within the group. Consequently, intercompany transactions between a parent and its subsidiaries or between subsidiaries are commonplace. If the effects of these intercompany sales are not eliminated from the consolidated financial statements, they will show the results of some sales twice— once when the intercompany sale occurs and a second time when the end product is sold to an outside entity. Consequently, a fundamental principle in consolidation theory is that all intercompany sales are eliminated.

The process of eliminating intercompany sales is complicated by the fact that inventory arising from intercompany sales is often resold to outside entities in the year following the intercompany sale. When the ending inventory of a company includes merchandise purchased from an affiliate, that inventory will be on the books of the purchaser at the intercompany price, which is an amount that normally exceeds the original cost to the affiliate producer. From a consolidated perspective, carrying inventory at an amount in excess of the affiliate producer's cost is a violation of the **realization** principle. Accordingly, any **intercompany profit** in inventory acquired from an affiliate must be eliminated in the consolidated statements worksheet. **The purpose of this entry is to defer the intercompany profit until the following year when the intercompany inventory is resold to an outside entity.**

The ending inventory of one year becomes the beginning inventory of the following year. As a result, the beginning inventory will contain intercompany profit if there was intercompany profit in the ending inventory of the preceding year. Since elimination entries are not booked, the consolidated financial statements of any year must be adjusted for intercompany transactions of the prior year that affect current year financial position and results of operations. Intercompany profit in beginning inventory is an important example of such a transaction. Therefore, elimination entries are made for profit in beginning inventory as well as for profit in ending inventory. **The purpose of these entries is to realize deferred intercompany profit from the previous year, thus including this profit in consolidated income in the year that the intercompany inventory is sold to an outside entity.**

Finally, the existence of intercompany sales often results in unpaid accounts receivable and accounts payable at the end of the year. These intercompany accounts receivable and accounts payable must also be eliminated. To summarize, intercompany inventory sales result in the need for four types of elimination entries:

1. Current year intercompany sales
2. Intercompany profit in ending inventory
3. Intercompany profit in beginning inventory (arising from prior year intercompany sales)
4. Intercompany accounts receivable and accounts payable

◀ CONCEPT QUESTION AND REFLECTION

> If the intercompany accounts payable were interest bearing, what additional elimination entries would be required?

COST AND EQUITY METHOD ISSUES

Recall from previous chapters that elimination entries are sometimes affected by the method of accounting used by the parent company to account for its investment in the subsidiary. Specifically, use of either the **cost method** or the **equity method** may alter the form of some elimination entries. In the case of intercompany profits, a parent company using the cost method would make no book entries for intercompany profits. A parent company using the equity method could choose to follow the so-called **modified equity method** where adjustments are **not** made for intercompany profits or it could choose the **full equity method** and make adjustments for intercompany profits. It should be emphasized that *APB Opinion 18* describes only one approach to accounting for substantial influence investments in common stock, and does not use the terms modified equity method and full equity method. These two terms serve merely to differentiate between the case where equity adjustments are not made for intercompany profits (the modified equity method) and the case where these adjustments are made (the full equity method). As this textbook has noted, an investment account to be consolidated is eliminated, an action that makes strict compliance with *APB Opinion 18* requirements unnecessary. Finally, remember that the **full equity method** is the "equity" method of *APB Opinion 18*, which specifies the approach for unconsolidated controlled subsidiaries and substantial influence investments. To clearly distinguish the two approaches, however, the terms *modified equity method* and *full equity method* will be used to differentiate the situations where equity adjustments are not made for intercompany profits and when these adjustments are made.

Sales by parent to subsidiary—the downstream case

To illustrate the full equity method entries for intercompany profit in inventories, assume that Plateau Company has a wholly-owned subsidiary, Solitaire Company, which was acquired in a purchase method combination on January 1, 20x2. The following additional data for the years ended December 31, 20x2 and 20x3 are available:

	20x2	20x3
Intercompany sales—Plateau to Solitaire	$25,000	$20,000
Mark-up percent on sales	20%	25%
Solitaire intercompany inventory on hand		
at year end	$ 8,000	$ 4,000
12/31 Unpaid Plateau accounts receivable from	$ 3,000	$ 2,500
intercompany sales		

At the end of the year 20x2, Plateau would record the following equity method entry on its books to account for the intercompany profit in inventory:

```
12/31/x2  Equity in Solitaire income            1,600
              Investment in Solitaire                      1,600
                 ($8,000 × 20%)
              (To defer intercompany profit in ending inventory)
```

The purpose of this entry is to reduce the equity earnings by the amount of the intercompany profit contained in the inventory of the subsidiary at the end of the year 20x2. Since the subsidiary has not resold this inventory, the profit is unrealized from the point of view of the parent company. In the following year, this entry is **reversed,** allowing the deferred intercompany profit to be recognized in the equity income in the year that the inventory is resold by the subsidiary to an external entity. Therefore, in the year 20x3, two equity adjustments are made, one to realize the deferred intercompany profit from the year 20x2 and one to defer the intercompany profit contained in the ending inventory for the year 20x3:

```
1/1/x3    Investment in Solitaire              1,600
              Equity in Solitaire income                   1,600
                 ($8,000 × 20%)
              (To realize deferred intercompany profit in beginning inventory)

12/31/x3  Equity in Solitaire income            1,000
              Investment in Solitaire                      1,000
                 ($4,000 × 25%)
              (to defer intercompany profit in ending inventory)
```

To illustrate the effect of these entries on the book balances of Plateau, assume that Plateau acquired 100% of Solitaire's outstanding common stock on January 1, 20x2, for $110,000. If Solitaire had income and dividends for the year 20x2 of $100,000 and $40,000 and for the year 20x3 of $150,000 and $60,000, the account balances under the equity method for the investment in Solitaire and income from Solitaire would be as follows:

	Investment in Solitaire	Income from Solitaire
Initial cost of common stock	$ 110,000	
Equity income for the year 20x2	100,000	$ 100,000
Dividends received 20x2	(40,000)	
Equity adjustment for profit in ending inventory	(1,600)	(1,600)
Balances 12/31/x2	168,400	98,400
Equity income for the year 20x3	150,000	150,000
Dividends received 20x3	(60,000)	
Equity adjustment for profit in beginning inventory	1,600	1,600
Equity adjustment for profit in ending inventory	(1,000)	(1,000)
Balances 12/31/x3	$ 259,000	$ 150,600

Sales by subsidiary to parent—the upstream case

If the intercompany sales are made by the subsidiary to the parent, **the equity adjustments are different from the downstream case only if there is a noncontrolling interest.** To illustrate, assume that the sales in the above example were made by Solitaire Company to Plateau Company and that Solitaire is a 90%-owned subsidiary. In this case, the entry at the end of the year 20x2 would be made for 90% of the amount of the intercompany profit:

12/31/x2	Equity in Solitaire income	1,440	
	Investment in Solitaire		1,440
	($8,000 × 20% × 90%)		
	(to defer intercompany profit in the ending inventory)		

The equity method adjustment is made for only 90% of the amount of the intercompany profit because the parent company only records 90% of the subsidiary's income under the equity method. The following year this entry is reversed, and an additional equity adjustment is made for the intercompany profit contained in the ending inventory of the year 20x3. Continuing our assumption that the Plateau-Solitaire intercompany sales were upstream and that Solitaire is a 90%-owned subsidiary, these two entries would be as follows:

1/1/x3	Investment in Solitaire	1,440	
	Equity in Solitaire income		1,440
	($8,000 × 20% × 90%)		
	(To realize deferred intercompany profit in beginning inventory)		
12/31/x3	Equity in Solitaire income	900	
	Investment in Solitaire		900
	($4,000 × 25% × 90%)		
	(To defer intercompany profit in ending inventory)		

Remember that equity adjustments only involve two accounts, the investment in subsidiary account and the equity in subsidiary income account. These are the only two accounts on the parent company's books related to its subsidiary investment. Also remember that the equity method adjustments are the only entries the parent company makes on its books because of the investment in the subsidiary. The elimination entries are only recorded on the consolidated statements worksheet. The purpose of the worksheet is to prepare financial statements under the assumption that all affiliated companies are to be treated as a single entity for financial reporting purposes. A comparison of the equity adjustments for upstream and downstream sales is shown in Exhibit 5-1.

EXHIBIT 5-1 Comparison of book equity method adjustments for intercompany transactions for the Plateau-Solitaire examples for the years ended December 31, 20x2 and 20x3

Cost Method or Modified Equity Method	*Full Equity Method*
Downstream case:	
12/31/20x2	Equity in Solitaire income 1,600
	Investment in Solitaire 1,600
	To defer unrealized profit in the 12/31/x2 ending inventory
	($8,000 × 20% = $1600)
1/1/20x3	Investment in Solitaire 1,600
	Equity in Solitaire income 1,600
No	To realize deferred profit in the 1/1/x3 beginning inventory
Entries	($8,000 × 20% = $1600)
Are	
12/31/20x3 **Made**	Equity in Solitaire income 1,000
	Investment in Solitaire 1,000
	To defer unrealized profit in the 12/31/x3 ending inventory
	($4,000 × 25% = $1,000)
Upstream case:	
12/31/20x2	Equity in Solitaire income 1,440
	Investment in Solitaire 1,440
	To defer unrealized profit in the 12/31/x2 ending inventory
	($8,000 × 20% × 90% = $1,440)
1/1/0x3 **No**	Investment in Solitaire 1,440
Entries	Equity in Solitaire income 1,440
Are	To realize deferred profit in the 1/1/x3 beginning inventory
Made	($8,000 × 20% × 90% = $1,440)
12/31/20x3	Equity in Solitaire income 900
	Investment in Solitaire 900
	To defer unrealized profit in the 12/31/x3 ending inventory
	($4,000 × 25% × 90% = $900)

ELIMINATION ENTRIES

The choice of cost method, modified equity method, or full equity method for the investment in subsidiary account affects some of the elimination entries for intercompany profits. Following is an illustration of two specific approaches to worksheet elimination entries for intercompany inventory transactions:

1. Elimination entries where no equity method adjustments have been made for the intercompany transactions. These procedures would be followed if the parent company accounts for its investment in subsidiary under either the cost method or modified equity method.
2. Elimination entries where equity method adjustments have been made for the intercompany transactions. These procedures would be followed if the parent company accounts for its investment in subsidiary under the full equity method.

Modified equity and cost method situations–downstream sales

Assume that Plateau Company and Solitaire Company had intercompany transactions over a three-year period as set forth in the following table:

	20x1	20x2	20x3
Intercompany sales—Plateau to Solitaire	$15,000	$25,000	$20,000
Markup percent on sales	20%	20%	25%
Solitaire intercompany inventory on hand at year end	$ 0	$ 8,000	$ 4,000
Unpaid Plateau accounts receivable from intercompany sales	$ 0	$ 0	$ 2,500
Solitaire markup on intercompany purchases resold	150%	150%	150%
Solitaire sales of merchandise purchased from Plateau	$22,500	$25,500*	$36,000**
Solitaire cost of goods sold on intercompany sales	$15,000	$17,000	$24,000

* Intercompany purchases of $25,000 less ending inventory of $8,000 = $17,000 × 150% = $25,500
**20x2 beginning inventory $8,000 × 150% = $12,000 plus $16,000 of 20x3 sales × 150% = $24,000; Total of $36,000

Four types of elimination entries may be required where intercompany sales have occurred.

1. **Intercompany sales**—All intercompany sales are eliminated. This entry is made for sales by the parent company to subsidiaries, by subsidiaries to the parent, and for sales between subsidiaries. The amounts eliminated are unaffected by the existence of a noncontrolling interest, **thus 100% of intercompany sales are eliminated in all cases.** In addition, the elimination entry is the same whether the intercompany buyer has resold the merchandise or whether the inventory has **not** been resold. For the data in the Plateau-Solitaire example for the year 20x1, the entry in the consolidated statements worksheet is:

12/31/x1	(1)	Sales	15,000	
		Cost of goods sold		15,000

Since there is no intercompany inventory and no unpaid accounts receivable, this is the only entry required for the year 20x1. A partial consolidated statements worksheet shows the effect of this elimination on the balances in the year 20x1:

Partial Worksheet	Plateau	Solitaire	Eliminations				Consolidated
Income statement 12/31/x1							
Sales	$ 15,000	$ 22,500	(1)	15,000			$ 22,500
Cost of goods sold	(12,000)	(15,000)			(1)	15,000	(12,000)

Note that the result of the elimination entry (1) above is that the consolidated balances **show Solitaire's sales and Plateau's cost of goods sold.** In effect, the consolidated income statement shows the original historical cost of the inventory as cost of goods sold and the sales amount of the final sale to an outside party. The effect of the intercompany transaction is completely eliminated. This result is as it should be. Otherwise, the sale of this inventory would have been included in the income statement twice—once as an intercompany sale and once when the inventory was sold to a customer external to the consolidated entity.

2. **Intercompany profit in the ending inventory**—intercompany profit in ending inventory is eliminated with a credit to the inventory account. The corresponding debit is to cost of goods sold. The entries to eliminate intercompany sales and profit in the ending inventory for the Plateau–Solitaire example in the year 20x2 is as follows:

12/31/x2	(1)	Sales		25,000	
		Cost of goods sold			25,000

12/31/x2	(2)	Cost of goods sold		1,600	
		Inventory			1,600

$$(\$8,000 \times 20\%)$$

Note that a reduction in ending inventory always increases cost of goods sold by the same amount. Recall from your study of inventory accounting that cost of goods sold is calculated by subtracting the ending inventory value from the total of beginning inventory plus purchases. This relationship is shown in the following expression:

$$CGS = BI + PUR - EI$$
where: CGS = Cost of goods sold
BI = Beginning inventory
PUR = Purchases
EI = Ending inventory

Thus, any change in ending inventory always changes cost of goods sold (CGS) by an equal amount. Since both ending inventory and CGS have a normal debit balance, a reduction in ending inventory increases CGS, and an increase in ending inventory decreases CGS. Note that a change in beginning inventory has the opposite effect on CGS because beginning inventory is added in determining CGS, whereas ending inventory is subtracted.

A partial worksheet for the above two entries in the year 20x2 for the Plateau-Solitaire consolidation would be as follows:

Partial Worksheet	Plateau	Solitaire	Eliminations				Consolidated
Income statement 12/31/x2							
Sales	$ 25,000	$ 25,500	(1)	25,000			$ 25,500
Cost of goods sold	(20,000)	(17,000)	(2)	1,600	(1)	25,000	(13,600)
Balance sheet							
Inventory	15,000	8,000			(2)	1,600	21,400

These two entries result in consolidated sales equal to the amount of sales by Solitaire to external entities during the year 20x2. The cost of goods sold of $13,600 is Plateau's original CGS on these sales of $13,600 (Solitaire's CGS of $17,000 less a 20% markup by Plateau of $3,400). Finally, the inventory is reported in the consolidated balance sheet at Plateau's original cost of $6,400 (the $8,000 intercompany price less a 20% markup).

3. **Intercompany profit in the beginning inventory**—Intercompany profit in the beginning inventory is eliminated. Recall that the ending inventory of the previous year becomes the beginning inventory of the current year. Since the worksheet elimination entries for the previous year's consolidated statements worksheet are not booked, they are not reflected in current-year book balances. Thus, the existence of unrealized profit in the beginning inventory of the current year means that the cost of goods sold at the end of the year will contain this unrealized profit **(BI + PUR − EI = CGS)**. Accordingly, unrealized profit in beginning inventory is eliminated by crediting the cost of goods sold account. The corresponding debit (in the downstream sale case) is to the retained earnings account of the parent company. The entries to eliminate intercompany sales, defer profit in the ending inventory, and realize deferred intercompany profit in the beginning inventory for the year 20x3 are as follows:

12/31/x3	(1)	Sales	20,000	
		Cost of goods sold		20,000

	(2)	Cost of goods sold	1,000	
		Inventory		1,000
		($4,000 × 25%)		

	(3)	Retained earnings—Plateau	1,600	
		Cost of goods sold		1,600
		($8,000 × 20%)		

The intercompany sales for the year 20x3 are $20,000, the profit in the ending inventory is $1,000 ($4,000 ending inventory from intercompany sales × a markup of 25%), and the profit in the beginning inventory is the amount of profit in the ending inventory of the previous year. The debit to Retained earnings—Plateau for entry (3) is a little complex and requires further explanation. This debit is explained by recalling that modified equity and cost method procedures do not adjust for unrealized intercompany profit when accounting for the investment in subsidiary on the books of the parent company. As a result, the equity method income of the parent company is overstated by the amount of unrealized profit in ending inventory—an overstatement corrected in the consolidated financial statements worksheet in the following year by debiting the (beginning) retained earnings account of the parent. A partial worksheet for all three of the above entries follows:

Partial Worksheet	Plateau	Solitaire	Eliminations				Consolidated
Income statement 12/31/x3							
Sales	$ 20,000	$ 36,000	(1)	20,000			$ 36,000
Cost of goods sold	(15,000)	(24,000)	(2)	1,000	(1)	20,000	(18,400)
					(3)	1,600	
Retained earnings statement							
Retained earnings—Plateau 1/1/x3			(3)	1,600			
Balance sheet							
Inventory	15,000	4,000			(2)	1,000	18,000

4. **Intercompany accounts payable and accounts receivable**—All intercompany reciprocal asset and liability balances are eliminated. As was discussed in previous chapters, the consolidated financial statements cannot show any intercompany assets and liabilities that are reciprocal in nature. Thus, consolidated financial statements require that such intercompany amounts be eliminated. For the Plateau-Solitaire example, this entry is as follows:

12/31/x3	Accounts payable	2,500	
	Accounts receivable		2,500

A partial worksheet for this entry for the year 20x3 is as follows:

Partial Worksheet	Plateau	Solitaire	Eliminations				Consolidated
Balance sheet							
Accounts receivable	$10,000	$15,000			(4)	2,500	$22,500
Accounts payable	12,000	13,000	(4)	2,500			22,500

Modified equity and cost method situations—upstream sales

In the case of upstream intercompany sales, where the subsidiary sells inventory to the parent, the procedures to be applied differ **only in the case where a noncontrolling interest exists,** and only for the entry that eliminates profit in the beginning inventory. All other elimination entries are the same as in the previous example. To illustrate, assume that the data in the Plateau-Solitaire example involved upstream sales and Solitaire was a 90%-owned subsidiary. The entry for profit in the beginning inventory would be as follows:

Entry 3:

12/31/x3	Retained earnings—Plateau*	1,440	
	Noncontrolling interest**	160	
	Cost of goods sold		1,600

*($8,000 × 20% × 90% = $1,440)
**($8,000 × 20% × 10% – $160)

A partial worksheet showing this entry with the other entries for the year 20x3 is as follows:

Partial Worksheet	Plateau	Solitaire		Eliminations			Consolidated
Income statement 12/31/x3							
Sales	$20,000	$36,000	(1)	20,000			$ 36,000
Cost of goods sold	(15,000)	(24,000)	(2)	1,000	(1)	20,000	(18,400)
					(3)	1,600	
Retained earnings statement							
Retained earnings — Plateau 1/1/x3			(3)	1,440			
Balance sheet							
Inventory	15,000	8,000			(2)	1,000	22,000
Noncontrolling interest*			(3)	160			XXX

*The consolidated balance in Noncontrolling interest is not shown because it is affected by other entries that are not illustrated.

Explanation of entry (3) is somewhat involved and requires an understanding of the relationship between the parent company equity method book adjustments and the elimination entries made in the consolidated statements worksheet. Note that elimination entries for intercompany profit are made to change the year in which the profits are realized rather than to eliminate them altogether. Since the existence of unrealized profit in the beginning inventory overstates the cost of goods sold at the end of the year (recall that **BI** + **PUR** − **EI** = **CGS**), the cost of goods sold account is credited for $1600. This credit increases consolidated net income, thereby realizing the deferred intercompany profit in beginning inventory. The two debits in this elimination entry are prorated between the retained earnings of the parent company and the noncontrolling interest account in the ratio of controlling interest percentage (90%) to noncontrolling interest percentage (10%). The debit to Retained earnings—Plateau is explained by the fact that Plateau's beginning retained earnings is overstated by $1,440 because Plateau did not make an equity method adjustment on its books for its share of the $1600 deferred intercompany profit. The $160 debit to noncontrolling interest is required to compensate for the fact that Solitaire's beginning retained earnings also includes this intercompany profit.[1] The debit is made for only 10% of the intercompany profit because only 10% of subsidiary retained earnings is included in the noncontrolling interest account. The remaining subsidiary retained earnings balance is eliminated when subsidiary equity is eliminated.

Full equity situations—downstream sales

For consolidations where the full equity method is used by the parent company to account for its investment in the subsidiary, the elimination entries for intercompany profit are slightly altered from the modified equity-cost method approach. **Specifically, the entry for realizing deferred intercompany profit in the beginning inventory is altered.** All of the other entries are the same as in the original example. For the data in the 20x3 Plateau-Solitaire consolidation, this entry is as follows:

---

[1] The subsidiary's financial statements are affected by intercompany profit in beginning inventory as follows: At the beginning of the year, the inventory account includes this profit. Accordingly, the opening balance of retained earnings also includes this profit. Recall from your study of financial accounting principles that an overstated asset balance is usually reflected as overstated retained earnings. This would always be the case when inventory is overstated and other asset and liability balances are correct.

Entry 3:

12/31/x3	**Investment in Solitaire**	1,600
	Cost of goods sold	1,600

($8,000 × 20%)

The partial worksheet for this situation would appear as follows:

Partial Worksheet	Plateau	Solitaire	Eliminations				Consolidated
Income statement 12/31/x3							
Sales	$ 20,000	$ 36,000	(1)	20,000			$ 36,000
Cost of goods sold	(15,000)	(24,000)	(2)	1,000	(1)	20,000	(18,400)
					(3)	1,600	
Balance sheet							
Inventory	15,000	8,000			(2)	1,000	22,000
Investment in Solitaire*	259,000		(3)	1,600			XXX

*The consolidated balance for the Investment in Solitaire account is not shown because it will be completely eliminated by other additional entries that are not illustrated.

As in the previous illustrations, the cost of goods sold is credited to realize the deferred profit in the beginning inventory arising from unsold intercompany inventory at the end of the year 20x2. The explanation for the debit to Investment in Solitaire (entry 3) is complex. To explain this debit, one must understand the equity method adjustments made by the parent company under the full equity method and the elimination entries to eliminate equity method income. To illustrate, assume that Plateau acquired a 100% interest in Solitaire at a cost of $100,000, on January 1, 20x2, an amount equal to the sum of Solitaire's capital stock of $20,000 and its retained earnings of $80,000. Further assume that Solitaire had net income and dividends for the years 20x2 and 20x3 as follows:

	20x2	20x3
Net income	$100,000	$150,000
Dividends	40,000	60,000

At the end of the year 20x2, Plateau makes three equity adjustments: one each for subsidiary income, subsidiary dividends, and for the intercompany profit in the ending inventory. The effects of these entries on the Investment in Solitaire as compared with the changes in Solitaire stockholders' equity are shown below:

	Investment in Solitaire	Solitaire Stockholders' Equity
Balances at acquisition, 1/1/x2	$100,000	$100,000
Solitaire net income for 20x2	100,000	100,000
Solitaire dividends for 20x2	(40,000)	(40,000)
Deferral of inventory profit	(1,600)	-
Ending balance 12/31/x2	$158,400	$160,000

The above analysis shows that the 20x2 ending balance in the investment in Solitaire account (and thus the beginning balance for the year 20x3) is reduced by the $1600 equity adjustment for deferred intercompany profit in ending inventory at the end of the year 20x2. The subsidiary retained earnings balance at 12/31/x2 (and 1/1/x3) reflects this intercompany profit. **Thus, the elimination entry for profit in the beginning inventory must debit the investment in Solitaire account, reestablishing reciprocity between Investment in Solitaire and the Solitaire equity. The 1/1/x3 beginning balance in Investment in Solitaire must be $160,000 when it is eliminated against the $160,000 of Solitaire stockholders' equity as of 1/1/x3 in the 20x3 consolidated statements worksheet. Otherwise, there would be a difference between these account balances and none should exist because there was no excess of cost over book value at the date of acquisition.**

Full equity situations—upstream sales

As in the modified equity case, upstream intercompany sales require **different procedures only in the case where a noncontrolling interest exists, and only for the entry that eliminates profit in the beginning inventory.** All other elimination entries are the same as in the original example. To illustrate, again assume that the data in the 20x3 Plateau-Solitaire example involved upstream sales and Solitaire was a 90%-owned subsidiary. The entry for profit in the beginning inventory would be as follows:

Entry 3:

12/31/x3	**Investment in Solitaire**	**1,440**	
	Noncontrolling interest	**160**	
	Cost of goods sold		1,600

($8,000 × 20% × 90% = $1,440)
($8,000 × 20% × 10% = $160)

A partial worksheet for the above entry is as follows:

Partial Worksheet	Plateau	Solitaire	Eliminations				Consolidated
Income statement 12/31/x3							
Sales	$ 20,000	$ 36,000	(1)	20,000			$ 36,000
Cost of goods sold	(15,000)	(24,000)	(2)	1,000	(1)	20,000	(18,400)
					(3)	1,600	
Statement of financial position							
Inventory	15,000	8,000			(2)	1,000	22,000
Investment in Solitaire*	259,000		(3)	**1,440**			XXX
Noncontrolling interest*			(3)	**160**			XXX

* The consolidated balances for these accounts are not shown because they are affected by other entries not illustrated. The Investment in Solitaire account will be fully eliminated from the consolidated statements.

Note that this entry differs from the modified equity example only in that the $1,440 debit is made to the investment in Solitaire account, rather than to Plateau Company retained earnings. Since Plateau made an equity adjustment for the intercompany profit in this case, its retained earnings account is not misstated. The purpose of the debit to the investment in Solitaire account is **to reestablish reciprocity between Investment in Solitaire and the Solitaire equity prior to**

eliminating the 1/1/x3 beginning of year balances of the Investment in Solitaire and the Solitaire stockholders' equity. Again, note the following comparison of the investment in Solitaire and the Solitaire stockholders' equity, assuming a 90% acquisition at a price ($90,000) that equals the book value of 90% of Solitaire stockholders' equity.

	Investment in Solitaire	Solitaire Stockholders' Equity	90% of Solitaire Stockholders' Equity
At acquisition, 1/1/x2	$ 90,000	$100,000	$ 90,000
Solitaire net income for 20x2	90,000	100,000	90,000
Solitaire dividends for 20x2	(36,000)	(40,000)	(36,000)
Deferral of inventory profit	(1,440)	-	-
Ending balance 12/31/x2	$142,560	$160,000	$144,000

In order to maintain the reciprocal relationship necessary to complete the consolidated statements worksheet, the balance of the account investment in Solitaire must equal 90% of $160,000 ($144,000) at the time the account is eliminated. This will only occur if the profit in the beginning inventory is eliminated with a debit of $1,440 to the investment in Solitaire account ($142,560 + $1,440 = $144,000). The $160 debit to noncontrolling interest is required to compensate for the fact that Solitaire's beginning retained earnings also includes the intercompany profit on the inventory sale. The entry is made for only 10% of the amount of the intercompany profit because only 10% of Solitaire Company's retained earnings is carried forward to the noncontrolling interest account. The remaining 90% of this account balance is eliminated when the subsidiary stockholders' equity is eliminated.

Summary—elimination entries for intercompany profit in inventory

Exhibit 5-2 summarizes the differences between the four situations:

1. Modified equity and cost method—downstream sales
2. Modified equity and cost method—upstream sales
3. Full equity method—downstream sales
4. Full equity method—upstream sales

It is important to reemphasize that entries for elimination of intercompany profit on upstream sales are different from the downstream case only if there is a noncontrolling interest. If the subsidiary is 100% owned, then elimination entries for downstream and upstream elimination of intercompany profit are the same. Exhibit 5-2 illustrates that changing from modified equity or cost to full equity changes only one of the four potential entries involving intercompany sales of inventory—**the entry to realize intercompany profit in beginning inventory.** In the modified equity and cost method situations, the parent company's retained earnings is debited for the controlling interest share of this realization, and the noncontrolling interest is debited for the noncontrolling interest share (upstream sales only). In the full equity situations, the parent company's investment in Subsidiary account is debited for the controlling interest share of this realization, and the noncontrolling interest is debited for the noncontrolling interest share (upstream sales only).

EXHIBIT 5-2 Comparison of worksheet elimination entries for intercompany transactions for the Plateau-Solitaire examples for the year ended December 31, 20x3

Cost Method or Modified Equity Method

Downstream case:
12/31/20x3

	Debit	Credit
Sales	20,000	
Cost of goods sold		20,000
To eliminate intercompany sales		
Cost of goods sold	1,000	
Inventory		1,000
To eliminate profit in the ending inventory ($4,000 × 25% = $1,000)		
Retained earnings—Plateau	1,600	
Cost of goods sold		1,600
To realized deferred profit in the beginning inventory ($8,000 × 20% = $1,600)		
Accounts payable	2,500	
Accounts receivable		2,500
To eliminate reciprocal payable and receivable		

Upstream case:
12/31/20x3

	Debit	Credit
Sales	20,000	
Cost of goods sold		20,000
To eliminate intercompany sales		
Cost of goods sold	1,000	
Inventory		1,000
To eliminate profit in the ending inventory ($4,000 × 25% = $1,000)		
Retained earnings—Plateau	1,440	
Noncontrolling interest	160	
Cost of goods sold		1,600
To realized deferred profit in the beginning inventory ($8,000 × 20% = $1,600)		
Accounts payable	2,500	
Accounts receivable		2,500
To eliminate reciprocal payable and receivable		

Full Equity Method

	Debit	Credit
Sales	20,000	
Cost of goods sold		20,000
To eliminate intercompany sales		
Cost of goods sold	1,000	
Inventory		1,000
To eliminate profit in the ending inventory ($4,000 × 25% = $1,000)		
Investment in Solitaire	1,600	
Cost of goods sold		1,600
To realized deferred profit in the beginning inventory ($8,000 × 20% = $1,600)		
Accounts payable	2,500	
Accounts receivable		2,500
To eliminate reciprocal payable and receivable		

	Debit	Credit
Sales	20,000	
Cost of goods sold		20,000
To eliminate intercompany sales		
Cost of goods sold	1,000	
Inventory		1,000
To eliminate profit in the ending inventory ($4,000 × 25% = $1,000)		
Investment in Solitaire	1,440	
Noncontrolling interest	160	
Cost of goods sold		1,600
To realized deferred profit in the beginning inventory ($8,000 × 20% = $1,600)		
Accounts payable	2,500	
Accounts receivable		2,500
To eliminate reciprocal payable and receivable		

Calculating the noncontrolling interest share of consolidated net income

Recall from Chapter 4 that the net income of a consolidated entity must be allocated between the controlling interest and the noncontrolling interest in all cases where the subsidiary is less than 100% owned. The general form of the calculation for noncontrolling interest share of consolidated net income was given in Chapter 4 as:

NISCNI = Subsidiary net income × NCI% − NCIA

Where: NISCNI = Noncontrolling interest share of consolidated net income

NCI% = Noncontrolling interest percentage

NCIA = Amortization of cost-book value differential applicable to the NCI

The calculation is slightly more complex where there are intercompany profits, when the expression becomes

NISCNI = (Subsidiary net income ± **IEU**) × NCI% − NCIA

Where: **IEU** = Income effects of upstream elimination entries

and other variables are as defined in the previous expression

The concept of income effects of upstream elimination entries requires further explanation. The **IEU** is the income effect of an elimination entry that changes consolidated net income where the subsidiary was the first party to the transaction. In the case of inventory, the first party is the seller. Only two entries involving intercompany profit in inventory potentially have such income effects: the entry to defer profit in the ending inventory and the entry to realize profit in the beginning inventory. These two entries have income effects because they change consolidated net income. Observe these two entries for the upstream, modified equity case using the Plateau-Solitaire data:

To defer profit in the ending inventory:

12/31/x1	Cost of goods sold	1,000	
	Inventory		1,000

($4,000 × 25%)

To realize profit in the beginning inventory:

12/31/x1	Retained earnings—Plateau	1,440	
	Noncontrolling interest	160	
	Cost of goods sold		1,600

($8,000 × 20% × 90% = $1,440)

($8,000 × 20% × 10% = $160)

The **IEU** (upstream income effect) of the above two entries is reflected in the cost of goods sold debit in the first entry and the cost of goods sold credit in the second entry. These elements of the entries have income effects because cost of goods sold is an income statement account. All the other accounts in these two entries (Inventory, Retained earnings—Plateau, and Noncontrolling interest) are balance sheet accounts. To determine whether the income effect is positive (increases income) or negative (decreases income), it is only necessary to observe whether cost of goods sold was debited (decreases income) or credited (increases income). In our example, we would thus subtract the $1,000 cost of goods sold debit from Solitaire's net income and add the

$1,600 cost of goods sold credit to Solitaire's net income in determining the noncontrolling interest share of consolidated net income. As previously stipulated, Solitaire had net income of $20,000 in the year 20x3, and the acquisition price of $90,000 did not result in any excess of cost over book value to be amortized. The calculation of the **NISCNI** in this example is thus:

$$\text{NISCNI} = (\text{Subsidiary net income} \pm \textbf{IEU}) \times \text{NCI\%} - \text{NCIA}$$
$$\text{NISCNI} = (\$20{,}000 + \mathbf{\$1{,}600} - \mathbf{\$1{,}000}) \times 10\% - (\$0)$$
$$\text{NISCNI} = \$2{,}060$$

COMPREHENSIVE ILLUSTRATION

The following comprehensive illustration of a purchase method consolidation with intercompany transactions in inventories is shown for three cases: the cost method case, the modified equity case, and the full equity case. Each of the three examples shows the entries that the parent company makes to account for the investment in subsidiary on its books, the elimination entries for the consolidated statements worksheet in journal form, and the completed worksheet.

Assume that Palmer Company acquires a 90% interest in Small Company for cash of $400,000 on January 1, 20x2 when Small has common stock outstanding consisting of 10,000 shares of $10 par common stock and retained earnings of $300,000. The excess of cost over book value at the date of acquisition is considered to be goodwill with an indefinite life. During the two years ended December 31, 20x2 and 20x3, Small Company had book net income of $40,000 and $60,000 respectively, and paid dividends of $10,000 each year.

For the two years ended December 31, 20x2 and 20x3, the two companies had intercompany transactions in inventory as illustrated in the following schedule:

	20x2	20x3
Intercompany sales—Small to Palmer	$50,000	$60,000
Markup percent on sales	30%	40%
Intercompany inventory on hand at year end	$10,000	$20,000
Unpaid Small accounts receivable from		
intercompany sales	$5,000	$7,000

An allocation schedule for the acquisition of Small Company by Palmer Company on 1/1/20x2 is shown in the following schedule:

Investment in Small 1/1/20x2		$400,000
Stockholders' equity of Small		
Common stock	$100,000	
Retained earnings	300,000	
	400,000	
Ownership percentage	90%	360,000
Goodwill		$ 40,000

COST METHOD CASE: The statements for the two companies for the year ended 20x3 are shown in the first two columns of Exhibit 5-3. Palmer Company's book entries to account for its investment in Small for the years 20x2 and 20x3 are shown below. The only entries necessary are the entries to record the dividends received from Small. Note that under the cost method, the account balance for the Investment in Small Company does not change. Since the dividends are the same each year, the entry for the year 20x2 is identical to the entry for the year 20x3.

12/31/x2 Cash	9,000	
Dividend income		9,000
12/31/x3 Cash	9,000	
Dividend income		9,000

The elimination entries for the consolidated statements worksheet, in journal form, are as follows:

(1) Sales   60,000
       Cost of goods sold   60,000
     To eliminate the intercompany sales for the year 20x3

(2) Cost of goods sold   8,000
       Inventory   8,000
     To eliminate intercompany profit in the ending inventory
       ($20,000 × 40% = $8,000)

(3) Retained earnings—Palmer   2,700
    Noncontrolling interest   300
       Cost of goods sold   3,000
     To realize deferred profit in the beginning inventory
       ($10,000 × 30% = $3,000; $3,000 × 90% = $2,700;
       $3,000 × 10% = $300)

(4) Accounts payable   7,000
       Accounts receivable   7,000
     To eliminate intercompany accounts receivable/payable

(5) Investment in Small   27,000
       Retained earnings—Palmer   27,000
     To adjust Palmer's Investment in Small balance to modified equity*
       ($330,000 − 300,000) × 90% = $27,000)

(6) Dividend income   9,000
       Dividends—Small   9,000
     To eliminate the intercompany dividend for the year 20x3

(7) Noncontrolling interest income   5,500
       Dividends—Small   1,000
       Noncontrolling interest   4,500
     To allocate the noncontrolling interest share of consolidated
       net income to the noncontrolling interest account**
       ($60,000 + 3,000 − 8,000 × 10% = $5,500)

(8)	Common stock—Small	100,000	
	Retained earnings—Small	330,000	
	Goodwill	40,000	
	Noncontrolling interest		43,000
	Investment in Small		427,000

To eliminate the stockholders' equity and investment in Small
and to establish the noncontrolling interest at 1/1/20x3

* Recall from Chapter 4 that the relationship between the Investment in Subsidiary and the Subsidiary equity accounts under the equity method is expressed as:

$$\Delta \text{ Investment}_{t...t+n} = [\Delta \text{ SubRE}_{t...t+n} \times \text{CI\%}] - \text{C/BVA}_{t...t+n}$$

Where: Δ Investment = Change in the Investment in Subsidiary

Δ SubRE = Change in Subsidiary Retained Earnings

CI% = Controlling interest percentage

C/BVA = Cost-Book Value Amortization

$_{t...t+n}$ = time period from t to t+n

In this instance, the subsidiary retained earnings has gone from a balance of $300,000 at the date of acquisition on January 1, 20x2, to a balance of $330,000 at the end of the year 20x2 (Net income of $40,000 less dividends declared of $10,000). Accordingly, the entry to convert the investment in Small account from the cost method to the modified equity method is made for 90% of $30,000. Cost-book value amortization is subtracted in this calculation, however, in this case, there is no amortization because the differential is attributable to goodwill.

** Recall from the previous section of this chapter that income effects of upstream intercompany transactions affect the noncontrolling interest share of consolidated net income. In this case, the $8,000 cost of goods sold debit (entry 2) and the $3,000 cost of goods sold credit (entry 3) must be subtracted and added respectively to subsidiary net income before multiplying by the noncontrolling interest percentage to compute noncontrolling interest income.

● **INTERPRETIVE EXERCISE**

How much will the adjustment be to convert the investment account to modified equity
as of 12/31/x3?

Exhibit 5-3 shows the completed worksheet for consolidated financial statements under the cost method with the above elimination entries posted. The existence of intercompany elimination entries does not change the procedures used to prepare a consolidated statements worksheet from those illustrated in previous chapters of this textbook.

MODIFIED EQUITY CASE: The 20x3 financial statements for Palmer and Small, assuming Palmer accounts for its investment in subsidiary using the modified equity method, are shown in the first two columns of Exhibit 5-4. Palmer Company's book entries to account for its investment in Small for the years 20x2 and 20x3 are shown below. Note that the use of the modified equity method causes the balance in the account, Investment in Small, to increase by the controlling interest share of the undistributed income of Small.

12/31/x2	Investment in Small	36,000	
	Equity in Small income		36,000

To record Palmer's share of Small income for the year 20x2
($40,000 × 90% = $36,000)

EXHIBIT 5·3 Palmer and Small
(Cost Method) Worksheet for Consolidated Financial Statements

Statement of Income	Park	Standard		Eliminations			Consolidated	
For the Year ended 12/31/x3								
Sales	$250,000	$190,000	(1)	60,000			$ 380,000	
Dividend income	9,000		(6)	9,000			-	
Cost of goods sold	(125,500)	(88,000)	(2)	8,000	(1)	60,000	(158,500)	
					(3)	3,000		
Operating expenses	(63,400)	(42,000)					(105,400)	
Net income	70,100	60,000					116,100	
Controlling interest income*							110,600	A
Noncontrolling interest income**			(7)	5,500			5,500	
Retained earnings - P Jan. 1	233,000		(3)	2,700	(5)	27,000	257,300	
Retained earnings - S Jan. 1		330,000	(8)	330,000			-	
Add controlling net income	70,100	60,000					110,600	A
Less: Dividends	(12,000)	(10,000)			(6)	9,000	(12,000)	
					(7)	1,000		
Retained earnings, Dec. 31	291,100	380,000					355,900	B
Balance sheet 12/31/x3								
Cash	18,500	23,700					42,200	
Accounts receivable	41,200	23,350			(4)	7,000	57,550	
Inventories	37,900	52,450			(2)	8,000	82,350	
Land	34,000	25,000					59,000	
Buildings - net	195,000	178,000					373,000	
Equipment - net	210,000	190,000					400,000	
Investment in Small	400,000		(5)	27,000	(8)	427,000	-	
Goodwill			(8)	40,000			40,000	
	936,600	492,500					1,054,100	
Accounts payable	45,500	12,500	(4)	7,000			51,000	
Long-term debt	250,000	-					250,000	
Common stock	350,000	100,000	(8)	100,000			350,000	
Retained earnings	291,100	380,000					355,900	B
Noncontrolling interest			(3)	300	(7)	4,500	47,200	
					(8)	43,000		
	$936,600	$492,500		$589,500		$589,500	$1,054,100	

* ($116,100 − $5,500) = $110,600   **($60,000 + $3,000 − $8,000) × 10% = $5,500

	Cash		9,000	
		Investment in Small		9,000
		To record Palmer's 20x2 dividend from Small		
		($10,000 × 90% = $9,000)		
12/31/x3	Investment in Small		54,000	
		Equity in Small income		54,000
		To record Palmer's share of Small income for the year 20x3		
		($60,000 × 90% = $54,000)		
	Cash		9,000	
		Investment in Small		9,000
		To record Palmer's 20x3 dividend from Small		
		($10,000 × 90% = $9,000)		

The use of the modified equity method as compared with the cost method changes three accounts on Palmer Company books. The account, Investment in Small, increases to $472,000 at the end of the year 20x3 as illustrated by the following T account:

Investment in Small Company

Cost 1/1/x2	400,000		
12/31/x2	36,000	9,000	
12/31/x3	54,000	9,000	
Balance 12/31/x3	472,500		

In addition, there is an account, Equity in Small Income, which did not exist under the cost method. For the year ended 12/31/20x3, this account has a balance of $54,000 and is also reflected in the above T account as a debit to the Investment in Small. Finally, both the beginning and ending retained earnings of Palmer are higher under the modified equity method than under the cost method because the equity in Small income under the equity method is higher in both years than the amount of dividend income reported under the cost method. Thus, the use of the modified equity method has the effect of increasing Palmer's 20x3 beginning retained earnings by $27,000 to $260,000 and its ending retained earnings by $72,000 to $363,100.

The elimination entries under the modified equity method are slightly different from those under the cost method. One entry made under the cost method is omitted. No "equity adjustment" is necessary to restate the Investment as was done in the cost method case because the books are already adjusted to reflect the equity basis. Also, another elimination entry is made to eliminate the "equity in Small income" in place of the entry to eliminate the dividend income from Small under the cost approach. The elimination entries for the modified equity approach are shown below:

(1) Sales   60,000
   Cost of goods sold   60,000
  To eliminate the intercompany sales for the year 20x3

(2) Cost of goods sold   8,000
   Inventory   8,000
  To eliminate intercompany profit in the ending inventory
   ($20,000 × 40% = $8,000)

(3) Retained earnings—Palmer   2,700
  Noncontrolling interest   300
   Cost of goods sold   3,000
  To realize deferred profit in the beginning inventory
   ($10,000 × 30% = $3,000; $3,000 × 90% = $2,700; $3,000 × 10% = $300)

(4) Accounts payable   7,000
   Accounts receivable   7,000
  To eliminate intercompany accounts receivable/payable

(5) Equity in Small income   54,000
        Dividends—Small   9,000
        Investment in Small   45,000

To eliminate the intercompany dividend for the year 20x3

(6) Noncontrolling interest income   5,500
        Dividends—Small   1,000
        Noncontrolling interest   4,500

To allocate the noncontrolling interest share of consolidated net income to the
noncontrolling interest account
($60,000 + 3,000 − 8,000 × 10% = $5,500)

(7) Common stock—Small   100,000
    Retained earnings—Small   330,000
    Goodwill   40,000
        Noncontrolling interest   43,000
        Interest in Small   427,000

To eliminate the stockholders' equity and investment in Small
and to establish the noncontrolling interest at 1/1/20x3

The above entries are reflected in the completed consolidated statements worksheet shown in Exhibit 5-4.

FULL EQUITY CASE: The 20x3 financial statements for Palmer and Small, assuming Palmer accounts for its investment in subsidiary using the full equity method, are shown in the first two columns of Exhibit 5-5. Palmer Company's book entries to account for its investment in Small for the years 20x2 and 20x3 are shown below. The entries to record the equity income and dividends received from the subsidiary are exactly the same as for the modified equity method. Also, additional equity entries are recorded for the intercompany profit in the beginning and ending inventory. The fact that the parent company records book entries under the equity method for intercompany profits does not negate the need to make elimination entries for these intercompany profits on the consolidations worksheet. As you will see, the use of the full equity method alters these elimination entries only slightly. Palmer's book equity method entries under this approach for the years 20x2 and 20x3 are as follows. (The equity adjustments for intercompany profit are shown in bold type for emphasis.)

12/31/x2 Investment in Small   36,000
        Equity in Small income   36,000
        To record Palmer's share of Small income for the year 20x2
            ($40,000 × 90% = $36,000)

      Cash   9,000
        Investment in Small   9,000
        To record Palmer's 20x2 dividend from Small: ($10,000 × 90% = $9,000)

      Equity in Small income   **2,700**
        Investment in Small   **2,700**
        To record the deferral of intercompany profit in the ending inventory
            ($3,000 × 90% = $27,000)

EXHIBIT 5·4 Palmer and Small
(Modified Equity Method) Worksheet for Consolidated Financial Statements

Statement of Income	Park	Standard	Eliminations				Consolidated	
For the Year ended 12/31/x3								
Sales	$ 250,000	$190,000	(1)	60,000			$ 380,000	
Equity in Small income	**54,000**		(5)	**54,000**			-	
Cost of goods sold	(125,500)	(88,000)	(2)	8,000	(1)	60,000	(158,500)	
					(3)	3,000		
Operating expenses	(63,400)	(42,000)					(105,400)	
Net income	115,100	60,000					116,100	
Controlling interest income*							110,600	A
Noncontrolling interest income**			(6)	5,500			5,500	
Retained earnings - P Jan. 1	260,000		(3)	2,700			257,300	
Retained earnings - S Jan. 1		330,000	(7)	330,000			-	
Add controlling net income	115,100	60,000					110,600	A
Less: Dividends	(12,000)	(10,000)			(5)	9,000	(12,000)	
					(6)	1,000		
Retained earnings, Dec. 31	363,100	380,000					355,900	B
Balance sheet 12/31/x3								
Cash	18,500	23,700					42,200	
Accounts receivable	41,200	23,350			(4)	7,000	57,550	
Inventories	37,900	52,450			(2)	8,000	82,350	
Land	34,000	25,000					59,000	
Buildings - net	195,000	178,000					373,000	
Equipment - net	210,000	190,000					400,000	
Investment in Small	472,000				(5)	45,000	-	
					(7)	427,000		
Goodwill			(7)	40,000			40,000	
	1,008,600	492,500					1,054,100	
Accounts payable	45,500	12,500	(4)	7,000			51,000	
Long-term debt	250,000	-					250,000	
Common stock	350,000	100,000	(7)	100,000			350,000	
Retained earnings	363,100	380,000					355,900	B
Noncontrolling interest			(3)	300	(6)	4,500	47,200	
					(7)	43,000		
	$1,008,600	$492,500		$607,500		$607,500	$1,054,100	

* ($116,100 − $5,500) = $110,600   ** ($60,000 + $3,000 − $8,000) × 10% = $5,500

12/31/x3	**Investment in Small**	2,700	
	Equity in Small income		2,700

To realize deferred intercompany profit in the beginning inventory
($3,000 3 90% 5 $2,700)

	Investment in Small	54,000	
	Equity in Small income		54,000

To record Palmer's share of Small income for the year 20x3
($60,000 × 90% = $54,000)

Cash	9,000	
Investment in Small		9,000

To record Palmer's 20x3 dividend from Small
($10,000 × 90% = $9,000)

Equity in Small income	**7,200**	
Investment in Small		**7,200**

To record deferred intercompany profit in the ending inventory
($8,000 × 90% = $7,200)

As the equity adjustment entries indicate, the use of the full equity method to account for the Investment in the subsidiary changes three account balances on Palmer's books: Investment in Small, Equity in Small income, and Retained earnings. These changes are, of course, also reflected in these account balances in the consolidated statements worksheet Exhibit 5-5. A T account for the Investment in Small is shown below:

Investment in Small Company

Cost 1/1/x2	400,000		
Equity adjustments	36,000	9,000	
12/31/x2		2,700	
Balance 12/31/x2	424,300		
Equity adjustments	2,700	9,000	
12/31/x3	54,000	7,200	
Balance 12/31/x3	464,800		

The balance of the account, "Equity in Small income," at 12/31/20x3, is reflected in the following T account:

Equity in Small income

12/31/x3		2,700
12/31/x3		54,000
12/31/x3	7,200	
Balance 12/31/x3		49,500

The elimination entries under the full equity method differ only slightly from those under the modified equity method. The use of the full equity method changes the account balances in the accounts Investment in Small and Equity in Small income, and the entry to realize deferred intercompany profit in the beginning inventory is altered slightly. These entries are shown below and in the consolidated statements worksheet Exhibit 5-5.

(1)
Sales	60,000	
Cost of goods sold		60,000

To eliminate the intercompany sales for the year 20x3

(2) Cost of goods sold   8,000
      Inventory   8,000

To eliminate intercompany profit in the ending inventory
($20,000 × 40% = $8,000)

(3) **Investment in Small**   **2,700**
Noncontrolling interest   300
      Cost of goods sold   3,000

To realize deferred profit in the beginning inventory
($10,000 × 30% = $3,000; $3,000 × 90% = $2,700;
$3,000 × 10% = $300)

(4) Accounts payable   7,000
      Accounts receivable   7,000

To eliminate intercompany accounts receivable/payable

(5) Equity in Small income   **49,500**
      Dividends—Small   9,000
      Investment in Small   **40,500**

To eliminate the intercompany dividend for the year 20x3

(6) Noncontrolling interest income   5,500
      Dividends—Small   1,000
      Noncontrolling interest   4,500

To allocate the noncontrolling interest share of consolidated net income to the
noncontrolling interest account
($60,000 + 3,000 − 8,000 × 10% = $5,500)

(7) Common stock—Small   100,000
Retained earnings—Small   300,000
Goodwill   40,000
      Noncontrolling interest   43,000
      Investment in Small   427,000

To eliminate the stockholders equity and investment in Small
and to establish the noncontrolling interest at 1/1/20x3

EXHIBIT 5·5 Palmer and Small
(Full Equity Method) Worksheet for Consolidated Financial Statements

Statement of Income	Park	Standard	Eliminations				Consolidated	
For the Year ended 12/31/x3								
Sales	$ 250,000	$190,000	(1)	60,000			$ 380,000	
Equity in Small income	**49,500**		(5)	**49,500**			-	
Cost of goods sold	(125,500)	(88,000)	(2)	8,000	(1)	60,000	(158,500)	
					(3)	3,000		
Operating expenses	(63,400)	(42,000)					(105,400)	
Net income	**110,600**	60,000					116,100	
Controlling interest income*							110,600	A
Noncontrolling interest income**			(6)	5,500			5,500	
Retained earnings - P Jan. 1	257,300						257,300	
Retained earnings - S Jan. 1		330,000	(7)	330,000			-	
Add controlling net income	110,600	60,000					110,600	A
Less: Dividends	(12,000)	(10,000)			(5)	9,000	(12,000)	
					(6)	1,000		
Retained earnings, Dec. 31	355,900	380,000					355,900	B
Balance sheet 12/31/x3								
Cash	18,500	23,700					42,200	
Accounts receivable	41,200	23,350			(4)	7,000	57,550	
Inventories	37,900	52,450			(2)	8,000	82,350	
Land	34,000	25,000					59,000	
Buildings - net	195,000	178,000					373,000	
Equipment - net	210,000	190,000					400,000	
Investment in Small	**464,800**		(3)	**2,700**	(5)	**40,500**	-	
					(7)	427,000		
Goodwill			(7)	40,000			40,000	
	1,001,400	492,500					1,054,100	
Accounts payable	45,500	12,500	(4)	7,000			51,000	
Long-term debt	250,000	-					250,000	
Common stock	350,000	100,000	(7)	100,000			350,000	
Retained earnings	**355,900**	380,000					355,900	B
Noncontrolling interest			(3)	300	(6)	4,500	47,200	
					(7)	43,000		
	$1,001,400	$492,500		$603,000		$603,000	$1,054,100	

* ($116,100 − $5,500) = $110,600   ** ($60,000 + $3,000 − $8,000) × 10% = $5,500

SUMMARY

Intercompany transactions create the need for elimination of intercompany accounts. These accounts make take the form of intercompany inventory sales, advances and loans, intercompany sales of plant assets, and other transactions. A common type of intercompany transaction is sale of inventory. When this type of transaction occurs, both the seller and the buyer record the events in a normal manner. From a consolidated perspective, however, these intercompany sales of inventory are an internal transaction. The effects of intercompany transactions on the consolidated financial statements must be eliminated in the consolidation process. Accordingly, for intercompany inventory transactions, four elimination entries are required for the following items:

1. **Intercompany sales.** This entry is made for 100% of intercompany sales whether or not a noncontrolling interest exists. This elimination entry is made in the same manner for both upstream and downstream sales. Intercompany purchases will eventually be resold, or more likely, become components in other products. However, the entry to eliminate intercompany sales is unaffected by the timing of the subsequent sale by the intercompany buyer. If any intercompany inventory is on hand at the consolidation date, an additional entry (entry 2 below) is made to eliminate the intercompany profit contained therein.

2. **Intercompany profit in ending inventory.** Any inventory on hand at the end of the year acquired from an affiliate will be on the buyer's books at the intercompany cost—an amount normally higher than the original producer's (seller's) cost. From a consolidated perspective, the intercompany profit is unrealized, resulting in the need for an entry that defers realization of the intercompany profit in ending inventory. This entry is always made by reducing the inventory account for the amount of unrealized intercompany profit contained therein and increasing the cost of goods sold account for the same amount. The amount and form of this entry is unaffected both by the existence of a noncontrolling interest and the circumstances of the sale, whether upstream or downstream. **The noncontrolling interest share of consolidated net income is, however, reduced by the noncontrolling interest share of deferred intercompany profit on upstream sales.**

3. **Intercompany profit in beginning inventory.** Intercompany profit in beginning inventory will occur in all circumstances where there was intercompany profit in the ending inventory of the previous year's consolidated statements worksheet. Since beginning inventory becomes a component of the cost of goods sold, the elimination entry for profit in beginning inventory is made to realize this intercompany profit with a credit to the cost of goods sold account. Two factors affect the appropriate debits for realization of deferred profit in beginning inventory: (1) the method of accounting used for the investment account—cost, modified equity, or full equity, and (2) for upstream sales, the presence of a noncontrolling interest. In cost and modified equity situations involving 100%-owned subsidiaries, the parent company retained earnings is debited. In full equity situations involving 100%-owned subsidiaries, the Investment in Subsidiary is debited. If there is an upstream sale and a noncontrolling interest, the noncontrolling interest share of the deferred profit realized is debited to the noncontrolling interest in all cases. Finally, the noncontrolling interest share of intercompany profit deferred or realized on upstream sales changes the noncontrolling interest share of consolidated net income. Review the appropriate sections of the chapter for a more detailed explanation and illustration of these issues.

4. **Intercompany accounts receivable and payable.** If any reciprocal accounts receivable and payable arise from either upstream or downstream intercompany transactions, these should always be eliminated using the same entry. There are no complications arising from the existence of noncontrolling interests, and no difference due to cost, modified equity, or full equity methods.

APPENDIX : # Estimating the Amount of Intercompany Profit in Inventory

This appendix reviews an analytical issue related to estimation of intercompany profit in inventory. These procedures are closely related to those used in estimating inventory under the gross profit method, a subject studied in intermediate accounting. The amount of intercompany profit in ending inventory is normally estimated by reference to markup, the percentage of sales or the percentage of cost that represents gross profit. Stated another way, gross profit rates can be expressed in terms of markup on sales or markup on cost.

MARKUP ON SALES

When markup is expressed as a percentage of sales, the calculation of gross profit in inventory is straightforward. For example, assume that the gross profit rate on sales is 40% and the amount of inventory containing inventory profit is $10,000. In this circumstance, the amount of profit in the inventory is $4,000 ($10,000 $\times$ 40%). In general terms, we can express this relationship as follows:

$$\pi = INV \times MU\%$$

where π = profit
INV = Inventory amount
MU% = Markup percent on sales

MARKUP ON COST

If the markup is given as a percentage of cost, the calculation is indirect. For example, assume that the gross profit rate on cost is 50% and the amount of inventory containing inventory profit is $15,000. Note the following:

Sales − Cost of Sales = Gross Profit

Thus,

Gross Profit + Cost of Sales = Sales

Substituting the percentages from the above paragraph gives

50% + 100% = 150%

And since markup on sales = gross profit / sales, we can estimate markup on sales in this case as

50% / 150% = 33 1/3%

This calculation allows us to estimate the profit in the inventory as

$$\pi = INV \times MU\%$$
$$\$5,000 = \$15,000 \times 33 \ 1/3\%$$

In general, a simple approach to calculating gross profit contained in inventory when the markup is given on cost is to first convert the markup on cost to a markup on sales. This conversion is done by adding 100% to the markup on cost and dividing the result into the markup on cost, resulting in the markup on sales percentage. This conversion allows the inventory profit to be estimated using the markup on sales formula.

The amount of inventory profit in situations where markup is expressed as a percentage of cost can also be estimated by dividing the amount of inventory by 100% plus the markup on cost:

$$\pi = \text{Sales} - \text{Sales} / (100\% + \text{MUC}\%)$$

where: π = profit
MUC% = markup on cost percentage

Using the data from the above example yields the following result:

$$\pi = \$15,000 - \$15,000 / (100\% + 50\%)$$
$$\pi = \$15,000 - \$10,000$$
$$\pi = \$5,000$$

QUESTIONS

1. Explain how the concept of the economic entity requires that intercompany transactions be eliminated in the preparation of consolidated financial statements.
2. Why must the effects of intercompany transactions in inventory be eliminated from consolidated financial statements? Identify what these potential effects are.
3. How does the existence of intercompany profit in ending inventory affect the consolidated financial statements in the following year? What type of elimination entry is required in the two years affected?
4. Does the existence of a noncontrolling interest affect the entry to eliminate intercompany sales?
5. If a company uses the equity method to account for an investment in an affiliate, what adjustments are necessary on account of intercompany transactions in inventory?
6. How does the existence of a noncontrolling interest affect the equity method entries for upstream sales of inventory? Explain.
7. Explain why the parent company Retained Earnings is debited in the elimination entry to realize deferred intercompany profit in beginning inventory in the downstream modified equity case.
8. Explain why the parent company Investment in subsidiary account is debited in the elimination entry to realize deferred intercompany profit in beginning inventory in the downstream (full) equity case.
9. What is meant by the term "Income effect of an elimination entry"? Give an example of an elimination entry with an "Income Effect."
10. Which elimination entries have an impact on the noncontrolling interest share of consolidated net income? How is this amount computed?
11. When the cost method is used to account for an investment in a subsidiary to be consolidated, an adjustment is required to restate the investment to the modified equity basis in all years except the year of acquisition prior to completing the consolidated statements worksheet. Explain why this adjustment is needed.
12. Explain why the method of accounting for the investment in subsidiary account has no impact on the balances in the consolidated financial statements.
13. Does the pooling-purchase issue have any impact on the procedures used to eliminate intercompany profit? Explain.

EXERCISES

Exercise 5-1   (Multiple choice: select the best answer for each item.)

1. Intercompany transactions between a parent and a subsidiary could involve
   a. sales of products or assets.
   b. loans.
   c. leases.
   d. investments in affiliate debt instruments.
   e. all of the above.
2. Which of the following transactions is **not** an intercompany transaction?
   a. Sale of inventory by a subsidiary to the parent company
   b. Sale of inventory by the parent company to a subsidiary
   c. Sale to a nonaffiliate of inventory purchased from an affiliate
   d. Sale of inventory by one subsidiary to another
   e. All of the above are intercompany transactions.
3. Equity adjustments on the books of a parent company for intercompany transactions
   a. are mandatory and must be recorded before a consolidated statements worksheet can be prepared.
   b. are optional and have no effect on the elimination entries for intercompany inventory transactions.
   c. are optional and alter the form of all elimination entries for intercompany inventory transactions.
   d. are optional, but alter the form of only the entry to realized deferred profit in beginning inventory.
4. Elimination entries are required for
   a. current year intercompany sales only.
   b. both current year and previous year intercompany sales.
   c. only those intercompany sales for which inventory remains in the possession of the affiliate.
   d. none of the above.
   Items 5–7 are based on the following information: Sub Company is a 90%-owned subsidiary of Parent Company. During the year ended 12/31/x3, Parent Company sells $4,000 of inventory to Sub Company, of which $3,000 remains in Sub Company's inventory as at the end of the year. Parent Company's markup on this inventory was 30% of sales price. Parent Company uses the modified equity method and does not make equity adjustments for intercompany profit.
5. What is the amount of intercompany sales to be eliminated?
   a. $3,000
   b. $4,000
   c. $1,200
   d. $3,600
6. What is the profit in the ending inventory to be eliminated?
   a. $4,000
   b. $ 900
   c. $1,200
   d. $ 810
7. Assume that the profit in the ending inventory was $1,000. The elimination entry would involve a
   a. debit to Inventory for $1,000.
   b. credit to Inventory for $900.
   c. debit to Cost of goods sold for $1,000.
   d. debit to Cost of goods sold for $900.

Items 8–10 are based on the following information: Standard Company is an 80%-owned subsidiary of Percell Company. During the year ended December 31, 20x4, Standard Company sold inventory with a cost of $4,000 to Percell for $5,000. One-half of this inventory was on hand at the end of the year 20x4 and was sold by Percell to an external entity during the month of January, 20x5. Percell accounts for its investment in Standard using the full equity method, recording adjustments for intercompany transactions.

8. The equity adjustment for profit in the ending inventory at December 31, 20x4, includes
   a. a debit to Income from subsidiary for $400.
   b. a debit to Income from subsidiary for $500.
   c. a debit to Income from subsidiary for $1,000.
   d. a debit to Income from subsidiary for $800.

9. What is the amount of intercompany sales to be eliminated in the December 31, 20x4, worksheet?
   a. $4,000
   b. $5,000
   c. $1,000
   d. $2,500

10. The elimination entry in the December 31, 20x5, worksheet to realize profit in the beginning inventory involves
    a. a debit to retained earnings—Percell for $500.
    b. a debit to retained earnings—Percell for $400.
    c. a debit to Investment in Standard for $500.
    d. a debit to Investment in Standard for $400.

Exercise 5-2

(Effect of intercompany transactions on sales and cost of goods sold)

Percival Company sold inventory to its wholly-owned subsidiary Seatex Company during the year 20x3. The inventory had a cost to Percival of $5,000 and was sold to Seatex for $8,000. Seatex sold this inventory to customers external to the consolidated entity for $12,000.

Required:

(1) Prepare a schedule computing the consolidated sales and cost of goods sold.
(2) Prepare a similar schedule assuming instead that Seatex Company was a 90%-owned subsidiary.

Exercise 5-3

(Effect of intercompany transactions on sales and cost of goods sold)

Subset Company sells 100% of its production of electrical components to its parent company, Giant Electric, a major appliance maker. During the year 20x1, Subset had total sales of $400,000. These sales were marked up 40% on sales price. In its separate financial statements, Giant Electric had sales of $2,000,000 and cost of sales of $1,200,000. Subset is a 100%-owned subsidiary of Giant Electric.

Required:

(1) Prepare a schedule computing the consolidated sales and cost of goods sold.
(2) Prepare a similar schedule, assuming instead that Subset Company was an 80%-owned subsidiary.

Exercise 5-4

(Effect of intercompany sales on cost of goods sold)

Passpoint Company made the following purchases from its wholly-owned subsidiaries during the years shown below. Also given is the balance of unsold inventory from intercompany purchases and the balance in consolidated cost of goods sold.

	20x2	20x3	20x4
Purchases	$ 10,000	$ 15,000	$ 22,000
Inventory on hand at year-end	3,000	5,000	7,000
Cost of goods sold	300,000	360,000	390,000

The markup on the purchases from subsidiaries was 20% on sales price in all cases.

Required:

(1) Assuming there were no intercompany transactions in inventory other than those shown in the schedule above, compute the consolidated cost of goods sold for the three years.
(2) Explain how your answer would change if the subsidiaries had been 75% owned.

Exercise 5-5

(Equity adjustments for intercompany sales)

Pensive Company and its wholly-owned subsidiary Surrogate Company had the following intercompany transactions:

	20x2	20x3	20x4
Sales Pensive to Surrogate	$50,000	$60,000	$30,000
Inventory on hand at year-end	5,000	3,000	7,500
% markup on sales price	40%	30%	40%

Required:

(1) Assuming that Pensive uses the full equity method to account for its investment in Surrogate, give the equity adjustments required on the books of Pensive to account for the profit in the inventories for the years 20x2 through 20x4.
(2) Explain or show how your answer would differ if the intercompany sales had been from Surrogate Company to Pensive Company.

Exercise 5-6

(Equity adjustments for intercompany sales)

Refer to the table in exercise 6-5 showing the intercompany sales. Assume that all sales were upstream and that Surrogate Company was a 90%-owned subsidiary.

Required:

Record the equity adjustments that the parent company would make on its books for the intercompany transactions in inventory for the years 20x2 through 20x4.

Exercise 5-7   **(Consolidation concepts)**

Parachute Company and its 90%-owned subsidiary, Sailboat Company, had the following separate income statements for the year ended December 31, 20x3:

	Parachute	Sailboat
Sales	$ 560,000	$ 245,000
Dividend income	27,000	-
Cost of goods sold	350,000	125,000
Depreciation expense	10,000	13,000
Operating expenses	35,000	45,000
Net income	$ 192,000	$ 62,000

The acquisition of the 90% interest in Sailboat occurred on December 31, 19x8. On December 31, 20x2, Parachute Company had inventory on its books purchased from its subsidiary in the amount of $20,000. This inventory was resold to customers external to the consolidated entity during the year 20x3. However, during 20x3, Parachute purchased additional inventory in the amount of $50,000 from Sailboat Company, of which $28,000 was on hand at December 31. The intercompany sales were marked up 100% on cost.

Required:

(1) What method of accounting is Parachute Company using to account for its investment in Sailboat Company?
(2) Assuming Parachute Company had no common stock investments other than the investment in Sailboat Company, what amount of dividends did Sailboat declare during the year 20x3?
(3) Compute consolidated sales and cost of goods sold for the year 20x3.
(4) Compute the noncontrolling interest share of consolidated net income.

Exercise 5-8   **(Consolidated income statement)**

Persimmon Company acquired an 80% interest in Starburst Company, a finance company, at a price equal to underlying book value on January 1, 20x1. The separate income statements for the two companies for the year 20x2 are shown below:

	Persimmon	Starburst
Sales revenue	$ 275,000	$ 120,000
Equity in Starburst income	16,000	-
Cost of goods sold	165,000	80,000
Depreciation expense	20,000	5,000
Operating expenses	34,000	15,000
Net income	$ 72,000	$ 20,000

During the year 20x2, Persimmon sold accounts receivable with a book value of $40,000 to Starburst for $38,000. The difference between these two amounts was reported as operating expenses by Persimmon and as Sales revenue (interest income) by Starburst.

Required:

Prepare a consolidated income statement for Persimmon Company and Starburst Company.

Exercise 5-9   **(Elimination entries)**

Pages Company and its 90%-owned subsidiary, Sawbuck Company, had the following inter-company transactions during the year 20x2:

Intercompany sales Pages to Sawbuck	$ 25,000
Intercompany sales Sawbuck to Pages	40,000
Unrealized intercompany profit in ending inventory of Pages	1,000
Unrealized intercompany profit in ending inventory of Sawbuck	3,000
Unrealized intercompany profit in beginning inventory of Pages	1,400
Unrealized intercompany profit in beginning inventory of Sawbuck	900

Required:

(1) Prepare the elimination entries in general journal form for the intercompany sales and for the profit in the ending inventory.
(2) Assume Pages Company accounted for its investment in Sawbuck using the modified equity method. Record the elimination entries for the unrealized profit in the beginning inventory.
(3) Assume Pages Company accounted for its investment in Sawbuck using the full equity method. Record the elimination entries for the unrealized profit in the beginning inventory.

PROBLEMS

Problem 5-1   **(Equity adjustments and elimination entries)**

Barge Company and its wholly-owned subsidiary, Severe Shipping, had the following inter-company transactions during the year ended December 31, 20x2:

	Downstream Transactions	Upstream Transactions
Intercompany sales during 20x2	$40,000	$25,000
Markup percentage on sales	25%	20%
Intercompany inventory on hand on 12/31/20x2	$ 8,000	$ 5,000
Intercompany payables on 12/31/20x2	$ 2,000	$ 4,000

During the year ended 12/31/20x2, Severe Shipping had net income of $35,000 and paid $15,000 in dividends. Barge uses the cost method to account for its subsidiary investment.

Required:

(a) Prepare the book entries that Barge Company would make to account for its investment in Severe Shipping.
(b) Prepare the elimination entries for the 12/31/20x2 consolidated statements worksheet on account of the above intercompany transactions.

Problem 5-2   **(Equity adjustments and elimination entries)**

Bi-Hi Company and its 90%-owned subsidiary, Sel-Lo Company, had the following intercompany transactions during the year ended December 31, 20x2:

	Downstream Transactions	Upstream Transactions
Intercompany sales during 20x2	$15,000	$30,000
Markup percentage on sales	10%	15%
Intercompany inventory on hand on 12/31/20x2	$10,000	$ 5,000
Intercompany payables on 12/31/20x2	$ 0	$ 2,500

Bi-Hi uses the equity method to account for its investment in Sel-Lo, and makes equity adjustments for intercompany transactions. During the year ended December 31, 20x2, Sel-Lo Company had net income of $30,000 and paid $10,000 in dividends.

Required:

(a) Prepare the equity adjustments required on the books of Bi-Hi Company to account for its investment in Sel-Lo.
(b) Assuming that the balance in Bi-Hi Company's Investment in Sel-Lo account had a balance of $65,000 on January 1, 20x2, compute the book balance in this account on December 31, 20x2.
(c) Give the elimination entries required for the intercompany transactions in inventory for the worksheet for consolidated financial statements as of December 31, 20x2 for the two companies.

Problem 5-3   **(Equity adjustments)**

On January 1, 20x1, Penny Company purchased 100% of the outstanding common stock of Silver Company for $125,000, a price that was equal to book value. During the year ended December 31, 20x1, Penny sold $50,000 in merchandise to its 100% owned subsidiary, Silver. This merchandise was marked up 25% on cost. At the end of the year, $12,500 of this merchandise remained on hand in Silver's warehouse. During the years 20x1 and 20x2, Silver had net income and dividends as follows:

	20x1	20x2
Net income	$20,000	$30,000
Dividends	5,000	8,000

Required:

Prepare all the equity method adjustments that Penny would record on its books for the years 20x1 and 20x2.

Problem 5-4   **(Elimination entries)**

During the year ended December 31, 20x0, ParGolf Company sold $100,000 in merchandise inventory to its 80%-owned subsidiary, Leaderboard, Inc. This merchandise was marked up 30% on sales price. At the end of the year, $25,000 of this merchandise remained on hand in Leaderboard's inventory. Leaderboard also had $20,000 of inventory acquired from ParGolf at the beginning of the year, which had been marked up 40% on sales price, by ParGolf. There were no intercompany accounts receivable and payable at the end of the year 20x0.

Required:

(a) Calculate the unrealized intercompany profit in the Leaderboard inventory on January 1, 20x0, and December 31, 20x0.

(b) Assume that ParGolf uses the so-called modified equity method to account for its investment in Leaderboard, Inc. Prepare the elimination entries for the ParGolf-Leaderboard consolidation as of December 31, 20x0, on account of the intercompany transactions in inventory.

Problem 5-5

(Elimination entries)

Bigfoot Company retails children's footwear manufactured by its 80%-owned subsidiary, Comfort Shoe Company. During the year ended December 31, 20x4, Bigfoot purchased $400,000 in inventory from Comfort. This inventory was marked up $100,000 by Comfort. At the end of the year 20x4, 20% of this merchandise was on hand in various retail locations operated by Bigfoot. During the year ended December 31, 20x5, Sales by Comfort Shoe to Bigfoot totaled $620,000. This inventory was marked up $155,000, and $50,000 of it was on hand in Bigfoot's retail locations at the end of the year 20x5. Of the total purchases by Bigfoot during the year 20x5, $20,000 had been returned to Comfort because of manufacturing defects and $570,000 had been paid for.

Required:

(a) Compute the amount of unrealized gross profit in the Bigfoot Company inventory as of December 31, 20x4 and 20x5.

(b) Assume that Bigfoot uses the modified equity method to account for its investment in Comfort Shoe Company. Prepare the elimination entries needed for the December 31, 20x5, consolidated statements worksheet implied by the above data.

Problem 5-6

(Equity conversion and elimination entries)

On January 1, 1999, Gold Company acquired a 100% interest in Bronze Company in a purchase business combination whereby Gold Company issued 10,000 shares of its $1 par common stock in exchange for all of the outstanding common stock of Bronze Company. The book values and fair values of Bronze Company net assets were approximately equal on this date. Gold Company accounted for its investment in Bronze Company using the cost method. On the date of acquisition, Bronze Company had the following balances in its Stockholders' equity.

Common stock	$20,000
Additional paid-in capital	10,000
Retained earnings	50,000
Total	$80,000

On January 1, 2003, Bronze Company had a retained earnings balance of $140,000. During the year ended December 31, 2003, Bronze Company had net income of $50,000 and paid $20,000 in dividends. There has been no change in the contributed capital accounts of Bronze company since being acquired by Gold Company. The following table summarizes the intercompany sales by Gold Company to its subsidiary for the five years ending December 31, 2003:

Year ended	12/31/99	12/31/00	12/31/01	12/31/02	12/31/03
Sales volume	$20,000	$40,000	$45,000	$60,000	$75,000
Unrealized profit in ending inventory	1,000	3,000	5,000	10,000	15,000
Intercompany accounts payable at year-end	400	1,500	$7,000	$23,000	12,000

Required:

(a) Prepare the worksheet entry necessary to convert Gold Company's investment in Bronze Company to the modified equity method in the December 31, 2003, worksheet for consolidated financial and to eliminate investment income.

(b) Prepare Gold's elimination entries for intercompany transactions in inventory in the December 31, 2003, consolidated statements worksheet.

Problem 5-7   **(Consolidated income statement)**

Southern Products Company is a 90%-owned subsidiary of Pacific Wholesale, Inc. Pacific Wholesale acquired Southern Products several years ago at a price equal to book value and uses the modified equity method to account for its investment in the subsidiary. The two companies had the following separate operating data for the year ended December 31, 20x1:

	Pacific	Southern
Sales revenue	$ 150,000	$ 120,000
Equity in Southern income	27,000	
Cost of goods sold	58,000	55,000
Operating expenses	36,000	35,000
	$ 83,000	$ 30,000

During the year ended December 31, 20x1, Southern purchased $30,000 in inventory from Pacific that was marked up 40% on sales price. One-fourth of this inventory was still on hand in Southern's warehouse at year-end. Pacific's beginning inventory contained $10,000 of inventory purchased from Southern at a markup of 25% on cost.

Required:

Prepare a consolidated income statement for Pacific Wholesale, Inc. and subsidiary for the year ended December 31, 20x1.

Problem 5-8   **(Consolidated statements worksheet)**

Patterson Company acquired a 90% interest in Schmidt Company for $500,000 cash on January 1, 20x2, when Schmidt had common stock outstanding consisting of 50,000 shares of $4 par common stock and retained earnings of $300,000. The excess of cost over book value at the date of acquisition was considered to be goodwill. During the two years ended December 31, 20x2 and 20x3, Schmidt Company had book net income of $60,000 and $80,000, respectively, and paid dividends of $30,000 in 20x2 and $40,000 in 20x3.

For the two years ended December 31, 20x2 and 20x3, the two companies had intercompany transactions in inventory as illustrated in the following schedule:

	20x2	20x3
Intercompany sales—Schmidt to Patterson	$75,000	$80,000
Markup percent on sales	30%	40%
Intercompany inventory on hand at year-end	$20,000	$30,000
Unpaid Schmidt accounts receivable from intercompany sales	$12,000	$14,000

Patterson accounted for its investment in Schmidt using the modified equity method as reflected in the following financial statements prepared immediately prior to consolidation on December 31, 20x3:

Statement of Income	Patterson	Schmidt
For the Year ended 12/31/x3		
Sales	$ 340,000	$ 160,000
Equity in Schmidt income	72,000	
Cost of sales	(210,000)	(58,000)
Operating expenses	(74,000)	(22,000)
Net income	128,000	80,000
Retained earnings - P Jan. 1	250,000	
Retained earnings - S Jan. 1		330,000
Add controlling net income	128,000	80,000
Less: Dividends	(10,000)	(40,000)
Retained earnings, Dec. 31	368,000	370,000
Balance sheet 12/31/x3		
Cash	24,500	15,000
Accounts receivable	33,200	23,000
Inventories	62,500	45,000
Land	74,000	91,000
Buildings - net	175,300	235,000
Equipment - net	320,000	195,000
Investment in Schmidt	563,000	
	1,252,500	604,000
Accounts payable	34,500	34,000
Long-term debt	450,000	-
Common stock	400,000	200,000
Retained earnings	368,000	370,000
	$ 1,252,500	$ 604,000

Required:

(a) Prepare an allocation schedule for the Patterson-Schmidt combination as of the date of acquisition.

(b) Prepare the elimination entries for the December 31, 20x3, consolidated statements worksheet in journal form.

(c) Complete the consolidated statements worksheet as of December 31, 20x3.

Problem 5-9

(Consolidated statements worksheet)

Refer to the data in the first two paragraphs of problem 5-8. Assuming that Patterson Company had used the cost method to account for its investment in Schmidt, the financial statements as of December 31, 20x3, immediately prior to consolidation would appear as follows:

Statement of Income	Patterson	Schmidt
For the Year ended 12/31/x3		
Sales	$ 340,000	$ 160,000
Dividend income	36,000	
Cost of sales	(210,000)	(58,000)
Operating expenses	(74,000)	(22,000)
Net income	92,000	80,000
Retained earnings - P Jan. 1	223,000	
Retained earnings - S Jan. 1		330,000
Add controlling net income	92,000	80,000
Less: Dividends	(10,000)	(40,000)
Retained earnings, Dec. 31	305,000	370,000
Balance sheet 12/31/x3		
Cash	24,500	15,000
Accounts receivable	33,200	23,000
Inventories	62,500	45,000
Land	74,000	91,000
Buildings - net	175,300	235,000
Equipment - net	320,000	195,000
Investment in Schmidt	500,000	
	1,189,500	604,000
Accounts payable	34,500	34,000
Long-term debt	450,000	–
Common stock	400,000	200,000
Retained earnings	305,000	370,000
	$ 1,189,500	$ 604,000

Required:

(a) Prepare the elimination entries for the December 31, 20x3, consolidated statements worksheet in journal form.

(b) Complete the consolidated statements worksheet as of December 31, 20x3.

Problem 5-10

(Consolidated statements worksheet)

Refer to the data in the first two paragraphs of problem 5-8. Assuming that Patterson Company had used the full equity method to account for its investment in Schmidt, the financial statements as of December 31, 20x3, immediately prior to consolidation would appear as follows:

Statement of Income	Patterson	Schmidt
For the Year ended 12/31/x3		
Sales	$ 340,000	$ 160,000
Equity in Schmidt income	66,600	
Cost of sales	(210,000)	(58,000)
Operating expenses	(74,000)	(22,000)
Net income	122,600	80,000
Retained earnings - P Jan. 1	244,600	
Retained earnings - S Jan. 1		330,000
Add controlling net income	122,600	80,000
Less: Dividends	(10,000)	(40,000)
Retained earnings, Dec. 31	357,200	370,000
Balance sheet 12/31/x3		
Cash	24,500	15,000
Accounts receivable	33,200	23,000
Inventories	62,500	45,000
Land	74,000	91,000
Buildings - net	175,300	235,000
Equipment - net	320,000	195,000
Investment in Schmidt	552,200	
	1,241,700	604,000
Accounts payable	34,500	34,000
Long-term debt	450,000	-
Common stock	400,000	200,000
Retained earnings	357,200	370,000
	$ 1,241,700	$ 604,000

Required:

(a) Prepare the elimination entries for the December 31, 20x3, consolidated statements worksheet in general journal form.
(b) Complete the consolidated statements worksheet as of December 31, 20x3.

Problem 5-11

(Accounting for substantial influence investments)

Julie Daniels is the CPA in charge of the 12/31/20x1 audit of the McPherson Chemical Company, a new client of her firm, Simpkins and Daniels. McPherson has a subsidiary, Coastal States Chemical, Inc., in which it owns a 45% interest. Joe Calder, controller of McPherson, gave Ms. Daniels the following schedule:

Acquisition price of Coastal States Chemical, 1/1/19x9	$200,000
5-year loan to Coastal on 1/15/20x0	20,000
Interest received on loan 1/15/20x1	(2,000)
Dividends received 12/15/x1	(5,000)
Account balance in Investment in Coastal, 12/31/20x1	$213,000

Coastal's net income and dividends since its acquisition by McPherson is shown in the following table:

	19x9	20x0	20x1
Net income (loss)	$(40,000)	$5,000	$120,000
Dividends declared and paid	none	none	30,000

McPherson also purchased chemicals from its subsidiary, which were used as raw materials in production. These purchases totaled $200,000 in 19x9, $240,000 in 20x0, and $265,000 in 20x1. Unsold inventories from these purchases at the end of each of the three years were $20,000 in 19x9, $60,000 in 20x0, and $50,000 in 20x1. The inventories were uniformly marked up 30% on sales price at the time of sale by Coastal.

Required:

Assuming that Coastal States is a substantial influence investee from the perspective of McPherson, what adjusting entries should Julie Daniels propose for the Investment in Coastal States Chemical on the books of McPherson?

Problem 5-12

(Consolidated statements worksheet)

Jackson Company acquired a 100% interest in the common stock of Moore Company on January 1, 20x1, for a price of $320,000, at a time when Moore Company had common stock of $100,000 and retained earnings of $190,000. The $30,000 excess of cost over book value was assumed to be goodwill. At the end of the year 20x1, a review of the goodwill for impairment indicated that goodwill should be amortized over a three-year period. During the year ended December 31, 20x1, Jackson sold Moore Company $65,000 in merchandise marked up 20% on sales price. At the end of the year, $20,000 of this merchandise remained in Moore Company's inventory. Jackson Company used the modified equity method to account for its investment in Moore Company.

The financial statements of Jackson and Moore at the end of the year 20x1 are as follows:

Statement of Income	Jackson	Moore
For the Year ended 12/31/x1		
Sales	$ 542,000	$ 425,500
Equity in Moore income	124,500	
Cost of sales	(220,500)	(235,000)
Operating expenses	(47,000)	(66,000)
Net income	399,000	124,500
Retained earnings Jan. 1	135,000	160,000
Add net income	399,000	124,500
Less: Dividends	(160,000)	(40,000)
Retained earnings, Dec. 31	374,000	244,500
Balance sheet 12/31/x1		
Cash	120,000	53,000
Accounts receivable	72,000	30,400
Notes receivable	10,000	
Inventories	102,300	43,000
Land	80,000	30,000
Buildings - net	225,000	190,000
Machinery - net	330,000	205,000
Investment in Moore	404,500	
	1,343,800	551,400

Accounts payable	210,000	114,900
Dividends payable	25,000	
Other liabilities	400,000	92,000
Capital stock	334,800	100,000
Retained earnings, Dec. 31	374,000	244,500
	$ 1,343,800	$ 551,400

Required:

Prepare a consolidated financial statements worksheet for Jackson Company and Moore Company for the year ended December 31, 20x1.

Problem 5-13   **(Consolidated statements worksheet)**

Snowboard Products, Inc. is a 90%-owned subsidiary of Poplar Manufacturing Company, having been acquired in a purchase acquisition on January 1, 20x0, in exchange for 10,000 shares of Poplar no par value stock. On the date of acquisition, the book value and fair market value of Snowboard's net assets were approximately equal. Immediately prior to the combination, the two companies had the following capital accounts:

	Popular	**Snowboard**
Common stock	$ 50,000	$100,000
Additional paid-in capital	100,000	-
Retained earnings	125,000	75,000
	$150,000	$100,000

Poplar used the modified equity method to account for its investment in Snowboard. The following information is available regarding intercompany transactions between the two companies for the two years ended December 31, 20x4 and 20x5:

	Intercompany transactions	
	P to S	**S to P**
20x4 Intercompany sales	$30,000	$40,000
20x4 Intercompany inventory	10,000	5,000
20x5 Intercompany sales	36,000	24,000
20x5 Intercompany inventory	15,000	8,000
Gross profit rate on intercompany sales	30%	50%
12/31/x5 intercompany receivables	$12,000	$ 8,000

The financial statements of the two companies immediately prior to consolidation on December 31, 20x5, would be as follows:

Statement of Income	Poplar	Snowboard
For the Year ended 12/31/x5		
Sales	$ 350,500	$ 234,500
Equity in Snowboard income	27,000	
Cost of sales	(213,800)	(160,000)
Operating expenses	(98,700)	(44,500)
Net income	65,000	30,000
Retained earnings, Jan. 1	210,000	115,000
Add net income	65,000	30,000
Less: Dividends		(10,000)
Retained earnings, Dec. 31	275,000	135,000
Balance sheet 12/31/x5		
Cash	43,200	30,000
Accounts receivable	52,100	17,500
Dividends receivable	4,500	
Notes receivable	11,800	5,000
Inventories	65,000	50,000
Land	120,000	75,000
Buildings - net	200,000	120,000
Machinery - net	210,000	90,000
Investment in Snowboard	144,000	
	850,600	387,500
Accounts payable	133,400	12,000
Dividends payable	-	5,000
Long-term debt	269,700	210,500
Capital stock	72,500	25,000
Additional paid-in capital	100,000	
Retained earnings, Dec. 31	275,000	135,000
	$ 850,600	$ 387,500

Required:

(a) Prepare the elimination entries in journal form for the Poplar-Snowboard Consolidation as of 12/31/20x5.

(b) Complete a consolidated statements worksheet as of 12/31/x5.

Problem 5-14   **(Consolidated statements worksheet)**

Refer to the data in the first two paragraphs of problem 5-13. Had Poplar prepared equity adjustments for the intercompany transactions, the financial statements of the two companies would have appeared as follows:

Statement of Income	Poplar	Snowboard
For the Year ended 12/31/x5		
Sales	$350,500	$234,500
Equity in Snowboard income	24,150	
Cost of sales	(213,800)	(160,000)
Operating expenses	(98,700)	(44,500)
Net income	62,150	30,000
Retained earnings, Jan. 1	204,750	115,000
Add net income	62,150	30,000
Less: Dividends		(10,000)
Retained earnings, Dec. 31	266,900	135,000
Balance sheet 12/31/x5		
Cash	43,200	30,000
Accounts receivable	52,100	17,500
Dividends receivable	4,500	
Notes receivable	11,800	5,000
Inventories	65,000	50,000
Land	120,000	75,000
Buildings - net	200,000	120,000
Machinery - net	210,000	90,000
Investment in Snowboard	135,900	
	842,500	387,500
Accounts payable	133,400	12,000
Dividends payable	-	5,000
Long-term debt	269,700	210,500
Capital stock	72,500	25,000
Additional paid-in capital	100,000	
Retained earnings, Dec. 31	266,900	135,000
	$842,500	$387,500

Required:

(a) Prepare the elimination entries in journal form for the Poplar-Snowboard Consolidation as of December 31, 20x5.
(b) Complete a worksheet for preparation of consolidated financial statements for the year ended December 31, 20x5.

CHAPTER 6

INTERCOMPANY TRANSACTIONS IN PLANT ASSETS

LEARNING OBJECTIVES

- Explain the conceptual issues underlying intercompany transactions in plant assets

- Record equity adjustments for intercompany transactions in plant assets

- Record consolidated statements worksheet elimination entries for intercompany transactions in plant assets

- Prepare consolidated statements worksheets, which include elimination entries for intercompany transactions in plant assets

CONCEPTUAL ISSUES UNDERLYING INTERCOMPANY TRANSACTIONS IN PLANT ASSETS

Intercompany transactions in plant assets are similar to the inventory transactions covered in Chapter 5. Recall that intercompany sale of inventory normally involves the sale of items that the buyer uses as components. Thus, intercompany sale of inventory affects accounting for the buyer's inventory and cost of goods sold. Intercompany sale of plant assets involves the sale of plant assets that are **used** in production. Accordingly, these transactions affect the subsequent accounting for plant assets. Because plant assets involved in the intercompany transactions, with the exception of land, are subject to depreciation, depreciation accounting may also be affected by the intercompany transactions in plant assets.

Equity adjustments and elimination entries for intercompany transactions in plant assets are similar to entries for intercompany inventory transactions. The objectives of these entries are to defer unrealized profit from intercompany transactions until the year in which the unrealized profit may be properly included in consolidated net income in accordance with the **realization** concept. The only complicating factor in analysis of intercompany plant asset transactions is that, unlike inventory, the intercompany buyer normally retains plant assets. Furthermore, building and equipment assets thus acquired are subsequently depreciated on the books of the buyer based on the intercompany price.

Because plant assets are held and used by the intercompany buyer, elimination entries for intercompany transactions in plant assets have several elements. First, the plant assets will be on the books of the intercompany buyer at the intercompany price. **The consolidated financial statements must show these assets at the original owner's cost.** Second, in the year of the intercompany transaction, there will be a gain or loss account on the books of the intercompany seller equal to the difference between the book value of the assets at the time of sale and the intercompany price. **This gain or loss is not reportable in the consolidated income statement.** Finally, the depreciation recorded by the intercompany buyer reflects the intercompany price of the assets in all years subsequent to the intercompany transaction. **Consolidated depreciation must be based on original owner's cost.** Since elimination entries are not booked, the above events must be taken into account in each consolidation worksheet subsequent to an intercompany transaction in plant assets as long as the assets are still in use.

To summarize, intercompany transactions in plant assets require elimination entries that accomplish the following objectives:

1. Adjust the carrying value of plant assets acquired in intercompany transactions to the original owner's historical cost.
2. Eliminate any gain or loss arising from intercompany sale of the plant assets in the current year financial statements.
3. Adjust the current year's depreciation expense to equal depreciation based on consolidated historical cost of plant assets.
4. Adjust the accumulated depreciation balances for assets acquired in prior years' intercompany to reflect consolidated historical cost.

COST AND EQUITY METHOD ISSUES

As in the case of intercompany transactions in inventor,y the parent company can choose to use the cost method or the modified equity method, making no equity adjustments for intercompany profit[1] transactions. Alternatively, the parent company can elect to make equity adjustments for intercompany profit transactions, following the full equity method. As will be illustrated, the exact form of some elimination entries for intercompany profit in plant assets is altered slightly depending upon whether any equity adjustments were recorded for these transactions on the books of the parent company. Following is an illustration of the equity adjustments for intercompany profit in plant assets that the parent company would make if it chooses to follow the full equity method. The illustrations differentiate between transactions involving land (a non-depreciable asset) and equipment (a depreciable asset). The illustrations for equipment would be equally applicable to other depreciable assets such as buildings.

Downstream sale of land

Assume that Parker Company sells land with a book value of $20,000 to its wholly-owned subsidiary Spencer Company for $30,000 on January 1, 20x1. The appropriate equity adjustment for this event is as follows:

12/31/20x1	Equity in Spencer Company Income	10,000	
	Investment in Spencer Company		10,000

The purpose of this entry is to reduce the parent company's book income by the amount of the gain it reported on the sale of the land asset to its subsidiary. Under the equity method, the gain account itself cannot be adjusted. This entry is required for unconsolidated subsidiaries by *APB Opinion 18*, and is optional for consolidated subsidiaries. As you will see, the form of the elimination entry for the intercompany gain is potentially affected by the parent company's decision to record or not record the above equity adjustment.

Recall that in the case of inventories, equity adjustments to defer intercompany profit **are reversed in the following accounting period,** in the year that the inventory is resold to outsiders[2]. In effect, this reversal realizes the deferred intercompany profit in the inventory. In the case of land, however, **no subsequent equity adjustment (reversal) is made unless the subsidiary resells the land to an outside entity.** The realization concept does not permit recognition of the deferred intercompany gain on land in absence of a subsequent resale. **Existence of a noncontrolling interest does not change the equity adjustments for downstream transactions. In the case of upstream sales, the entries are altered only if there is a noncontrolling interest.**

Upstream sale of land with a noncontrolling interest

Now assume that Spencer Company is a 90%-owned subsidiary of Parker Company. If Spencer Company sells land with a book value of $20,000 to Parker Company for $30,000, the equity adjustment is altered slightly from the downstream case:

---

[1] Intercompany transactions in plant assets could result in either losses or gains. All of the illustrations in this chapter depict scenarios involving gains. The accounting principles illustrated are equally applicable to loss transactions. In the opinion of the author, intercompany transactions involving losses are likely to occur only rarely in actual practice.

[2] The statement "resold to outsiders" includes the case of inventory being used in the production process as a component of a product that is then sold in the ordinary course of business.

| 12/31/20x1 | Equity in Spencer Company Income | **9,000** | |
| | Investment in Spencer Company | | **9,000** |

In this case, the equity adjustment is made for the controlling interest share of the gain: $10,000 × 90% = $9,000. Parker's entry to record equity income is based on the book income of Spencer, which includes the intercompany gain. The equity adjustment is necessary to reduce the parent company's equity income account by $9,000. This entry is based on the assumption that the 10% noncontrolling interest share of the intercompany gain is not deferred. As in the case of the downstream sale, this entry is not reversed in a subsequent accounting period unless the land is resold to an outside party by the parent company. Also, as will be shown, some of the elimination entries for intercompany profit on the consolidated statements worksheet are affected by the election to record or not record equity adjustments for subsidiaries on the parent company books.

Downstream sale of equipment

Equity adjustments for intercompany transactions in depreciable assets are more complex than for land. It is assumed that deferred intercompany gains on depreciable assets **are realized through use.** This procedure is accomplished by reversing the deferral entry in increments over the years of remaining life of the depreciable asset. To illustrate, assume that on January 1, 20x1, Parker Company sells equipment with a remaining useful life of five years, an original cost of $40,000, and a book value of $10,000 to its wholly-owned subsidiary, Spencer Company, for $15,000. Note that this transaction results in a book gain of $5,000 on Parker's books.

Sale price of equipment		$ 15,000
Original cost	$ 40,000	
Accumulated depreciation	30,000	
Book value		10,000
Gain		$ 5,000

Two equity adjustments are required. One entry defers the intercompany gain of $5,000 and another entry realizes the portion of the deferred gain assumed to be realized through the use of the asset for the year ended 12/31/20x1. These two entries are shown below:

12/31/20x1	Equity in Spencer Company Income	5,000	
	Investment in Spencer Company		5,000
	To defer the intercompany gain ($15,000 sales price − book value of $10,000)		

12/31/20x1	Investment in Spencer Company	1,000	
through	Equity in Spencer Company Income		1,000
12/31/20x5			
	To realize one-fifth of the deferred gain ($5,000/5 = $1,000)		

The first entry reduces equity income to compensate for the parent company's reporting of the $5,000 gain on the sale of equipment. The gain account itself cannot be adjusted under the equity method. The second entry realizes one-fifth of the deferred gain. This second entry is repeated each year until the original deferred gain of $5,000 is fully realized. In this case, the second entry would be recorded at the end of the years 20x1 through 20x5. The upstream sale case is recorded in exactly the same manner, unless there is a noncontrolling interest.

Upstream sale of equipment with a noncontrolling interest

In the case of a noncontrolling interest, the entries are made only for the controlling interest share of the intercompany gain. Assume that Spencer Company is a 90%-owned subsidiary of Parker Company and that on January 1, 20x1, it sells equipment with an original cost of $40,000, a book value of $10,000, and a remaining useful life of five years to the parent Company, Parker, for $15,000. The appropriate equity adjustments recorded by Parker on December 31, 20x1, are:

12/31/20x1	Equity in Spencer Company Income	**4,500**	
	Investment in Spencer Company		**4,500**

Intercompany gain × controlling interest % = $5,000 × 90% = $4,500

12/31/20x1	Investment in Spencer Company	**900**	
through	Equity in Spencer Company Income		**900**
12/31/20x5			

To realize one-fifth of the deferred gain ($4,500/5 = $900)

The first entry compensates for the fact that the parent's equity income account includes 90% of the gain. As in the downstream case, the second entry is repeated in each of the following four years, until the gain is fully realized. Remember that equity adjustments are reflected only in the two accounts, **Investment in Subsidiary** and **Equity in Subsidiary Income,** and that these entries are the only entries made on the books of the parent company with respect to intercompany transactions. Also remember that these equity method adjustments are **required only for unconsolidated subsidiaries or for substantial influence investments** in which the investor does not exercise a controlling interest. In the case of a parent company using the cost method or modified equity method to account for its investment in subsidiary, equity adjustments are not made for intercompany transactions. **The exact form of some of the elimination entries made for intercompany transactions, however, are affected by the parent company's choice of the cost method, modified equity method, or full equity method in accounting for its Investment in Subsidiary.** These procedures are illustrated in the remaining sections of this chapter.

ELIMINATION ENTRIES

As was the case for inventory transactions, the choice of **cost method, modified equity method,** or **full equity method** for the Investment in subsidiary account affects **some** of the elimination entries for intercompany sales of plant assets. Specifically, there are two approaches to elimination entries based on the parent company's method of accounting for its Investment in Subsidiary:

1. Elimination entries where no equity method adjustments are made for the intercompany transactions. These procedures would be followed if the parent company uses either the **cost method** or the **modified equity method.**
2. Elimination entries where equity method adjustments are made for the intercompany transactions. These procedures would be followed if the parent company accounts for its investment in subsidiary under the **full equity** method.

All of the following illustrations are based on the data used in the equity method illustrations shown above. This data, for the Parker Company and Spencer Company illustrations, is summarized in the following tables:

Intercompany Land Sale on January 1, 20x1	
Original historical cost of land	$20,000
Intercompany price	30,000

Intercompany Equipment Sale on January 1, 20x1	
Original historical cost of equipment	$40,000
Accumulated depreciation at the time of intercompany sale	30,000
Intercompany price	15,000
Remaining useful life	5 years

Modified equity and cost method situations—downstream sales
Land sale

1. Year 1 (12/31/x1)

In the year of the intercompany sale, an elimination entry is needed to eliminate the intercompany gain on Parker's books and restate the land account to its original historical cost of $20,000.

12/31/20x1	Gain on Sale of Land	10,000	
	Land		10,000

A partial worksheet showing how the above entry appears in the Parker-Spencer consolidated statements worksheet for the year 20x1is shown below:

Partial Worksheet	Parker	Spencer	Eliminations		Consolidated
Income statement 12/31/x1					
Gain on sale of land	$10,000	$ –	(1) $10,000		$ –
Balance sheet					
Land*		30,000	(1)	10,000	20,000

*The book balance of Spencer's land account is assumed to be $30,000 for illustration purposes. The consolidated balance in Spencer's land account is reduced $10,000 by entry (1).

2. Years 2–n (12/31/x2 and thereafter until land is disposed of)

In subsequent years' consolidated statements worksheets, the retained earnings of Parker will be overstated from a consolidated perspective because it reflects the gain on the sale of land in the year 20x1, which was included in Parker's book income for that year. This entry is made on every consolidated statements worksheet subsequent to the year 20x1 until the land is sold or otherwise disposed of.

12/31/20x2 through year **n**	**Retained Earnings—Parker**	10,000	
	Land		10,000

A partial worksheet showing how the above entry appear in the Parker-Spencer consolidated statements worksheet for the year 20x2 and thereafter is shown below:

Partial Worksheet—years 2–n	Parker	Spencer	Eliminations		Consolidated
Retained earnings statement					
Retained earnings—Parker*	$ XXX	$ –	(1) $10,000		$ XXX
Balance sheet					
Land*		30,000	(1)	10,000	20,000

*Whatever the balance in Parker book retained earnings, the consolidated retained earnings will be $10,000 less as a result of entry (1). The book balance of Spencer's land account is assumed to be $30,000 for illustration purposes and is reduced $10,000 by entry (1).

Equipment sale

1. Year 1 (12/31/x1)

An entry is required to eliminate the gain on the intercompany sale of the equipment on Parker's books and increase the book balance of the equipment from the intercompany purchase price of $15,000 to its original purchase price of $40,000. The accumulated depreciation account balance, $0 after the intercompany sale, is restated to its presale balance of $30,000. The second entry realizes $1,000 of the gain, which was deferred in the first entry, by reducing the depreciation expense on the equipment.

12/31/x1	Gain on Sale of Equipment	5,000	
	Equipment	25,000	
	Accumulated Depreciation—Equipment		30,000

| 12/31/x1 | Accumulated Depreciation—Equipment | 1,000 | |
| | Depreciation Expense | | 1,000 |

Theoretically, the second entry is a realization through use. Parker Company's separate financial statements prior to consolidation show a $5,000 gain on the sale of the equipment to its subsidiary Spencer. Spencer's separate financial statements show the asset at $15,000, an amount that is $5,000 more than Parker's book value of $10,000 immediately prior to the intercompany sale. As a result of the higher book value, the book depreciation (Spencer's books) on the asset is $3,000 ($15,000 ÷ 5), whereas depreciation based on the original $10,000 book value of Parker would have been $2,000 ($10,000 ÷ 5). Accordingly, the second elimination entry reduces the depreciation expense by $1,000, the amount that would have been recorded based on a consolidated equipment book value of $10,000 and a remaining life of five years.[3] This entry has the effect of increasing income by reducing depreciation expense and thus constitutes a partial realization of $1,000 of the $5,000 deferred gain. A partial worksheet for the Parker-Spencer Consolidation showing the two entries for the equipment sale is as follows:

---

[3] All illustrations assume the use of straight-line depreciation.

Partial Worksheet 12/31/x1	Parker	Spencer	Eliminations				Consolidated
Income statement							
Gain on sale of equipment	$ 5,000	$ –	(1)	$ 5,000			$ –
Depreciation expense*	(4,500)	(5,300)			(2)	1,000	(8,800)
Balance sheet							
Equipment*	45,000	53,000	(1)	25,000			123,000
Accumulated depreciation*	(15,000)	(32,000)	(2)	1,000	(1)	30,000	(76,000)

*The unconsolidated balances for Depreciation Expense, Equipment, and Accumulated Depreciation are assumed for purposes of illustration.

2. Year 2 (12/31/x2)

In the consolidated statements worksheet for the second year, Parker's separate financial statements do not show a gain since that account was closed to Retained Earnings on December 31, 20x1. Thus, an elimination entry is needed to reduce Parker's Retained Earnings by $4,000, the difference between the $5,000 deferred gain and the $1,000 gain realized in **year 1.** The credit to Accumulated Depreciation is likewise made for the $29,000 difference between the Accumulated Depreciation credit of $30,000 and the Accumulated Depreciation debit of $1,000 recorded in the two elimination entries for **year 1.** A second entry realizes an additional $1,000 of the deferred intercompany gain. This entry is identical to the second entry for the year 20x1. These two entries are shown below:

12/31/20x2	**Retained Earnings—Parker**	**4,000**	
	Equipment		25,000
	Accumulated Depreciation—Equipment		**29,000**

12/31/20x2	Accumulated Depreciation—Equipment	1,000	
	Depreciation Expense		1,000

Remember that elimination entries are not booked, so the effects of the elimination entries for previous years must be recorded each year when the consolidated statements worksheet is prepared anew. The effect of the 20x2 elimination entries on the accumulated depreciation account for this asset are shown in the following T account:

	Accumulated Depreciation Equipment	
Spencer accumulated depreciation 12/31/20x2		6,000
Elimination entries as of 12/31/20x2	1,000	29,000
Balance		34,000

Posting the two elimination entries in the worksheet at the end of the year 20x2 results in an accumulated depreciation balance equal to what Parker would have shown had it not sold the asset. This balance of $34,000 is equal to the accumulated depreciation balance of $30,000 prior to the intercompany sale plus two years depreciation based on a 5-year remaining life applied to the $10,000 book value at the time of the intercompany sale ($30,000 + $2,000 + $2,000 = $34,000). A partial worksheet for the Parker-Spencer Consolidation showing the two entries for the equipment sale in the year x2 is as follows:

Partial Worksheet 12/31/x2	Parker	Spencer		Eliminations			Consolidated
Income statement							
Depreciation expense*	(4,500)	(5,300)			(2) 1,000		(8,800)
Retained earnings statement							
Retained earnings—Parker*	XXX		(1)	**4,000**			XXX
Balance sheet							
Equipment*	45,000	53,000	(1)	25,000			123,000
Accumulated depreciation*	(15,000)	(32,000)	(2)	1,000	(1)	**29,000**	(75,000)

*The unconsolidated balances for Depreciation Expense, Equipment, and Accumulated Depreciation are assumed for purposes of illustration. Whatever the balance in Parker Retained Earnings, entry (1) would reduce it by $4,000.

3. Subsequent years (12/31/x3–x5)

Comparing the entries for the years 20x1 and 20x2 reveals the general pattern that the elimination entries follow. In the first year, the intercompany gain is eliminated. In each subsequent year, the retained earnings account of the parent company is debited for **the unrealized deferred intercompany gain.** (In this illustration, that amount is $4,000 in 20x2; $3,000 in 20x3; etc.) In all years, the asset balance is restated to original historical cost, and accumulated depreciation is adjusted to the correct balance for each date based on original historical cost. Finally, depreciation expense is adjusted to reflect realization of the appropriate amount of deferred intercompany gain (or loss) based on the remaining life of the asset at the time of the intercompany sale.

The above procedures are unaffected by the existence of a noncontrolling interest. The entries are likewise unaffected in the case of upstream sales if the subsidiary is 100% owned. However, the upstream sale case is somewhat different if there is a noncontrolling interest. These procedures are shown in the following section.

Modified equity and cost method situations— upstream sales with a noncontrolling interest

Land sale

1. Year 1 (12/31/x1)

Now assume that Spencer is a 90%-owned subsidiary of Parker and that the intercompany transactions were upstream sales. **In the case of an upstream sale of land, the elimination entry is identical to that for the downstream case in the year of the intercompany transaction.** The gain on the sale of land is now on the subsidiary's books, but the elimination entry, whose purpose is to eliminate the gain and reduce the land account to its presale balance, is the same.

12/31/20x1	Gain on Sale of Land	10,000	
	Land		10,000

A partial worksheet showing how the above entry appears in the Parker-Spencer consolidated statements worksheet for the year 20x1is shown below:

Partial Worksheet 12/31/x1	Parker	Spencer	Eliminations		Consolidated
Income statement					
Gain on sale of land	$ –	$10,000	(1) $10,000		$ –
Balance sheet					
Land*	45,000		(1) 10,000		35,000

*The book balance of Parker's land account is assumed for purposes of illustration and is reduced $10,000 by entry (1).

2. Years 2–n (12/31/x2 and thereafter until land is disposed of)

In the second year, the fact that the intercompany transaction was upstream has an impact on the noncontrolling interest balance. The land account must still be reduced by $10,000, so that the land is reported at $20,000, its historical cost prior to the intercompany sale. Since the gain was on the subsidiary's books, the noncontrolling interest is affected, resulting in the following entry:

12/31/20x1	**Retained Earnings—Parker**	**9,000**	
	Noncontrolling Interest	**1,000**	
	Land		10,000

The debit to Retained earnings—Parker is analogous to a correction of prior years' earnings. Under cost and modified equity procedures, Parker does not make equity adjustments for intercompany profits. If the cost method is used, an adjustment is needed to convert Parker's books to modified equity as of the beginning of the year being consolidated. Thus, under either cost or modified equity, Parker's beginning Retained Earnings will include $9,000 of the intercompany gain because the gain was included in the subsidiary income in the year of the intercompany sale. Since the intercompany gain is not a proper component of consolidated retained earnings, it may not be included in consolidated retained earnings. The debit to noncontrolling interest is made for the same reason. The elimination entry establishing the noncontrolling interest is based on subsidiary book Retained Earnings, a balance that includes the intercompany gain from the prior year. Since the gain cannot be recognized in the consolidated financial statements, the noncontrolling interest is reduced to eliminate recognition of the noncontrolling interest share of the prior year gain. A partial worksheet showing how the above entry appear in the Parker-Spencer consolidated statements worksheet for the year 20x2 and thereafter is shown below:

Partial Worksheet—years 2–n	Parker	Spencer	Eliminations		Consolidated
Retained earnings statement					
Retained earnings—Parker*	$ XXX		(1) 9,000		$ XXX
Balance sheet					
Land*	45,000		(1) 10,000		35,000
Noncontrolling interest*			(1) 1,000		XX*

*Whatever the balance in Parker's retained earnings account, it is reduced $9,000 by entry (1). The book balance Parker's land account is assumed for illustration purposes and is reduced $10,000 by entry 1. The consolidated balance for Noncontrolling Interest is not given because it is affected by other entries not illustrated.

Equipment sale

1. Year 1 (12/31/x1)

In the case of an upstream sale of equipment, the elimination entry is identical to that for the downstream case in the year of the intercompany

transaction. The gain is now on the subsidiary's books, but the first elimination entry, whose purpose is to eliminate the gain and restate the equipment cost and accumulated depreciation to the presale balances, is the same. The second entry is also identical to the downstream case. This entry adjusts the subsidiary's depreciation account to reflect the reduction in depreciable basis caused by the first entry, and in the process, realizes one-fifth of the deferred gain.

12/31/20x1	Gain on Sale of Equipment	5,000	
	Equipment	25,000	
	Accumulated Depreciation—Equipment		30,000

| 12/31/20x1 | Accumulated Depreciation—Equipment | 1,000 | |
| | Depreciation Expense | | 1,000 |

A partial worksheet for the Parker-Spencer Consolidation showing the two entries for the equipment sale is as follows:

Partial Worksheet 12/31/x1	Parker	Spencer		Eliminations			Consolidated
Income statement							
Gain on sale of equipment	$ –	$ 5,000	(1)	$ 5,000			$ –
Depreciation expense*	(4,500)	(5,300)			(2)	1,000	(8,800)
Balance sheet							
Equipment*	45,000	53,000	(1)	25,000			123,000
Accumulated depreciation*	(15,000)	(32,000)	(2)	1,000	(1)	30,000	(76,000)

*The unconsolidated balances for Depreciation Expense, Equipment, and Accumulated Depreciation are assumed for illustration purposes.

2. Year 2 (12/31/x2)

In the consolidated statements worksheet for the second year, Spencer's separate financial statements do not show a gain since that account was closed to Retained Earnings on December 31, 20x1. The modified equity procedures or the equity conversion entry (in the case of the cost method) result in 90% of this gain also being reflected in parent company Retained Earnings. Furthermore, since 90% of Spencer's Retained Earnings are eliminated, with 10% going to the noncontrolling interest account, the appropriate elimination entry for the second year reduces Parker's Retained Earnings and the noncontrolling interest by 90% and 10%, respectively, of the deferred unrealized gain.

12/31/20x2	**Retained Earnings—Parker**	3,600	
	Noncontrolling Interest	400	
	Equipment	25,000	
	Accumulated Depreciation—Equipment		**29,000**

| 12/31/20x2 | Accumulated Depreciation—Equipment | 1,000 | |
| | Depreciation Expense | | 1,000 |

Note that the only difference between the above entry and the entry for the downstream transaction is that the $4,000 debit to Parker's Retained Earnings in the downstream case becomes, in the upstream case, a $3,600 debit with the remaining $400 being debited to the noncontrolling interest. Prorating the debits for the

$4,000 deferred gain to Parker Retained Earnings and Noncontrolling Interest is required because Parker's Retained Earnings includes only 90% of this gain and because 10% of the subsidiary's Retained Earnings becomes part of the noncontrolling interest in the consolidated financial statements. A partial worksheet for the Parker-Spencer Consolidation showing the two entries for the equipment sale in the year x2 is as follows:

Partial Worksheet 12/31/x2	Parker	Spencer		Eliminations			Consolidated
Income statement							
Depreciation expense*	(4,500)	(5,300)			(2) 1,000		(8,800)
Retained earnings statement							
Retained earnings—Parker*	XXX		(1)	3,600			XXX
Balance sheet							
Equipment*	45,000	53,000	(1)	25,000			123,000
Accumulated depreciation*	(15,000)	(32,000)	(2)	1,000	(1)	29,000	(75,000)
Noncontrolling interest*			(1)	400			XXX

*The unconsolidated balances for Depreciation Expense, Equipment, and Accumulated Depreciation are assumed for illustration purposes. Whatever the balance for Parker Retained Earnings, it is reduced $3,600 by entry (1). The ending balance of Noncontrolling Interest is not given because it is affected by other elimination entries not illustrated.

3. Subsequent years (12/31/x3–x5)

The subsequent years' elimination entries through the year 20x5 (five years after the intercompany sale) follow the pattern established above. The amount of the unrealized deferred gain on the intercompany sale declines by $1,000 each year so that its balance is as follows:

Year	Unrealized Gain 1/1	Amount Realized	Unrealized Gain 12/31
20x1	$ 5,000	$ 1,000	$ 4,000
20x2	4,000	1,000	3,000
20x3	3,000	1,000	2,000
20x4	2,000	1,000	1,000
20x5	1,000	1,000	–

The amount of the unrealized gain at the end of each year is prorated between the parent's retained earnings and the noncontrolling interest, in the ratio of controlling interest % to noncontrolling interest % in each of the subsequent years. Note that this entry is made for the amount of the unrealized gain as of the beginning of each year with a second entry made for the amount of the gain realized in that year.

Full equity situations—downstream sales

Land sale

1. Year 1 (12/31/x1)

Both the entry to eliminate gain on the sale of land in the year of the sale and the worksheet procedures are the same under the *full equity method* as for the *modified equity* or *cost method.* The gain account on the books of Parker Company is eliminated and the land account is reduced to the original owner's cost. The entry and partial worksheet illustration follow:

| | 12/31/20x1 | Gain on Sale of land | 10,000 | |
| | | Land | | 10,000 |

Partial Worksheet 12/31/x1	Parker	Spencer		Eliminations				Consolidated	
Income statement									
Gain on sale of land	$10,000	$ –	(1)	$10,000		$	–	$	–
Balance sheet									
Land*		30,000			(1)	10,000		20,000	

*The book balance of Spencer's land account is assumed to be $30,000 for illustration purposes and is reduced $10,000 by entry (1).

2. Years 2–n (12/31/x2 and thereafter until the land is disposed of)

When the full equity method is employed, the Retained earnings of subsequent years is not overstated because the equity adjustment reduces parent company Retained Earnings by debiting the account Equity in Subsidiary Earnings for the amount of the intercompany gain and **crediting the investment in subsidiary account.** Accordingly, the elimination entry for years 2–n under the full equity method requires a debit to the account for Investment in Subsidiary. This entry and the example partial worksheet are shown below:

| | 12/31/20x2 through year *n* | *Investment in Spencer* | 10,000 | |
| | | Land | | 10,000 |

Partial Worksheet —years 2–n	Parker	Spencer		Eliminations				Consolidated	
Balance sheet									
Investment in Spencer*	$ XXX	$ –	(1)	$10,000		$	–	$ XXX	
Land*		30,000			(1)	10,000		20,000	

*Whatever the balance in Investment in Spencer, entry (1) increases it by $10,000. Its consolidated balance will be zero, having been fully eliminated by other entries not shown in this illustration. The book balance for Spencer's land account is assumed to be $30,000 for illustration purposes and is reduced $10,000 by entry (1).

Had no equity adjustment been made for the deferred intercompany profit, the Investment account would have been $10,000 higher. The elimination entry in *years 2–n* thus substitutes a debit to Investment in Spencer for the debit to Retained Earnings, which was made under the modified equity and cost method approaches. An alternative way to explain the debit to Investment in Spencer for $10,000 is to note that the equity adjustment to defer the intercompany profit credits the Investment in Spencer for the amount of the deferred gain. This entry alters the reciprocal relationship between the Investment in Spencer and the stockholders' equity of the subsidiary because the subsidiary retained earnings account reflects the gain, while the investment in subsidiary does not. It is therefore necessary to debit the Investment in Spencer account when eliminating the deferred intercompany gain in order to reestablish the proper reciprocal relationship between the investment in subsidiary and the stockholders' equity accounts of the subsidiary. Failure to do so will result in an incorrect balance in the unamortized differential when the subsidiary's stockholders' equity is eliminated against the investment in subsidiary account. The above entry is made in every subsequent worksheet as long as the land remains on the books of the subsidiary at the intercompany price—essentially until it is sold or otherwise disposed of.

Equipment sale

1. Year 1 (12/31/x1)

As was the case for the land sale, the entries under the full equity method to eliminate intercompany profit under the **full equity method** are identical to the entries under the **modified equity** and **cost methods.** The first entry eliminates the intercompany gain and restates both the asset and accumulated depreciation accounts to their presale balances. The second entry realizes an appropriate portion of the deferred gain via a reduction of depreciation expense. These two entries along with a partial worksheet are shown below:

12/31/20x1	Gain on Sale of Equipment	5,000	
	Equipment	25,000	
	Accumulated Depreciation—Equipment		30,000

| 12/31/20x1 | Accumulated Depreciation—Equipment | 1,000 | |
| | Depreciation Expense | | 1,000 |

Partial Worksheet 12/31/x1	Parker	Spencer		Eliminations			Consolidated
Income statement							
Gain on sale of equipment	$ 5,000	$ –	(1)	$ 5,000			$ –
Depreciation expense*	(4,500)	(5,300)			(2)	1,000	(8,800)
Balance sheet							
Equipment*	45,000	53,000	(1)	25,000			123,000
Accumulated depreciation*	(15,000)	(32,000)	(2)	1,000	(1)	30,000	(76,000)

*The book balances for Depreciation Expense, Equipment, and Accumulated Depreciation are assumed for illustration purposes.

2. Year 2 (12/31/x2)

In the consolidated statements for the second year, Parker Company's financial statements will not show a gain since that account was closed to Retained Earnings on December 31, 20x1. In addition, Parker Company would have reduced its Retained Earnings and its Investment in Spencer by a net of $4,000 in its equity method adjustments when using the full equity method.[4] Thus, the entry to eliminate deferred intercompany profit in the second year requires a debit to the investment in Spencer in place of the debit to Retained Earnings, which was made under the modified equity and cost method scenarios. The second entry realizes an additional $1,000 of the deferred intercompany gain in accordance with the concept of **realization through use.** This entry is identical to the second elimination entry for the year 20x1. These two entries and the related partial worksheet are shown below:

12/31/20x2	**Investment in Spencer**	**4,000**	
	Equipment	25,000	
	Accumulated Depreciation—Equipment		**29,000**

---

[4] Refer to the previous section of this chapter on the subject of equity adjustments under the full equity method for an illustration and discussion of these journal entries.

12/31/20x2	Accumulated Depreciation—Equipment	1,000	
	Depreciation expense		1,000

Partial Worksheet 12/31/x2	Parker	Spencer		Eliminations			Consolidated
Income statement							
Depreciation expense*	$(4,500)	$(5,300)		(2)	$ 1,000		$ (8,800)
Balance sheet							
Investment in Spencer*	XXX		(1)	**4,000**			XXX
Equipment*	45,000	53,000	(1)	25,000			123,000
Accumulated depreciation*	(15,000)	(32,000)	(2)	1,000	(1)	**29,000**	(75,000)

*The book balances for Depreciation Expense, Equipment, and Accumulated Depreciation are assumed for illustration purposes. Whatever the balance for Investment in Spencer, it is increased $4,000 by entry (1) and is fully eliminated in the consolidated financial statements.

3. Subsequent years (12/31/x3–x5)

The journal entries in subsequent years follow the pattern shown above. The amount of unrealized deferred gain eliminated by a debit to the investment in Spencer account declines by $1,000 each year until it is fully realized. Thus, the amount of the debit to Investment in Spencer for the year 20x3 in the first elimination entry would be $3,000; in the year 20x4, it would be $2,000; etc. The second entry is recorded in the same manner in each year's worksheet through the year 20x5, after which time the deferred gain is fully realized and no further realizations are made. If and when Spencer Company disposes of the asset, no additional entries are made except to recognize any unrealized deferred intercompany gain in the year the asset is sold or retired.

▶ INTERPRETIVE EXERCISE

If Spencer sold the asset for $6,000 on December 31, 20x3, what elimination entries would be made for the deferred intercompany gain in the consolidated statements worksheet on that date?

The above procedures for **full equity** situations apply to all downstream transactions and to all upstream transactions unless a noncontrolling interest exists. An example for an upstream transaction with a noncontrolling interest follows.

Full equity situations—upstream sales with a noncontrolling interest

As the following examples will show, the only difference between elimination entries for upstream plant and equipment sales for the full equity case as compared with the modified equity or cost method case is the following. **All debits to parent company Retained Earnings in the modified equity or cost method cases are replaced with debits to Investment in Subsidiary.** This variation results from the fact that parent's recording of equity adjustments for deferred intercompany profit results in a correct Retained Earnings balance from a consolidated perspective and reduces the balance of Investment in Subsidiary. Since there is no corresponding reduction in subsidiary Stockholders' Equity, Investment in Subsidiary is debited for deferred intercompany profit in order to establish its reciprocity with the subsidiary equity accounts prior to their elimination in the consolidated statements worksheet.

Land sale

1. Year 1 (12/31/x1)

The elimination of the $10,000 intercompany gain on the sale of land is unaffected by either the upstream case or the use of the full equity method by the parent company—**thus, this entry is identical to the previous cases.** While the gain is on the subsidiary's books in the upstream case, the elimination entry is still made to reduce the land balance and eliminate the gain. The only difference between this example and the downstream case is that the gain is on Spencer's books and the land account is on Parker's books. However, this difference does not affect the consolidated balances. The entry and a partial worksheet are shown below.

12/31/20x1	Gain on Sale of Land	10,000	
	Land		10,000

Partial Worksheet 12/31/x1	Parker	Spencer	Eliminations				Consolidated
Income statement							
Gain on sale of land	$ –	$10,000	(1)	$10,000	$ –		$ –
Balance sheet							
Land*	45,000			(1)	10,000		35,000

*The book balance for Parker's land account is assumed to be $45,000 for purposes of illustration.

2. Years 2–n (12/31/x2 and thereafter)

As was the case under the modified equity and cost methods, the fact that the intercompany transaction was an upstream sale has an impact on the noncontrolling interest. The land account is reduced by $10,000, so that it is shown at the $20,000 original owner's cost. Debiting the Investment in Spencer and the noncontrolling interest for their pro-rata share of the deferred gain eliminates the deferred gain. As stated in the previous paragraph, the only difference between this entry and the entry for the modified equity and cost method cases is the debit to the investment in subsidiary account for the controlling interest share of the deferred gain. This entry and the related partial worksheet are shown below:

12/31/20x1	**Investment in Spencer**	**9,000**	
	Noncontrolling Interest	1,000	
	Land		10,000

Partial Worksheet—years 2–n	Parker	Spencer	Eliminations				Consolidated
Balance sheet							
Investment in Spencer*	$ XXX	$ –	(1)	**9,000**			$ XXX
Land*	45,000			(1)	10,000		35,000
Noncontrolling interest*			(1)	1,000			XXX

*Whatever the balance of Investment in Spencer, it is increased by $9,000 and the land account is decreased by $10,000 by entry (1). The book balance of land is assumed to be $45,000 for illustration purposes. The noncontrolling interest balance is not shown because it is affected by other elimination entries not illustrated.

Recall that the equity adjustment for an upstream $10,000 intercompany gain would be made with a debit to Equity in Investee Earnings and a credit to the investment in subsidiary account, resulting in a correct balance in the parent's retained earnings account on a consolidated basis. Accordingly, the debit to

Investment in Spencer in the above entry is made to establish reciprocity with the equity accounts of the subsidiary prior to their elimination. This elimination entry is made in each subsequent year as long as the land is still in the accounts of the parent company. Since the land is a non-depreciable asset, the deferred intercompany gain on the sale is not recognized in the consolidated statements unless the land is resold to an external entity.

▶ INTERPRETIVE EXERCISE

Assume that Parker resells the land to an external entity in the year 20x5. What elimination entry would be made for the deferred intercompany gain? Construct a proof of your answer using a series of journal entries showing how Parker's book gain is adjusted to the correct consolidated gain with the elimination entry.

Equipment sale

1. Year 1 (12/31/x1)

In the case of an upstream sale of equipment with a minority interest, in the year of the intercompany transaction, the elimination entry is the same as for the **modified equity** and **cost method** cases. The only difference between this (the upstream case) and the downstream case is that the gain to be eliminated is on the subsidiary books. This difference has no effect, however, on either the form of the elimination entry or on the consolidated balances. The required entries and the example partial worksheet are shown below:

12/31/20x1	Gain on Sale of Equipment	5,000	
	Equipment	25,000	
	Accumulated Depreciation—Equipment		30,000

12/31/20x1	Accumulated Depreciation—Equipment	1,000	
	Depreciation Expense		1,000

Partial Worksheet 12/31/x1	Parker	Spencer		Eliminations			Consolidated
Income statement							
Gain on sale of equipment	$ –	$ 5,000	(1)	$ 5,000			$ –
Depreciation expense*	(4,500)	(5,300)			(2)	1,000	(8,800)
Balance sheet							
Equipment*	45,000	53,000	(1)	25,000			123,000
Accumulated depreciation*	(15,000)	(32,000)	(2)	1,000	(1)	30,000	(76,000)

*The book balances of Depreciation Expense, Equipment, and Accumulated Depreciation are assumed for illustration purposes.

2. Year 2 (12/31/x2)

In the consolidated statements worksheet for the second year, the elimination entry changes from the **modified equity** and **cost method** cases only in that the debit to Parker Company's Retained Earnings is now made to the account Investment in Parker. This change is necessary for the same reasons previously described. The use of the full equity method results in a balance in Parker Company's Retained Earnings that is correct on a consolidated basis. However, the equity adjustments reduce the Investment in Spencer account by the amount of the deferred intercompany profit. Thus, a debit to Investment in Spencer is needed to establish reciprocity with the Spencer equity accounts (which are not adjusted for deferred intercompany profit) prior to their elimination in the consolidated statements worksheet. As in the **modified equity case** for an upstream sale of equipment, the noncontrolling interest share of the deferred intercompany gain is debited to the noncontrolling interest account because 10% of Spencer's Retained Earnings are carried to noncontrolling interest in the worksheet. The appropriate elimination entry and partial worksheet example are as follows:

12/31/20x2	**Investment in Spencer**	3,600	
	Noncontrolling Interest	400	
	Equipment	25,000	
	Accumulated Depreciation—Equipment		29,000

| 12/31/20x2 | Accumulated Depreciation—Equipment | 1,000 | |
| | Depreciation Expense | | 1,000 |

Partial Worksheet 12/31/x2	Parker	Spencer		Eliminations			Consolidated
Income statement							
Depreciation expense*	$(4,500)	$(5,300)		(2)	$ 1,000		$ (8,800)
Balance sheet							
Investment in Spencer*	XXX		(1)	3,600			XXX
Equipment*	45,000	53,000	(1)	25,000			123,000
Accumulated depreciation*	(15,000)	(32,000)	(2)	1,000	(1)	29,000	(75,000)
Noncontrolling interest*			(1)	400			XXX

*The book balances of Depreciation Expense, Equipment, and Accumulated Depreciation are assumed for illustration purposes. Whatever the balance in Investment in Spencer, entry (1) increases it by $3,600, and its balance will be fully eliminated in the consolidated worksheet. The balance for Noncontrolling Interest is not shown because it is affected by other elimination entries not illustrated.

3. Subsequent years

The subsequent years' elimination entries through the year 20x5 (five years after the intercompany sale) follow the pattern established above. The amount of the unrealized deferred gain on the intercompany sale declines by $1,000 each year so that its balance at the end of year 20x1 is $4,000; year 20x2, $3,000, etc. The debit in entry (1) is pro-rated between Parker's investment in Spencer account and the noncontrolling interest account in the ratio of controlling interest percentage to noncontrolling interest percentage in the year of the intercompany sale and in each subsequent year until the deferred gain is fully realized.

Calculating the noncontrolling interest share of consolidated net income

Recall from Chapter 5 that the net income of a consolidated entity is allocated between the controlling interest and the noncontrolling interest in all cases where the subsidiary is less than 100% owned, using the following formula.

$$\text{NISCNI} = (\text{Subsidiary net income} + \text{IEU}) \times \text{NCI\%} - \text{NCIA}$$

Where: NISCNI = Noncontrolling interest share of consolidated net income

IEU = Income effects of upstream elimination entries

NCI% = Noncontrolling interest percentage

$$NCIA = \text{Amortization of cost-book value differential applicable to the NCI}$$

An illustration of this calculation can be made using the Parker-Spencer data from the previous sections. Assume that Spencer Company had net income during the two years ending December 31, 20x1 and 20x2, of $100,000 and $120,000, respectively, and that Spencer is a 90%-owned subsidiary. Finally, assume that the only intercompany transaction was an upstream sale of equipment as described in the previous illustrations:

Intercompany Equipment Sale on January 1, 20x1	
Original historical cost of equipment	$40,000
Accumulated depreciation at the time of intercompany sale	30,000
Intercompany price	15,000
Remaining useful life	5 years

Note that the method of accounting used by the parent company (cost method, modified equity method, full equity method) has no impact on this analysis. The key issue is assuring that the **income effects** of all intercompany transactions are included in the calculation of noncontrolling interest share of consolidated net income. Following are the elimination entries (modified equity or cost method) for the two years 20x1 and 20x2 for the upstream equipment sale with the income effects highlighted in bold:

Year 20x1

12/31/20x1	**Gain on sale of equipment**	**5,000**	
	Equipment	25,000	
	Accumulated Depreciation—Equipment		30,000

12/31/20x1	Accumulated Depreciation—Equipment	1,000	
	Depreciation Expense		**1,000**

Year 20x2

12/31/20x2	Retained Earnings—Parker	3,600	
	Noncontrolling Interest	400	
	Equipment	25,000	
	Accumulated Depreciation—Equipment		29,000

12/31/20x2	Accumulated Depreciation—Equipment	1,000	
	Depreciation Expense		**1,000**

The bold lines in the journal entries show that the income effects of the elimination entries in the year 20x1 are a net reduction in consolidated net income of $4,000. This amount is the net effect of a $5,000 debit to the gain on sale of equipment and a $1,000 credit for a partial realization of the gain through use. In the year 20x2, the only income effect is a $1,000 credit for partial realization through use. A calculation of the noncontrolling interest share of consolidated net income using the above formula, assuming that noncontrolling interest amortization was $0 and that Spencer earned $100,000 and $120,000 during each of the two years, gives the following results:

Year 20x1: NISCNI = [($100,000 − $5,000 + $1,000) × 10%] − $0 = $9,600
Year 20x2: NISCNI = [($120,000 + $1,000) × 10%] − $0 = $12,100

COMPREHENSIVE ILLUSTRATION

This illustration of a purchase method consolidation with intercompany transactions in plant assets is shown for three cases: the cost method case, the modified equity case, and the full equity case. Each of the three examples uses the same set of financial statements and the same intercompany transactions for comparison purposes. The illustrations show the entries that the parent company makes to account for the investment in subsidiary on its books, the elimination entries for the consolidated statements worksheet in journal form, and the completed worksheet.

Assume that Parasol Company acquires a 90% interest in Spinnaker Company for $300,000 cash on January 1, 20x2, when Spinnaker has common stock outstanding consisting of 50,000 shares of $1 par common stock and retained earnings of $250,000. The excess of cost over book value at the date of acquisition is considered to be goodwill with an indefinite life. During the two years ended December 31, 20x2 and 20x3, Spinnaker Company had book net income of $50,000 and $70,000, respectively, and paid dividends of $15,000 in the year 20x2 and $20,000 in the year 20x3.

For the two years ended December 31, 20x2 and 20x3, the two companies had intercompany transactions in plant assets as illustrated in the following schedule:

Downstream transaction: 12/31/20x2

Sales price of land	$ 30,000
Cost of land sold	5,000

Upstream transaction: 1/1/20x3

Sales price of equipment	25,000
Original cost of equipment sold	50,000
Accumulated depreciation on the date of sale	35,000
Remaining useful life of the equipment	five years

An allocation schedule for the acquisition of Spinnaker Company by Parasol Company on 1/1/20x2 is shown in the following schedule:

Investment in Spinnaker 1/1/20x2		$300,000
Stockholders' equity of Spinnaker		
Common stock	$ 50,000	
Retained earnings	250,000	
	300,000	
Ownership percentage	90%	270,000
Goodwill		$ 30,000

COST METHOD CASE: The statements for the two companies for the year ended 20x3 are shown in the first two columns of Exhibit 6-1. Parasol Company's book entries to account for its investment in Spinnaker for the years 20x2 and 20x3 are shown below. The only entries necessary are those that record the dividends received from Spinnaker. Note that under the cost method, the account balance for the Investment in Spinnaker Company does not change.

12/31/x2 Cash	13,500	
Dividend Income		13,500
12/31/x3 Cash	18,000	
Dividend Income		18,000

The elimination entries for the 20x3 consolidated statements worksheet, in journal form, are as follows:

(1)
Retained Earnings—Parasol	25,000	
Land		25,000

    To eliminate deferred gain on 20x2 land sale

(2)
Gain on Sale of Equipment	10,000	
Equipment	25,000	
Accumulated Depreciation—Equipment		35,000

    To eliminate intercompany gain on sale of equipment
    (Sales price of $25,000 less book value of $15,000)

(3)
Accumulated Depreciation	2,000	
Operating Expenses		2,000

    To realize 1/5 of the deferred equipment gain
    ($10,000/5 = $2,000)

(4)
Investment in Spinnaker	31,500	
Retained Earnings—Parasol		31,500

    To adjust Parasol's 1/1/20x3 Investment in Spinnaker balance to
    modified equity [($285,000 − $250,000) × 90% = $31,500]

(5)
Dividend Income	18,000	
Dividends—Spinnaker		18,000

    To eliminate the intercompany dividend for the year 20x3

(6)
Noncontrolling Interest Income	6,200	
Dividends—Spinnaker		2,000
Noncontrolling Interest		4,200

    To allocate the noncontrolling interest share of consolidated net
    income to the noncontrolling interest account
    [($70,000 − $10,000 + $2,000) × 10% = $6,200]

(7)
Common Stock—Spinnaker	50,000	
Retained Earnings—Spinnaker	285,000	
Goodwill	30,000	
Noncontrolling Interest		33,500
Investment in Spinnaker		331,500

    To eliminate the stockholders' equity and investment in Spinnaker and
    to establish the noncontrolling interest at 1/1/20x3

Entry (1) above requires a debit to Retained Earnings—Parasol because the intercompany transaction for the sale of the land occurred in a prior year. The intercompany transaction for sale of the equipment occurred in 20x3, the current year.

As a result, Spinnaker Company has an account, Gain on the Sale of Equipment, representing the amount of book gain it recorded at the time of the intercompany sale. This elimination entry (2) debits the gain for the account balance and restates the equipment account to its original historical cost. This entry also reestablishes the accumulated depreciation balance at the beginning of the year, which the subsidiary wrote off when it sold the equipment. Entry (3) reduces accumulated depreciation and operating expenses for the $2,000 portion of the deferred gain assumed to be realized through use of the asset in the year 20x3. This elimination entry results in an operating expense balance equal to the amount that would have been reported had the equipment not been sold in an intercompany transaction.

■ CONCEPTUAL QUESTIONS AND REFLECTION

1. How would entry (1) above differ had the intercompany transaction been an upstream sale?
2. How would entries (2) and (3) above differ had the intercompany transaction been a downstream sale?
3. Compute the noncontrolling interest share of consolidated net income if both intercompany transactions had been downstream.

The remaining elimination entries under the cost method are all based on accounting principles that were illustrated and discussed in previous chapters. Entry (4) converts the investment in Spinnaker account and Parasol's Retained Earnings to reflect the modified equity basis as of the beginning of the year to be consolidated. The procedures involve computing the controlling interest share of the cumulative undistributed income of the subsidiary from the date of acquisition to January 1 of the current year less cumulative amortization of the cost-book value differential arising from the original acquisition of the subsidiary. This calculation is done in the following manner:

Subsidiary retained earnings, 1/1/20x3	$285,000
Subsidiary retained earnings, 1/1/20x2	250,000
Increase in subsidiary retained earnings	35,000
Controlling interest percentage	90%
Adjustment from cost to modified equity	$ 31,500

Entry (5) eliminates the current year dividend income of the parent company against the subsidiary's dividends declared account. Entry (6) establishes the noncontrolling interest share of consolidated net income. Note that this calculation involves adjusting the subsidiary net income for the income effects of upstream elimination entries prior to multiplying by the noncontrolling interest percentage. In this example, there are two such income effects—the $10,000 debit to gain in entry (2) and the $2,000 credit to operating expenses in entry (3). The net income effect of these two entries results in a reduction of subsidiary income from $70,000 to $62,000 for purposes of computing noncontrolling interest share of consolidated net income. This calculation is as follows:

Subsidiary net income	$ 70,000
Less: Gain on sale of equipment	(10,000)
Plus: Realization of 1/5 of equipment gain	2,000
	62,000
Noncontrolling interest percentage	10%
Noncontrolling interest share of consolidated net income	$ 6,200

Entry (7) eliminates the subsidiary equity accounts, the remaining balance in the investment in Subsidiary, and records the difference between these amounts as goodwill. Since goodwill has an indefinite life, it is not amortized. Entries (1) through (7) are posted in the consolidated statements worksheet Exhibit 6-1, which also illustrates the other procedures used to complete the analysis for consolidated financial statements.

MODIFIED EQUITY CASE: The 20x3 financial statements for Parasol and Spinnaker, assuming that Parasol accounts for its investment in subsidiary using the modified equity method, are shown in the first two columns of Exhibit 6-2.

EXHIBIT 6·1   Parasol and Spinnaker
(Cost Method) Worksheet for Consolidated Financial Statements

Statement of Income	Parasol	Spinnaker	Eliminations				Consolidated	
For the Year ended 12/31/x3								
Sales	$325,000	$200,000					$525,000	
Gain on sale of equipment		10,000	(2)	10,000			–	
Dividend income	18,000		(5)	18,000			–	
Cost of sales	(125,500)	(75,000)					(200,500)	
Operating expenses	(97,500)	(65,000)			(3)	2,000	(160,500)	
Net income	120,000	70,000					164,000	
Controlling interest income*							157,800	A
Noncontrolling interest income**			(6)	6,200			6,200	
Retained earnings - P Jan. 1	210,000		(1)	25,000	(4)	31,500	216,500	
Retained earnings - S Jan. 1		285,000	(7)	285,000			–	
Add controlling net income	120,000	70,000					157,800	A
Less: dividends	(25,000)	(20,000)			(5)	18,000	(25,000)	
					(6)	2,000		
Retained earnings, Dec. 31	305,000	335,000					349,300	B
Balance sheet 12/31/x3								
Cash	34,500	25,000					59,500	
Accounts receivable	38,750	33,000					71,750	
Inventories	71,250	45,500					116,750	
Land	55,000	65,000			(1)	25,000	95,000	
Buildings	335,000	260,000					595,000	
Accumulated depr—buildings	(100,000)	(50,000)					(150,000)	
Equipment	20,000	250,000	(2)	25,000			295,000	
Accumulated depr—quipment	(40,000)	(60,000)	(3)	2,000	(2)	35,000	(133,000)	
Investment in Spinnaker	300,000		(4)	31,500	(7)	331,500	–	
Goodwill			(7)	30,000			30,000	
	714,500	568,500					980,000	
Accounts payable	49,500	23,500					73,000	
Long-term debt	110,000	160,000					270,000	
Common stock	250,000	50,000	(7)	50,000			250,000	
Retained earnings	305,000	335,000					349,300	B
Noncontrolling interest					(6)	4,200	37,700	
					(7)	33,500		
	$714,500	$568,500	$482,700		$482,700		$980,000	

* ($164,000 − $6,200) = $157,800   ** ($70,000 − $10,000 + $2,000) × 10% = $6,200

Parasol Company's book entries to account for its Investment in Spinnaker for the years 20x2 and 20x3 are shown below. Note that use of the modified equity method causes the investment in Spinnaker to increase by the controlling interest share of the undistributed income of Spinnaker.[5]

12/31/20x2 Investment in Spinnaker	45,000	
Equity in Spinnaker income		45,000
To record Parasol's share of Spinnaker income for the year 20x2		
($50,000 × 90% = $45,000)		
Cash	13,500	
Investment in Spinnaker		13,500
To record Parasol's 20x2 dividend from Spinnaker ($15,000 × 90% = $13,500)		
12/31/20x3 Investment in Spinnaker	63,000	
Equity in Spinnaker income		63,000
To record Parasol's share of Spinnaker income for the year 20x3		
($70,000 × 90% = $63,000)		
Cash	18,000	
Investment in Spinnaker		18,000
To record Parasol's 20x3 dividend from Spinnaker ($20,000 × 90% = $18,000)		

The use of the modified equity method as compared with the cost method changes three accounts on Parasol Company's books. The account, Investment in Spinnaker, increases to $376,500 from its acquisition cost of $300,000 as illustrated by the following T account:

Investment in Spinnaker Company

1/1/20x2	300,000		
12/31/20x2	45,000	13,500	
12/31/20x3	63,000	18,000	
	376,500		

In addition, there is an account, Equity in Spinnaker Income, which did not exist under the cost method. For the year ended December 31, 20x3, this account has a balance of $63,000. This amount is shown in the above T account as a debit on 12/31/x3 and also appears in the Parasol beginning balances in the consolidated statements worksheet, Exhibit 6-2. Finally, both the beginning and ending retained earnings of Parasol are higher under the equity method than under the cost method because the amount of **Equity in Spinnaker Income** is higher than the amount of **Dividend Income** reported under the cost method. Thus, use of the modified equity method has the effect of increasing Parasol's 20x3 beginning Retained Earnings by $31,500 to $241,500, and its ending Retained Earnings by an additional $45,000 to $381,500.

The following elimination entries for the **modified equity method** differ very little from the previous example. Recall that elimination entries for intercompany profits following the modified equity method are the same as for the cost method. Accordingly, the only differences between the **modified equity** case and the **cost method** case are that: (1) the **cost method** entry to adjust the investment to the

---

[5] Since differential in this example is applicable to goodwill with an indefinite life, there is no differential amortization reflected in the equity income.

modified equity method basis is omitted and, (2) the entry to eliminate dividend income is replaced with an entry to eliminate equity income (entry 4 below). These entries are posted in the consolidated statements worksheet Exhibit 6-2.

(1) Retained Earnings—Parasol   25,000
       Land   25,000
    To eliminate deferred gain on 20x2 land sale

(2) Gain on Sale of Equipment   10,000
   Equipment   25,000
       Accumulated Depreciation—Equipment   35,000
    To eliminate intercompany gain on sale of equipment
    (Sales price of $25,000 less book value of $15,000)

(3) Accumulated Depreciation   2,000
      Operating Expenses   2,000
    To realize 1/5 of the deferred equipment gain
    ($10,000/5 = $2,000)

(4) **Equity in Spinnaker Income**   63,000
     Dividends—Spinnaker   18,000
     Investment in Spinnaker   45,000
    To eliminate equity in investee income and intercompany dividends

(5) Noncontrolling Interest Income   6,200
     Dividends—Spinnaker   2,000
     Noncontrolling Interest   4,200
    To allocate the noncontrolling interest share of consolidated net
    income to the noncontrolling interest account
    [($70,000 − $10,000 + $2,000) × 10% = $6,200]

(6) Common Stock—Spinnaker   50,000
   Retained Earnings—Spinnaker   285,000
   Goodwill   30,000
      Noncontrolling Interest   33,500
      Investment in Spinnaker   331,500
    To eliminate the stockholders equity and investment in Spinnaker and
    to establish the noncontrolling interest at 1/1/20x3

FULL EQUITY CASE: The 20x3 financial statements for Parasol and Spinnaker, assuming that Parasol accounts for its investment in Spinnaker using the full equity method, are shown in the first two columns of Exhibit 6-3. Parasol's book entries to account for its Investment in Spinnaker for the years 20x2 and 20x3 are shown below. Note that use of the full equity method uses the same entries as the modified equity method, but also requires additional equity adjustments for the intercompany transactions.

12/31/x2 Investment in Spinnaker   45,000
      Equity in Spinnaker Income   45,000
     To record Parasol's share of Spinnaker income for the year 20x2
      ($50,000 × 90% = $45,000)

EXHIBIT 6-2 Parasol and Spinnaker
(Modified Equity Method) Worksheet for Consolidated Financial Statements

Statement of Income	Parasol	Spinnaker	Eliminations				Consolidated	
For the Year ended 12/31/x3								
Sales	$325,000	$200,000					$525,000	
Gain on sale of equipment		10,000	(2)	10,000			–	
Equity in Spinnaker income	63,000		(4)	63,000			–	
Cost of sales	(125,500)	(75,000)					(200,500)	
Operating expenses	(97,500)	(65,000)			(3)	2,000	(160,500)	
Net income	165,000	70,000					164,000	
Controlling interest income*							157,800	A
Noncontrolling interest income**			(5)	6,200			6,200	
Retained earnings—P Jan. 1	241,500		(1)	25,000			216,500	
Retained earnings—S Jan. 1		285,000	(6)	285,000			–	
Add controlling net income	165,000	70,000					157,800	A
Less: dividends	(25,000)	(20,000)			(4)	18,000	(25,000)	
					(5)	2,000		
Retained earnings, Dec. 31	381,500	335,000					349,300	B
Balance sheet 12/31/x3								
Cash	34,500	25,000					59,500	
Accounts receivable	38,750	33,000					71,750	
Inventories	71,250	45,500					116,750	
Land	55,000	65,000			(1)	25,000	95,000	
Buildings	335,000	260,000					595,000	
Accumulated depr—buildings	(100,000)	(50,000)					(150,000)	
Equipment	20,000	250,000	(2)	25,000			295,000	
Accumulated depr—equipment	(40,000)	(60,000)	(3)	2,000	(2)	35,000	(133,000)	
Investment in Spinnaker	376,500				(4)	45,000	–	
					(6)	331,500		
Goodwill			(6)	30,000			30,000	
	791,000	568,500					980,000	
Accounts payable	49,500	23,500					73,000	
Long-term debt	110,000	160,000					270,000	
Common stock	250,000	50,000	(6)	50,000			250,000	
Retained earnings	381,500	335,000					349,300	B
Noncontrolling interest					(5)	4,200	37,700	
					(6)	33,500		
	$796,000	$568,500	$496,200		$496,200		$980,000	

* ($164,000 − $6,200) =$157,800   ** ($70,000 − $10,000 + $2,000) × 10% = $6,200

Cash		13,500	
Investment in Spinnaker			13,500

To record Parasol's 20x2 dividend from Spinnaker ($15,000 × 90% = $13,500)

Equity in Spinnaker Income   **25,000**
   Investment in Spinnaker   **25,000**
To adjust for deferred profit on the sale of land of $25,000

12/31/x23 Investment in Spinnaker   60,000
   Equity in Spinnaker Income   60,000
To record Parasol's share of Spinnaker income for the year 20x3
($70,000 × 90% = $63,000)

Cash	18,000	
Investment in Spinnaker		18,000

To record Parasol's 20x3 dividend from Spinnaker ($20,000 × 90% = $18,000)

Equity in Spinnaker Income	**9,000**	
Investment in Spinnaker		**9,000**

To adjust for deferred profit on the sale of equipment of $10,000 × 90% = $9,000

Investment in Spinnaker	**1,800**	
Equity in Spinnaker Income		**1,800**

To realize 1/5 of the deferred gain on the sale of the equipment

The balances in the accounts of the two companies immediately prior to consolidation on 12/31/20x3 are shown in Exhibit 6-3. The use of the full equity method as compared with the modified equity method changes the balances in three accounts in the separate financial statements of the two companies. Parasol's beginning retained earnings is $25,000 lower under the full equity method than under modified equity because of the equity adjustment to defer the gain on the sale of land in the year 20x2. The investment in Spinnaker account is also reduced by this same $25,000 amount and by the amount of the ***unrealized*** deferred intercompany gain on the intercompany sale of the equipment ($9,000 − $1,800 = $7,200), resulting in a balance of $344,300 in this account as of 12/31/20x3. Finally, the account Equity in Spinnaker income in Exhibit 6-3 shows a balance of $55,800, having also been reduced by the $7,200 deferred gain on the equipment sale. The elimination entries for the full equity worksheet (Exhibit 6-3) are as shown below. Only entry (1) and entry (4) differ from the entries under the modified equity method. Entry (1) requires a debit to Investment in Spinnaker in place of the Retained Earnings debit under the modified equity method. The investment account debit is necessary because the equity adjustment for intercompany gain on the sale of the land corrects the Retained Earnings balance. This debit to Investment in Spinnaker is also necessary to establish reciprocity between the investment in Spinnaker account and the subsidiary equity balances prior to their elimination in entry (6). The other entry that differs from the modified equity approach is entry (4), which changes because the full equity method results in a lower balance in the account for Equity in Spinnaker Income. These entries are posted in the consolidated statements worksheet Exhibit 6-3.

(1)	**Investment in Spinnaker**	25,000	
	Land		25,000

To eliminate deferred gain on 20x2 land sale

(2)	Gain on Sale of Equipment	10,000	
	Equipment	25,000	
	Accumulated Depreciation—Equipment		35,000

To eliminate intercompany gain on sale of equipment
(Sales price of $25,000 less book value of $15,000)

(3)	Accumulated Depreciation	2,000	
	Operating Expenses		2,000

To realize 1/5 of the deferred equipment gain
($10,000/5 = $2,000)

EXHIBIT 6-3 Parasol and Spinnaker
(Full Equity Method) Worksheet for Consolidated Financial Statements

Statement of Income	Parasol	Spinnaker		Eliminations			Consolidated	
For the Year ended 12/31/x3								
Sales	$325,000	$200,000					$525,000	
Gain on sale of equipment		10,000	(2)	10,000			–	
Equity in Spinnaker income	55,800		(4)	55,800			–	
Cost of sales	(125,500)	(75,000)					(200,500)	
Operating expenses	(97,500)	(65,000)			(3)	2,000	(160,500)	
Net income	157,800	70,000					164,000	
Controlling interest income*							157,800	A
Noncontrolling interest income**			(5)	6,200			6,200	
Retained earnings - P Jan. 1	216,500						216,500	
Retained earnings - S Jan. 1		285,000	(6)	285,000			–	
Add controlling net income	157,800	70,000					157,800	A
Less: dividends	(25,000)	(20,000)			(4)	18,000	(25,000)	
					(5)	2,000		
Retained earnings, Dec. 31	349,300	335,000					349,300	B
Balance sheet 12/31/x3								
Cash	34,500	25,000					59,500	
Accounts receivable	38,750	33,000					71,750	
Inventories	71,250	45,500					116,750	
Land	55,000	65,000			(1)	25,000	95,000	
Buildings	335,000	260,000					595,000	
Accumulated depr—buildings	(100,000)	(50,000)					(150,000)	
Equipment	20,000	250,000	(2)	25,000			295,000	
Accumulated depr—equipment	(40,000)	(60,000)	(3)	2,000	(2)	35,000	(133,000)	
Investment in Spinnaker	344,300		(1)	25,000	(4)	37,800	–	
					(6)	331,500		
Goodwill			(6)	30,000			30,000	
	758,800	568,500					980,000	
Accounts payable	49,500	23,500					73,000	
Long-term debt	110,000	160,000					270,000	
Common stock	250,000	50,000	(6)	50,000			250,000	
Retained earnings	349,300	335,000					349,300	B
Noncontrolling interest					(5)	4,200	37,700	
					(6)	33,500		
	$758,800	$568,500		$489,000		$489,000	$980,000	

* ($164,000 − $6,200) = $157,800   ** ($70,000 − $10,000 + $2,000) × 10% = $6,200

(4)	Equity in Spinnaker Income	55,800	
	Dividends—Spinnaker		18,000
	Investment in Spinnaker		37,800

To eliminate equity in investee income and intercompany dividends

(5)

Noncontrolling Interest Income		6,200	
Dividends—Spinnaker			2,000
Noncontrolling Interest			4,200

To allocate the noncontrolling interest share of consolidated net income to the noncontrolling interest account

[($70,000 − $10,000 + $2,000) × 10% = $6,200]

(6)

Common stock—Spinnaker		50,000	
Retained Earnings—Spinnaker		285,000	
Goodwill		30,000	
Noncontrolling Interest			33,500
Investment in Spinnaker			331,500

To eliminate the stockholders' equity and investment in Spinnaker and to establish the noncontrolling interest at 1/1/20x3

SUMMARY

Intercompany transactions in plant assets fall into two categories. Sales of land require elimination of intercompany gain or loss in the year of the sale. The land account must also be adjusted to consolidated historical cost in the year of sale and in all subsequent years, unless the land is resold to an external entity. Intercompany sales of depreciable assets also require elimination of the intercompany gain or loss in the year of the intercompany transaction. Furthermore, in the case of depreciable assets, the gain or loss deferred is realized over the remaining useful life of the asset. This realization is accomplished by annually decreasing (in the case of gains) or increasing (in the case of losses) the depreciation expense by the amount of the deferred gain or loss divided by the remaining life of the asset (assuming straight-line depreciation). Annually, the asset and accumulated depreciation accounts are restated to the appropriate consolidated historical cost balance, for as long as the assets remain on hand.

Elimination entries for intercompany profit in plant assets vary slightly depending upon whether the parent company has made equity method adjustments for the intercompany transactions. *APB Opinion 18* requires these adjustments for unconsolidated investees accounted for by the equity method, but they are optional for consolidated investees because the effects of these entries are eliminated upon consolidation of the subsidiary. If the cost method or modified equity method is used to account for the investment in subsidiary, the income effects of prior year intercompany sales of plant assets are closed to Retained Earnings. In the case of downstream sales, only parent company Retained Earnings is affected. In the case of upstream sales, both the parent company Retained Earnings and Noncontrolling Interest are adjusted for the amount of deferred intercompany profit. If the full equity method is used to account for the investment in subsidiary, the income effects of prior year intercompany sales of plant assets are closed to the investment in subsidiary account for downstream sales. In the upstream sale case, both the investment in subsidiary account and the noncontrolling interest account are adjusted for their pro-rata share of the deferred intercompany profit.

QUESTIONS

1. Explain how the realization concept applies to deferral and recognition of intercompany profit in plant assets.
2. Explain how an intercompany sale of land at a gain affects the separate financial statements of a parent company and its subsidiary. What consolidation statements elimination entries are required in the year of the sale as a result of such a transaction?
3. Refer to the first part of question 2. What elimination entries are required in the years subsequent to an intercompany sale of land?
4. Explain how an intercompany sale of a depreciable asset affects the separate financial statements of a parent company and its subsidiary. What consolidated statements elimination entries are required in the year of the sale as a result of such a transaction?
5. Refer to the first part of question 4. What elimination entries are required in the years subsequent to an intercompany sale of a depreciable asset?
6. If a company uses the full equity method to account for an investment in an affiliate, what adjustments are necessary on account of intercompany sales of plant assets?
7. How does the existence of a noncontrolling interest affect the equity method entries for upstream sales of plant assets?
8. Explain when and why the parent company retained earnings account is debited for deferred intercompany profit on a prior year downstream intercompany sale of land.
9. Refer to question 8 above. Explain when and why this debit is made to the investment in subsidiary account.
10. Explain why the noncontrolling interest account is affected when deferred intercompany profit from prior year upstream intercompany plant assets sales are eliminated.
11. Which plant asset intercompany elimination entries have an impact on the noncontrolling interest share of consolidated net income?
12. Explain how the noncontrolling interest share of consolidated net income is computed in a situation involving intercompany sales of plant assets.

EXERCISES

Exercise 6-1

(Multiple choice: select the best answer for each item.)

1. Consolidated financial statements should report plant assets acquired in intercompany transactions at
   a. the intercompany buyer's purchase price, less accumulated depreciation from the date of the intercompany purchase.
   b. at the intercompany seller's original cost adjusted for accumulated depreciation through the financial statement date.
   c. at the intercompany seller's original cost adjusted for accumulated depreciation only if higher than the intercompany price.
   d. appraised value on the financial statement date.
2. When preparing consolidated financial statements,
   a. gains on the intercompany sale of plant assets are eliminated, but losses are reported.
   b. losses on the intercompany sale of plant assets are eliminated, but gains are reported.
   c. both gains and losses on the intercompany sale of plant assets are eliminated.
   d. both gains and losses on the intercompany sale of plant assets are reported.
3. Pearson Company sells land with an original historical cost of $10,000 to its 100%-owned subsidiary, Simon Company, for $12,000. An equity method adjustment for this event would require
   a. a debit to Gain on the sale of land for $2,000.
   b. a debit to Land for $2,000.
   c. a credit to Income from Simon for $2,000.
   d. a credit to Investment in Simon for $2,000.

The following information pertains to questions 4–6. SUB Company is a 90%-owned subsidiary of PAR Company. PAR acquired its interest in SUB on January 1, 20x1, in exchange for 50,000 shares of its own common stock in a business combination where investment cost was equal to underlying book value. During the year 20x1, SUB Company had net income of $10,000 and paid $4,000 in dividends.

4. Assume that PAR also sold land with a book value of $15,000 to SUB for $18,000 on December 31, 20x1. What would be the correct balance in the account Income from SUB on December 31, 20x1, after all equity adjustments were made?
   a. $9,000
   b. $6,000
   c. $6,300
   d. $12,000

5. Assume instead that SUB sold land with a book value of $4,000 to PAR for $5,000 on July 1, 20x1. What would be the correct balance in the account Income from SUB on December 31, 20x1, after all equity adjustments were made?
   a. $9,000
   b. $12,600
   c. $11,600
   d. $8,100

6. Assume instead that PAR sold equipment with a 4-year remaining life to PAR on January 1, 20x1, at a gain of $8,000. What would be the correct balance in the account Income from SUB on December 31, 20x1, after all equity adjustments were made?
   a. $1,000
   b. $9,000
   c. $3,000
   d. $8,100

The following information pertains to items 7–10. On January 1, 20x2, Periwinkle Company gave 25,000 shares of common stock in exchange for 90% of the voting common stock of Sunflower Company in a transaction where investment cost was equal to underlying book value. During the year 20x3, Sunflower purchased land with a book value of $20,000 from Periwinkle for $25,000. Periwinkle uses the modified equity method for its Investment in Sunflower and does not make equity adjustments for intercompany transactions.

7. The elimination entry for intercompany profit on the land in the December 31, 20x3, worksheet requires a
   a. debit to Land for $5,000.
   b. debit to Gain on sale of land for $5,000.
   c. debit to Gain on sale of land for $4,500.
   d. debit to Retained Earnings for $5,000.

8. The elimination entry for the deferred intercompany profit on the land in the December 31, 20x4, worksheet requires a
   a. debit to Gain on sale of land for $5,000.
   b. debit to Gain on sale of land for $4,500.
   c. debit to Retained Earnings—Periwinkle for $5,000.
   d. debit to Retained Earnings—Periwinkle for $4,500.

9. If Periwinkle and Sunflower had income from their own operations in the year 20x4 of $20,000 and $8,000, respectively, how much was consolidated net income for the year 20x4?
   a. $27,200
   b. $28,000
   c. $23,000
   d. $22,700

10. Assume all the facts as described above except that the land sale was a sale by Sunflower to Periwinkle. The elimination entry for intercompany profit on the land in the December 31, 20x3 worksheet requires a
   a. debit to Land for $5,000.
   b. debit to Gain on sale of land for $5,000.
   c. debit to Gain on sale of land for $4,500.
   d. debit to Retained Earnings for $5,000.

Exercise 6-2

(Entries for intercompany transactions in equipment)

The Montana Mining Company and its wholly owned subsidiary, Western Trucking Company, had the following intercompany transactions during the year ended December 31, 20x3:

Downstream sale of equipment (On January 1, 20x3)	Account Balances
Original cost to Montana Mining	$50,000
Accumulated depreciation on date of sale	30,000
Intercompany sales price	25,000
Estimated remaining life on date of sale	5 years

Required:

(a) Prepare the book entries that Montana Mining and Western Trucking would record to reflect the intercompany sale.
(b) Prepare the 20x3 equity method entries that would be made if Montana Mining makes equity adjustments for intercompany transactions.
(c) Prepare the elimination entries for the 12/31/20x3 consolidated statements working papers.

Exercise 6-3

(Elimination entries for intercompany building sale)

On January 1, 20x1, Max Company purchased a building from its 90%-owned subsidiary, Mini Company, for $100,000. The building had an original historical cost to Mini of $80,000 and was 25% depreciated using the straight-line method of depreciation. The building had an expected remaining life of 10 years on the date of the intercompany transaction. Max Company uses the modified equity method to account for its investment in Mini and does not make equity adjustments for intercompany transactions. The companies prepared consolidated financial statements annually on a calendar-year basis.

Required:

(a) Record the elimination entries needed in the December 31, 20x1, consolidated statements worksheet.
(b) Record the elimination entries needed in the December 31, 20x3, consolidated statements worksheet, assuming that the building is still in use.

Exercise 6-4

(Elimination entries for intercompany sale of equipment)

Bama Ball Club, Inc. is a wholly owned subsidiary of Crimson, Inc. On January 1 20x0, Bama purchased a building from Crimson for $60,000. The building had an original cost to Crimson of $50,000 and was 20% depreciated at the time of the intercompany sale. Crimson uses the cost method to account for its investment in Bama. On January 1, 20x2, Bama sold the building to an external entity for $66,000. The estimated remaining life of the building on January 1, 20x0, was 10 years.

Required:

(a) Give the elimination entries required for the consolidated statements worksheets for the years ended December 31, 20x0 and 20x1.

(b) Give the elimination entry required in the consolidated statements worksheet for the year ended December 31, 20x2, the year the building is sold by Bama to an outside entity.

Exercise 6-5   (Elimination entries for intercompany sale of equipment)

Refer to the data in exercise 6-4. Assume that Bama is a 90%-owned subsidiary of Crimsom, that the intercompany transaction was an upstream sale, and that the final sale to an outside party was made by Crimson.

Required:

(a) Give the elimination entries required for the consolidated statements worksheets for the years ended December 31, 20x0, and 20x1.

(b) Give the elimination entry required in the consolidated statements worksheet for the year ended December 31, 20x2, the year the building is sold by Crimson to an outside entity.

Exercise 6-6   (Computing equity income)

Soapstone Company is an 90%-owned subsidiary of Pathway Company. On January 1, 20x4, Soapstone purchased equipment from Pathway for a price of $5,000. This equipment had an original cost of $8,000, a book value of $2,000, and an estimated remaining life of three years on this date. On December 31, 20x4, Pathway purchased land with a book value of $15,000 from Soapstone for a price of $25,000. The land is to be used in operations. For the years ended December 31, 20x4, and 20x5, Soapstone had net incomes of $40,000 and $50,000, respectively. Each year Soapstone declared and paid $10,000 in dividends.

Required:

(a) Compute equity income, including adjustments for intercompany transactions, for the years ended December 31, 20x4, and 20x5, assuming the original acquisition of Soapstone by Pathway was a purchase method acquisition where price = underlying book value.

(b) Compute the noncontrolling interest share of consolidated net income for the Pathway-Soapstone consolidation for the years ended December 31, 20x4, and 20x5.

Exercise 6-7   (Effects of the cost, modified equity, and full equity methods)

Ptarmigan Company owns 80% of the outstanding common stock of Seaside Company and consolidates it in its annual financial statements. During the year 20x4, the two companies had separate net income and paid dividends as follows:

	Ptarmigan	Seaside
Net income (excluding equity income)	$60,000	$40,000
Dividends	6,000	10,000

On January 1 20x2, Ptarmigan sold a machine with a book value of $20,000 to Seaside for $30,000. The machine had a remaining useful life of five years. There is no cost-book value differential amortization.

Required:

(1) Compute Ptarmigan's 20x4 income from Seaside using the (a) cost method, (b) modified equity method, and (c) full equity method of accounting for its investment in Seaside.

(2) Provide the same three amounts, assuming that the intercompany sale was made by the subsidiary to the parent company.

Exercise 6-8

(Noncontrolling interest share of consolidated net income)

Refer to the data in exercise 6-7 for Ptarmigan and Seaside companies.

Required:

Compute the noncontrolling interest share of 20x4 consolidated net income, assuming that (a) the intercompany inventory sale was downstream, and (b) that the intercompany sale was upstream.

Exercise 6-9

(Realization of intercompany profit)

Intercompany profit on the sale of inventory is realized in the consolidated financial statements when the inventory is resold to an outside entity or, if used in the production of goods or services, when those goods or services are sold to an outside entity. Intercompany profit on the sale of a plant asset is realized **though use of the plant asset.** Explain what is meant by the concept of realization through use.

Exercise 6-10

(Computing consolidated income with an intercompany transaction)

On January 1, 20x2, Bigtime Company sold a building with an original cost of $100,000 and accumulated depreciation of $60,000 to its 100%-owned subsidiary, Smalltown Company, for $50,000. On this date, the building had a remaining useful life of five years.

Required:

(a) Compute the amount of book depreciation that Smalltown would report on this asset during the years 20x2 through 20x6 using straight line depreciation and zero salvage value.
(b) Assume that Bigtime and Smalltown had net income during the years 20x2 and 20x3 as shown below. Compute consolidated net income after elimination entries for the intercompany transaction for both years.

	Bigtime	Smalltown
20x2 Net income (excluding equity income)	$125,000	$80,000
20x3 Net income (excluding equity income)	105,000	66,000

PROBLEMS

Problem 6-1

(Consolidated income statement)

Pelton Company acquired 90% of Southwest Company several years ago in a purchase business combination as a cost equal to book value of net assets acquired. Pelton has accounted for its investment in Southwest using the modified equity method. The two companies had the following separate operating data for the year ended December 31, 20x1·

	Pelton	Southwest
Sales revenue	$325,000	$150,000
Gain on the sale of equipment		5,000
Equity in Southwest income	22,500	
Cost of goods sold	(125,000)	(88,000)
Operating expenses	(95,000)	(42,000)
	$127,500	$ 25,000

On January 1, 20x1, Southwest sold equipment with a book value of $30,000 to Pelton for $35,000. This equipment had a remaining useful life of five years on the date of the sale.

Required:

(a) Prepare a consolidated income statement for Pelton Company and subsidiary for the year ended December 31, 20x1.
(b) Prove your net income answer in (a) above by computing the parent company's net income using the full equity method.

Problem 6-2

(Worksheet for consolidated statements)

On January 1, 20x1, Pierce Company acquired a 100% interest in SPI Company in a purchase method business combination for $100,000 cash. Any excess of cost over book value is assumed to be goodwill with an indefinite life. On the date of acquisition, SPI Company had the following balances in its Stockholders' equity. Pierce Company accounted for its investment in SPI Company using the cost method.

Common stock	$20,000
Additional paid-in capital	10,000
Retained earnings	50,000
Total	$80,000

The following table summarizes the intercompany inventory transactions for sales by Pierce Company to its subsidiary for the two years ending December 31, 20x2:

Year ended	12/31/x1	12/31/x2
Sales volume	$30,000	$50,000
Unrealized profit in ending inventory	6,000	14,000
Intercompany accounts payable at year-end	3,000	12,000

During the year 20x2, SPI sold land with an original cost basis of $5,000 to Pierce for $12,000. The financial statements of the two companies immediately prior to consolidation are shown below:

Statement of Income for the year ended 12/31/x2	Pierce	SPI
Sales	$400,000	$180,000
Dividend income	35,000	
Gain on sale of land		7,000
Cost of sales	(240,000)	(67,000)
Operating expenses	(120,000)	(50,000)
Net income	75,000	70,000
Retained earnings – Pierce, January 1	245,000	
Retained earnings – SPI, January 1		80,000
Add: net income	75,000	70,000
Less: dividends	(10,000)	(35,000)
Retained earnings, December 31	310,000	115,000

Balance sheet 12/31/x3

Cash	18,000	15,000
Accounts receivable	21,000	25,000
Inventories	76,000	50,000
Land	35,000	100,000
Buildings – net	150,000	150,000
Equipment – net	200,000	60,000
Investment in SPI	100,000	
Total assets	600,000	400,000
Accounts payable	25,000	13,000
Long-term debt	65,000	242,000
Common stock	200,000	20,000
Additional paid-in capital		10,000
Retained earnings	310,000	115,000
Total liabilities and equity	$600,000	$400,000

Required:

(a) Prepare the worksheet entry necessary to convert Pierce Company's investment in SPI Company to the modified equity method in the December 31, 20x2, worksheet for consolidated financial statements.
(b) Complete the consolidated financial statements worksheet for the year ended December 31, 20x2.

Problem 6-3   **(Consolidated income statement)**

Switzer Company is a 90%-owned subsidiary of Peccolo Company. Peccolo acquired Switzer several years ago at a price equal to book value and uses the modified equity method to account for its investment in the subsidiary. The two companies had the following separate operating data for the year ended December 31, 20x1:

	Peccolo	Switzer
Sales revenue	$200,000	$150,000
Equity in Switzer income	56,700	
Cost of goods sold	(75,000)	(65,000)
Operating expenses	(28,000)	(22,000)
Net income	$153,700	63,000

During the year ended December 31, 20x1, Switzer purchased $20,000 in inventory from Peccolo that was marked up 40% on sales price. One-half of this inventory was still on hand in Switzer's warehouse at year-end. Peccolo's beginning inventory contained $8,000 of inventory purchased from Switzer at a markup of 33-1/3% on cost. On January 1, 20x0, Peccolo purchased a building from Switzer for $75,000 cash. At the time of the purchase, the building had a cost basis of $100,000, accumulated depreciation of $40,000, and an estimated remaining useful life of five years.

Required: Prepare a consolidated income statement for Peccolo Company and subsidiary for the year ended December 31, 20x1.

Problem 6-4   **(Worksheet for consolidated statements)**

Power Company acquired a 90% interest in Sand Company for $400,000 cash on January 1, 20x2, when Sand had common stock outstanding consisting of 40,000 shares of $5 par common stock and retained earnings of $200,000. The excess of cost over book value at the date of acquisition was considered to be goodwill with an indefinite life. During the two years ended December 31, 20x2, and 20x3, Sand Company had book net income of $40,000 and $70,000, respectively, and paid dividends of $20,000 in 20x2 and $30,000 in 20x3.

For the two years ended December 31, 20x2 and 20x3, the two companies had intercompany transactions in inventory as illustrated in the following schedule:

	20x2	20x3
Intercompany sales – Power to Sand	$20,000	$30,000
Markup percent on sales	30%	40%
Intercompany inventory on hand at year-end	$10,000	$15,000
Unpaid Sand accounts receivable from intercompany sales	$ 8,000	$12,000

In addition, on January 1, 20x3, Power sold equipment to Sand for $35,000 that had an original cost of $50,000 and accumulated depreciation of $30,000. The equipment had a remaining useful life of five years at the time of the intercompany transaction. Power accounted for its investment in Sand using the modified equity method as reflected in the following financial statements prepared immediately prior to consolidation on December 31, 20x3:

Statement of Income for the year ended 12/31/x3	**Power**	**Sand**
Sales	$ 325,000	$145,000
Equity in Sand income	63,000	
Gain on sale of equipment	15,000	
Cost of sales	(190,000)	(54,000)
Operating expenses	(35,000)	(21,000)
Net income	178,000	70,000
Retained earnings, Power, Jan. 1	247,000	
Retained earnings, Sand, Jan. 1		220,000
Add: Net income	178,000	70,000
Less: Dividends	(40,000)	(30,000)
Retained earnings, Dec. 31	385,000	260,000
Balance sheet 12/31/x3		
Cash	20,000	12,000
Accounts receivable	26,000	55,000
Inventories	55,000	32,000
Land	37,500	64,500
Buildings – net	135,500	180,500
Equipment – net	200,000	150,000
Investment in Sand	454,000	
Total assets	928,000	494,000
Accounts payable	45,000	34,000
Long-term debt	198,000	
Common stock	300,000	200,000
Retained earnings	385,000	260,000
Total liabilities and equity	$ 928,000	$ 494,000

Required:

(a) Prepare an allocation schedule for the Power-Sand combination as of the date of acquisition.
(b) Prepare the elimination entries for the December 31, 20x3, consolidated statements worksheet in journal form.
(c) Complete the consolidated statements worksheet as of December 31, 20x3.

Problem 6-5   (Workbook for consolidated financial statements)

Peppermint Company acquired a 100% interest in the common stock of Sunburst Company on January 1, 20x1, for a price of $220,000, at a time when Sunburst had common stock of $50,000 and retained earnings of $130,000. The $40,000 excess of cost over book value was assumed to be goodwill with an indefinite life. During the year ended December 31, 20x1, Peppermint sold Sunburst $60,000 in merchandise marked up 20% on sales price. At the end of the year, $30,000 of this merchandise remained in Sunburst inventory. There were no unpaid intercompany payables and receivables arising from intercompany sales on December 31, 20x1. On July 1, 20x1, Sunburst also sold land with an original cost of $12,000 to Peppermint for $15,000. Peppermint used the full equity method to account for its investment in Sunburst.

The financial statements of Peppermint and Sunburst at the end of the year 20x1 are as follows:

Statement of Income for the year ended 12/31/x1	Peppermint	Sunburst
Sales	$ 425,000	$ 290,000
Equity in Sunburst income	71,000	
Gain on sale of land		3,000
Cost of sales	(275,000)	(127,000)
Operating expenses	(68,000)	(86,000)
Net income	153,000	80,000
Retained earnings, Jan. 1	190,000	130,000
Add: Net income	153,000	80,000
Less: Dividends	(70,000)	(30,000)
Retained earnings, Dec. 31	273,000	180,000
Balance sheet 12/31/x1		
Cash	45,000	34,000
Accounts receivable	49,000	25,000
Notes receivable	20,000	
Inventories	95,000	42,500
Land	50,000	32,500
Buildings – net	150,000	25,000
Machinery – net	200,000	124,000
Investment in Sunburst	261,000	
	870,000	283,000
Accounts payable	72,000	15,000
Dividends payable	25,000	
Other liabilities	200,000	38,000
Common stock	300,000	50,000
Retained earnings, Dec. 31	273,000	180,000
	$ 870,000	$ 283,000

Required:

(1) Prepare a schedule that computes the account balance, Equity in Sunburst Income, under the full equity method.
(2) Prepare a worksheet for consolidated financial statements for Peppermint Company and Sunburst Company for the year ended December 31, 20x1.

Problem 6-6   **(Worksheet for consolidated financial statements)**

Paris Company acquired a 90% interest in the common stock of Strasbourg Company on January 1, 20x1, at a price equal to the book value of Strasbourg's net assets. During the year 20x1, Paris sold land with an original cost of $22,000 to Strasbourg for $27,000. Also during the year 20x1, Strasbourg sold Paris used equipment with an original cost of $30,000 and accumulated depreciation of $25,000 for $20,000. The equipment had an estimated useful life of five years from the date of the intercompany sale. Paris used the modified equity method to account for its investment in Strasbourg. The financial statements of Paris and Strasbourg at the end of the year 20x1 are as follows:

Statement of Income for the year ended 12/31/x1	Paris	Strasbourg
Sales	$700,000	$335,000
Equity in Strasbourg income	135,000	
Gain on sale of land	5,000	
Gain on sale of equipment		15,000
Cost of sales	(320,000)	(140,000)
Operating expenses	(110,000)	(60,000)
Net income	410,000	150,000
Retained earnings Jan. 1	125,000	175,000
Add net income	410,000	150,000
Less: Dividends	(80,000)	(60,000)
Retained earnings, Dec. 31	455,000	265,000
Balance sheet 12/31/x1		
Cash	166,200	28,000
Accounts receivable	74,300	22,600
Notes receivable	10,000	
Inventories	75,700	77,200
Land	90,000	20,000
Buildings - net	160,000	225,000
Equipment - net	275,000	110,000
Investment in Strasbourg	328,500	
Total assets	1,179,700	482,800
Accounts payable	123,400	52,400
Dividends payable	25,000	
Bonds payable	151,300	65,400
Capital stock	300,000	100,000
Additional paid-in capital	125,000	
Retained earnings, Dec. 31	455,000	265,000
Total liabilities and equity	$1,179,700	$482,800

Required:

Prepare a worksheet for consolidated financial statements for Paris Company and Strasbourg Company for the year ended December 31, 20x1.

Problem 6-7   **(Worksheet for consolidated statements)**

Peerless Company acquired a 90% interest in the common stock of Sundown Company on January 1, 20x2, at a price equal to book value of underlying net assets. The financial statements of Peerless and Sundown at the end of the year 20x2 are as follows:

Statement of Income for the year ended 12/31/x2	Peerless	Sundown
Sales	$ 725,000	$320,000
Equity in Sundown income	135,000	
Gain on sale of machinery		10,000
Cost of sales	(340,000)	(120,000)
Operating expenses	(110,000)	(60,000)
Net income	410,000	150,000
Retained earnings, Jan. 1	125,000	150,000
Add net income	410,000	150,000
Less: Dividends	(80,000)	(60,000)
Retained earnings, Dec. 31	455,000	240,000
Balance sheet 12/31/x2		
Cash	176,200	18,000
Accounts receivable	74,300	32,600
Notes receivable	10,000	
Inventories	65,700	77,200
Land	80,000	25,000
Buildings – net	160,000	220,000
Machinery – net	285,000	110,000
Investment in Sundown	328,500	
Total assets	1,179,700	482,800
Accounts payable	145,400	70,400
Dividends payable	20,000	
Bonds payable	134,300	47,400
Capital stock	300,000	125,000
Additional paid-in capital	125,000	
Retained earnings, Dec. 31	455,000	240,000
Total liabilities and equity	$1,179,700	$482,800

Additional information:

1. Peerless uses the modified equity method to account for its investment in Sundown.
2. During the year 20x2, Sundown sold $20,000 in merchandise to Peerless at a markup of 100% on cost. At the end of the year, Peerless had $5,000 of this merchandise on hand. The unpaid accounts payable on these purchases at 12/31/x2 were $6,000.
3. On July 1, 20x2, Sundown sold machinery with a book value of $10,000 to Peerless for $20,000. This equipment had a remaining useful life of five years at the time of the sale.

Required:

Prepare a worksheet for consolidated financial statements for Peerless Company and Sundown Company for the year ended December 31, 20x2.

Problem 6-8   **(Elimination entries)**

Pointer Company acquired 80% of Sensible Company on January 1, 20x1, at a price of $100,000 at a time when Sensible had common stock of $40,000 and retained earnings of $60,000. The excess of cost over book value is assumed to be applicable to patents with a 10-year life. Pointer and Sensible had the following net income and dividends from their separate operations for the years 20x1 through 20x4:

	20x1	20x2	20x3	20x4
Pointer:				
Net income	$70,000	$50,000	$30,000	$80,000
Dividends	5,000	5,000	8,000	10,000
Sensible:				
Net income	20,000	25,000	40,000	30,000
Dividends	$10,000	$10,000	$20,000	$20,000

Additional information:

1. On January 1, 20x2, Pointer sold land with a book value of $20,000 to Sensible for $30,000. Sensible sold this land to the Outside Company (an unrelated entity) on December 31, 20x4, for $50,000.
2. On January 1, 20x3, Sensible sold a building with an original cost of $100,000 and accumulated depreciation of $40,000 to Pointer for $80,000. The building had a remaining useful life of five years at the time of the intercompany sale.

Required:

1. Assuming that Pointer uses the modified equity method to account for its investment in Sensible, prepare the elimination entries required for the intercompany transactions during the years 20x2 through 20x4 for the consolidated statements worksheet.
2. Compute the parent company's income under the full equity method for each of the four years ended December 31, 20x1 through 20x4.

Problem 6-9   **(Concepts underlying intercompany sale of assets)**

Intercompany sale of plant assets involves transferring plant assets from the parent company to a subsidiary, from the subsidiary company to a parent company, or from one subsidiary company to another. What are some of the business reasons why such transfers might occur? Based on your understanding of the principles of accounting involving the purchase and sale of assets, what valuation bases might be used for such transfers? Give arguments in support of and against each of the alternatives you suggest.

Problem 6-10   **(Concepts of intercompany transactions)**

This textbook illustrates the elimination entries that are required for two types of intercompany transactions—intercompany sales of inventory and intercompany sales of plant assets. Other types of intercompany transactions include intercompany loans and intercompany leases. Identify the types of intercompany accounts that might arise in connection with an intercompany loan or lease and explain whether or not these should be eliminated from the consolidated financial statements.

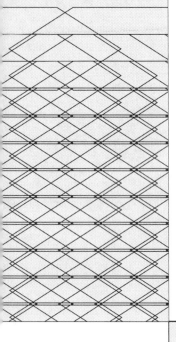

CHAPTER 7

BUSINESS COMBINATIONS USING THE POOLING OF INTERESTS METHOD

LEARNING OBJECTIVES

- State the conceptual basis for the pooling of interests method
- Describe the criteria for use of the pooling of interests method
- Record an acquisition under the pooling of interest method
- Account for a merger/consolidation using the pooling of interests method
- Prepare a consolidated statements worksheet for a stock acquisition accounted for as a pooling of interests

THE CONCEPTUAL BASIS FOR A POOLING OF INTERESTS

Banned after June 2001, pooling accounting uses the **book values** of the target company's net assets as a basis for the combination transactions. As was illustrated in the previous four chapters, the **purchase method** is based upon the **fair market values** of the target company's net assets. The differences in financial statement effects between the two accounting methods (purchase vs. pooling) can be enormous. For example, note the following data relevant the Boeing-McDonnell Douglas combination, which was accounted for as a pooling of interests in 1997:[1]

	March 31, 1997
(1) Stockholders' equity of McDonnell Douglas, per books	$ 3,204 million
(2) Outstanding common shares of McDonnell Douglas	210 million
(3) Ratio of exchange for Boeing common stock	1 for 1.3
(4) Average price of Boeing common stock 1/1–3/31/97	$53
(5) Approximate Fair Market value of shares given (210 × 1.3 × $53)	$14,469 million
(6) Excess of fair value of Boeing stock over book value of McDonnell Douglas stockholders' equity (5) – (1)	$10,439 million

While the above data are approximate, they clearly demonstrate that the pooling method may result in significantly different financial position and results of operations than would the purchase method. Following the pooling method, the net assets of McDonnell Douglas would be reported in an immediate postacquisition consolidated statement of financial position at about $3,204 million (book value), whereas under the purchase method, these same net assets would be reported at $14,469 million (fair market value). Thus, use of the purchase method would have more than quadrupled the reported net assets as compared with the (pooling) values actually used. More significant, perhaps, are the potential net income differences in the postacquisition years. Using the purchase method, the Combined Boeing-McDonnell Douglas would likely have reported increased plant and equipment valuations and a significant amount of goodwill arising from the combination. If all of the cost-book value differential was amortized, the result of using purchase accounting would be a materially lower net income as compared with the pooling method. Allowing for a little speculation, assume that the Boeing-McDonnell Douglas combination was accounted for using the purchase method and all of the excess of cost over book value was amortized. Using a 40-year amortization period, the reduction in net income would be $282 million annually [($14,469 million − $3,204 million)/40 years]. Using a 20-year amortization period would result in an annual charge for amortization of $564 million. Pro-forma consolidated net income for the two companies for the year ended December 31, 1996, was $1,818 million under the pooling of interests method.[2] Thus, a $564 million amortization charge would have reduced consolidated net income by about 31%. If goodwill was not amortized, the income differences under purchase accounting as compared with pooling accounting would likely be much smaller. In this case, only the excess of cost over book value attributable to identifiable assets would be amortized or depreciated.

---

[1] Source of items (1) to (4) is the *Joint Proxy Statement* announcing the Boeing-McDonnell combination of June 20, 1997. The author estimated Rows (5) and (6).

[2] Boeing-McDonnell Douglas *Joint Proxy Statement* on June 20, 1997, p. 64.

If two different methods of accounting for a business combination could potentially result in materially different financial reports in the postacquisition years, there should be strong conceptual justification for these differences. Continuing the analogy with the Boeing-McDonnell Douglas combination, there should be a legitimate reason why the market values were ignored in recording the exchange of stock. The combination was a transaction whereby the common shareholders of McDonnell Douglas exchanged their shares for those of Boeing in the ratio of 1.3 shares of Boeing for each share of McDonnell Douglas owned. Were the market values relevant to this transaction? Again, a look at the data would clearly indicate that they were. On June 19, 1997, the last trading day before the proxy statement, the market prices of Boeing, McDonnell Douglas, and the McDonnell Douglas (as exchanged) equivalent were as follows:

Boeing market value per share	$56.500
McDonnell Douglas market value per share	69.750
McDonnell Douglas equivalent in Boeing shares ($56.500 × 1.3)	73.450

The data indicate, as do the disclosures in the proxy statement, that the exchange ratio for the combination is based on the market value per share for the two companies. In fact, during the first three months of 1997, Boeing stock was split two for one. This split resulted in a change in the exchange ratio to be used in the acquisition from .65 shares of Boeing for 1 share of McDonnell Douglas to 1.3 shares of Boeing for 1 share of McDonnell Douglas.[3] The market price of the equivalent shares exceeds the actual McDonnell price by $3.70 ($73.450 − $69.750), a spread that one would presume resulted from the uncertainty that the combination would actually occur.[4]

Since the Boeing-McDonnell Douglas combination was a transaction governed by market forces and since the share exchange was based on market values, why was the pooling method used and why does pooling disregard the market values of shares exchanged in a business combination? The answer to these questions is that **pooling of interests accounting assumes that no sale has occurred, but rather the combination is simply an agreement between the two groups of shareholders to combine their interests and operate jointly in the future. The absence of a sale allows the conclusion that no market transaction has occurred and market values are not relevant to the exchange.** For the vast majority of pooling combinations, including the Boeing-McDonnell Douglas combination, this argument is spurious. Recognizing this fact, the FASB moved to eliminate the use of pooling in 1997, but opposition by the business community stalled its efforts. Pooling is a long-standing accounting practice that is favored by companies involved in acquisitions because they will report higher net incomes in the postacquisition years due to an absence of additional fixed charges arising from amortization of goodwill and depreciation of upwardly adjusted plant assets. Their motivation is apparently based on the belief that the choice of accounting method will have an effect on stock price performance in the postacquisition years, although abundant empirical research questions the existence of this effect. More recent FASB decisions prohibit pooling,

---

[3] Boeing-McDonnell Dougles *Joint Proxy Statement* of June 20, 1997, p. 17.

[4] This combination could not have occurred without the approval of both the Federal Trade Commission and the European Economic Community (EC). Substantial doubt existed as to whether either would approve the combination for some weeks after the announcement. The EC acquiesced to the merger only after Boeing agreed to void exclusive supplier contracts with major U.S. airlines—thereby allowing the European company, Airbus Industrie, to compete for business with these airlines.

allowing only the purchase method. As explained in earlier chapters, purchased goodwill will not be amortized in the post-pooling era. However, it will be subject to tests for impairment if circumstances occur indicating that an impairment might exist.[5]

▶ CONCEPTUAL QUESTION AND REFLECTION

In early 1998, the U.S. Department of Defense announced its opposition to a proposed acquisition of Northrup Grumman by Lockheed Martin because of its potential impact on competition in the defense industry.[6] In the days immediately following this announcement, Northrup Grumman common stock fell about $25 per share from its all-time high of $139 per share. During the same period, Lockheed Martin's common stock price was relatively unchanged, except for minor day-to-day fluctuations.[7] What inferences regarding the economic forces affecting the merger can be made from the stock price changes?

THE CRITERIA FOR USE OF THE POOLING OF INTERESTS METHOD

The pooling method was based on the presumption that a business combination **may not** constitute a purchase of the target company when the shareholders of the two separate companies become shareholders in the combined company. The proponents of this method of accounting argued that a business combination accomplished by issuing common stock was fundamentally different from one where cash or other consideration was given. Opponents took the position that pooling ignored the economic substance of the transactions—a position supported by examples such as the Boeing-McDonnell Douglas combination.

The authoritative literature on pooling combinations was principally contained in *APB Opinion 16*.[8] There were 12 separate criteria, contained in 3 categories, which were required to be met if a combination was to be accounted for as a pooling of interests. If any of the criteria were not met, the combination was to be accounted for by the purchase method. **It should be emphatically noted that the choice of accounting method for a business combination was not a random event. When a combination is planned and negotiated, management of the companies involved do so with knowledge of the accounting and reporting consequences of their decisions. Thus, the use of pooling was a deliberate decision made during the planning process.**

APB Opinion 16 allowed the use of pooling for certain combinations where the sole consideration given in the combination was the common stock of the acquiring company. In the authoritative literature, the acquiring company was referred to as the **issuer,** and the target or acquired company was referred to as the **combiner.** According to *APB 16*, pooling transactions were characterized by an exchange of stock

---

[5] Statement of Financial Accounting Standards No. 141, *Business Combinations* (Norwalk, CT: FASB, 2001).

[6] On July 16, 1998, CNN reported that Lockheed Martin called off this merger because of opposition to it by the Pentagon.

[7] Source: http://quicken.excite.com/investments.

[8] Accounting Principles Board Opinion No. 16, *Business Combinations* (New York: American Institute of Certified Public Accountants, 1970).

whereby 90% or more of the common stock of the combiner company were acquired. Pooling rules further prohibited this transaction from being accomplished over a protracted period of time. They also prohibited use of pooling accounting for combiner companies that were subsidiaries of other entities within the two years immediately preceding the acquisition. Pooling criteria are stated more specifically below. All conditions must have been met if pooling accounting was to be used.

Attributes of combining companies. The combining companies must have essentially been independent entities that are combined together in such a way as to continue previously separate ownership interests. This requirement thus states that both the following conditions be met: (1) A combining company may not have been a subsidiary of another company during the two years prior to the date the plan of combination is adopted. And, (2) Each combining company (if there is more than one) must be independent of other combining companies prior to the acquisition.

Method of combining. The combination must be accomplished with an exchange of common stock. More specifically: (1) The combination must be accomplished in a single transaction completed within one year of the date of adoption of the plan of combination. And, (2) only common stock (with rights identical to those held by current shareholders) may be given for 90% or more of the voting common stock of the combiner. Subsequent to the exchange of stock, the combiner may continue as a subsidiary or be liquidated and merged into the issuer.

Absence of planned transactions. Any transactions that occured in the postcombination period that were inconsistent with the combining of the entire interests of previous shareholder groups disallowed the use of pooling. Such transactions were characterized by buy-out agreements, subsequent adjustments in the amounts exchanged, guarantees of share prices, or similar conditions. Specifically, the combined company could not (a) agree to retire or reacquire any shares issued in the combination; (b) enter into any financial arrangements for the benefit of the former shareholders of a combining company, or (c) intend or plan to dispose of significant parts of the combining companies within two years of the date of the combination.

In conclusion, the essence of a pooling transaction was the combination of two companies in a stock exchange where both shareholder groups became shareholders in the combined entity. The argument for nonrecognition of market values in the exchange was based on the presumption that no exchange had occurred because the cash resources of the constituent owners had not been disbursed. This arrangement allowed the book values of the constituent companies to be carried forward to the combined corporation. It is, perhaps, important to note that the relative size of the issuer and combiner companies was not a factor in determining if the pooling method was permitted.

■ CONCEPT QUESTION AND REFLECTION

> Could a parent company agree to revise the common stock exchange ratio six months following the completion of a pooling of interests acquisition if the parent company stock price falls?

RECORDING A POOLING ACQUISITION

A pooling of interests transaction involves the acquisition of an investment in the common stock of another company, giving only common stock in exchange. You have already studied the stock for stock acquisition where the transaction was accounted for at fair market value using the purchase method of accounting. A pooling acquisition differs from the purchase acquisition both in terms of the value assigned to the investment account and in terms of the equity accounts adjusted by the issuing company. In general, all pooling acquisitions take the following form:

Investment in Combiner Company	(at book value)
Common stock	(par value issued)
Additional paid-in capital	*
Retained earnings	*

* The amounts of the credits to additional paid-in capital and retained earnings are determined as illustrated in cases 1–5 on the following pages.

The basic principle in a pooling combination is that the common stock acquired is recorded on the issuer's books at an amount equal to the combiner's book value. This approach has the effect of carrying forward the book values of the constituents in the combined financial statements of the two companies. The only analytical aspect of the journal entry is determining the proper amount of the credits to additional paid-in capital and retained earnings (the amounts marked by an asterisk in the above journal entry). Normally, these amounts are rather simply determined. However, in one or two circumstances, the calculations are somewhat confusing. Accordingly, the following four cases provide the appropriate examples. Each of the cases is based on the following acquisition:

Poole Company acquires 100% of the outstanding common stock of Spinner Company on January 1, 20x1, issuing 10,000 shares of its own common stock. Immediately prior to the acquisition, Poole Company and Spinner Company had the following stockholders' equity accounts:

	Poole	**Spinner**
Common stock	$100,000	$ 40,000
Additional paid-in capital	30,000	60,000
Total contributed capital	130,000	100,000
Retained earnings	175,000	50,000
Total stockholders' equity	$305,000	$150,000

CASE 1: THE COMMON SHARES ISSUED HAVE NO PAR VALUE If Poole Company issues no par common stock, it will be recorded at an amount equal to the total contributed capital of the shares acquired. Accordingly, a schedule that allocates the equity of Spinner to the 10,000 shares issued by Poole would appear as follows:

Case 1—no par stock issued

	Poole	**Spinner**
Common stock (10,000 shares issued)	$100,000	$ 40,000
Additional paid-in capital	0	60,000
Total contributed capital	100,000	100,000
Retained earnings	50,000	50,000
Total stockholders' equity	$150,000	$150,000

The schedule shows the credits that Poole would make in its journal entry recording the acquisition of the Spinner Common stock as a pooling of interests. The arrows represent the values of Spinner's stockholders' equity that are assigned to the Poole accounts in recording the pooling. The remaining amounts are determined by implication. Recall that the basic principle of pooling accounting is that the stockholders' equity of the combiner is assigned to the securities issued. If the common stock issued is no par stock, as in the above case, then the common stock issued is recorded at the amount of the combiner's total contributed capital. Total contributed capital recorded in the combination should equal the total contributed capital of the combiner company. Thus, the credit to additional paid-in capital is the dependent variable in the journal entry—shown in the previous entry surrounded by a dotted line box. In the case of no par common stock, that amount is zero. The retained earnings of the combiner are assigned to the issuer's entry. For the above combination, Poole Company's entry on January 1, 20x1, would appear as follows:

Investment in Spinner Company	150,000	
Common stock		100,000
Retained earnings		50,000

CASE 2: PAR VALUE COMMON SHARES ARE ISSUED IN THE COMBINATION; PAR VALUE OF COMMON SHARES ISSUED IS LESS THAN COMBINER TOTAL CONTRIBUTED CAPITAL Now assume the 10,000 common shares issued have a par value of $1 per share. In this case, the credit to common stock in the acquisition entry must be $10,000 (10,000 shares issued = $1 per share par value). Accordingly, the credit to additional paid-in capital in the acquisition entry (the dependent variable) must be $90,000, as shown in the following analysis:

Case 2—10,000 shares of $1 par stock issued

	Poole	Spinner
Common stock (10,000 shares × $1) →	$ 10,000	$ 40,000
Additional paid-in capital	90,000	60,000
Total contributed capital	100,000 ←	100,000
Retained earnings	50,000 ←	50,000
Total stockholders' equity	$150,000	$150,000

Notice that the key to this analysis is that only two combiner balances are carried to the issuer's journal entry. The total contributed capital is carried forward, resulting in the $90,000 credit to additional paid-in capital. Finally, the combiner's retained earnings of $50,000 are recorded on the issuer's books. This analysis gives the following January 1, 20x1, journal entry:

Investment in Spinner Company	150,000	
Common stock		10,000
Additional paid-in capital		90,000
Retained earnings		50,000

CASE 3: PAR VALUE OF COMMON SHARES ISSUED IS GREATER THAN COMBINER TOTAL CONTRIBUTED CAPITAL In this case, assume that Poole

Company's common stock has a par value of $12 per share, resulting in an issuance of $120,000 of par value when Spinner's contributed capital totals only $100,000. This scenario will require a debit to additional paid-in capital in the acquisition entry as illustrated by the following analysis:

Case 3—10,000 shares of $12 par stock issued

	Poole	Spinner
Common stock (10,000 shares × $12)→	$ 120,000	$ 40,000
Additional paid-in capital	(20,000)	60,000
Total contributed capital	100,000 ←	100,000
Retained earnings	50,000 ←	50,000
Total stockholders' equity	$150,000	$150,000

Notice that this scenario requires a debit to additional paid-in capital in the acquisition journal entry—thus the additional paid-in capital account of Poole must have a credit balance at least as large as the amount of the required debit. In this case, Poole has a pre-acquisition additional paid-in capital balance of $30,000, so the following January 1, 20x1, entry records the acquisition:

Investment in Spinner Company	150,000	
Additional paid-in capital	20,000	
Common stock		120,000
Retained earnings		50,000

Should the required debit to additional paid-in capital exceed the issuer's additional paid-in capital balance, an alternative approach is required as illustrated by case 4 below.

CASE 4: PAR VALUE OF COMMON SHARES ISSUED IS GREATER THAN COMBINER TOTAL CONTRIBUTED CAPITAL PLUS ISSUER ADDITIONAL PAID-IN CAPITAL Finally, consider the case where the Poole Company common stock has a par value of $15 per share. Under this assumption, the par value of the common stock issued in the pooling of interests acquisition is larger than the sum of the combiner company's total contributed capital and the additional paid-in capital balance of Poole. Note the following equity analysis:

Case 4—10,000 shares of $15 par stock issued

	Poole	Spinner
Common stock (10,000 shares = $15 par) →	$150,000	$ 40,000
Additional paid-in capital	(30,000)	60,000
Total contributed capital	120,000	100,000
Retained earnings	30,000	50,000
Total stockholders' equity	$150,000 ←	$150,000

In this scenario, the par value of the common stock and the number of shares issued determine the common stock credit by Poole. This $150,000 credit to common stock would normally require a $50,000 debit to additional paid-in capital in order to equate the total contributed capital of Spinner ($100,000) to the contributed capital credited in the acquisition entry. This $50,000 debit to additional paid-in capital is not possible because Poole has only a $30,000 additional paid in capital balance. Accordingly, the amount of the retained earnings credit must be reduced to $30,000 in order that the total credits to stockholders' equity of common stock, additional paid-in capital, and retained earnings in the acquisition entry equal Spinner's total equity. This January 1, 20x1, entry would appear as follows:

Investment in Spinner Company	150,000	
Additional paid-in capital	30,000	
Common stock		150,000
Retained earnings		30,000

Incidental costs associated with acquisitions accounted for by the pooling method

Any incidental costs incurred in connection with a business combination accounted for as a pooling of interests must be expensed. Three types of costs are commonly incurred: (1) direct acquisition costs, (2) issue costs, and (3) internal costs. All three were described in Chapter 1. In a purchase method acquisition, direct acquisition costs are capitalized as part of the investment, and issue costs are debited to additional paid-in capital. However, both of the first two cost categories must be expensed in a pooling of interests situation. The justification for expensing these two items rests on the requirement to record the acquisition at combiner book value, a result that can only occur if all incidental costs are charged to expense. The third item, internal costs, is expensed in both purchase and pooling accounting.

Less than 100% acquisitions

Recall that a pooling must involve an acquisition of at least 90% of the combiner company's common stock. With a less than 100% pooling, the equity analysis is altered slightly. For example, if the combination involves an acquisition of 90% of the combiner's equity, then the stockholders' equity accounts of the combiner are multiplied by 90% in order to determine the pooling result. The following schedule illustrates the Poole-Spinner combination where 10,000 shares of $1 par value Poole common are issued for 90% of the common stock of Spinner. For future reference, let us refer to this illustration as case 5.

Case 5—90% acquisition, 10,000 shares of $1 par stock issued

	Poole	90% Spinner
Common stock (10,000 shares × $1) →	$ 10,000	$ 36,000
Additional paid-in capital	80,000	54,000
Total contributed capital	90,000 ←	90,000
Retained earnings	45,000 ←	45,000
Total stockholders' equity	$135,000	$135,000

Since 90% of the total contributed capital of Spinner equals only $90,000, the contributed capital of Poole is credited for $90,000 as well. The credit to Poole's additional paid-in capital must be $80,000 because the par value of the common stock issued equals $10,000. Spinner's retained earnings are carried forward to the Poole acquisition entry in the amount of 90% of its balance, or $45,000. This analysis results in the following January 1, 20x1, acquisition entry:

Investment in Spinner Company	135,000	
Common stock		10,000
Additional paid-in capital		80,000
Retained earnings		45,000

● **INTERPRETIVE EXERCISE**

Record the acquisition entry for the Poole-Spinner combination if Poole issues 10,000 shares of **$10** par common stock for 90% of Spinner's common stock.

Postacquisition accounting

The illustrations in the previous section of this chapter show how an acquisition of stock should be recorded under the pooling of interest method. Recall from Chapter 1 that a stock acquisition business combination can take two forms.

In an **asset merger,** the target company is **liquidated.** Its assets and liabilities are then recorded on the books of the parent company in a journal entry that closes the investment in common stock account. Since the target company is liquidated, an asset merger requires 100% ownership by the issuer company. You may recall that this process can be somewhat involved in a purchase method acquisition. In a purchase method asset merger, the identifiable net assets of the target company are recorded by the acquiring company at fair market value, with the difference between fair market values and investment cost being recorded as goodwill (or negative goodwill). These complications do not arise in a pooling acquisition because the net assets of the combiner (target) company are recorded on the books of the issuer at combiner book value. Thus, there is **never** any adjustment of identifiable net asset basis or additional goodwill recorded in an asset merger accounted for as a pooling of interests.

If the target company is **not liquidated,** the only entry the acquiring company makes is the entry to record the acquisition. Since the subsidiary remains a separate entity, as little as 90% of the voting common stock of the combiner company can be acquired under pooling of interests rules. Subsequently, at the financial statement date, consolidated financial statements are prepared for the parent company and the subsidiary company. As was illustrated in chapters 3 and 4, this process can be rather elaborate under the purchase method of accounting. **In a pooling of interest, the preparation of consolidated financial statements is less complex. Since the investment in subsidiary account is recorded at book value on the date of acquisition, there is no cost-book value differential. The absence of cost-book value differential means that all subsidiary assets and liabilities are consolidated at book values and no goodwill is recorded.** A pooling consolidation is identical to the case of a purchase situation where the investment in subsidiary is acquired at a price exactly equal to underlying book value. This process will be illustrated later in this chapter.

ASSET MERGERS UNDER THE POOLING METHOD

Continuing the illustration of the Poole-Spinner combination in the previous section, assume that the two companies have the following balance sheets on 1/1/20x1, immediately prior to the acquisition:

Poole and Spinner
Balance Sheet (before acquisition)
January 1, 20x1

Assets	Poole	Spinner
Cash	$ 124,500	$ 25,000
Accounts receivable	45,600	40,000
Inventories	33,400	33,500
Land	65,500	27,750
Building - net	175,000	45,000
Equipment - net	186,000	73,750
	630,000	245,000
Liabilities and Equity		
Current liabilities	75,000	30,000
Long-term debt	250,000	65,000
Common stock	100,000	40,000
Additional paid-in capital	30,000	60,000
Retained earnings	175,000	50,000
	$ 630,000	$ 245,000

Further assume the facts in case 2, where Poole issues, on January 1, 20x1, 10,000 shares of $1 par value common stock for all of the outstanding common stock of Spinner in the following entry:

(1)	Investment in Spinner Company	150,000	
	Common stock		10,000
	Additional paid-in capital		90,000
	Retained earnings		50,000

To complete the asset merger, Poole would also make the following entry, eliminating the investment in Spinner account and recording the assets and liabilities of Spinner.

(2)	Cash	25,000	
	Accounts receivable	40,000	
	Inventory	33,500	
	Land	27,750	
	Building - net	45,000	
	Equipment - net	73,750	
	Current liabilities		30,000
	Long-term debt		65,000
	Investment in Spinner Company		150,000

A postacquisition balance sheet for Poole can be constructed by posting entries (1) and (2) to the Poole balances before acquisition. This procedure is illustrated in Exhibit 7-1.

EXHIBIT 7-1   Poole and Spinner
Worksheet for Merged Balance Sheet, January 1, 20x1

Assets	Poole Pre-Acquisition		Acquisition Entries			Poole Post-acquisition
Cash	$ 124,500	(2)	25,000			$ 149,500
Accounts receivable	45,600	(2)	40,000			85,600
Inventories	33,400	(2)	33,500			66,900
Land	65,500	(2)	27,750			93,250
Building - net	175,000	(2)	45,000			220,000
Equipment - net	186,000	(2)	73,750			259,750
Investment in Spinner		(1)	150,000	(2)	150,000	–
Total assets	630,000					875,000
Liabilities and Equity						
Current liabilities	75,000			(2)	30,000	105,000
Long-term debt	250,000			(2)	65,000	315,000
Common stock	100,000			(1)	10,000	110,000
Additional paid-in capital	30,000			(1)	90,000	120,000
Retained earnings	175,000			(1)	50,000	225,000
Total liabilities and equity	$ 630,000		$395,000		$395,000	$ 875,000

◢ CONCEPT QUESTION AND REFLECTION

Could an asset merger be done if Poole had acquired only 90% of Spinner's common, as described in case 5? Explain.

As was the case in a purchase method asset merger, no additional accounting related to the merger is necessary after the target company is liquidated. Only Poole Company continues to operate because Spinner has been liquidated and its assets and liabilities transferred to the books of Poole. Note again that **the transfer of net assets was made at book value, therefore, no asset or liability reevaluations are recorded, nor does any goodwill result from the acquisition. Goodwill can only arise when the purchase method is employed.**

CONSOLIDATED FINANCIAL STATEMENTS UNDER THE POOLING METHOD

As an alternative to the asset merger, Spinner Company could remain as a separate entity. In this case, Spinner would be a **subsidiary** of Poole and the two companies would prepare consolidated financial statements. Consolidation of pooling method acquisitions is normally less complex than purchase method acquisitions. Since pooling requires consolidation of subsidiary assets and liabilities at book value rather than fair market value (as in the purchase method case), there is no cost-book value differential to be assigned to the assets and liabilities of the subsidiary in the consolidated statements worksheet. For the same reason, there is no additional goodwill and no differential amortization to be recorded.

Consolidated balance sheet at the date of acquisition (100% acquisition)

Exhibit 7-2 shows the consolidated balance sheet of Poole Company and Spinner Company immediately after the acquisition of 100% of Spinner's common stock by Poole using the case 2 scenario, where 10,000 shares of $1 par value Poole common stock is issued. Note that the only entry that Poole makes on its books is an entry to acquire the common stock. This entry is identical to the first entry made by Poole in the previous asset merger scenario.

(1)	Investment in Spinner Company	150,000	
	Common stock		10,000
	Additional paid-in capital		90,000
	Retained earnings		50,000

The balance sheets of Poole (after posting this entry) and Spinner would appear as shown in Exhibit 7-2, which also shows the only elimination entry required to complete the worksheet. This entry eliminates the balance of the account Investment in Spinner and the stockholders' equity accounts of Spinner. Note that the consolidated balance sheet in Exhibit 7-2 results in the same account balances that appear in the postmerger statement in Exhibit 7-1.

● INTERPRETIVE EXERCISE

Prepare an analysis similar to Exhibit 7-2, assuming that Poole issues 10,000 shares of **$12** par value common stock in exchange for 90% of Spinner's common stock as described in case 3.

EXHIBIT 7-2 Poole and Spinner
Worksheet for Consolidated Balance Sheet, January 1, 20x1

Assets	Poole	Spinner	Elimination entry		Consolidated
Cash	$ 124,500	$ 25,000			$ 149,500
Accounts receivable	45,600	40,000			85,600
Inventories	33,400	33,500			66,900
Land	65,500	27,750			93,250
Building - net	175,000	45,000			220,000
Equipment - net	186,000	73,750			259,750
Investment in Spinner	150,000		(1)	150,000	-
Total assets	780,000	245,000			875,000
Liabilities and Equity					
Current liabilities	75,000	30,000			105,000
Long-term debt	250,000	65,000			315,000
Common stock	110,000	40,000	(1) 40,000		110,000
Additional paid-in capital	120,000	60,000	(1) 60,000		120,000
Retained earnings	225,000	50,000	(1) 50,000		225,000
Total liabilities and equity	$ 780,000	$ 245,000	$150,000	$150,000	$ 875,000

Consolidated balance sheet at the date of acquisition (<100% acquisition)

A stock acquisition pooling can be done for as little as 90% of the voting common stock of the target company. Referring to the analysis in case 5, an entry to acquire 90% of the common stock of Spinner in exchange for 10,000 shares of $1 par value Poole Common resulted in the following January 1, 20x1, entry:

Investment in Spinner Company	135,000	
Common stock		10,000
Additional paid-in capital		80,000
Retained earnings		45,000

As was the case for the 100% acquisition, only one elimination entry is made to complete the worksheet for a consolidated balance sheet immediately after acquisition. Exhibit 7-3 shows the January 1, 20x1, Poole (after the acquisition entry) and Spinner balance sheets, the elimination entry, and the consolidated balances. Note that the elimination entry requires establishment of a $15,000 noncontrolling interest account equal to 10% of the book value of Spinner Company's stockholders' equity on the date of acquisition.

Consolidated financial statements subsequent to the date of acquisition—100% ownership

Except for the absence of a cost-book value differential, consolidated financial statements subsequent to the date of acquisition for a pooling of interests follow the same procedures as do those for a purchase method acquisition. The absence of a differential

EXHIBIT 7-3   Poole and Spinner
Worksheet for Consolidated Balance Sheet, January 1, 20x1

Assets	Poole	Spinner	Elimination entry		Consolidated
Cash	$ 124,500	$ 25,000			$ 149,500
Accounts receivable	45,600	40,000			85,600
Inventories	33,400	33,500			66,900
Land	65,500	27,750			93,250
Building - net	175,000	45,000			220,000
Equipment - net	186,000	73,750			259,750
Investment in Spinner	135,000		(1)	135,000	–
Total assets	765,000	245,000			875,000
Liabilities and Equity					
Current liabilities	75,000	30,000			105,000
Long-term debt	250,000	65,000			315,000
Common stock	110,000	40,000	(1) 40,000		110,000
Additional paid-in capital	110,000	60,000	(1) 60,000		110,000
Retained earnings	220,000	50,000	(1) 50,000		20,000
Noncontrolling interest			(1)	15,000	15,000
Total liabilities and equity	$ 765,000	$ 245,000	$ 150,000	$ 150,000	$ 875,000

makes the required elimination entries substantially less complex.[9] As in the case of a purchase situation, the parent company must account for the Investment in subsidiary during the year, using either the cost method or the equity method. Assume that the results of operations and financial position of Poole and Spinner are as shown in the first two columns of Exhibit 7-4. In addition, assume that Poole acquired 100% of Spinner's outstanding common stock on January 1, 20x1, in exchange for 10,000 shares of $1 par value common stock as described in the case 2 scenario. If Poole accounts for its investment using the equity method of accounting, it would make the following equity method adjustments on its books based on the results of operations of Spinner for the year ended December 31, 20x1.

Investment in Spinner	60,000	
Equity in Spinner income		60,000
Cash	10,000	
Investment in Spinner		10,000

The beginning balances for Poole and Spinner in Exhibit 7-4 reflect the above two entries. As the exhibit illustrates, the elimination entries for the worksheet for consolidated financial statements are very straightforward. Only two elimination entries are required. Entry (1) eliminates the current year's equity income and the dividend account of Spinner. The Investment in Spinner account is credited for the differences between these two amounts, thereby restating the Investment in Spinner account to its beginning of year balance. Entry (2) eliminates the Spinner stockholders' equity accounts and the Investment in Spinner account. In general journal form, these two entries are as follows:

(1)	Equity in Standard income	60,000	
	Dividends—Spinner		10,000
	Investment in Spinner		50,000

(2)	Common stock—Spinner	40,000	
	Additional paid-in capital—Spinner	60,000	
	Retained earnings—Spinner	50,000	
	Investment in Spinner		150,000

Because the pooling of interests method was used, the total of the subsidiary stockholders' equity account and the Investment in Spinner account are equal. Especially note that **in a pooling of interests there is never any excess of cost over book value when comparing the balance of the investment in subsidiary with the underlying subsidiary equity accounts. It follows that there is also never any differential amortization.** The absence of these complications makes the consolidated statements working paper less complex than in the case of the purchase method acquisition, where subsidiary net assets are adjusted to fair market value.

---

[9] A pooling of interests acquisition is similar to a purchase method acquisition where the investment cost to the parent company equals the book value of the subsidiary net assets.

EXHIBIT 7-4 Poole and Spinner
Worksheet for Consolidated Financial Statements
Year Ended December 31, 20x1

Assets	Poole	Spinner	Elimination entry				Consolidated
Sales	$ 350,000	$ 175,000					$ 525,000
Equity in Spinner income	60,000		(1)	60,000			–
Cost of goods sold	(180,000)	(95,000)					(275,000)
Operating expenses	(68,000)	(20,000)					(88,000)
Net income	162,000	60,000					162,000
Retained earnings 1/1	225,000	50,000	(2)	50,000			225,000
Add net income	162,000	60,000					162,000
Dividends	(30,000)	(10,000)			(1)	10,000	(30,000)
Retained earnings 12/31	357,000	100,000					357,000
Cash	146,000	33,000					179,000
Accounts receivable	54,000	41,000					95,000
Inventories	32,500	28,700					61,200
Land	65,500	27,750					93,250
Building (net)	168,000	40,000					208,000
Equipment (net)	190,000	71,500					261,500
Investment in Spinner	200,000				(1)	50,000	–
					(2)	150,000	
Total assets	856,000	241,950					897,950
Liabilities and Equity							
Current liabilities	69,000	26,950					95,950
Long-term debt	200,000	15,000					215,000
Common stock	110,000	40,000	(2)	40,000			110,000
Additional paid-in capital	120,000	60,000	(2)	60,000			120,000
Retained earnings	357,000	100,000					357,000
Total liabilities and equity	$ 856,000	$ 241,950		$ 210,000		$ 210,000	$ 897,950

Consolidated financial statements subsequent to the date of acquisition (<100% ownership)

Exhibit 7-5 shows the worksheet for the Poole-Spinner consolidation at December 31, 20x1, assuming an acquisition of 90% of Spinner common stock on January 1, 20x1, in exchange for 10,000 shares of Poole common stock, as depicted in case 5. The unconsolidated balances of Poole and Spinner at December 31, 20x1, are shown in the first two columns of Exhibit 7-5. Poole's book balances assume the use of the equity method to account for its investment in Spinner, having recorded the following two equity method adjustments on its books at the end of the year:

Investment in Spinner	54,000	
Equity in Spinner Income		54,000
(Spinner net income of $60,000 × 90%)		
Cash	9,000	
Investment in Spinner		9,000
(Spinner dividends of $10,000 × 90%)		

Exhibit 7-5 shows three elimination entries rather than the two entries shown in Exhibit 7-4. The additional entry results because there are noncontrolling interest shareholders. Entry (1) eliminates the account Equity in Spinner income, 90% of the Spinner dividends account, and credits Investment in Spinner for the difference, thereby restating the Investment in Spinner account to its beginning of year balance. Entry (2) allocates $6,000 (10%) of Spinner's net income, net of the $1,000 of dividends received by the noncontrolling shareholders to the noncontrolling interest equity account. This entry produces a credit of $5,000 ($6,000 − $1,000) to the noncontrolling interest equity account. **Note that there is no noncontrolling interest account until this entry is made.** Entry (3) eliminates the stockholders' equity of Spinner, establishes an opening noncontrolling interest account balance equal to 10% of the total stockholders' equity of Spinner at the beginning of the year, and credits Investment in Spinner for its beginning of year balance. In general journal form, these entries are as follows:

(1)	Equity in Spinner income	54,000	
	Dividends—Spinner		9,000
	Investment in Spinner		45,000
(2)	Noncontrolling interest income	6,000	
	Dividends—Spinner		1,000
	Noncontrolling interest		5,000
(3)	Common stock—Spinner	40,000	
	Additional paid-in capital—Spinner	60,000	
	Retained earnings—Spinner (1/1/20x1)	50,000	
	Noncontrolling interest		15,000
	Investment in Spinner		135,000

Exhibit 7-5 differs from Exhibit 7-4 only in that a 10% noncontrolling interest exists. The entries made for the noncontrolling interest are made in the same manner as was done for purchase method subsidiaries as illustrated in Chapter 4.

EXHIBIT 7·5 Poole and Spinner
Worksheet for Consolidated Financial Statements
Year Ended December 31, 20x1

Assets	Poole	Spinner	Elimination entry				Consolidated
Sales	$ 350,000	$ 175,000					$ 525,000
Equity in Spinner income	54,000		(1)	54,000			-
Cost of goods sold	(180,000)	(95,000)					(275,000)
Operating expenses	(68,000)	(20,000)					(88,000)
Net income	156,000	60,000					162,000
Noncontrolling interest income			(2)	6,000			6,000
Controlling interest income							156,000
Retained earnings 1/1	225,000	50,000	(3)	50,000			225,000
Add net income	156,000	60,000					156,000
Dividends	(30,000)	(10,000)			(1)	9,000	(30,000)
					(2)	1,000	
Retained earnings 12/31	351,000	100,000					351,000
Cash	160,000	33,000					193,000
Accounts receivable	54,000	41,000					95,000
Inventories	32,500	28,700					61,200
Land	65,500	27,750					93,250
Building (net)	168,000	40,000					208,000
Equipment (net)	190,000	71,500					261,500
Investment in Spinner	180,000				(1)	45,000	-
					(3)	135,000	
Total assets	850,000	241,950					911,950
Liabilities and Equity							
Current liabilities	69,000	26,950					95,950
Long-term debt	200,000	15,000					215,000
Common stock	110,000	40,000	(3)	40,000			110,000
Additional paid-in capital	120,000	60,000	(3)	60,000			120,000
Retained earnings	351,000	100,000					351,000
Noncontrolling interest					(2)	5,000	
					(3)	15,000	20,000
Total liabilities and equity	$ 850,000	$ 241,950		$ 210,000		$ 210,000	$ 911,950

SUMMARY

The following learning objectives were stated at the beginning of the chapter.

- State the conceptual basis for the pooling of interests method
- Describe the criteria for use of the pooling of interests method
- Record an acquisition under the pooling of interests method
- Account for a merger/acquisition using the pooling of interests method
- Prepare a consolidated statements worksheet for a stock acquisition accounted for as a pooling of interests

The pooling of interests method of accounting for a business combination combines the entities involved in the combination using the book values of their assets and liabilities immediately prior to the combination. When the combiner companies are liquidated and merged into the issuer company, the assets and liabilities acquired are recorded in the merger transactions at combiner book value. If the combiner companies remain as separate subsidiaries, book values serve as the basis for preparation of consolidated financial statements. Fair market values of the assets and liabilities of the combiner companies are ignored. Support for this approach is based on the somewhat unrealistic assumption that a pooling of interests does not involve an acquisition of one company by another, but rather is the result of the two groups of constituent shareholders agreeing to operate jointly in the future. In the opinion of the author, pooling of interest accounting is based on a weak theoretical argument. In 2001, the FASB reaffirmed a decision to ban pooling accounting, but the changes are not retroactive.

Under the rules set forth in *APB Opinion 16*, the pooling of interest method was used only in business combinations involving an exchange of common stock, whereby 90% or more of the voting common stock of the combiner companies are acquired, giving only common stock of the issuer in exchange. The pooling was also accomplished in a single transaction, completed within one year of the date of adoption of the plan of combination. Any contingent clauses in the plan of merger that would benefit any shareholder group, to the economic detriment of other shareholders, resulted in a disallowance of the pooling method. Furthermore, the combiner companies involved in a combination must have been independent of each other and of other companies prior to the combination.

The use of book values in a pooling of interests business combination means that the transaction recording the acquisition ignores the fair market value of the securities given in the combination, even where the evidence indicates that market values were the basis of the exchange agreement. As a result, no goodwill is recorded in either the resulting merger or in a consolidation of financial statements. In the case of an acquisition involving consolidated financial statements, the use of book values does eliminate some of the complexity in the consolidated statements worksheet because of the absence of the need to adjust subsidiary company assets and liabilities to fair market value and to record purchased goodwill.

QUESTIONS

1. Explain the rationale underlying the use of combiner book values in a business combination accounted for as a pooling of interests.
2. Why does *APB 16* stipulate that a business combination accounted for as a pooling of interests involve an exchange of common stock between the issuer company and the stockholders of the combiner company?
3. Describe the required *attributes of combiner companies* in a business combination accounted for as a pooling of interests.
4. Describe the *method of combining* requirements of *APB 16* as related to the pooling of interests method.
5. What type of postcombination transactions are prohibited if the pooling of interests method is to be used in a business combination?
6. What is meant by the statement "combiner book value is assigned to the securities issued" in a pooling of interests combination?
7. Why is there never any goodwill recorded in a business combination accounted for as a pooling of interests?
8. Critique the argument that a pooling of interests does not involve an exchange, therefore making it inappropriate to record a stock exchange combination at fair market value.

9. What additional procedures related to the business combination are required subsequent to an asset merger transaction? Explain your answer.
10. How will the immediate postacquisition balance sheet of an asset merger differ from the consolidated balance sheet of a parent–subsidiary consolidation? Explain.
11. Explain why differential amortization is never required in a business combination accounted for as a pooling of interests.
12. What alternative methods of accounting may be used for pooling method subsidiary investments to be consolidated?
13. How is the ending noncontrolling interest equity account determined in a pooling of interests consolidation of less than a 100% interest.

EXERCISES

Exercise 7-1 **(Multiple choice: select the best answer for each item.)**

1. In an asset merger accounted for as a pooling of interests, the assets and liabilities of the combiner company are
   a. recorded at fair market value on the effective date of the acquisition.
   b. recorded at the lower of combiner book value or fair market value on the effective date of the acquisition.
   c. recorded at combiner book value on the effective date of the acquisition.
   d. recorded at either combiner book value or fair market value at the option of the issuer.
2. The pooling of interests method may be used
   a. for any stock acquisition.
   b. for only acquisitions where no cash is given by the acquiring company.
   c. for certain acquisitions where only common stock is given by the acquiring company.
   d. for only those acquisitions where the target company remains an independent subsidiary.
3. Goodwill
   a. can only arise in business combinations accounted for by the pooling method.
   b. can only arise in business combinations accounted for by the purchase method.
   c. can arise in business combinations accounted for by either the purchase method or the pooling method.
   d. is recorded in the general ledger of the parent company in acquisition-type business combinations.
4. The use of book values in pooling of interests acquisitions is based on which of the following concepts?
   a. The argument that fair market values are too subjective to be reliable
   b. The idea that book values are reasonable measures of the economic substance of the transaction
   c. The idea that a pooling of interests does not constitute an exchange because the shareholders of both the issuer and the combiner become owners of the combined entity
   d. All of the above form the basis for the pooling of interests concept.
5. The total par value of common stock issued in a pooling of interests combination is recorded at
   a. an amount equal to the total par value of the combiner common stock acquired.
   b. an amount equal to the issuer's share of the combiner's total stockholders' equity.
   c. an amount equal to the total fair market value of the shares issued.
   d. an amount equal to the issuer's par value per share times the number of shares issued..
6. Direct acquisition costs in a business combination accounted for as a pooling of interests are
   a. charged to expense.
   b. capitalized as a component of the investment in subsidiary account.
   c. charged to additional paid-in capital of the issuer.
   d. charged to retained earnings of the issuer.

7. Issue costs in a business combination accounted for as a pooling of interests are
   a. charged to expense.
   b. capitalized as a component of the investment in subsidiary account.
   c. charged to additional paid-in capital of the issuer.
   d. charged to retained earnings of the issuer.
8. In a pooling of interests business combination, the excess of the combiner contributed capital over the par value of the issuer stock given
   a. is credited to retained earnings of the issuer.
   b. is debited to additional paid-in capital of the combiner.
   c. is credited to additional paid-in capital of the issuer.
   d. is debited to additional paid-in capital of the issue.
9. In a pooling of interests of 90% of the common stock of a combiner, the investment in common stock account is recorded at
   a. an amount equal to the par value of the issuer shares exchanged.
   b. an amount equal to the book value of the stock acquired.
   c. an amount equal to the fair market value of the stock issued.
   d. an amount equal to the fair market value of the stock acquired.
10. Which of the following events would disallow use of the pooling of interest method for a business combination?
   a. An agreement to retire or reacquire any shares issued in the combination
   b. An agreement to guarantee share prices of shares received by former combiner company shareholders
   c. A plan to spin off or sell significant portions of the combiner company's operations
   d. All of the above events would disallow pooling accounting.

Exercise 7-2　**(Pooling of interest concepts)**

Do an Internet search on the term "pooling accounting" or "pooling of interests accounting". Write a one-page report summarizing the business issues surrounding this controversial procedure.

Exercise 7-3　**(Journal entries for a pooling of interests; 100% acquisition)**

On July 1, 20x3 Poole Company acquired 100% of the outstanding common stock of Standstill Company in exchange for shares of its own $10 par common stock. The acquisition qualified as a pooling of interests. Immediately prior to the acquisition Standstill had the following stockholders' equity balances:

Common stock, $1 par	$ 50,000
Additional paid-in capital	60,000
Retained earnings	120,000
Total	$230,000

Required:

(a) Record the acquisition on the books of Poole assuming the number of Poole shares issued was 10,000.
(b) Assuming Poole Company has an additional paid-in capital account balance of $125,000, record the acquisition entry assuming the number of Poole shares issued was 15,000.

Exercise 7-4　**(Journal entries for a pooling of interests; 100% acquisition)**

On January 1, 20x1 Pintail Company acquired 100% of the outstanding common stock of Stardust Company in exchange for 50,000 shares of its own no par common stock. The acquisition qualified as a pooling of interests. Immediately prior to the acquisition, Stardust Company had the following stockholders' equity balances.

Common stock, $5 par	$ 100,000
Additional paid-in capital	50,000
Retained earnings	350,000
Total	$500,000

Required:

(a) Record the acquisition on the books of Pintail.
(b) Record the acquisition on the books of Pintail assuming instead that Pintail common stock has a par value of $1 per share.

Exercise 7-5

(Journal entries for a pooling of interests; less than 100% acquisition)

Poland Company acquired 90% of the outstanding common stock of Sublette Company on January 1, 20x4 in exchange for 10,000 shares of its common stock. Poland incurred $5,000 in issue costs and accounted for the acquisition as a pooling of interests. Immediately prior to the acquisition, Sublette Company had the following stockholders' equity.

Common stock, $1 par	$ 10,000
Additional paid-in capital	90,000
Retained earnings	200,000
Total	$300,000

Required:

(a) Record Poland Company's entries for the acquisition assuming its stock has no par value.
(b) Record Poland Company's entries for the acquisition assuming its stock has a par value of $2 per share.

Exercise 7-6

(Journal entries for a pooling of interests; less than 100% acquisition)

Parr Company acquired 90% of the outstanding common stock of Stencil Company in a business combination accounted for as a pooling of interests. Parr issued 20,000 shares of $5 par value common stock in exchange for the Stencil common. On the acquisition date, Stencil had the following stockholders' equity balances.

Common stock, $2 par	$ 10,000
Additional paid-in capital	40,000
Retained earnings	200,000
Total	$250,000

Required: Assume Parr Company does not have a balance in additional paid-in capital. Record its entry for the acquisition of the Stencil Company common stock.

Exercise 7-7

(Pooling and merger)

Mega Company and Mini Company had the following balance sheets immediately prior to a transaction where Mega acquired 100% of the outstanding common stock of Mini. Mega then merged Mini Company into its operations and liquidated Mini. The exchange involved issuance of 10,000 shares of Mega no par stock for all of the outstanding common stock of Mini.

Assets	Mega	Mini
Cash	$ 50,000	$10,000
Inventory	125,000	35,000
Plant Assets, net	110,000	50,000
	285,000	95,000
Current liabilities	5,000	10,000
Long-term debt	55,000	30,000
Common stock, no par value	50,000	10,000
Additional contributed capital	100,000	
Retained earnings	75,000	45,000
	$285,000	$95,000

Required: Prepare a combined balance sheet for Mega and Mini subsequent to the acquisition and liquidation of Mini Company.

| Exercise 7-8 | **(Pooling and merger)** |

Refer to the pre-acquisition balance sheets of Mega Company and Mini Company in Exercise 7-7. Assume that Mega Company common had a par value of $1 per share. Prepare a post-acquisition balance sheet for the combined companies assuming Mega issued 5,000 shares of $1 par common stock for all of the outstanding no par shares of Mini Company.

| Exercise 7-9 | **(Comparison of pooling and purchase)** |

Shown below are the balance sheets of PXT Company and SOFWARE Company immediately prior to a merger of the two companies:

Assets	PXT	SOFWARE
Cash	$ 65,000	$ 5,000
Inventory	105,000	15,000
Office equipment	230,000	60,000
	300,000	80,000
Current liabilities	25,000	10,000
Long-term debt	80,000	20,000
Common stock, $1 par value	50,000	5,000
Additional paid-in capital	30,000	
Retained earnings	15,000	45,000
	$300,000	$ 80,000

Assume that PXT Company acquired 100% of the outstanding common stock of SOFWARE Company in exchange for 10,000 shares of its $1 par value common stock. On the acquisition date, PXT Company common stock had a market value of $40 per share. All of SOFWARE's assets and liabilities had book values approximately equal to fair market values, except for software assets with a zero basis but with fair market values of $200,000. These assets were the result of internal research and development activities that were charged to operations as R&D expense.

Required:

Assume that SOFWARE remains a subsidiary of PXT but consolidated financial statements for the two companies are prepared. What amount of software and other intangible assets will appear in the consolidated balance sheet if the combination is accounted for as a pooling of interests? What values will be assigned to software and other intangibles if the combination is accounted for as a purchase? Comment on the propriety of the two possibilities.

Exercise 7-10

(Criteria for using pooling accounting; internet research)

International accounting standards (see http://www.IASB.org) allow pooling accounting only when the business combination is organized in such a way as it is not possible to determine which company is the parent company and which company is the subsidiary company.

Required:

(a) Go to the IASB web site and find the accounting standard that discusses pooling accounting. Describe a hypothetical case where it might not be possible to identify a parent and its subsidiaries in a business combination.
(b) Compare the IASB criteria with current pooling criteria in the United States. Which of these do you believe is more appropriate? Justify your position.

Exercise 7-11

(Effect of pooling on balance sheet)

The following quote is from the 1999 Annual report of Pfizer Inc., a multinational pharmaceutical company whose corporate headquarters is in New York City.

> *"On February 7, 2000, we announced an agreement to merge with Warner-Lambert Company (Warner-Lambert). Under terms of the merger agreement, which has been approved by the Board of Directors of both Pfizer and Warner-Lambert, we will exchange 2.75 shares of Pfizer voting common stock for each outstanding share of Warner-Lambert voting common stock in a tax-free transaction valued at $98.31 per Warner Lambert share, or an equity value of $90 billion based on the closing price of our stock on February 4, 2000 of $35.75 per share."*

The transaction was to be accounted for as a pooling of interests. On December 31, 1999 Warner-Lambert had stockholders' equity with a book value of $3.6 billion.

Required:

(a) Why would Pfizer be willing to exchange common stock worth $90 billion for ownership of a company with a book value of $3.6 billion? What were the likely immediate effects on the stock prices of the two companies of the merger announcement?
(b) Comment on the long-term financial reporting implications of using pooling of interest accounting for this transaction.

Exercise 7-12

(Assumptions of pooling accounting)

The following quote is taken from the joint proxy statement for Pfizer Inc. and Warner-Lambert Company dated March 10, 2000.

> *"The merger is intended to qualify as a pooling-of-interests. The pooling-of-interests method of accounting assumes the companies had always been combined, and the historical financial statements for periods prior to closing of the merger are restated as though the companies had always been combined as required under United States generally accepted accounting principles."*

On December 31, 1999, four days prior to announcement of the merger, Warner-Lambert Common stock had a market value of $81 per share. The ratio of exchange of Pfizer stock for Warner-Lambert stock was 2.75 shares of Pfizer for each share of Warner-Lambert. Following is a table comparing the stock prices of the two companies on selected dates:

Date	Approximate market value of Pfizer	Pfizer market value × 2.75	Approximate market value of Warner-Lambert
9/3/99	39 – 1/8	107 – 5/8	68 – 13/16
10/1/99	37 – 5/16	102 – 5/8	68 – 1/2
11/5/99	34 – 1/4	94 – 3/16	89 – 7/8
12/31/99	32 – 7/16	89 – 3/16	81 – 15/16
1/28/00	35 – 3/16	96 – 3/4	91 – 1/8
3/31/00	36 – 9/16	100 – 9/16	97 – 15/16
4/28/00	42 – 1/8	115 – 13/16	114 – 11/16
5/26/00	44 – 15/16	123 – 9/16	125 – 1/8

Note that beginning approximately two months before the merger announcement the Pfizer equivalent (column 3) price of Warner-Lambert and the actual price of Warner-Lambert (Column 4) begin to merge. By April 28, 2000 as the financial news revealed that the merger was likely to be approved and finalized, the two prices were virtually the same.

Required:

Discuss the implications of the above data for the pooling of interests assumption that "the two companies had always been combined" therefore the market values of the assets of Warner-Lambert should not be considered in recording the merger.

PROBLEMS

Problem 7-1

(Acquisition, merger, and statement of financial position)

On January I, 20x3, Pittman Company acquired 100% of the outstanding common stock of Spirit Company in exchange for 10,000 shares of its own $1 par common stock in a transaction accounted for as a pooling of interests. Pittman Company also incurred $5,000 of direct acquisition costs in the form of consulting fees and $4,000 of issue costs. Immediately after the stock acquisition, Spirit Company was merged into Pittman Company and dissolved. The balance sheets of the two companies immediately prior to the merger were as follows:

	Pittman Company	Spirit Company
Cash	$ 75,000	45,000
Other current assets	155,000	65,000
Plant assets	250,000	140,000
Total assets	480,000	250,000
Current liabilities	35,000	50,000
Long-term debt	180,000	100,000
Capital stock, $1 par	100,000	
Capital stock, $5 par		25,000
Retained earnings	165,000	75,000
	$480,000	$250,000

At the date of acquisition, the book values and fair market values of the net assets of both companies were approximately equal, except for Spirit Company plant assets that had an estimated fair value of $160,000.

Required:

(1) Prepare the Pittman Company journal entries to record the acquisition of the Spirit Company common stock and the other related costs.
(2) Prepare the Pittman Company journal entries to merge Spirit Company and close the investment in Spirit Common account.
(3) Prepare a statement of financial position for Pittman immediately subsequent to the merger.

Problem 7-2

(Acquisition, merger, and statement of financial position)

Refer to the data in problem 5-1. Assume that Pittman acquired 100% of the outstanding common stock of Spirit Company in exchange for 10,000 shares of its own $3 par value common stock. Further assume that there were no direct acquisition costs, but Pittman did pay $5,000 for issue expenses incurred and internal expenses of $15,000 in connection with the merger. The acquisition qualifies as a pooling of interests.

Required:

(1) Prepare Pittman Company's journal entries to record the acquisition of Spirit Company common stock and the other related costs .
(2) Prepare the Pittman Company entries to record the merger.
(3) Prepare a postacquisition statement of financial position for Pittman Company.

Problem 7-3

(Acquisition and merger, comparison of purchase and pooling)

On January 1, 20x4, Pro-Golf Company and Spillover Company agree to a business combination whereby Pro-Golf acquires all of the outstanding common stock of Spillover. Spillover Company is to be liquidated and merged into Pro-Golf Company on March 1, 20x4, the effective date of the merger. On the date of acquisition, Pro-Golf has 100,000 common shares authorized and 50,000 common shares issued and outstanding. The Pro-Golf common has a par value of $1.50 per share and a market value of $10 per share.

On March 1, 20x4, immediately prior to the merger, Spillover had the following book and fair market values:

Assets	Book Value	Fair Value
Cash	$ 15,000	$ 15,000
Other current assets	25,000	40,000
Plant and equipment	165,000	275,000
	205,000	

Liabilities and Equity		
Current liabilities	10,000	10,000
Long-term liabilities	40,000	50,000
Common stock: $1 par	50,000	
Retained earnings	105,000	
	$205,000	

Required:

1. Assume the acquisition qualifies as a pooling of interests. Prepare the entries to record the acquisition of Spillover common and the merger on the books of Pro-Golf if the consideration given is 20,000 shares of Pro-Golf $1.50 par value common stock, and direct acquisition cost are $15,000.
2. Assume the acquisition does **not** qualify as a pooling of interests. Prepare the entries to record the acquisition of Spillover common and the merger on the books of Pro-Golf if the consideration given is 30,000 shares of $1.50 par value common stock, and direct acquisition costs are $15,000.

Problem 7-4	**(Acquisition, merger, and statement of financial position)**

Refer to the data in problem 7-3. Prepare the entries to record the acquisition as a pooling of interests if Pro-Golf issues 40,000 shares of $1.50 par value common stock for all of the outstanding common stock of Spillover, and also pays $10,000 in issue costs. Assume Pro-Golf has a preacquisition additional paid-in capital balance of $100,000. There are no direct acquisition costs.

Problem 7-5	**(Acquisition and merger, conceptual basis for pooling of interests)**

On July l, 20x1, Big-O Corporation and Rocky Top Company agree to a business combination whereby Big-O acquires all of the outstanding common stock of Rocky Top in exchange for 100,000 shares of Big-O no par value common stock. Rocky Top is to be liquidated and merged into Big-O on September 1, 20x1, the effective date of the merger. On September l, 20x1, Big-O common has a market value of $3.00 per share. Big-O also pays $15,000 to a consulting firm in connection with the merger. The internal costs of the Big-O acquisitions department are estimated to be $15,000 for this acquisition.

On September 1, 20x1, immediately prior to the merger, Rocky Top had the following book and fair market values:

	Book Value	**Fair Value**
Cash	$ 15,000	$ 15,000
Other current assets	135.000	160,000
Plant and equipment	205,000	250,000
Patents	55,000	30,000
	410,000	
Current liabilities	45,000	45,000
Bonds payable	180,000	190,000
Common stock, no par value	20,000	
Retained earnings	165,000	
	$ 410,000	

Required:

(1) Record all the journal entries on the books of Big-O to record the acquisition and merger of Rocky Top, assuming that the acquisition is to be accounted for as a pooling of interests.
(2) Compare the financial statements of this combination as compared with the financial statements that would result had the purchase method of accounting been used. Indicate your opinion about the propriety of the pooling of interests method based on your comparisons.

Problem 7-6	**(Acquisition and merger, consolidated balance sheet in a pooling of interests)**

Partridge Company acquired 100% of the outstanding voting common stock of Dove Company on January 1, 20x1, in exchange for 15,000 shares of its own $5 par common stock. The transaction qualifies as a pooling of interests. Immediately prior to the acquisition, the two companies had the following statements of financial position:

Assets	Partridge	Dove
Cash	$ 100,000	$ 33,000
Accounts receivable	37,500	44,000
Inventories	200,000	47,500
Land	125,500	20,000
Building	204,750	54,500
Equipment	177,400	86,000
	845,150	285,000

Liabilities and Equity

Current liabilities	44,650	65,000
Long-term debt	305,000	100,000
Common stock, $5 par	250,000	
Common stock, $1 par		80,000
Retained earnings	245,500	40,000
	$ 845,150	$ 285,000

Required:

1. Analyze the pooling of interests transaction and record the journal entry for acquisition of Dove Company on January 1, 20x1.
2. Prepare a worksheet for preparation of a consolidated balance sheet immediately subsequent to the acquisition. (Hint: be sure to adjust Partridge Company accounts for the acquisition entry prior to setting up the worksheet.)

Problem 7-7

(Acquisition and consolidated statement of financial position—pooling of interests)

Statements of financial position for Detroit Corporation and Toledo Company as of December 31, 20x3, are shown below:

Assets	Detroit	Toledo
Cash	$ 224,000	$ 25,000
Accounts receivable	321,000	33,250
Inventories	88,500	45,850
Land	35,000	10,000
Buildings	87,400	50,000
Equipment	135,450	33,000
Investment in Toledo	116,415	
	1,007,765	197,100
Liabilities and Equity		
Current liabilities	88,000	27,750
Long-term debt	200,000	40,000
Common stock, $1 par	250,000	
Common stock, $5 par		25,000
Additional paid-in capital	100,000	20,000
Retained earning	369,765	84,350
	$ 1,007,765	$ 197,100

On this date, Detroit acquired 90% of the outstanding voting common stock of Toledo in a pooling of interests method acquisition by issuing 10,000 shares of its $1 par value common stock. Detroit also paid $5,000 to a consulting firm for a finder's fee. All of Toledo's assets and liabilities had book values approximately equal to fair market values except for Buildings that had a fair market value of $60,000 and book values of $50,000.

Required:

1. Prepare a worksheet for a consolidated statement of financial position as of December 31, 20x3, based on the above data.
2. Give the journal entries that Detroit recorded for the acquisition on its separate books.

Problem 7-8

(Acquisition and consolidated financial statements—pooling of interests)

Pearl Company acquired a 90% interest in the common stock of Satin Company on January 1, 20x1, in exchange for 75,000 shares of its $1 par common stock, at a time when Satin Company had common stock of $100,000 and retained earnings of $175,000 The acquisition qualifies as a pooling of interests. The financial statements of Pearl and Satin at the end of the year 20x1 are as follows:

Statement of Income	Pearl	Satin
For the Year ended 12/31/x1		
Sales	$ 705,000	$ 350,000
Equity in Satin income	135,000	
Cost of sales	(320,000)	(140,000)
Operating expenses	(110,000)	(60,000)
Net income	410,000	150,000
Retained earnings, Jan. 1	125,000	175,000
Net income	410,000	150,000
Dividends declared	(80,000)	(60,000)
Retained earnings, Dec. 31	455,000	265,000
Balance sheet 12/31/x1		
Cash	166,200	28,000
Accounts receivable	74,300	22,600
Notes receivable	10,000	
Inventories	75,700	77,200
Land	90,000	20,000
Buildings - net	160,000	225,000
Machinery - net	275,000	110,000
Investment in Satin	328,500	
	1,179,700	482,800
Accounts payable	123,400	52,400
Dividends payable	25,000	
Bonds payable	151,300	65,400
Capital stock	300,000	100,000
Additional paid-in capital	125,000	
Retained earnings, Dec. 31	455,000	265,000
	$ 1,179,700	$ 482,800

Required:

Prepare a worksheet for consolidated financial statements for Pearl Company and Satin Company for the year ended December 31, 20x1.

Problem 7-9   **(Acquisition and consolidated financial statements—pooling of interests, cost method)**

Refer to the data in problem 7-8. Assume the same facts except that Pearl used the cost method to account for its investment in Satin. In this case, the balances in the accounts of the two companies at December 31, 20x1, would be as follows:

Statement of Income	Pearl	Satin
For the Year ended 12/31/x1		
Sales	$ 705,000	$ 350,000
Dividend income	54,000	
Cost of sales	(320,000)	(140,000)
Operating expenses	(110,000)	(60,000)
Net income	329,000	150,000
Retained earnings, Jan. 1	125,000	175,000
Net income	329,000	150,000
Dividends declared	(80,000)	(60,000)
Retained earnings, Dec. 31	374,000	265,000
Balance sheet 12/31/x1		
Cash	166,200	28,000
Accounts receivable	74,300	22,600
Notes receivable	10,000	
Inventories	75,700	77,200
Land	90,000	20,000
Buildings - net	160,000	225,000
Machinery - net	275,000	110,000
Investment in Satin	247,500	
	1,098,700	482,800
Accounts payable	123,400	52,400
Dividends payable	25,000	
Bonds payable	151,300	65,400
Capital stock	300,000	100,000
Additional paid-in capital	125,000	
Retained earnings, Dec. 31	374,000	265,000
	$ 1,098,700	$ 482,800

Required:

Assume the acquisition was accounted for as a pooling of interests. Prepare a worksheet for consolidated financial statements for Pearl Company and Satin Company for the year ended December 31, 20x1.

Problem 7-10 **(Conceptual basis of pooling of interests)**

In September 1996, a joint proxy statement of the Bell Atlantic Corporation and NYNEX Corporation announced the intention of the two companies to merge in a business combination to be accounted for as a pooling of interests. Bell Atlantic was to become the parent company, and NYNEX would survive as a separate wholly-owned subsidiary. Bell Atlantic and NYNEX were both telecommunications companies originally created in the aftermath of the court-ordered breakup of AT&T in the early 1980s. The stock exchange agreement, which was subject to the approval of the shareholders of both companies, contained the following information:

	Bell Atlantic	**NYNEX**
Market price on announcement date 4/19/96	$65	$53
Market price on 9/5/96, just prior to printing of the Joint Proxy Statement	55.25	42.625
Ratio of Bell Atlantic shares to be received for each NYNEX share		.768
Book value of the stockholders' equity on June 30, 1996	$7.1 l billion	$6.5 billion
Weighted average outstanding common shares, six months ended 6/30/96 (in millions of shares)	439.5	435.5

Required:

1. What is the market value of the NYNEX common stock acquired by Bell Atlantic in this acquisition? What is the apparent market value of the Bell Atlantic shares given to NYNEX shareholders in exchange?
2. If the transaction was accounted for as a pooling of interests, at what pro-forma amount would the combined shareholders' equity be?
3. Is the accounting treatment to be followed consistent with the economic circumstances of the merger? Explain.

FOREIGN EXCHANGE AND TRANSLATION

2

Globalization of economic activity has created the need for all business students to have a greater understanding of international business issues. Part 2 of this book introduces the student to two such issues. Chapter 8 reviews the nature of foreign exchange and explains the complexities created when a transaction is denominated in a currency other than the domestic currency. Transactions denominated in foreign exchange have additional risks, caused by fluctuations in the value of the foreign exchange, that do not occur in connection with domestic transactions. Chapter 8 explains some managerial actions that can be taken to mitigate or **hedge** these risks and how these hedging transactions are accounted for.

Globalization has also resulted in multinational business organizations where companies have subsidiaries domiciled in many different nations. Consolidation of the financial statements of these business organizations requires that the financial statements of foreign subsidiaries be **translated** prior to consolidation. This process requires translation of not only the language, but also the effects of differences in both accounting principles and the currency values. Chapter 9 introduces the subject of foreign currency translation by explaining the theory and practice of translating foreign currency financial statements, assuming that both language and accounting principles differences have already been resolved.

CHAPTER 8

INTERNATIONAL ACCOUNTING—FOREIGN CURRENCY CONCEPTS AND TRANSACTIONS

LEARNING OBJECTIVES

- Identify accounting-related business problems that arise in connection with international business

- Explain what is meant by the need to manage risk associated with foreign currency transactions

- Demonstrate an understanding of the key terminology associated with international accounting

- Account for import and export transactions

- Account for forward exchange contracts and other hedging transactions, including contracts that hedge foreign exchange assets and liabilities, foreign exchange commitments, and contracts whose purpose is to speculate in foreign currency

ACCOUNTING PROBLEMS IN INTERNATIONAL BUSINESS

Today, many companies have international operations. They import from foreign suppliers, export to foreign customers, and have subsidiaries domiciled in other nations. For example, in 1997, Exxon Corporation had net sales of $135 billion—of which $28 billion were domestic, $21 billion were from other Western Hemisphere operations, and $83 billion were from Eastern Hemisphere operations. Pharmaceutical manufacturer Pfizer, Inc. had total annual revenue in 1997 of $12.5 billion of which only $6.8 billion came from domestic customers. Business operations conducted across international boundaries are affected by factors that either do not exist for domestic operations or are substantially less significant. These factors include differences in language, culture, social customs, laws, and level of economic development. In addition, business transactions that are denominated in a foreign currency are potentially affected by changes in the value of the foreign currency relative to the domestic currency.

Translation of foreign currency financial statements

Even nations that speak the same language have different social customs, laws, and needs that affect business practices. In addition, the relative level of economic development, the scope of capital markets, and the role of government in economic activity have an impact on business practices. When language differences, different banking practices, and the use of a foreign currency are combined with these other factors, measurement and reporting problems arise that are not present in purely domestic transactions. Some of these reporting problems are not easily resolved. For example, Japanese corporations make greater use of debt financing than do U.S. corporations. Debt financing has a direct impact on a company's debt to equity ratio—a key factor in evaluating risk. However, comparisons of debt equity ratios of Japanese and U.S. companies cannot be made without taking into account the differences in business and lending practices. Just as we cannot always effectively translate language (when we do so, some of the context is removed), we cannot remove the context from a business transaction or from a financial statement and analyze from our own perspective.

To explore this point a little further, consider the following stanza from popular French singer Michel Sardou's song "S'enfuir et Après,"[1] in which he expresses the futility of trying to escape life's problems by fleeing from them:

> S'enfuir et après
> Revivre à peu près
> Les mêmes choses qu'on fuit

Translated into English, much of the emotion in the words is lost because the poetic character of the phrases is lost in translation. To some degree, we can overcome this problem with skillful translation, but the result is always different from the original. The same problem will happen to a greater degree with the translation of a foreign financial statement because more variables are involved. In order to translate a foreign currency financial statement, we must (1) translate the language (including all the technical terminology) (2) recast the financial statements into U.S. accounting principles, and (3) translate the foreign currency amounts into the U.S. dollar. Even after these translations are done, the financial statements still reflect differences in laws, business practices, and economic conditions. Thus, expert use of accounting information from a foreign company requires understanding the business practices and other unique

---

[1] "S'enfuir et Après" by J. Reveaux and M. Sardou, from the CD *Salut*, sung by M. Sardou, TREMA, 1997.

conditions that affect the statements. A foreign language is not English that has been translated into that language, and foreign business practices and foreign exchange transactions are (usually) not American practices and transactions adopted by other nations. Therefore, we must always remember that some relevance is potentially lost anytime we perform translations and use translated data. Conceding this limitation, we still must translate foreign financial statements in an international business environment. In particular, translation of foreign financial statements is a prerequisite to applying the equity method of accounting to a foreign investment, to complying with reporting requirements for listing foreign company stock on a domestic stock exchange, and to consolidating the financial statements of a foreign subsidiary.

Foreign currency transactions

In addition to the issue of translation of foreign currency financial statements, the denomination of import and export transactions in foreign currency introduces the issue of foreign exchange risk into managerial decisions and transaction analysis. The risk associated with an import or export transaction results from the agreement to receive or pay foreign currency in settlement of an account payable or receivable. Since units of a foreign currency fluctuate continuously in price (in terms of domestic currency), an account payable or receivable will likely have a different value on its settlement date than on its origination date. Import and export transactions give rise to unique accounting problems **only** if the transactions are denominated in a foreign currency. For example, a sale of products or services to a Japanese customer is no different from a sale to a domestic customer unless the Japanese customer is going to pay its bill in foreign currency, say the Japanese Yen (¥). Whether an import or export transaction is denominated in a foreign currency is dependent on what the parties to the transaction agree to. Again, refer to the example of a sale of goods or services to a Japanese customer. The sales contract could specify payment in U.S. $, Japanese ¥, or perhaps the currency of a third nation. For international transactions between a U.S. company and a company in a developed nation, the currency of the transaction is usually that of one of the two countries where companies are located. When a transaction involves two smaller countries, the currency of the transaction is unlikely to be currency of either nation. Most international transactions are denominated in a so-called "hard" currency, such as the U.S. $, the European Community Euro (EU), the Japanese ¥, or that of another developed nation. For example, international transactions in crude oil, one of the most widely traded commodities, are usually denominated in U.S. $. Thus, an import into the United States of crude oil from a Saudi Arabian supplier, denominated in U.S. $, does not expose the importer to reportable foreign exchange risk in its U.S. $ financial statements.

▶ INTERPRETIVE EXERCISE

In a credit sale of goods from a U.S. supplier to a Canadian customer denominated in U.S. $, which parties have foreign exchange risk? Explain.

Risk management of foreign exchange assets and liabilities

Because exchange gains and losses may result from import and export transactions denominated in a foreign currency, business corporations often engage in risk management transactions to minimize the effect of potential exchange losses on overall profitability. These transactions are called hedging transactions and include the purchase and sale of **forward exchange contracts.** A forward contract is an agreement between two parties (one of whom is almost always a financial institution) to purchase or sell a fixed quantity of foreign exchange for future delivery at a pre-determined price.[2] These contracts are similar to commodity futures contracts such as those used by grain merchants to manage the risks associated with the purchase and sale of grain for future delivery. Commodities futures contracts involve the agreement by two parties to exchange (on a preset future date) a quantity of a com-modity for a fixed dollar price. Futures contracts for foreign exchange are also traded on commodity exchanges. A forward exchange contract differs from a futures contract in that forward contracts may be arranged for the exact amount of foreign exchange desired and can be specified to mature on any given date. Another differ-ence is that futures contracts are settled for cash on the maturity date and the com-modity is never actually delivered. Forward contracts, however, are transactions between business entities and financial institutions, and the foreign exchange is deliv-ered on the maturity date of the contract.

In summary, companies commonly encounter two classes of accounting problems related to international business. Companies with investments in foreign companies and foreign companies whose stock is listed on domestic exchanges must translate their financial statements. In addition, companies that engage in international trade may encounter business problems associated with foreign exchange risk. The remain-der of this chapter explains some economic issues associated with foreign trade, illus-trates accounting for import and export transactions, and explains accounting for risk management transactions. Chapter 9 covers the theory and practice of translating for-eign currency financial statements.

ECONOMIC ISSUES IN IMPORT AND EXPORT TRANSACTIONS

Foreign exchange is a commodity in the same sense that gold, corn, and soybeans are commodities. As such, it has a market price that fluctuates in response to supply and demand for the currency. The most important economic fact to remember when learning to analyze transactions involving foreign exchange is that **the market value of foreign exchange is constantly changing.** If a company holds a foreign exchange asset—a bank balance, a receivable, or an investment security denominated in foreign exchange—**the company will realize a loss if the value of the foreign currency declines and a gain if the value of the foreign currency increases.** By the same logic, a company that has liabilities to be settled in foreign exchange will **realize a gain if the value of the foreign exchange declines and a loss if the value of the foreign exchange increases.** In general, these foreign exchange gains and losses are included in income in the year realized.[3] The following section explains these rela-tionships in the context of day-to-day business transactions.

Foreign exchange assets and liabilities

When a company makes a credit purchase or a credit sale denominated in a foreign currency, the transaction creates a foreign currency liability (for a purchase) or a

[2] Statement of Financial Accounting Standards No. 52, *Foreign Currency Translation* (Norwalk, CT: FASB, 1981).
[3] *Ibid.*, par. 15.

foreign currency asset (for a sale). These assets and liabilities are monetary items with a readily determinable market value and must be accounted for at fair market value. Since the price of foreign exchange floats, the value of foreign exchange assets and liabilities is unlikely to be worth the same on the date they are settled as they were on the date they were initially recorded. Thus, a foreign exchange transaction has an additional element of risk associated with it that does not exist with respect to transactions denominated in domestic currency. Sometimes the values of foreign currencies can change substantially over very short periods of time. Other long-term changes in foreign exchange values have also been observed. For example, the number of Japanese Yen that can be exchanged for one U.S. dollar varied over the five years ending in November 1999 from as low as about 80 to around 140. However, the long-term trend shows that the dollar has declined in value relative to the Yen.

Since foreign currency assets and liabilities are accounted for at fair market value, gains and losses must be accrued on these items as a result of changes in the value of foreign exchange. If a domestic company holds a foreign currency asset (a receivable, for example) a rise in the market price of the foreign currency makes the receivable worth more, giving rise to a **gain.** Likewise, a fall in the market value of the foreign currency makes the receivable worth less, giving rise to a **loss.** These price changes have the opposite effect on foreign currency liabilities. A fall in the market value of a foreign currency makes a foreign currency liability worth less because the amount of foreign currency needed to pay the liability can be purchased for fewer dollars. This event would be reflected in the accounts by reducing the carrying value of the liability and reporting a gain. Conversely, a rise in the market value of the foreign currency results in the need to spend more dollars to purchase the foreign exchange needed to pay the liability, giving rise to an adjustment that increases the carrying value of the liability and recording an equal amount of loss. The following table summarizes the above concepts:

Type of transaction	Effect on income if the market value of the foreign currency rises	Effect on income if the market value of the foreign currency falls
Credit sale denominated in foreign currency, creating a receivable	*Gain*	*Loss*
Credit purchase denominated in foreign currency, creating a payable	*Loss*	*Gain*

▶ INTERPRETIVE EXERCISE

West Creek Company had the following assets in its balance sheet at 12/31/20x1:

	Book value	Fair market value
Trading securities	$45,000	$38,000
Investment in Euros	21,500	21,900
Accounts receivable in Euros	24,500	22,300

How much gain or loss would be included in net income as a result of the above book value-fair market value differences?

Foreign exchange rates for foreign currency transactions

Foreign exchange rates may be expressed in the domestic currency price of the foreign currency (the **direct rate**) or the number of units of foreign currency that can be exchanged for one unit of domestic currency (the **indirect rate**). For example, the recent range of the French franc in comparison with the U.S. dollar is a direct rate from around \$.16 = 1FF to \$.22 = 1FF. In indirect terms, a direct rate of \$.16 for the French franc equals an indirect rate of 6.25 (1/\$.16) francs for one dollar and a direct rate of \$.22 equals 4.545 francs (1/\$.22). By the year 2002, many of the nations in the European Community (EC) will have adopted the Euro as a common currency. The transition period for the early adopters of a common currency began on January 1, 1999. On Wednesday, February 3, 1999, the Euro was quoted in *The Wall Street Journal*[4] at \$1.1304 per Euro (the direct rate) or .8846 Euros per \$1.00 U.S. (the indirect rate). As the above French franc example demonstrates, either rate can be calculated by computing the reciprocal of the other. Here are the conversions for the Euro example:

Indirect to direct: 1/.8846 = \$1.1304
Direct to indirect: \$1/1.304 = .8846

Foreign exchange transaction data is most easily calculated using direct rates. The financial pages of major newspapers report one or both exchange rates on a daily basis for many currencies.

Foreign exchange rates also may be described as either **fixed** or **floating.** Fixed exchange rates are set by government and do not change. However, a fixed exchange rate system will generally be ineffective unless the governments are willing to redeem currencies into something else of value, such as gold coin or bullion. From the end of World War II until 1973, the United States and other large nations operated under a system of fixed exchange rates, and the United States redeemed dollar reserves of other nations in gold bullion. In 1971, the United States suspended redemption of dollar reserves in gold bullion because of pressure on the dollar, which was in excess supply relative to other currencies. Within a few years, no country remained on the international gold standard. Under the current exchange rate system, the major currencies are allowed to float although central banks occasionally intervene in the market. Smaller countries "peg" their currency to one of the major currencies or to a composite currency.

A business or an individual may purchase or sell foreign exchange for immediate delivery or for future delivery with a forward exchange contract. Normally these transactions are arranged through banks and currency brokers. For purposes of recording foreign exchange transactions, two exchange rate concepts are essential. The **spot rate** for a currency is today's price for immediate delivery. A **forward rate** is today's price for future delivery. For example, the 90-day forward rate for the German Mark is the price in U.S. dollars that would be paid or received today for delivery of German Marks in 90 days. Forward rates can be obtained from a financial institution for any desired date. Forward rates are also quoted in *The Wall Street Journal* for 30, 90, and 180-day delivery. For example, on Wednesday, February 3, 1999, *The Wall Street Journal* had the following quotes for the German Mark:

---

[4] *The Wall Street Journal*, February 4, 1999, p. C16.

Germany (Mark)	.5780
1 – month forward	.5787
3 – months forward	.5806
6 – months forward	.5836

Based on the above table, we can conclude that DM 10,000 could be purchased on February 3, 1999 for $5,780. However, DM 10,000 would cost $5,787 if bought on February 3, 1999, but not exchanged until one month had elapsed.

The difference between the spot rate and the forward rate for a particular currency at any point in time is caused by the fact that interest rates for instruments of equal risk are different in the two countries. For example, assume that the six-month interest rates in the United States and Germany are 2.5% and 2.8% for investments of the same relative risk. Further assume that the spot rate for the German Mark is $.5600 per Mark. Under these conditions, the purchase of DM 10,000 for $5600 would produce the following sum after six months:[5]

$$DM\ 10,000 + (10,000 \times 2.8\%) = DM\ 10,280.00$$

Whereas an investment of the same sum in $ at the U.S. interest rate would yield:

$$\$5,600 + (\$5,600 \times 2.5\%) = \$5,740$$

The equilibrium forward rate for the Mark is the rate that sets the two investments equal in terms of return, thus eliminating arbitrage profits:

$$Fwd\ rate = \$\ 5,740/DM\ 10,280 = \$.55837$$

In this example, the forward rate can be determined by the following expression:

(1)   Fwd rate = Spot rate $\times (1+ i_d)/(1+ i_f)$
       Where: i_d = domestic interest rate per period of time
              i_f = foreign interest rate per period of time

And applying formula (1) above to our example data yields the following forward rate calculation:

$$\$.55837 = \$.56 \times (1.025/1.028)$$

Foreign exchange rates for translation of foreign currency financial statements

Two other exchange rate concepts are important in translating foreign currency financial statements. While this subject is not covered until the following chapter, these two terms are introduced now. The so-called **current rate** is the spot rate on the balance sheet date. A **historical rate** is the exchange rate on any particular day in the past when a transaction has occurred that must be translated. Thus, there may be as many historical rates as there are dates of relevance to the translation. In addition, the **weighted average rate** is determined by averaging the daily spot rates for a specific period of time, say for the last three months of a given year or for the entire year.

---

[5] A 360-day year is assumed in the following formula for purposes of simplification.

ACCOUNTING FOR IMPORT AND EXPORT TRANSACTIONS

Import and export transactions denominated in foreign exchange are straightforward transactions. Assuming the transaction involves a credit purchase or sale, there are income statement consequences related to the resulting account receivable or account payable because these accounts are to be settled in foreign exchange. In the case of a receivable, the asset is essentially an investment with a fluctuating market value. In the case of a payable, the liability fluctuates in value. If the spot rate for the relevant foreign currency rises, both the value of a foreign currency receivable and the value of a foreign currency payable will rise. If the value of the foreign currency falls, both the value of a foreign currency receivable and a foreign currency payable will fall. Thus, it is necessary to adjust foreign currency assets and liabilities to their fair market value in the financial statements and include the corresponding foreign exchange gain or loss in income. It is also necessary to report foreign exchange gains or losses on settlement of foreign currency assets and liabilities equal to the difference between book value and fair market value of the assets and liabilities on their settlement date.

Accounting for a purchase of inventory

As an illustration, assume that Domestic Company (a U.S. Company) purchases inventory from Overseas Company (a Dutch Company) on December 1, 20x1, terms net 60 days, to be paid in the amount of EU 100,000. Further assume that Domestic Company has a fiscal year ending December 31 and that the direct spot rates for the Euro were as follows:

December 1, 20x1	$1.13
December 31, 20x1	$1.16
January 29, 20x1	$1.15

Assuming the use of the perpetual inventory method, the journal entry to record the purchase is:

12/01/x1 Inventory	113,000	
Accounts payable		113,000

To record purchase of inventory
(EU 100,000 × $1.13)

On December 31, 20x1, the account payable balance must be adjusted to its fair market value based on the spot rate for the Euro on that date. Since the spot rate for the Euro has risen to $1.16, the value of the liability has increased and Domestic Company will record a foreign exchange loss equal to the increase in the value of the 100,000 Euros needed to settle the account payable.

12/31/x1 Foreign exchange loss	3,000	
Accounts payable		3,000

To adjust the liability to the spot rate on December 31
EU 100,000 × (1.16 − 1.13)

Finally, the entry to record payment of the liability on January 29, 20x2, when the price of the Euro has fallen to $1.15 would be as follows:

01/29/x2 Accounts payable	116,000	
Foreign exchange gain		1,000
Investment in Euros		115,000

To record settlement of the liability at the spot rate on January 29, 20x2
(EU 100,000 × 1.15 = $115,000)

The effect of the three entries on the accounts payable balance is summarized in the following T account:

Accounts payable—Overseas Company

		113,000	12/01/x1
01/29/x2	116,000	3,000	12/31/x1
	0		

Notice that the 01/29/x2 entry involves a credit to "Investment in Euros" rather than to cash. The payment is not being made in U.S. $. If you assume that Domestic Company does not maintain any bank accounts denominated in Euros, then the credit would be to cash for the $115,000 required to purchase the EU 100,000 draft used to pay the account. This illustration assumes that Domestic has a Euro bank account called "Investment in Euros," which it uses to pay its Euro obligations. This would be a standard business practice of companies that import on a regular basis.

● INTERPRETIVE EXERCISE

Assume that the spot rate for the Euro was $1.11 on December 31, 20x1 and $1.095 on January 29, 20x2. Give the appropriate adjusting journal entry on December 31, 20x1 and the entry to pay the account on January 29, 20x2.

Illustration of the sale of inventory

Assume that Domestic Company sells inventory to Yokahama Trading Company of Japan on November 1, 20x1 for a price of ¥ 10,000,000, with payment due on February 28, 20x2. Further assume that Domestic Company has a fiscal year end on December 31 and that relevant direct exchange rates for the Japanese Yen are as follows:[6]

November 1, 20x1	$.0070922
December 31, 20x1	$.0074074
February 28, 20x1	$.0069444

The entry to record the sale on November 1, 20x1 is as follows:

11/01/x1 Accounts receivable	70,922	
Sales		70,922

To record a sale of 10,000,000 Yen at a spot rate of $.0070922

---

[6] The reader will note that the prices for the Japanese Yen are given to seven decimal places. Unlike the U.S. currency, which uses decimals to differentiate between dollars and cents, Japan uses a single currency unit—the Yen. While exchange rates between currencies are determined strictly by market forces, the nominal exchange ratios between a non-decimal currency (such as the Japanese Yen) and a decimal currency (such as the U.S. dollar) will usually be larger than between two decimal currencies. At the time this book was written, the indirect rate of exchange for the Yen was in the range of 120 to 145 Yen for one U.S. dollar. The rates used in this example fall within that range after conversion to direct rates.

On December 31, 20x1, when Domestic Company closes its books, the value of the Yen has risen substantially to a direct rate of ¥1 = $.0074074. The rise in the price of the Yen means that Domestic Company's receivable has increased in value, requiring an adjusting entry recording an exchange gain on December 31. Had the value of the Yen fallen, the receivable would have declined in value, requiring the recording of an exchange loss. The correct entry at December 31 is as follows:

12/31/x1	Accounts receivable	1,152	
	Exchange gain		1,152

> To record an increase in the carrying amount of the receivable equal to 10,000,000 Yen × ($.0074074 − $.0072922)

Finally, on the settlement date, the value of the Yen has declined in value to $.0069444 resulting in an exchange loss during the year 20x2 equal to the decrease in the value of the receivable as of February 28, 20x2 as compared with its book value on January 1.

2/28/x2	Investment in Yen	69,444	
	Exchange loss	2,630	
	Accounts receivable		72,074

> To record collection of the receivable when (10,000,000 Yen × $.0069444 = $69,444)

The effect of the three entries on the accounts receivable balance is summarized in the following T account:

Accounts receivable—Yokahama Company

11/01/x1	70,922		
12/31/x1	1,152	72,074	02/28/x2
	0		

Notice that the collection of the receivable results in a debit to an account "Investment in Yen" rather than to "Cash." Unless the foreign exchange was immediately sold, there would be no cash asset received in this transaction; the customer pays with a check or draft in Japanese currency. The normal business practice of a company that regularly exports to Japan would be to maintain a bank account denominated in Japanese currency.

● **INTERPRETIVE EXERCISE**

> Assuming the spot rate for the Yen was $.0068668 on December 31, 20x1 and $.0067556 on February 28, 20x2, give the required adjusting journal entry on December 31 and the entry to collect the receivable on February 28, 20x2.

Other foreign exchange transactions

In addition to purchase of inventory items or sale of products and services, companies may engage in other types of transactions that create foreign currency assets and liabilities. These include purchase of plant and equipment, sale of investments (including subsidiaries), or the sale of assets other than inventory. The accounting principles illustrated above regarding accrual and realization of gains and losses on foreign exchange assets and liabilities apply equally to these other transactions.

MANAGING FOREIGN EXCHANGE RISK WITH FORWARD EXCHANGE CONTRACTS

Business corporations buying and selling internationally may wish to minimize the risks associated with foreign exchange assets and liabilities. There are several reasons why this action may be desirable. Most significantly, companies may desire to focus their managerial and technical expertise on their primary business activity, whatever that may be. For example, a company engaged in the production and sale of products for industrial or retail customers worldwide may not wish to complicate its forecasting effort by trying to anticipate exchange rate changes in foreign currencies. Furthermore, the sheer volume of transactions that any particular company has may make the risks associated with foreign exchange unacceptable. Related to this second point is the fact that movement in foreign exchange rates is very unpredictable and may be material over very short periods of time. For example, during the years 1997–1998 the Korean Won depreciated more than 50% against the U.S. dollar in the aftermath of a financial crisis in several developed and developing Asian nations.

Foreign exchange risk exists whenever a company has an asset or a liability denominated in a foreign currency. The accounting records of a company are kept in domestic currency. As a result, foreign currency assets and liabilities are similar to marketable securities in that their value rises or falls with changes in the spot rate for the foreign currency. As we have already learned, a purchase denominated in foreign currency creates a foreign currency liability. Likewise, a credit sale denominated in foreign currency creates a foreign currency asset. Since the accounts receivable or payable from these transactions change in value as the value of the relevant foreign currency changes, foreign exchange risk results. A common way of minimizing the risk associated with these transactions is to **hedge** the risk using a forward exchange contract. This type of hedge is often called **a hedge against an exposed net asset or liability position.** This term simply denotes that the company has entered into a primary business transaction creating an asset or a liability that will be settled by payment or receipt of foreign exchange. The foreign currency risk associated with a foreign currency asset is that the **value of the asset will decline if the spot rate for the foreign currency declines.** A company may avoid (hedge) virtually all of this risk by entering into a forward exchange contract (on or about the date the foreign currency asset is received) to **sell** an equal amount of foreign currency (on or about the date the account is to be collected). If a forward contract is made for the exact amount of the foreign currency asset for the exact time period the asset is held, the risk is fully hedged. Essentially, hedging involves entering into a forward exchange contract creating a foreign exchange liability that offsets the foreign exchange risk associated with the foreign exchange asset. Exactly the opposite type of action is appropriate if the foreign exchange risk to be hedged is associated with a foreign exchange liability. The risk associated with a foreign currency liability is that **the value of resources needed to pay the liability will rise if the spot rate for the foreign currency rises.** In this case, the appropriate action is to enter into a forward contract to **buy** an equal amount of foreign exchange for delivery on or about the day the liability is to be paid. The only negative economic consequences associated with hedging are that (1) the spread between spot and forward exchange rates often results in a small cost of hedging, and (2) the natural result of hedging against exchange losses is that any potential foreign exchange gains will also be hedged. That is, a forward contract hedges potential losses, but it also hedges potential gains. The loss (or gain) on the original purchase or sale transaction is offset by the gain (or loss) on the hedging transaction in a fully hedged arrangement. The accounting procedures associated with these two types of hedges will be illustrated shortly.

The second type of foreign exchange risk that can be hedged is the risk associated with executory contracts. An executory contract is a contract that has been **formed but not performed.** An example would be a contract to manufacture and deliver equipment that has not yet been produced. Visualize an order placed by a U.S. airline company to purchase airplanes from Airbus Industrie with payment to be made in Euros. Large commercial airliners are not manufactured without a customer order; the airplanes are very expensive and are only manufactured to order. Accordingly, no transaction is recorded by either seller or purchaser at the time the sales contract is signed. This type of agreement creates what is called **an identifiable foreign currency commitment.** The airline company has a foreign currency commitment because it has agreed to a fixed price for the purchase of airplanes, however, it has no recorded liability because the accounting criteria for recognition of a liability have not been met. A company with substantial foreign currency commitments of this type may wish to hedge the risk associated with such executory contracts. It is also possible to have an identifiable foreign currency commitment that will involve a receipt of foreign currency—an event that would occur if a domestic company signs a contract for future manufacture and delivery of machinery to be paid for in foreign exchange. Forward contracts to hedge identifiable foreign currency commitments are identical to those used for hedging foreign currency assets and liabilities. **However, the accounting procedures for each type of contract are somewhat different.** We will first illustrate accounting for hedges on assets and liabilities and then illustrate hedges on identifiable foreign currency commitments.

Accounting for hedges on foreign currency assets

The following table explains the type of forward contract needed to hedge both foreign currency assets and foreign currency liabilities. It is important to understand exactly what the hedge does and does not do before trying to learn the accounting procedures. You will find these procedures to be confusing if the nature of the exchanges that comprise the hedge itself is not clearly understood.

Foreign currency position	Description of the forward contract
Foreign currency asset	A contract to **sell** foreign currency for future delivery
Foreign currency liability	A contract to **buy** foreign currency for future delivery

A company with a foreign exchange asset arising from credit sales in foreign currency or other similar transactions would hedge the risk associated with this transaction by **selling foreign exchange for future delivery.** This forward contract offsets the foreign currency asset from the sales transaction with a foreign currency liability from the forward contract. The forward contract to sell foreign currency is an agreement to receive dollars and deliver foreign currency. The foreign currency portion of this contract is accounted for at fair market value because it is a liability to deliver foreign exchange—a commodity with a market value that changes daily as the spot rate for the foreign currency changes. For example, assume that on December 1, 20x1, USA Corporation sells Canadian Corporation merchandise to be paid for in Canadian dollars on January 30, 20x2 in the amount of C$100,000. USA Corporation immediately enters into a forward contract with an exchange broker to sell C$100,000 on January 31, 20x1. Relevant exchange rates for this transaction are:

Rate–Date	Exchange rate
Spot rate on December 1, 20x1	$.80U.S. = C$1
60-day forward rate on December 1, 20x1	$.79U.S. = C$1
Spot rate on December 31, 20x1	$.77U.S. = C$1
Spot rate on January 30, 20x2	$.81U.S. = C$1

On December 1, USA Corporation records a sale and account receivable based on the **spot rate** for the Canadian dollar on that date based on the spot price for Canadian dollars of $.80 U.S. This entry is as follows:

12/01/x1	Accounts receivable C$	80,000	
	Sales		80,000

($80,000 = C$100,000 × .80)

The forward contract to delivery the Canadian dollars to the broker on January 30 consists of a U.S. $ portion and a foreign currency (C$) portion. Since the contract is to sell foreign exchange, the liability in this contract is the foreign currency portion. The foreign currency portion of the contract is recorded at the spot rate because it **represents a liability to deliver foreign exchange and the value of the foreign exchange is measured by the spot rate.** The U.S. $ portion of this contract is a fixed dollar receivable that does not have a fluctuating value. The difference between the spot rate and the forward rate is determined by interest rate differentials as was explained earlier in the chapter. You cannot, however, assume that the spot rate will be higher or lower than the forward rate in any given circumstances, therefore it is essential to remember which portion of the contract is recorded at the spot rate and which portion is recorded at the forward rate. The difference between these two amounts is a discount if the spot rate is higher than the forward rate and a premium if the forward rate is higher than the spot rate. The discount or premium may have either a debit or a credit balance and is treated as a period cost and amortized over the life of the forward contract as contract expense. For the above transaction, the entry to record the forward contract on December 1, 20x1 is:

12/01/x1	Contracts receivable $U.S.	79,000	
	Discount on forward contract	1,000	
	Contracts payable C$		80,000

(C$100,000 × .79 fwd rate = 79,000)
(C$100,000 × .80 spot rate = 80,000)

Especially note that the forward contract has a C$ liability because its purpose is to hedge a C$ receivable. This offsetting of a foreign currency liability against a foreign currency asset creates the hedge. Over the life of the forward contract, any change in the value of the account receivable due to changes in the spot rate for the C$ will be offset by changes in the value of the C$ contract payable. If the spot rate for the C$ rises, both the value of the foreign currency asset and the foreign currency liability will rise. If the spot rate for the C$ falls, the value of both the C$ asset and the C$ liability will fall.

On December 31, 20x1, USA Corporation should make three adjusting entries. The account receivable from the sale should be adjusted to fair market value with a corresponding exchange gain or loss included in income. The foreign currency liability on the foreign contract should also be adjusted to fair market value with a corresponding exchange gain or loss included in income. Finally, any contract premium or discount on the forward contract should be amortized. In cases where the forward contract was recorded on the same date as the sales transaction (as in our example), there will be no **net** foreign exchange gain or loss because the gain or loss on the forward contract will offset the loss or gain on the sales transaction. The entries for our example are shown below:

12/31/x1	Foreign Exchange loss	3,000	
	Accounts receivable C$		3,000

To adjust the Account receivable to the spot rate on 12/31/x1
C$ 100,000 × ($.80 − $.77) = $3,000

	Contracts payable C$	3,000	
	Foreign exchange gain		3,000

To adjust the Contract payable to the spot rate on 12/31/x1
C$ 100,000 × ($.80 − $.77) = $3,000

	Amortization expense	500	
	Discount on forward contract		500

To amortize 1/2 of the contract discount = $1,000/2

Assuming the account receivable is collected on the due date, the foreign exchange received is recorded at the spot rate in an account, "Investment in C$," and this foreign exchange is immediately used to settle the forward contract. In addition, cash is recorded to settle the contract receivable in U.S. $ and the remainder of the contract discount is amortized. These entries are as follows:

01/31/x2	Investment in C$	81,000	
	Accounts receivable C$		77,000
	Foreign exchange gain		4,000

To record collection of the C$100,000 receivable
C$ 100,000 × spot rate of $.81 = $81,000

	Contracts payable C$	77,000	
	Foreign exchange loss	4,000	
	Investment in C$		81,000

To record delivery of the C$100,000 to the broker
C$ 100,000 × spot rate of $.81 = $81,000

	Cash	79,000	
	Contracts receivable $US		79,000

To record settlement of the $US portion of the forward contract

	Amortization expense	500	
	Discount on forward contract		500

To amortize the balance of the contract discount

Accounting for hedges on foreign currency liabilities

A forward contract to hedge a foreign currency liability is almost the mirror image of the forward contract to hedge a foreign currency asset. In the case of a foreign currency liability, the appropriate forward contract is to **buy** foreign currency for future delivery. This contract creates a foreign exchange asset whose changes in value will offset the changes in value of the foreign currency liability, thus hedging against potential losses. As an example, assume that American Products Company purchases inventory from Spanish Concepts Company on June 1, 20x2 in the amount of EU 50,000 with payment to be made on August 31, 20x2. Further assume that American Products Company has a fiscal year ending June 30, 20x2. Relevant spot and forward rates for the Euro are as follows:

Rate–Date	Exchange rate
Spot rate on June 1, 20x2	$1.12U.S. = EU 1
60-day forward rate on June 1, 20x2	$1.15U.S. = EU 1
Spot rate on June 30, 20x2	$1.14U.S. = EU 1
Spot rate on August 31, 20x2	$1.18U.S. = EU 1

A comprehensive illustration of all journal entries required on American Products Company books on account of these transactions are shown in Exhibit 8-1. Note that the forward contract involves a contract receivable in Euros and a contract payable in U.S. $. Accordingly, the rise in the value of the spot rate from $1.12 on June 1, 20x2 to $1.14 on June 30, 20x2 results in a foreign exchange gain on June 30. A further rise in the spot rate for the Euro to $1.18 on August 31, 20x2 results in an additional foreign exchange gain on the forward contract of $2,000 on August 31. These gains, however, are offset by equal amounts of losses arising from an increase in the value of the liability to the Spanish vendor that it is payable in Euros. Since the forward rate for the Euro is higher than the spot rate, the differential on the forward contract is a premium and is amortized as a period cost over the 90-day life of the forward contract.

Accounting for hedges on foreign currency commitments

As discussed previously, a foreign currency commitment arises from executory contracts denominated in a foreign currency. A contract is executory if neither party has substantially performed its contractual obligations. In the case of purchase or sale of services, inventory, plant assets, and other similar transactions, no purchase or sale is recorded until revenue realization occurs. In order to recognize a purchase or sale under the rules of accrual accounting, services must have been rendered or title to merchandise must have passed from the seller to the buyer. In legal terms, substantial performance on the part of the seller must have taken place. Even though unrecorded, executory contracts create foreign exchange risk because the normal expectation is that the parties will fulfill their contractual obligations and legal liability could result in the case of breach of contract. Thus, an appropriate risk management strategy for foreign currency commitments is the use of forward contracts to hedge these risks. The appropriate action can be easily inferred from the previous illustrations. If a U.S. company has entered into a sales contract, it has the expectation of receiving foreign currency in the future, an event that can be hedged by contracting to deliver foreign currency. On the other hand, if a U.S. company has entered into a purchase contract, it has the expectation of paying foreign currency in the future, an event that can be hedged by contracting to receive foreign currency.

EXHIBIT 8·1 Purchase of inventory and hedge

06/01/x2	Inventory	56,000	
	Accounts payable—EU		56,000

To record purchase of Inventory for EU 50,000
EU 50,000 × spot rate of $1.12 = $56,000

	Contacts receivable EU	56,000	
	Premium on the forward contract	1,500	
	Contracts payable U.S. $		57,500

To record a forward exchange contract for the purchase of EU 50,000
FC portion: EU 50,000 × spot rate of $1.12 = $56,000
U.S. $ portion: EU 50,000 × forward rate of $1.15 = $57,500

06/30/x2	Foreign exchange loss	1,000	
	Accounts payable—EU		1,000

To record an increase in the value of the account payable
EU 50,000 × increase in spot rate ($1.14 − $1.12) = $1,000

	Contacts receivable EU	1,000	
	Foreign exchange gain		1,000

To record an increase in the value of the Contract Receivable EU
EU 50,000 × increase in spot rate ($1.14 − $1.12) = $1,000

	Amortization expense	500	
	Premium on the forward contract		500

To amortize the premium on the forward contract for one month
Contract premium of $1,500/3 = $500

08/31/x2	Contract payable U.S. $	57,500	
	Cash		57,000

To record the payment of the U.S. $ contract payable on the forward contract

	Investment in EU	59,000	
	Foreign exchange gain		2,000
	Contracts receivable EU		57,000

To record collection of the contracts receivable in EU
EU 50,000 × spot rate of $1.18 = $59,000

	Amortization expense	1,000	
	Premium on forward contract		1,000

To amortize the balance of the premium on the forward contract
Contract premium of $1,500 × 2/3 = $1,000

	Accounts payable—EU	57,000	
	Foreign exchange loss	2,000	
	Investment in EU		59,000

To record payment of the account payable to the Spanish supplier
EU 50,000 × spot rate of $1.18 = $59,000

A forward contract used to hedge a foreign currency commitment is **identical** to a forward contract used to hedge a foreign currency asset or liability. However, the two contracts are accounted for differently. On a foreign currency commitment hedge, all exchange gains and losses on the forward contract, together with the contract premium or discount are deferred until the settlement date. These items are then closed against the asset (when the foreign currency commitment is a purchase) or against sales revenue (when the foreign currency commitment is a sale). This approach is necessary because the balance sheet or income statement effects of the foreign currency commitment are also deferred due to the executory nature of the foreign currency commitment.

As an example, assume that on October 1, 20x1 Stars and Stripes Company of New York City signs a purchase commitment to buy machinery from a Japanese supplier with delivery and payment to be made on March 30, 20x2. The total invoice price of the machinery is ¥ 50,000,000. Relevant exchange rates for accounting for the purchase contract and for the forward contract are as follows:

Rate–Date	Exchange rate
Spot rate on October 1, 20x1	$.008333U.S. = ¥1
Six-month forward rate on October 1, 20x1	$.008130U.S. = ¥1
Spot rate on December 31, 20x1	$.008696U.S. = ¥1
Spot rate on March 31, 20x2	$.008521U.S. = ¥1

All required entries to account for the purchase and the forward contract are shown in Exhibit 8-2. The purchase commitment is an executory contract, therefore, no entry is made for this contract on October 1, 20x2, the date it is signed. The forward contract is recorded and accounted for in the same way as for a hedge of a foreign currency liability **except that the contract discount and all foreign exchange gains and losses are deferred until the date of settlement. On the settlement date, these accounts are closed against the Inventory account recorded when the purchase contract is performed.** These procedures result in an inventory balance equal to the amount that would have been recorded for the purchase had it been recorded on October 1, 20x1, adjusted for the discount on the hedge.

On October 1, 20x1, the forward contract is recorded with the foreign currency portion being recorded at the spot rate and the dollar portion at the forward rate. The difference between these amounts is a discount because the forward rate is lower than the spot rate. Recall from our earlier discussion that the difference between forward rates and spot rates is a result of differences in interest rates in the two countries. Thus, the **discount** (when the spot rate is higher than the forward rate) or **premium** (when the forward rate is higher than the spot rate) will have either a debit or credit balance depending on the type of contract (buy or sell) and the interest rate differentials at the time. In this particular example, the combination of contract discount and contract to purchase Yen results in a forward contract discount with a credit balance. This balance is deferred and closed out to the Inventory account when the contract is settled.

The adjusting entry on December 31, 20x1 is made to adjust the Contracts Receivable—Yen account to its fair market value as determined by the spot rate for the Yen on December 31. The resulting foreign exchange gain is deferred until the settlement date. Note that the purchase agreement is unrecorded, hence there is no foreign exchange loss recorded on the purchase commitment even though the value of the Yen has risen from $.008333 to $.008696. There is, however, an economic loss on this purchase commitment that the hedge offsets because there is an expectation of a loss based on the increase in the spot rate for the Yen. No entry is made for amortization of the contract discount because, as noted above, it is also deferred.

EXHIBIT 8-2   Hedge of a purchase commitment

10/01/x1	Contract receivable—Yen	416,650	
	Discount on forward contract		10,150
	Contract payable—$		406,500

       To record a forward contract to buy 50,000,000 Yen
          FC portion = Y50,000,000 × .00833332 = $416,650
          U.S. $ portion = Y50,000,000 × $.008130 = $406,500

12/31/x1	Contract receivable—Yen	18,150	
	Deferred foreign exchange gain		18,150

       To adjust the contract receivable—Yen to the spot rate on 12/31/x1
          Y50,000,000 × ($.0088696 − $.008333) = $18,150

03/31/x2	Contract payable— $	406,500	
	Cash		406,500

       To pay the Contract Payable—$ on the settlement date

	Investment Yen	426,050	
	Deferred foreign exchange loss	8,750	
	Contracts receivable—Yen		434,800

       To record collection of the Contracts Receivable—Yen
          Y50,000,000 × spot rate of $.008521 = $426,050

	Inventory	426,050	
	Investment in Yen		426,050

       To record purchase of the Inventory for Y50,000,000
          Y50,000,000 × spot rate of $.008521 = $426,050

	Discount on forward contract	10,150	
	Deferred foreign exchange gain	18,150	
	Deferred foreign exchange loss		8,750
	Inventory		19,550

       To close the discount on the forward contract, the deferred exchange gain,
        and the deferred exchange loss to the Inventory account

On the settlement date, March 31, 20x2, the broker is paid the $406,500 agreed upon when the forward contract was arranged. The Yen received on this contract is recorded at the spot rate on that date, resulting in a foreign exchange loss based on the decline in the value of the Yen from $.008696 on December 31 to $.008521 on March 31. The settlement of the purchase commitment is also recorded at the spot rate on March 31. Finally the deferred discount, the deferred foreign exchange gain from the December 31 adjustment, and the deferred foreign exchange loss from settlement of the forward contract are all closed against the inventory account. Following is a reconciliation of the effects of these entries on the purchase commitment:

Inventory cost on March 31 (based on spot rate for Yen)	$426,050
Less foreign exchange gain from December 31 adjustment	(18,150)
Add foreign exchange loss from March 31 settlement	8,750
Value of the inventory at the time of the purchase agreement	416,650
Less discount on forward exchange contract	(10,150)
Final cost of inventory (equal to forward rate on October 1)	$406,500

EXHIBIT 8-3   Hedge of a sales commitment

10/01/x1	Contract receivable—$	406,500	
	Discount on forward contract	10,150	
	Contract payable—Yen		416,650

      To record a forward contract to sell 50,000,000 Yen
          FC portion = Y50,000,000 × .00833332 = $416,650
          U.S. $ portion = Y50,000,000 × $.008130 = $406,500

12/31/x1	Deferred foreign exchange loss	18,150	
	Contract payable—Yen		18,150

      To adjust the contract payable—Yen to the spot rate on 12/31/x1
          Y50,000,000 × ($.0088696 − $.008333) = $18,150

03/31/x2	Investment in Yen	426,050	
	Sales		426,050

      To record the sale for Y50,000,000 at the spot rate on 3/31/x2
          Y50,000,000 × spot rate of $.008521 = $426,050

	Cash	406,500	
	Contract receivable—$		406,500

      To collect the Contract Payable—$ on the settlement date

	Contract payable—Yen	434,800	
	Deferred foreign exchange gain		8,750
	Investment in Yen		426,050

      To record payment of the Contract payable—Yen
          Y50,000,000 × spot rate of $.008521 = $426,050

	Deferred foreign exchange gain	8,750	
	Sales	19,550	
	Deferred foreign exchange loss		18,150
	Discount on forward contract		10,150

      To close the discount on the forward contract, the deferred exchange gain,
      and the deferred exchange loss to the Sales account

A foreign currency commitment can also be a commitment to **receive** foreign currency. For example, assume Stars and Stripes Company had signed a **sales** contract to delivery machinery to a Japanese customer with the same terms and conditions as used in the previous example. The journal entries for this example are shown in Exhibit 8-3. In this case, the sales commitment produces unrecorded foreign exchange risk similar to a foreign currency **asset** because Stars and Stripes has committed to receive foreign exchange in the future. Accordingly, the forward contract is a contract to **deliver** foreign exchange, resulting in a foreign currency **liability.** Only the forward contract may be recorded. Thus, any foreign exchange gains or losses and the discount on the forward contract (now with a debit balance) are deferred until the settlement date. The accounting principles that the foreign currency portion of the forward contract be recorded at the spot rate and adjusted to the spot rate at year end are applicable, resulting in the journal entries as illustrated on 10/1/x1 and 12/31/x1.

On the settlement date, 3/31/x2, the sale to the Japanese customer is recorded at the spot rate on that date. Note that the account Investment in Yen is recorded at the time of the sale because the customer has paid in Yen rather than U.S. dollars. The foreign exchange broker pays the fixed dollar contract receivable in the amount of $406,500, and the 50,000,000 Yen received from the customer is delivered to the exchange broker. Since the value of the 50,000,000 Yen on March 31 (based on the spot rate) is now $426,050, a foreign exchange gain is reported equal to the difference between $426,050 and the book value of the contract payable of $434,800 balance as last adjusted on December 31. In the last entry, the deferred exchange gain and loss and the discount on the forward contract are closed to sales. This entry results in a sales account balance equal to the forward rate on the date the sales contract was signed on October 1 as shown in the following table:

Sale amount recorded on March 31	$426,050
Less foreign exchange loss from December 31 adjustment	(18,150)
Add foreign exchange gain from March 31 settlement	8,750
Value of the sale at the time of the sales agreement on October 1	416,650
Less discount on forward exchange contract	(10,150)
Final amount of the sale (equal to forward rate on October 1)	$406,500

SPECULATING IN FOREIGN EXCHANGE

The purchase of either speculative forward exchange contracts or futures contracts in foreign exchange should not be accounted for as hedges, with the difference between the forward price and the spot price of the foreign exchange being assigned to a contract discount or premium account. **In a forward exchange contract arranged for speculative purposes, the entire contract cost should be treated as a gain or loss within the period in which it occurs.** This objective is accomplished by initially recording both the $ portion of the forward contract and the foreign currency portion at forward rates. Any interim adjustments on the foreign currency portion of the forward contract are made for **the forward rate for the settlement date.** Finally the contract is settled at the spot rate on the settlement date. The only difference between a forward exchange contract and a futures contract for foreign currency is that the foreign exchange is normally delivered in the forward contract, whereas cash is paid to or received from the broker for the net loss or gain on a futures contract. The following illustration illustrates these procedures.

Assume that Domestic Risque Company enters into a forward exchange contract to buy EU 40,000 on November 1, 20x1 to be delivered on January 30, 20x2. Domestic Risque has a calendar year-end and closes its books on December 31. Relevant exchange rates for the Euro are as follows:

Rate–Date	Exchange rate
Spot rate on November 1, 20x1	$1.125 = EU 1
3-month forward rate on November 1, 20x1	$1.140 = EU 1
1-month forward rate on December 31, 20x1	$1.135 = EU 1
Spot rate on January 30, 20x2	$1.145 = EU 1

Note that the key exchange rate on this contract on November 1, 20x1 is the forward rate because this is the price of the EU for future delivery. By taking a so-called **long** position in the Euro (buying Euros), Domestic Risque Company is essentially

wagering that the spot rate for the Euro on the settlement date will be higher than the forward rate of $1.140 on November 1, 20x1. If this expectation is realized, the company will make a profit on its speculative arrangement. If the spot rate for the Euro on the settlement date is less than the forward rate on November 1, 20x1, the company will incur a loss. If Domestic Risque had expected that the spot rate for the Euro would fall over the contract period, the appropriate action would have been to take a so-called **short** position (selling Euros) in the forward market.

The entries for the above contract are shown in Exhibit 8-4. On November 1, 20x1, Domestic records a contract receivable—EU and a contract payable—$ for the forward contract, recording both elements of the entry at the **forward rate.** Using only the forward rate avoids recording a contract premium or discount on the forward contract and results in all income effects of the transactions being reflected in an exchange gain or loss account. Essentially what Domestic Risque Company is doing is wagering that the value of the Euro on the settlement date will be greater than the forward rate on the date the contract is signed. In this context, the forward rate is the only relevant rate on November 1 because it is the value of the EU for delivery on January 30, the settlement date.

Following similar logic, the EU portion of the forward contract is adjusted to **the forward rate for the settlement date** ($1.135) on December 31, 20x1. Since the EU for delivery one month later is then worth only $1.135, the contract receivable—EU is written down by $200 [EU 40,000 × ($1.14 − $.135)] to its fair value for the settlement date. Assuming that the foreign exchange is delivered, two entries are required on January 30. The first entry pays the foreign exchange broker $45,600 in accordance with the terms of the forward contract as originally recorded on November 1. The second entry records receipt of EU with a value of $45,800, recording it at the spot rate on January 30 (EU 40,000 × $1.145 = $45,800). The difference between the fair value of the 40,000 Euros on January 30 ($45,800) and the book value of the Contract receivable—EU after the 12/31/x1 adjustment ($45,400) determines the foreign exchange gain recorded in this entry.

An alternative arrangement with the exchange broker might also exist. If the forward contract is arranged exclusively for speculative purposes, there may be no particular reason for Domestic Risque to take delivery of the foreign exchange on the settlement date. Consequently the agreement could be simply "closed out" in the manner commonly done for commodities futures contracts. The second part of Exhibit 8-4 shows this entry. In this entry, the broker pays a cash settlement to Domestic Risque equal to the $200 net gain over the full three-month period of the contract. Note that the contract loss for Domestic was $200 in the year 20x1 and the contract gain was $400 in the year 20x2, resulting in a **net gain of $200** over the entire life of the contract. This entry also records the $400 exchange gain for the year 20x2 equal to EU 40,000 times the difference between the spot rate on January 30 and the one-month forward rate on December 31 [EU 40,000 × ($1.145 − $1.135) = $400]. The entry is completed by closing the balances of both the contract receivable—EU ($45,400) and the contract payable—$ ($45,600).

● INTERPRETIVE EXERCISE

Prepare entries similar to Exhibit 8-4, assuming instead that Domestic Risque **sold** Euros for future delivery. Use the same dates exchange rates as in the illustration.

EXHIBIT 8-4   Speculative Forward Contract—Long Position

11/01/x1	Contracts receivable—EU	45,600	
	Contracts payable—$		45,600
	To record the purchase of EU 40,000 at the forward rate of $1.14		
12/31/x1	Foreign Exchange loss	200	
	Contracts Receivable—EU		200
	To adjust the Contracts receivable to the forward rate for the settlement date		
	EU 40,000 × ($1.140 − 1.135) = $200		
1/30/x2	Contract payable—$	45,600	
	Cash		45,600
	To record the payment of the $45,600 liability to the broker		
	Investment in EU	45,800	
	Foreign exchange gain		400
	Contracts receivable—EU		45,400
	To record collection EU 40,000 from the broker		
	EU 40,000 × $1.145 = $45,800		
	$45,600 − $200 = $45,400		

Entries for 1/30/x2 assuming the account is settled with the broker
without delivery of the foreign exchange

1/30/x2	Contracts payable—$	45,600	
	Cash	200	
	Foreign exchange gain		400
	Contracts receivable—EU		45,400

HEDGING INVESTMENTS IN FOREIGN CURRENCY

In addition to the all the usual risks associated with investments, multinational investments have foreign exchange risk. Professional mutual fund managers engage in a variety of risk management techniques to hedge the risks arising from foreign investments in their international funds. In particular, these fund managers make use of forward contracts and future contracts for the period of time they expect to hold their investments. These techniques work well for investments of relatively short duration, however, forward contracts may not be well suited for investments held for long periods of time. Companies with long-term investments in foreign companies have a similar problem with respect to the risk. Another risk management technique available for investments in foreign companies is to arrange long-term debt denominated in the foreign currency. This type of hedge offsets the long-term investment in the foreign company with a long-term liability of approximately equal size. Before illustrating accounting procedures associated with hedging long-term investments, it is necessary to discuss the unique accounting procedures associated with accounting for investments in foreign companies. Both accounting for foreign investments and risk management transactions associated with foreign investments are discussed in Chapter 9.

SUMMARY

The following learning objectives were stated at the beginning of this chapter:

- Identify accounting-related business problems that arise in connection with international business
- Explain what is meant by the need to manage risk associated with foreign currency transactions
- Demonstrate an understanding of the key terminology associated with international accounting
- Account for import and export transactions
- Account for forward exchange contracts and other hedging transactions, including contracts that hedge foreign exchange assets and liabilities, foreign exchange commitments, and contracts whose purpose is to speculate in foreign currency

Two important business problems with implications for accounting managers arise in connection with international business. Companies with foreign investments, foreign companies traded on a domestic exchange, and companies with foreign subsidiaries will all have to translate their financial statements into a format acceptable for domestic reporting purposes. Problems associated with different language, technical terminology, accounting principles, and currency have to be addressed in this process. A related set of accounting problems are those that result from import and export transactions denominated in a foreign currency. Understanding these problems requires becoming conversant in some new terminology and learning some basic economic principles related to foreign exchange.

Accounting for import and export transactions involves translating the resulting foreign exchange assets and liabilities into U.S. dollars because the books and accounts of the domestic company are kept in U.S. dollars. Because foreign exchange assets and liabilities are carried at fair market values, changes in foreign exchange prices (rates) create foreign exchange gains and losses that are normally included in income in the year realized. The existence of foreign exchange risk associated with these assets and liabilities adds an additional dimension to management's responsibilities regarding their profit plan. Management will often wish to control their exposure to foreign exchange risk by entering into hedging transactions whose purpose is to mitigate the risk associated with foreign exchange assets and liabilities. The particular type of hedging activity used and the methods of accounting required for these transactions varies according to the terms of the transaction creating the foreign exchange risk.

QUESTIONS

1. Explain the steps involved in translating a foreign currency financial statement.
2. What is foreign exchange risk? How does foreign exchange risk affect the operating profit of a company engaged in foreign trade?
3. Does an import or export transaction denominated in domestic currency carry foreign exchange risk? Explain.
4. What is meant by the concept of risk management of foreign currency assets and liabilities?
5. What is a forward exchange contract? Describe the sequence of events that comprise a forward exchange contract.
6. Explain how a forward exchange contract differs from a foreign currency futures contract.
7. Explain how a change in the value of foreign exchange affects the value of foreign currency assets and liabilities.

8. How does a direct foreign exchange rate quote differ from an indirect quote? How can each be converted into the other? Which rate is easiest to use when analyzing foreign currency transactions? Explain.
9. Explain the difference between fixed exchange rates and floating exchange rates in an international trade context.
10. What is a forward rate for a foreign currency? A spot rate? Explain why these two rates are almost always different.
11. Derive the 180 forward rate for the Euro if the spot rate is U.S. $1.15 = EU 1 and the six-month interest rates are as follows: New York (U.S. dollar accounts): 4.5% APR; Major European Cities (Euro accounts): 4.75% APR.
12. Why must foreign exchange accounts payable and accounts receivable be adjusted to fair market value on a financial statement date?
13. What type of risk management transaction might a company arrange if it wished to hedge the risks associated with a foreign currency receivable of 100,000 Euros with a value of U.S. $108,000.
14. Explain the difference between an exposed net liability position and an identifiable foreign currency commitment to pay foreign currency.
15. Why are transactions not recorded for executory contracts?
16. Explain why exchange gains and losses on identifiable commitment hedges are deferred until the settlement date of the identifiable commitment.
17. Explain why speculative forward contracts are accounted for using forward rates exclusively.

EXERCISES

Exercise 8-1

(Multiple choice: select the best answer for each item.)

Questions 1 and 2 are based on the following information:
On April 1, 20x1, Argo Company imported 10,000,000 barrels of oil from a Venezuelan Company at a price of U.S.$17.00 per barrel. The invoice was paid 30 days later. Indirect exchange rates for the Venezuelan Bolivar were:

April 1, 20x1: U.S.$1 = VEB 587
April 30, 20x1: U.S.$1 = VEB 570

1. What is the cost of the oil?
   a. VEB 99,790 million
   b. VEB 96,900 million
   c. U.S.$ 170 million
   d. U.S.$165.08 million
2. When the invoice is paid, Argo will report
   b. a U.S.$ 8637 exchange gain.
   c. a U.S.$ 8637 exchange loss.
   d. a debit to accounts payable of $170 million.
   e. a debit to inventory of $170 million.
3. Domestic Company has an account payable in the amount of 100,000 Euros on its books on October 1, 20x2. This account was unpaid at the end of the fiscal year, October 31, 20x2. The spot rate for the Euro was:

   October 1, 20x1: EU 1 = U.S.$ 1.10
   October 31, 20x1: EU 1 = U.S.$ 1.12

   On October 31, 20x1, Domestic Company should report:
   a. an account payable of $110,000.
   b. an account payable of $112,000.
   c. an account payable of EU 100,000.
   d. an exchange gain of $2,000.

4. Pristine Company sold merchandise to Gomez Company, a Mexican corporation, on January 1, 20x1. The invoice was for U.S.$ 200,000 payable in 60 days. On January 31, 20x1,
   a. Pristine Company has a foreign currency asset.
   b. Gomez Company has a foreign currency liability.
   c. both a and b are correct.
   d. none of the above is correct.

5. Parker Company signs a contract to deliver machinery to a Japanese customer on March 1, 20x2. The contract calls for Parker to manufacture and deliver the machinery to its customer in six months. Payment is to be 10,000,000 Yen. Which of the following is true?
   a. If Parker Company wishes to hedge its foreign exchange risk, it should enter into a contract to sell 10,000,000 Yen.
   b. If Parker Company wishes to hedge its foreign exchange risk, it should enter into a contract to buy 10,000,000 Yen.
   c. Parker has no foreign exchange risk because the contract is substantially unperformed.
   d. Parker has foreign exchange risk, but it cannot hedge this risk because the amount to be paid by the Japanese customer has not been recorded as a receivable.

6. In a forward exchange contract,
   a. the spot rate is always higher than the forward rate on short positions.
   b. the forward rate is always higher than the spot rate on long positions.
   c. the spot rate and the forward rate are set so that the spread between the rates always results in a debit balance in the premium or discount account.
   d. none of the above is correct.

7. A forward contract is purchased for future receipt of 100,000 Euros when the spot rate for the Euro is $1.08 and the forward rate is $1.09. In this example,
   a. a debit premium of $1,000 will be recorded.
   b. a credit premium of $1,000 will be recorded.
   c. a debit discount of $1,000 will be recorded.
   d. a credit discount of $1,000 will be recorded.

8. On April 1, 20x1, the direct exchange rate for the Euro in New York was $1.12. On this date, the indirect exchange rate for the Euro in Toronto was C$ 1 = .74 Euros. Based on this information, the price of the U.S. dollar in Toronto would be
   a. C$ 1.2065.
   b. C$ .8288.
   c. C$ 1.5235.
   d. C$ .6607.

9. Homegrown Company enters into a forward contract to hedge an exposed net asset position of 100,000,000 Korean Won. Any exchange gain or loss over the life of the contract
   a. should be included in income currently.
   b. should be deferred and closed out against the foreign currency asset on the settlement date.
   c. cannot be determined from the information given.
   d. Either a or b may be selected at the discretion of the company.

10. Contract premium on forward contracts that hedges exposed asset or liability positions
    a. should be deferred and closed out on the settlement date to balances resulting from the primary transaction.
    b. should be amortized over the life of the contract.
    c. should always be zero unless the contract is speculative.
    d. will only be recorded in cases where the premium or discount has a debit balance.

Exercise 8-2 **(Computing exchange rates)**

(a) Compute the direct exchange rate for the following indirect rates:

U.S. $1 =

.90 Euros

125 Yen

C$ 1.25

(b) Explain why some foreign currency prices are (nominally) more than $1 per unit while most others are less an $1.

Exercise 8-3

(Understanding exchange rates)

Given the following exchange rates involving Euros (EU), Canadian dollars (C$), Japanese Yen (¥) and U.S. $:

EU 1 = C$ 1.40

EU 1 = U.S. $ 1.09

EU 1 = ¥135

Required:

(a) Compute the number of Canadian $ that can be exchanged for one U.S. $.
(b) Compute the price of the Japanese ¥ in U.S. $.
(c) Explain the apparent significance of the lack of a decimal in Japanese currency on its nominal exchange ratios.

Exercise 8-4

(Understanding spot and forward exchange rates)

Given the following exchange data:

Spot rate for the Euro on 1/1/20x2	EU 1 = U.S. $ 1.15
Average 90-day interest rate (APR) for Euro loans in London	4.8% APR
Average 90-day interest rate (APR) for U.S. $ loans in New York	4.4% APR

Required:

(a) Compute the 90-day forward rate for the Euro in U.S. $ on 1/1/20x1.
(b) Assume the New York interest rate was 5.20%. Compute the 90-day forward rate. Explain how this result differs from the answer in requirement (a).

Exercise 8-5

(Import transaction denominated in foreign currency)

Presto Company imported 5,000 television receivers manufactured in Japan at a price of 50,000 Yen each. The televisions were shipped F.O.B. Tokyo on April 1, 20x1. Payment is due three months after that date. Relevant exchange rates are:

Spot rate 4/1/x1	U.S. $ 1 = 125 Yen
90-day forward rate 4/1/x1	U.S. $ 1 = 127 Yen
Spot rate 6/30/x1	U.S. $ 1 = 128 Yen
90-day forward rate 6/30/x1	U.S. $ 1 = 130 Yen

Required:

(a) Record all required entries by Presto Company, assuming the invoice was paid on the due date.
(b) Assume Presto Company decided to partially hedge the contract by acquiring a forward contract for 60% of the liability on 4/1/x1. Record the required entries for purchase and settlement of the forward contract.

Exercise 8-6

(Import transaction denominated in foreign currency)

Oneida Company purchased 300 tons of wood pellets for inventory from a Canadian supplier on July 1, 20x1. Payment is due in 60 days. Oneida Company maintains bank accounts in both U.S. $ and C$. The following exchange rates were effective for the Canadian dollar on the dates indicated.

Spot rate on 7/1/x1	$.675
60-day forward rate on 7/1/x1	.678
Spot rate on 8/31/x1	.677
60-day forward rate on 8/31/x1	.695

Required:

(a) Assume that the purchase price of the wood pellets was U.S. $ 78 per ton. Record the entries for the purchase on July 1, 20x1 and payment of the vendor invoice on the due date.

(b) Assume that the purchase price of the wood pellets was C$ 105 per ton. Record the entries for the purchase on July 1, 20x1 and payment of the vendor invoice on the due date.

(c) Assume that Oneida Company entered into a forward contract to hedge the purchase in (b) above for the period from July 1 to August 31. Record the entries for the hedge.

Exercise 8-7

(Risk management using forward exchange contracts)

Match the following actions with the transactions listed below by placing the appropriate letter in the space provided.

Action:

(a) Hedge the transaction by purchasing foreign exchange for future delivery.

(b) Hedge the transaction by selling foreign exchange for future delivery.

(c) The transaction does not need to be hedged.

Transaction:

_____ 1. Purchase of 500 automobiles to be paid for in Euros in 60 days.

_____ 2. Signed a contract to sell 300,000 bushels of corn to be delivered in 90 days. Payment to be made in Euros.

_____ 3. Signed a contract to buy 40,000 automobile tires from a Mexican manufacturer, payment to be made in U.S. dollars in 90 days.

_____ 4. Sold two airliners to a customer in Singapore with payment to be made in 120 days in Japanese Yen.

Exercise 8-8

(Understanding the effects of changes in foreign exchange rate)

Tug Hill Company had the following accounts or events to report in its December 31, 20x2 financial statements. Indicate whether each of the following events will result in a foreign gain, loss, or have no effect on income. If the item will result in an exchange gain or loss, indicate the amount. The spot price of the Euro on December 31, 20x2 is $1.015.

_____ 1. A current liability of 400,000 Euros. The spot rate for the Euro on October 31, 20x2, the date the liability was recorded, was $.985.

_____ 2. A bank account denominated in Euros with a balance of EU 40,000. The spot rate for the Euro on the day the account was opened, December 15, 20x2, was $1.025.

_____ 3. An executory contract to purchase 5,000 copying machines from an Italian supplier for 1,500 Euros each. The machines have not been shipped. The spot price for the Euro on the date of the order, August 1, 20x2, was $1.01.

_____ 4. A forward contract to purchase 5,000,000 Euros to partially hedge the liability described in (3) above. The contract was signed on October 1, 20x2, when the Euro was trading at a spot rate of $1.02.

_____ 5. A receivable from a French customer in the amount of 500,000 Euros. The exchange rate for the Euro on the date of the sale, September 1, 20x2, was $.9924.

Exercise 8-9

(Understanding foreign exchange rates)

You are planning a business trip to London. When you booked your hotel for a one-week stay, the price of the hotel room was £120 per day and the price of the British Pound was $1.45 per unit of British currency. Your flight leaves tomorrow. You notice in _The Wall Street Journal_ that the British Pound closed yesterday at $1.55.

(1) Has the Pound appreciated or depreciated against the dollar since you made your travel plans?

(2) How will the change in the exchange rates likely affect the cost of your trip?

Exercise 8-10

(Understanding foreign exchange rates)

You read in _The Wall Street Journal_ that the exchange rates for the Japanese Yen are as follows:

Spot rate for today's date	$.0098800
30-day forward rate	.0098808

You also know that the New York prime interest rate for 30-day loans is 5.6% per annum.

(a) What does the above information tell you, if anything, about the expected movement of foreign exchange rates over the next 30 days?

(b) What does the difference in the spot and forward rates for the Yen tell you, if anything, about interest rates in Japan as compared with interest rates in the United States?

(c) Is the 60-day forward rate likely to be higher or lower than the 30-day forward rate? Explain.

PROBLEMS

Problem 8-1

(Export transaction denominated in a foreign currency)

Power Golf Company exported 50,000 golf balls to a British retail chain at a price of EU 65,000 on July 1, 20x3. Payment was received on August 15, 20x3, and Power Golf deposited the check in a London Bank denominated in Euros. The following exchange rate information is available:

Spot rate July 1, 20x3	EU 1 = $ 1.050
45-day forward rate 4/1/x1	EU 1 = $ 1.060
Spot rate August 15, 20x3	EU 1 = $ 1.08

Required:

(a) Record all necessary journal entries by Power Golf for the sale and collection of the receivable.

(b) Explain the significance of the fact that Power Golf deposited the payment in a Euro denominated bank account with a balance of 125,000 Euros immediately prior to the deposit. Would the exchange gain or loss have been different had Power Golf sold the foreign exchange for dollars on August 15, 20x3?

(c) Assume that Power Golf had elected to hedge the foreign currency asset by selling Euros on the forward exchange market on July 1, 20x3. Record the journal entries necessary to account for the forward contract.

(d) Assume the customer's payment was deposited in a Euro denominated account as described in (b) above and that Power Golf settles the forward contract with a check drawn on this account. Explain the significance of the forward contract to the Euro balance remaining in the London bank after settlement of the contract.

Problem 8-2   **(Hedge on an asset position with interim adjustments)**

On October 1, 20x3, Big Sky Grain Company executed a forward contract to sell 100 million Yen to be delivered on March 31, 20x4. The purpose of the forward contract was to hedge an exposed net asset position arising from a sale of agricultural commodities to several Japanese customers. Relevant exchange rates for the Yen were as follows:

October 1, 20x3, spot	¥ 1 = U.S. $ .0083000
October 1, 20x3, 6-month forward	¥ 1 = U.S. $ .0082940
December 31, 20x3, spot	¥ 1 = U.S. $ .0083125
December 31, 20x3, 3-month forward	¥ 1 = U.S. $ .0082975
March 31, 20x4, spot	¥ 1 = U.S. $ .0083080

Required:

(a) Record the entry for the forward exchange contract on October 1, 20x3.
(b) Assuming that Big Sky Grain Company closes its books on December 31, 20x3, record the required adjusting journal entries related to the forward contract.
(c) Record the entries required to settle the forward contract on March 31, 20x4.

Problem 8-3   **(Managing foreign exchange risk)**

International Engineering Company, a Chicago-based consulting company, had the following assets on October 1, 20x1 (all values are in U.S. $):

Canadian dollar demand deposits	$125,000
Canadian dollar certificates of deposit, maturing 3/31/20x2	400,000
U.S. $ demand deposits	100,000
U.S. $ certificates of deposit maturing 12/31/20x1	250,000
Total	$875,000

International Engineering also has recently signed a contract for C$ 1,000,000 to provide consulting services in connection with a power plant being built in Canada. International will begin work on the contract on October 1, 20x1 and plans to complete all work within six months. The budget (in U.S. $) for the contract is as follows:

Contract price	$1,000,000
Salaries to be paid in C$	400,000
Salaries to be paid in U.S. $	200,000
Expenses to be paid in C$	150,000

On October 1, 20x1, the spot rate for the C$ was C$ 1 = U.S. $.75.

Required:

(a) Construct a sensitivity analysis for International Engineering's exposure to a 10% decline in the exchange rate over the next six months. Your analysis should show the potential impact on both the balance sheet and on the consulting contract.

(b) Based on your answer to (a), outline a strategy for managing the foreign exchange exposure for this company during the period of the contract.

Problem 8-4

(Hedge on a liability position with interim adjustments)

Fine Apparel, Inc., an upscale department store chain based in Philadelphia, imported 2,000 wool coats from an Italian supplier at a price of 300 Euros each. The coats were shipped F.O.B. Milan, Italy, on March 1, 20x2. Payment is due three months from the shipment date. Fine Apparel immediately entered into a three-month forward exchange contract to purchase 600,000 Euros. Fine apparel closes its books annually on April 30. Relevant exchange rates for the Euro are as follows:

Spot rate on March 1, 20x1	EU 1 = U.S. $ 1.08
3-month forward rate on March 1, 20x1	EU 1 = U.S. $ 1.085
Spot rate on April 30, 20x1	EU 1 = U.S. $ 1.075
Spot rate on May 31, 20x1	EU 1 = U.S. $ 1.09

Required:

Record all required entries by Fine Apparel for purchase of the coats, payment of the invoice, and the forward contract for the three months ending May 31, 20x1.

Problem 8-5

(Strategy and transactions for an identifiable foreign currency commitment)

On July 1, 20x3, Walker Company signed a contract to buy 25,000 electric motors from a Canadian supplier for C$40 each. The motors are to be delivered in two shipments. Half of the motors are due to be shipped on October 1, 20x3 and the remaining half on December 31, 20x3. Payment is due by electronic cash transfer on the shipment date.
(a) Outline a strategy for managing the foreign exchange risk associated with this contract.
(b) Given the following exchange rates for the Canadian dollar, record all required entries for your strategy.

July 1, 20x3 spot rate	C$ 1 = U.S. $ .7110
July 1, 20x3 3-month forward rate	C$ 1 = U.S. $ .7180
July 1, 20x3 6-month forward rate	C$ 1 = U.S. $ .7220
October 1, 20x3 spot rate	C$ 1 = U.S. $ .6990
December 31, 20x3 spot rate	C$ 1 = U.S. $ .6940

Problem 8-6

(Managing foreign exchange risk)

Double H Company had the following foreign currency assets and liabilities on January 1, 20x2:

Accounts receivable	Spot exchange rate per 1 US $
Australian – $ 20,000	1.5454
Euros – EU 100,000	.94
Greek Drachma – GD 5,000,000	305.46
Mexican Pesos – MP 10,000,000	9.385
Accounts payable	
Swedish Krona – SK 1,000,000	8.3735
Taiwan dollars – T$ 1,000,000	32.72

The accounts receivable, except for the Mexican Peso account, have an average maturity of 30 days. The Peso account is due in 90 days and is from a single customer. Both the accounts payable are due in 30 days.

Required:

(a) Describe the nature of the business risks, credit risks, and foreign exchange risks associated with the above accounts.

(b) Which, if any, of these accounts might be appropriate accounts to hedge with a forward contract? Explain the reasons for your answer.

Problem 8-7

(Foreign exchange transactions and hedging)

(a) Record the following transactions of Znono Company for the year 20x2.

1/1 Purchased 25,000 kilos of cheese from a French Wholesale Cooperative for 225,000 Euros. The spot rate for the Euro is U.S.$ 1.08 = EU 1. Payment is to be made on March 1.

1/31 The price of the Euro has risen to $1.10. Znono decides to hedge 200,000 Euros of the account payable with a 30-day forward contract. On this day, the 30-day forward rate for the Euro is U.S. $ 1.05 = EU 1.00.

3/1 Both the forward contract and the account payable are settled at a spot rate of U.S. $ 1.12 = EU1.

(b) How much did Znono lose by failing to hedge the account payable on 1/1, assuming the spot rate for EUI on 1/1 was $1.09 and the forward rate was $1.106.

Problem 8-8

(Speculating in foreign exchange)

On May 1, 20x1, UBETCHA Company purchased a forward exchange contract to deliver C$ 100,000 in six months. UBETCHA closes its books annually on June 30. The purpose of this forward contract was to speculate on future price movement of the Canadian $ relative to the U.S. $. Relevant exchange rates are as follows:

Spot rate on May 1, 20x1	C$ 1 = U.S. $ .765
6-month forward rate on May 1, 20x1	C$ 1 = U.S. $ .75
Spot rate on June 30, 20x1	C$ 1 = U.S. $ .74
4-month forward rate on June 30, 20x1	C$ 1 = U.S. $ .73
Spot rate on October 31, 20x1	C$ 1 = U.S. $ .78

Required:

(a) Is UBETCHA Company's forward position long or short? Explain. Based on their action, what can be inferred about UBETCHA Company management's expectations about future movement in the price of the C$ on May 1, 20x1?

(b) Record all entries that UBETCHA Company should make on account of the above forward contract.

Problem 8-9

(Speculating in forward exchange)

GAAP requires that speculative forward contracts be accounted for exclusively at forward rates until settlement of the contract at the spot rate on the settlement date.

Required:

(a) Explain how this procedure is different from a forward contract whose purpose is to hedge either an exposed asset or liability position or an exposed foreign currency commitment.

(b) What is the justification for the difference that you describe in (a)?

Problem 8-10

(Managing foreign exchange risk)

On December 31, 20x2, HOTSHOT Company has investments in four different European Companies. One of these companies transacts 90% of its business in Euros. The other three investments are in currencies that are tied to the Euro as a result of central bank policy in each of the three countries. The total amount of these investments is $15,000,000 at the spot rate for the Euro on December 31, 20x2. HOTSHOT Company management is concerned that the Euro, which is at a three-year high relative to the dollar, may fall as much as 15% during the next six months.

Required:

Outline three strategies that HOTSHOT could take in response to this situation and discuss the circumstances under which each might be appropriate.

Problem 8-11

(Speculative forward contracts)

On November 1, 20x4, ABC Company purchases a forward exchange contract to acquire 50,000,000 Yen to be delivered in three months. ABC has no other Yen denominated assets or liabilities and closes its book annually on December 31. Relevant exchange rates for the Yen are as follows:

Spot rate on November 1, 20x4	¥ 1 = U.S. $ .0082
3-month forward rate on November 1, 20x4	¥ 1 = U.S. $ .00835
Spot rate on December 31, 20x4	¥ 1 = U.S. $ .0083
1-month forward rate on December 31, 20x4	¥ 1 = U.S. $ .0084
Spot rate on January 31, 20x5	¥ 1 = U.S. $ .00845

Required:

(a) What is the expectation of ABC management with respect to movement of the Yen over the period of the forward contract? Were their expectations met? Explain.
(b) Record all necessary journal entries to account for the forward contract based on the data given.

Problem 8-12

(Hedging foreign exchange transactions)

Syntax Company had the following foreign exchange transactions during the year 20x1. Syntax closes its books on June 30 and prepares annual financial statements as of that date.

January 1: Syntax sold 200,000 English-German dictionaries to a European book distributor at a price of EU 2,000,000, payment to be made in 60 days.

March 1: Syntax signed a sales contract to print and deliver 30,000 literature textbooks to a Canadian distributor at a price of C$ 40 each. Deliver will take place on August 1.

June 1: Syntax signed a purchase contract to buy an offset press from a British manufacturer at a price of £100,000. Delivery of the equipment is to take place on October 1.

Syntax hedged all three of the above transactions with forward exchange contracts.

The following exchange rate data are available:

	Euro	C$	£
January 1 spot rate	$ 1.12		
60-day forward rate on January 1	1.11		
Spot rate on March 1	1.09	$ .80	
5-month forward rate on March 1		.78	
June 1 spot rate			$ 1.57
4-month forward rate on June 1			1.555
June 30 spot rate	1.095	.785	1.56
30-day forward rate		.775	
August 1 spot rate		.79	
October 1 spot rate			1.54

Required:

For each of the three primary events, record all required entries for the event and the related hedging transactions. Record the complete series of entries for the first event before going to the subsequent event.

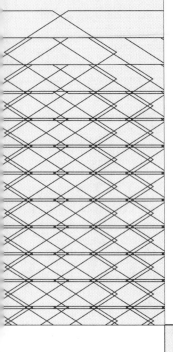

CHAPTER 9

TRANSLATION OF FOREIGN CURRENCY FINANCIAL STATEMENTS

LEARNING OBJECTIVES

- Explain the need for financial statement translation
- Demonstrate an understanding of the terminology used in translation
- Translate a foreign currency financial statement
- Remeasure a foreign currency financial statement
- Use the equity method to account for a foreign subsidiary
- Consolidate a foreign subsidiary
- Explain how to manage foreign exchange risk associated with foreign investments

THE NEED FOR TRANSLATED FINANCIAL STATEMENTS

In addition to the issues of international transactions and hedging discussed in Chapter 8, companies may also have a need to prepare financial statements that can be used to facilitate international investments. A company with no international operations may wish to make its financial statements more understandable to international investors, particularly to international mutual fund managers. A company that lists its securities for trading in another country will have to prepare financial statements that comply with the disclosure laws in that country. Finally, a U.S. company with investments required to be either accounted for by the equity method or consolidated with the parent company must translate the financial statements of its investees in order to accomplish these tasks.

Translation of a foreign currency financial statement is more complex than translating a document for several reasons. Three distinct phases are involved:

1. Translation of the language
2. Translation of the accounting principles
3. Translation of the currency

In absence of a legal requirement to follow a particular translation approach (such as in the case of reporting requirements for listing on a stock exchange), a foreign company wanting to provide financial information to U.S. investors has several alternatives. It could simply provide its foreign language financial statements to the U.S. investors. It could also provide what is called a **convenience statement,** which essentially involves translating only the language in the statements. A slightly more user-friendly form of the convenience statement involves translation of both the language and the currency, but does not translate any accounting principles. Neither of these alternatives is likely to be particularly satisfactory to U.S. investors, however. Assuming that the U.S. investor can read the foreign language of the reporting country, all three of the above alternatives fail to adjust for the most critical element of all in translation—the translation of the accounting principles. In order to understand the problem of financial statement translation more fully, let us examine the three steps in translation more fully.

Translation of the language

Any reader of this textbook is likely to have studied a foreign language and is thus aware that a literal translation of a sentence or phrase from another language may be inaccurate, nonsensical, or even misleading. This problem is particularly true for idiomatic speech or for technical terminology. Translation of financial statements is complicated by the fact that virtually all the words in the face of the statements are technical terms. These terms almost never translate literally. For example, the financial statements of the Michelin Group[1] report Net sales using the term "Chiffre d'affaires net," a term which when translated literally could mean something like "distinct business number." The terminology problem essentially means that even an accountant who is fluent in a foreign language would have difficulty with some of the terminology unless he or she had studied or worked in the country in question.

---

[1] A French Company, Groupe Michelin financial statements can be found in French and in English convenience translations at www.Michelin.fr.

Translation of the accounting principles

Differences in accounting principles make financial statements difficult to understand and interpret even after dealing with the technical terminology. For example, following French civil law requirements, Michelin reports goodwill amortization and income taxes as "Exceptional expenses" in a separate section of its income statement after previous sections that report "Trading income," "Financial income," and "Financial income and expense"—totals that are labeled as "Income from ordinary activities."[2] There has been some effort toward making financial statements more harmonious but barriers exist that will not be easily eliminated, even over very long periods of time. One important barrier to international harmonization of accounting principles rests in the legal systems. English-speaking countries such as the United States, Canada, Australia, and the United Kingdom all have a common law legal system[3] in which court precedents serve as an important source of future legal decisions. Civil law countries (most nations in Europe, Latin American, and some countries in Asia) have a legal system derived from the Justinian Code of ancient Rome. During the nineteenth century, European countries codified their legal systems for civil law, criminal law, commercial law, civil and criminal procedures, and for the penal codes. In a civil law country, legal decisions are almost exclusively based on interpretations of the code and not on legal precedent, which has little status in the courts. The implication for financial statements from this evolution is that **accounting principles are statues in civil law countries.** Whereas, in common law countries such as the United States, accounting principles are usually set in the private sector and the legal system only has oversight authority and responsibility. These fundamental differences in legal systems lead to the conclusion that full harmonization of accounting standards is unlikely to exist in the foreseeable future. Accordingly, a really useful translation of a foreign financial statement will require translation of accounting principles as well as language. Often, translation of the effects of different accounting principles is likely to be only an estimate because information may simply not be available to do more.

Translation of the currency

Upon initially reflecting on the translation process for the elements of a foreign currency financial statement, it would appear to be a relatively straightforward activity. Recall, however, from the previous chapter that exchange rates change from day to day and may change significantly over time. In theory, it is not well established which exchange rates should be used to translate the elements of financial statements. There have been, in fact, several different sets of translation procedures used by U.S. companies in the past, and current accounting principles allow for two different translation techniques depending upon the circumstances of each case. *FASB Statement 52,* which states current guidelines for financial statement translation, was passed by only a 4–3 vote of the board.[4] A separate section of this chapter discusses the theoretical

---

[2] If you find these captions unfamiliar based upon your study of U.S. accounting principles, it is because French company financial statement formats are at best only generally similar to those used in the United States, even after translating the language and technical terminology.

[3] The State of Louisiana and the Canadian province of Québec have legal systems based on French civil law.

[4] Statement of Financial Accounting Standards No. 52, *Foreign Currency Translation* (Norwalk, CT: Financial Accounting Standards Board, 1981), par. 38.

alternatives to translating the foreign currency numbers in financial statements and illustrates the currently accepted techniques.

TRANSLATION TERMINOLOGY

In addition to the terms introduced in Chapter 8, a number of technical terms are needed to explain the issues associated with translation of foreign currency financial statements. For purposes of this textbook, a **foreign currency** is any currency other than the U.S. dollar. The **local currency** is the currency of the local economy of any particular foreign company. We would normally expect that a foreign subsidiary would keep its books and records and prepare its financial statement in the local currency. There are, however, individual situations where a company may keep its accounting records in the currency of the parent company or that of another nation because of economic circumstances existing at the time. The weaker and less stable a local currency happens to be, the more likely that a company will find it useful or necessary to maintain its accounting records and denominate its transactions in the currency of another country.

The **reporting currency** of a company is the currency of the primary financial statements. In the case of a foreign subsidiary, the reporting currency is the currency of the parent company. For example, the reporting currency of a U.S. corporation with subsidiaries in several foreign countries is the U.S. dollar. Consequently, the reporting currency of the foreign subsidiaries is also the U.S. dollar. A parent company whose subsidiaries' financial statements are prepared in any currency other that the reporting currency must translate those statements prior to making equity adjustments or preparing consolidated financial statements. **The particular translation technique required depends on determination of the functional currency of the subsidiary.** This concept is discussed more fully in the following section.

Functional currency

The first step in translation of a foreign currency financial statement is determination of the **functional currency.** The functional currency of a foreign subsidiary is the currency of the primary economic environment in which the subsidiary operates. Upon first glance, we would normally expect that the local currency of a foreign subsidiary and its functional currency would be the same. For example, an Italian subsidiary of a U.S. parent company may be a semiautonomous operation, where labor and materials are purchased locally with payment made in the local currency (either the Euro or Italian Lire). In addition, the subsidiary may obtain a substantial amount of debt financing from banks or other institutions in Italy, with the interest and principal on these obligations payable in local currency. Under these circumstances, we would almost certainly conclude that the functional currency for this subsidiary would be the local currency.

There are a number of circumstances, however, where the functional currency of a foreign subsidiary might be other than the local currency. If a foreign subsidiary is little more than an entity that serves as a conduit through which export transactions are processed (essentially acting as a sales office), then its functional currency would likely be that of the parent company. *FASB Statement 52*[5] lists six **indicators** that provide guidance in determining the appropriate functional currency of a foreign entity.

---

[5] *Ibid.*, par. 42.

1. Cash flow indicators are concerned with whether the entity's cash flows are primarily in the local currency and have little impact on the parent company's cash flows or whether the parent company's cash flows are directly affected by the subsidiary's cash flows.
2. Sales price indicators are concerned with whether the sales prices of the foreign subsidiary's products are determined by local cost, demand, and supply conditions or are strongly affected by exchange rates between the foreign entity and its U.S. parent.
3. Sales market indicators allude to the question of whether the products of the foreign subsidiary are marketed locally on a widespread basis or whether the subsidiary was created to take advantage of lower labor costs with most of the production being shipped to the parent company domestic markets.
4. Expense indicators relate to the extent to which production inputs are obtained in the local market or whether these inputs are primarily components exported from the parent company and its domestic subsidiaries.
5. Financing indicators deal with whether financing is obtained from local sources or is primarily in dollar denominated obligations.
6. Intercompany transaction indicators deal with whether there is a low or high volume in intercompany transactions between the foreign subsidiary and its U.S. parent.

All of these indicators speak to the issue of autonomy of the foreign entity. The more autonomous the subsidiary is, the more evidence we have that indicates that the functional currency of the subsidiary is the local currency.

A final additional issue may also affect determination of functional currency. The stability and ease of convertibility of a local currency into other currencies affects the functional currency specification issue. A currency that is nonconvertible because of political instability or hyperinflation should not be designated as the functional currency of a foreign subsidiary. In extreme cases, the local currency may be so unstable as to not even be acceptable to local merchants in payment for purchases. In other cases, it may be accepted but not as desirable as the foreign currency. U.S. citizens who have traveled in less-developed nations have commonly experienced circumstances where they pay for purchases in dollars and receive "change" in the local currency that cannot be easily re-exchanged for dollars. Because of the inherent instability of the currency in a highly inflationary economy, the FASB has ruled that the functional currency in such a country is assumed to be the reporting currency without regard to other factors.[6]

Exchange rates used in translation

Three exchange rate terms are helpful in explaining the theory and practice of translating foreign currency financial statements. The **current rate** is defined as the spot rate on the date of the statement of financial position. *FASB 52* refers to the term *current rate* in a more general way, suggesting that a current rate is the rate on the date of any particular recent transaction, however, a more precise definition of the term *current rate* is used here. A **historical rate** is defined at the spot rate on any previous date—a date when a particular transaction of interest has occurred. Therefore, there are as many potential historical rates as there are dates (prior to the date of the statements) relevant to the translation. Finally, an **average rate** is defined at the weighted-average exchange rate for a

---

[6] *Ibid.*, par. 11. *FASB 52* operationally defines *highly inflationary* as a cumulative inflation rate over three years of approximately 100% or more.

time period relevant to the translation. As we shall see, the use of weighted average rates serves as a practical substitute for actual rates for most revenue and expense transactions.

TRANSLATING THE CURRENCY IN FOREIGN FINANCIAL STATEMENTS

Once the language and accounting principles of a foreign financial statement have been translated, the foreign currency values for the elements in the financial statements must be converted into the reporting currency. At first glance, this procedure would not appear to be particularly complex. Because exchange rates change over time, however, translation of the foreign currency amounts in a financial statement can constitute an accounting principle change as well. We shall see how choice of translation approach can affect accounting principles shortly. A second important issue is whether the gain or loss from the translation of a foreign currency financial statement should be included in income. Note that foreign financial statements are translated to make communication of financial position and performance more effective—an absolute necessity in the case of stock exchange listing, consolidation, or the need to make equity adjustments for a substantial influence common stock investment. The translation process does not involve or create cash flows; thus, translation gain or loss is not a cash flow. A translation gain or loss arises when the exchange rates used to translate the trial balance of a company vary according to the particular account being translated. The gain or loss is, quite simply, the "plug" figure in the translation. When the account balances in a trial balance are multiplied by several different exchange rates, the resulting trial balance will be out of balance by the amount of the translation effect, which will be a loss if the difference is a debit and a gain if the difference is a credit.

Historical issues in foreign currency translation

During the post-World War II era when the United States and other free enterprise countries were on the international gold standard, foreign currency translation was a minor topic in financial accounting for two reasons. In the first place, insofar as the United States was concerned, international trade was a significantly smaller component of gross national product than it is today. In 1945, both Europe and Japan were in ruins and much of the rest of the world was undeveloped. Secondly, the system of fixed exchange rates meant that all financial statement elements were translated at the same exchange rate. Whether an element was translated at a current rate, a historical rate, or an average rate was an unimportant question because all three rates were always the same. When necessary, foreign financial statements were usually translated using either the **current–non-current method** or the **monetary–non-monetary method**. These two approaches can be summarized as follows:

1. Current non-current method: Translate current assets and liabilities at current rates, non-current assets and liabilities at historical rates, income elements at actual or average rates, and capital at historical rates.
2. Monetary–non-monetary method: Translate monetary assets and liabilities at current rates, non-monetary assets and liabilities at historical rates, income elements at actual or average rates[7], and capital at historical rates.

---

[7] Generally, cost of goods sold, depreciation expense, amortization of prepaids, and amortization of intangible assets are translated at actual historical rates, while other expenses and revenues are translated at average rates.

Of these two alternatives, only the second approach had much theoretical merit. The monetary–non-monetary method of translation is internally consistent in that it applies the same exchange rate to items that are fundamentally alike. For example, the current exchange rate is used to translate both current liabilities and long-term liabilities if they are to be settled in cash (if they are both monetary items). This internal consistency also applies to items translated using historical rates. Under the monetary–non-monetary method, both inventory (a current asset) and plant and equipment (a non-current asset) are translated at historical rates. Since the current–non-current method is not consistent in this way, it has little merit as a means of translating the account balances in a foreign currency financial statement.

By the end of the decade of the 1960s, the countries ravaged by World War II had redeveloped to the point where they could again compete in the international marketplace. The resulting growth in international business continues to this day on an unprecedented scale. The United States, in particular, went from being a relatively self-sufficient economy to being completely involved in the international economy in the last third of the twentieth century. Thus, the subject of translation of foreign financial statements changed from being a non-issue for business corporations to one of major importance. The redevelopment of the European and Japanese economies after 1945 dramatically altered the United States balance of trade. The growing balance of payments deficits in the 1960s forced abandonment of the international gold standard, and the fixed exchange rate system was replaced by the floating exchange rate system we have today. Floating exchange rates meant that foreign financial statement translations would require reporting of translation gains and losses. As a consequence of these events, the subject of financial statement translation became an important current issue and the FASB initiated a currency translation project almost immediately after becoming fully operational.

The FASB ruled out use of either the current–non-current method or the monetary–non-monetary method of translation in favor of a variant of the monetary–non-monetary method called the temporal method. These conclusions were formalized in *FASB Statement No. 8*.[8] This approach is called **remeasurement** because it "remeasures" the foreign currency amounts in the financial statements without changing basic accounting principles, most importantly without violating the historical cost concept. A definition of remeasurement can serve as a basis for explaining how the historical cost basis is maintained by remeasurement.

> Remeasurement: Translate monetary items at current rates; non-monetary items carried at fair market value at current rates; non-monetary items carried at historical cost at historical rates; revenue and expense items at the rate on the date of the transaction (weighted average may be substituted); and contributed capital at historical rates. The remeasurement (translation) gain or loss is included in income.

To illustrate why remeasurement preserves the historical cost basis, consider the hypothetical case of an asset purchased by a German subsidiary for DM 100,000 in 19x3 when the price of one German Mark = $.25. The translated cost of that asset into U.S. dollars on the date of acquisition is $25,000 (DM 100,000 × $.25). Now assume three years had passed and the current exchange rate on the balance sheet date for December 31, 19x6 was $.40 = 1 DM. If the current exchange rate were used to translate the asset, its translated value would be $40,000 even though the historical

---

[8] *Statement of Financial Accounting Standards No. 8*, Foreign Currency Translation (Norwalk, CT: Financial Accounting Standards Board, 1975).

cost of the asset was $25,000. **Only the use of the historical rate will preserve the historical cost basis.** In *FASB Statement No. 8*, the FASB also took the position that a translation gain or loss reflected a change in the value of the Investment in a subsidiary and should therefore be included in income.

FASB Statement No. 8 was released during a period of time when exchange rates were particularly volatile and was very unpopular with U.S. business corporations that had significant international operations. They particularly disliked the requirement that translation gains and losses be included in income because those gains and losses were not represented by an actual cash flow. Companies actually adopted the practice of writing footnotes stating that the reported results under *FASB 8* were not representative of what had actually occurred, suggesting that financial statement readers should disregard the *FASB 8* disclosures. In 1981, the FASB superceded *FASB Statement No. 8* with *FASB Statement No. 52*. *FASB 52* specified that the method of translation be determined after the functional currency of the subsidiary was specified. **For relatively autonomous subsidiaries whose functional currency was the local currency, the FASB decided that the current rate method was appropriate.** While departing from the strict historical cost basis, the current rate method provides a measure of the current reporting currency values of the assets and liabilities, as well as the revenues and expenses. A definition of the current rate method **(Translation)** helps explain how this effect is accomplished.

> Translation: Translate all assets and liabilities at current rates; revenue and expense items at actual historical or weighted average rates; and contributed capital at the historical rate on the date of acquisition of the subsidiary or date of issue if later. The translation gain or loss is reported as an element of other comprehensive income.

This approach sidesteps the major objection to remeasurement by excluding the translation gain or loss from net income. Translation will also almost always produce a lower translation gain or loss than the remeasurement gain or loss in a remeasurement procedure. The translation gain or loss will be lower than the remeasurement gain or loss because translation makes virtually no use of historical rates for balance sheet elements (only contributed capital is translated at historical rates). Proponents of current rate translation also point out that the non-cash nature of translation gains and losses makes it appropriate to exclude them from determination of income. These proponents also point out that exchange rates for foreign currency often fluctuate up and down over time, thus the effects of short-term temporary exchange rate changes are often canceled out by later changes in the opposite direction.

FASB Statement 52 further specified that **remeasurement** using the temporal approach was required if the functional currency of the foreign entity was the reporting currency. In the unusual case of an entity whose functional currency was neither the local currency nor the reporting currency, a two-step approach would be necessary. First the local currency financial statements would be remeasured into the functional currency (a foreign currency other than the local currency). The resulting remeasured amounts would then be **translated** into the reporting currency using the current rate approach. Both translation and remeasurement are illustrated in the following sections.

Example of translation

As an example of translation for a foreign subsidiary whose functional currency is the local currency, assume that CanArt Corporation, a Canadian subsidiary of a U.S.

parent company, had a trial balance at December 31, 20x1, as shown in the first column of Exhibit 9-1. Further assume that CanArt was acquired by its U.S. parent on January 1, 19x8 and that ending retained earnings in the translated financial statements at December 31, 20x0 was U.S. $286,500. CanArt capital stock is unchanged since the date the subsidiary was acquired and the 20x1 dividends were declared on May 15, 20x1. Relevant direct exchange rates for one Canadian dollar are as follows:

	C$ 1 = U.S. $
January 1, 19x8	$.7522
May 15, 20x1—day the dividends were paid	.7650
Weighted average for the year 20x1	.7445
December 31, 20x1	.7710

Exhibit 9-1 shows the translation worksheet for CanArt Corporation for the year ended December 31, 20x1. The assets and liabilities are translated at the spot rate on December 31 of $.7710. The revenues and expenses are translated at the weighted average rate of $.7445, and the dividends are translated at the rate on the date of declaration of $.7650. Capital stock is translated at the historical rate—in this case, the date of acquisition of the subsidiary on January 1, 19x8 of $.7522.

The retained earnings balance in the trial balance is the beginning balance. Accordingly, this amount is determined in translation worksheets as follows:

1. The retained earnings on the acquisition date of the subsidiary is translated using the historical rate for the date of acquisition in the translation worksheet at the end of that year.
2. **Ending** retained earnings for any year is calculated: Ending retained earnings = beginning retained earnings + translated net income − translated dividends.[9]
3. **Beginning** retained earnings for all translation worksheets after the year of acquisition = ending retained earnings for the previous year as calculated in step 2.

After all of the above accounts are translated, the **equity adjustment from translation** is entered into the worksheet as the amount necessary to balance the trial balance. This account is an unrealized loss or gain and is reported as an element of other comprehensive income. Accumulated other comprehensive income is reported separately as an element of stockholders' equity. The translated trial balance is used by the parent company to account for the subsidiary investment on its books, using either the cost method or the equity method. After being recast into financial statement format, the trial balance is entered into the consolidated statements worksheet for purposes of preparing consolidated financial statements. This procedure is illustrated later in this chapter.

Example of remeasurement

Now assume that CanArt Corporation has a functional currency of the U.S. dollar. In this case, the trial balance must be **remeasured** using the temporal method. Recall that under the temporal method, monetary items (and non-monetary items carried at fair market value) are translated at current rates, and non-monetary items are translated at historical rates. The resulting translation gain or loss is included in income. As in the previous example, assume that CanArt was acquired on January 1, 19x8 and

---

[9] This calculation assumes that no other retained earnings transactions (stock dividends, treasury stock transactions) have occurred.

that ending retained earnings from the December 31, 20x0 translation was $284,000. Also assume that CanArt capital stock is unchanged since the date the subsidiary was acquired and the 20x1 dividends were declared on May 15, 20x1. In addition, the following information is available:

1. On January 1, 20x1 CanArt purchased equipment costing $20,000. All other plant and equipment was on hand on the date of acquisition of the subsidiary on January 1, 19x8. All equipment is depreciated using the straight-line method over 10 years, and buildings are depreciated using the straight-line method over 20 years.
2. CanArt uses the first-in, first-out method of inventory valuation. Its beginning inventory in Canadian dollars from the 12/31/x0 translation worksheet was C$ 21,000 and U.S.$ 16,000. Purchases in C$ occurred evenly throughout the year and were C$ 134,500. Ending inventory of C$ 30,000 was acquired during the last quarter of the year 20x1.
3. Other current assets consist of C$ 15,000 of prepaid insurance purchased on January 1, 20x1 and marketable securities of C$ 30,000 carried at fair market value.

EXHIBIT 9·1 CanArt Corporation
Translation from Canadian dollars to U.S. dollars—12/31/x1

Debits	Canadian Dollars	Translation Rate	Translated US $
Cash	C$ 118,500	0.7710	$ 91,364
Accounts receivable	76,550	0.7710	59,020
Inventories	30,000	0.7710	23,130
Other current assets	45,000	0.7710	34,695
Land	65,000	0.7710	50,115
Buildings	160,000	0.7710	123,360
Equipment	300,000	0.7710	231,300
Dividends	25,000	0.7650	19,125
Cost of goods sold	125,500	0.7445	93,435
Depreciation expense	38,000	0.7445	28,291
Other operating expenses	210,000	0.7445	156,345
Equity adjustment from translation			22,663
	1,193,550		932,843
Credits			
Accounts payable	25,150	0.7710	19,391
Long-term debt	70,000	0.7710	53,970
Accumulated depreciation—buildings	40,000	0.7710	30,840
Accumulated depreciation—equipment	145,000	0.7710	111,795
Capital stock	100,000	0.7522	75,220
Retained earnings January 1	336,400	**	286,500
Sales Revenue	477,000	0.7445	355,127
	C$1,193,550		$932,843

** This amount is carried forward from the previous years translation worksheet.

Relevant direct exchange rates for the Canadian dollar are as follows:

	C$ 1 = U.S. $
January 1, 19x8	$.7522
May 15, 20x1—day the dividends were paid	.7650
Weighted average for the year 20x1	.7445
January 1, 20x1	.7540
Weighted average for the last quarter of 20x1	.7690
December 31, 20x1	.7710

As Exhibit 9-2 shows, a remeasurement worksheet is substantially more complex than a translation worksheet. The general principles are that the monetary items of cash, accounts receivable, accounts payable, and long-term debt are translated at the current rate on the financial statement date. The non-monetary elements of inventories, plant and equipment, and contributed capital are translated at historical rates. The revenues and expenses are translated at average rates except for those elements that are derived from an asset translated at historical rates, particularly cost of goods sold and depreciation expense. Transactions associated with a specific date, such as dividends, are translated at the historical rate for the day of the transaction. Exhibit 9-2 shows that several complications arise in constructing a remeasurement worksheet. These complexities arise principally from the requirement to use historical rates for the translation of non-monetary assets. As the subsidiary acquires plant assets over time, it becomes necessary to make multiple calculations for the translated amounts of these assets because the historical rates for the various acquisitions are all different. These differences in turn affect the calculation of both accumulated depreciation and depreciation expense because, in remeasurement, the amounts for these accounts are derived from the asset balances. A similar problem occurs when translating cost of goods sold. In remeasurement, the beginning inventory, the purchases for the year, and the ending inventory are all translated at different exchange rates. The calculations for these amounts are shown in the sub-schedules for Exhibit 9-2. After all the accounts are translated, the **translation loss** is entered into the accounts as the amount necessary to balance the trial balance. In remeasurement, this amount is included in income rather than deferred as in the case of translation using the current rate method. The theory underlying remeasurement is that the financial statement should report financial position and results of operations as if the books and records of the subsidiary had been kept in the reporting currency. The use of historical rates for non-monetary assets and the inclusion of the translation gain or loss in income accomplish this objective.

ACCOUNTING FOR AN INVESTMENT IN A FOREIGN SUBSIDIARY

An investment in a foreign company accounted for by the cost method is done in exactly the same way as for a domestic investment. The only periodic entry required under the cost method is for dividends received. A dividend from a foreign investment is reported as income under the cost method and translated using the spot rate on the date received. Under the equity method, an investment in a foreign company must report unrealized "equity adjustment" income in addition to equity income. This equity adjustment amount is obtained from the equity adjustment account in the subsidiary's translated trial balance. In addition, an amortization of cost-book value differential in a current rate translation must be based on an allocation schedule initially prepared in foreign currency.

EXHIBIT 9·2   CanArt Corporation
Remeasurement from Canadian dollars to U.S. dollars—12/31/x1

Debits	Canadian Dollars	Translation Rate	Translated US $
Cash	C$ 118,500	0.7710	$ 91,364
Accounts receivable	76,550	0.7710	59,020
Inventories	30,000	(a)	23,070
Other current assets	45,000	(c)	34,440
Land	65,000	0.7522	48,893
Buildings	160,000	0.7522	120,352
Equipment	300,000	(d)	225,696
Dividends	25,000	0.7650	19,125
Cost of goods sold	125,500	(b)	93,065
Depreciation expense	38,000	(e)	28,587
Other operating expenses	210,000	0.7445	156,345
Translation loss			26,911
	1,193,550		926,868
Credits			
Accounts payable	25,150	0.7710	19,391
Long-term debt	70,000	0.7710	53,970
Accumulated depreciation—buildings	40,000	0.7522	30,088
Accumulated depreciation—equipment	145,000	(f)	109,073
Capital stock	100,000	0.7522	75,220
Retained earnings January 1	336,400	*	284,000
Sales Revenue	477,000	0.7445	355,127
	C$1,193,550		$926,868

Calculations for worksheet

Cost of goods sold:				
Beginning inventory	C$ 21,000	**	$ 16,000	
Purchases	134,500	0.7445	100,135	
Goods available	155,500		116,135	
Ending inventory	(30,000)	0.7690	(23,070)	(a)
	125,500		93,065	(b)
Other current assets:				
Prepaid insurance	15,000	0.7540	11,310	
Marketable securities	30,000	0.7710	23,130	
	45,000		34,440	(c)
Equipment:				
On hand January 1, 19x8	280,000	0.7522	210,616	
Purchased January 1, 20x1	20,000	0.7540	15,080	
	300,000		225,696	(d)
Depreciation expense:				
On equipment on hand 1/1/19x8	28,000	0.7522	21,062	
On equipment purchased 1/1/20x1	2,000	0.7540	1,508	
On buildings	8,000	0.7522	6,017	
	38,000		28,587	(e)
Accumulated depreciation—equipment:				
Balance 1/1/20x1	115,000	0.7522	86,503	
Depreciation expense for 20x1	30,000	***	22,570	
Balance 12/31/20x1	C$ 145,000		$109,073	(f)

* This amount is carried forward from the previous years translation worksheet.   ** Beginning inventory balance from the previous year's translation worksheet.   *** From depreciation calculation above ($21,062 + $1,508 = $22,570)

Applying the equity method to a translated financial statement

Referring again to Exhibit 9-1, assume that U.S. Parent Company, acquired 100% of CanArt Corporation on January 1, 19x8 for C$ 300,000 when CanArt stockholders' equity consisted of C$ 100,000 of capital stock and C$ 150,000 of retained earnings. The excess of cost over book value was considered to be patents with a 10-year life. An allocation schedule in C$ as of the date of acquisition is as follows:

		Canadian $
Price of investment		C$300,000
Stockholders equity of CanArt		
Common stock	C$100,000	
Retained earnings	150,000	250,000
Patents		50,000
Amortization per year (10 years)		C$ 5,000

The equity adjustments for the year 20x1 are derived from the translated trial balance (Exhibit 9-1) and the above allocation schedule. The net income from Exhibit 9-1 is:

		U.S. $
Sales		$355,127
Cost of goods sold	$ 93,435	
Depreciation expense	28,291	
Other operating expenses	156,345	278,071
		$ 77,056

Four equity adjustments are recorded, one each for the income from subsidiary, dividends from subsidiary, the equity adjustment from translation, and the amortization of cost-book value differential. These entries are shown in Exhibit 9-3. Entry (1) for the income from subsidiary is taken from the translation worksheet as calculated above. Entry (2) for the dividend from subsidiary is also taken from the translation worksheet (U.S.$ 19,125 from Exhibit 9-1). Entry (3), the equity adjustment, results from the fact that the equity adjustment account in the translation worksheet is not included in income under the current rate method. Since the equity adjustment is essentially an **unrealized income** account, an entry is required for it just as for **realized** income. Since the equity adjustment account is an unrealized income account, the parent company equity entry is made for the current year's change in this account. This amount is determined by comparing the balance in the equity adjustment on the translation worksheet for the current year with the ending balance for the previous year. Assume that the **20x0** equity adjustment from the translation worksheet was an $18,400 debit. The equity entry for the year **20x1** is determined as follows:

20x1 Equity adjustment balance per Exhibit 9-1	$ 22,663 debit
20x0 Equity adjustment balance (assumed)	18,400 debit
Current year equity entry for the change in equity adjustment	$ 4,263 debit

Thus entry (3) in Exhibit 9-3 records the equity adjustment as a debit on U.S. Parent Company books and reduces the investment in CanArt Corporation account. The equity adjustment recorded under the equity method is included in the stockholders' equity accounts of the parent company.

Entry (4) records the amortization of cost-book value differential. This calculation has two components. First, the foreign currency amount of cost-book value differential amortization is translated at the average rate for the year. Second, the change in the unamortizated differential over the year is determined as the difference between the beginning balance for the year at the appropriate historical rate less the ending balance at the current rate. The difference between the amortization amount at average rates and the decline in the unamortized balance of differential is an addition to (or deduction from) the equity adjustment recorded in entry (3). This calculation for the CanArt Corporation illustration is as follows:

	C$	Rate	U.S. $
Unamortized differential 1/1/x1	C$35,000	0.7540	$26,390
Unamortized differential 12/31/x1	30,000	0.7710	23,130
Decrease in unamortized differential (credit investment)			3,260
Amortization of differential (debit income from Sub)	5,000	0.7445	3,723
Equity adjustment (credit)			$ (463)

EXHIBIT 9-3

(1)	Investment in CanArt Corporation	77,056	
	Income from CanArt Corporation		77,056
	(To record equity income for the year 20x1)		
(2)	Cash	19,125	
	Investment in CanArt Corporation		19,125
	(To record dividends received in the year 20x1)		
(3)	Equity adjustment	4,263	
	Investment in CanArt Corporation		4,263
	(To record equity adjustment)		
(4)	Income from CanArt Corporation	3,723	
	Equity adjustment		463
	Investment in CanArt		3,260
	(To record differential amortization per schedule)		

Applying the equity method to a remeasured financial statement

Under remeasurement, the equity method is applied as if the books of the subsidiary had been kept in the reporting currency. As a result, the equity adjustments are virtually identical to the case of a domestic subsidiary. In our example for the CanArt Corporation, an allocation schedule for the acquisition is translated using the historical rate as of the date of acquisition. The exchange rate on this date, January 1, 19x8, was C$ 1= U.S. $ .7522 as used in Exhibit 9-2. The allocation schedule for the acquisition, translated into U.S. $, is as follows:

		Canadian $	Exchange Rate	U.S. $
Price of investment		C$300,000	0.7522	$225,660
Stockholders' equity of CanArt				
Common stock	C$100,000		0.7522	–
Retained earnings	150,000	250,000	0.7522	188,050
Patents		50,000	0.7522	37,610
Amortization per year (10 years)		5,000	0.7522	3,761

CanArt Corporation net income for the year 20x1 can be calculated from the translation worksheet (Exhibit 9-2) as follows:

Sales		$355,127
Cost of goods sold	$ 93,065	
Depreciation expense	28,587	
Other operating expenses	156,345	
Translation loss	26,911	304,908
		$ 50,219

The entries to account for the Investment in CanArt under the equity method for the year 20x1, assuming the functional currency of CanArt is the U.S. $, are shown in Exhibit 9-4. Only two entries are required. The subsidiary net income under remeasurement includes the translation loss as calculated above. The dividend entry is identical to the translation case.

EXHIBIT 9-4

(1)	Investment in CanArt Corporation	50,219	
	Income from CanArt Corporation		50,219
	(To record equity income for the year 20x1)		
(2)	Cash	19,125	
	Investment in CanArt Corporation		19,125
	(To record dividends received in the year 20x1) (per Exhibit 9-1)		

COMPREHENSIVE ILLUSTRATION—CONSOLIDATION OF A FOREIGN SUBSIDIARY

As in the previous illustrations, a foreign subsidiary of a U.S. Parent Company could have as its functional currency either the local currency or the reporting currency. Perhaps the most common case is that of the functional currency being the local foreign currency. In both cases, four steps are required for the analysis and consolidation of the subsidiary:

1. Analyze the acquisition using an allocation schedule.
2. Translate the foreign currency financial statements of the subsidiary.
3. Account for the investment in the subsidiary on the books of the parent company.
4. Prepare a consolidated statements worksheet for the parent and the subsidiary.

Case of functional currency = local currency

Assume that U.S. Intl Company, a domestic corporation, acquires 100% of Continental, SA (a French Company) whose functional currency is the Euro (EU). The acquisition occurred on January 1, 20x1 for a price of EU 250,000. The excess of cost over book value is attributable to copyrights with a 5-year life.

ALLOCATION SCHEDULE. The allocation schedule in Euros and the relevant exchange rates are shown below:

		Euros	Spot rate 1/1/x1	U.S. $
Price of Continental, SA		€250,000	1.10	$275,000
Common stock	100,000			
Retained earnings	125,000	225,000	1.10	247,500
Copyrights (5-year life)		25,000	1.10	27,500
Amortization		5,000	1.14	5,700
Exchange rates for the year 20x1				
January 1		$ 1.10		
November 15—dividend date		1.12		
Weighted average for the year		1.14		
December 31		1.15		

TRANSLATION WORKSHEET. A translation worksheet for the year 20x1 for Continental, SA is shown in Exhibit 9-5. The assets and liabilities are translated at the current (December 31) rate and income/expense accounts are translated at the weighted average rate for the year. The dividends are translated at the rate in existence on the date the dividends were paid of $1.12. The capital accounts are translated at the historical rate for the date of acquisition (January 1). Note that only the date of acquisition retained earnings is translated using an exchange rate. At the end of the year 20x1 and for all future years, ending retained earnings will be calculated by taking beginning retained earnings, adding net income, and subtracting dividends.

BOOK ENTRIES FOR THE INVESTMENT IN THE SUBSIDIARY. The equity adjustments for the Investment in Continental, SA are shown in Exhibit 9-6. The amounts for these entries are derived from the translation worksheet. The first entry records the acquisition of $275,000 of 100% of Continental's capital stock (see the allocation schedule above). The second entry records receipt of the dividends on November 15, 20x1 in the amount of $11,200 based on the spot rate on that date. Continental's net income for the year is shown at the bottom of Exhibit 9-5, calculated from the translated trial balance. This income is recorded by the parent company in the third entry. The income is composed of two elements: (1) the realized net income of $35,910 as calculated and (2) the unrealized income—the **equity adjustment** of $11,265. Since the unrealized equity adjustment is a credit, the combined debit to the investment account is $47,175. The last entry amortizes the $27,500 of copyrights for the year. This entry has two components. The amortization amount of $5,700 is determined by multiplying the foreign currency amortization of EU 5,000 times the average exchange rate for the year (EU 5,000 × $1.14 = $5,700). For a domestic subsidiary, the credit to the investment account equals the amount of the differential amortization. However, in this case, the credit to the investment account is equal to the decrease in the unamortized differential as measured by the difference between the translated differential at the beginning of the year as compared with the end of the year. This decrease is shown below the amortization entry in Exhibit 9-6 as $4,500. The difference between these two amounts represents the increase in the value of the investment due to change in exchange rates and is a $1,200 unrealized gain, credited to the equity adjustment account.

EXHIBIT 9-5   Continental, SA
Translation from Euros to U.S. dollars—12/31/x1

Debits	Euros EU	Translation Rate	Translated US $
Cash	€15,000	1.15	$ 17,250
Accounts receivable	44,000	1.15	50,600
Inventories	37,500	1.15	43,125
Other current assets	12,000	1.15	13,800
Land	20,000	1.15	23,000
Buildings	150,000	1.15	172,500
Equipment	36,000	1.15	41,400
Dividends	10,000	1.12	11,200
Cost of goods sold	48,500	1.14	55,290
Depreciation expense	11,000	1.14	12,540
Other operating expenses	18,000	1.14	20,520
	402,000		461,225
Credits			
Accounts payable	30,000	1.15	34,500
Accumulated depreciation—buildings	20,000	1.15	23,000
Accumulated depreciation—equipment	18,000	1.15	20,700
Capital stock	100,000	1.10	110,000
Retained earnings January 1	125,000	1.10	137,500
Sales Revenue	109,000	1.14	124,260
Equity adjustment			11,265
	€402,000		$ 461,225

Translated Net Income of Continental, SA

Sales		$124,260
Expenses:		
Cost of goods sold	$ 55,290	
Depreciation expense	12,540	
Other operating expenses	20,520	88,350
Net Income		$ 35,910

ELIMINATION ENTRIES. The elimination entries for the consolidation are shown in Exhibit 9-7. The only difference between these entries and the entries for a domestic subsidiary is in the second entry where the subsidiary equity adjustment account is also eliminated. Note that equity adjustment is an equity account and thus would be eliminated on consolidation, along with all other equity accounts. The worksheet for consolidated financial statements is shown in Exhibit 9-7. The only difference between this worksheet and that for a domestic subsidiary is the existence of the equity adjustment on the parent's books, which is carried forward on consolidation. This account is its unrealized gain or loss resulting from changes in exchange rates.

EXHIBIT 9-6 Equity adjustments for Investment in Continental, SA

1/1/x1	Investment in Continental, SA	275,000	
	Cash		275,000
11/15/x1	Cash (or Investment in Euros)	11,200	
	Investment in Continental, SA		11,200
12/31/x1	Investment in Continental, SA	47,175	
	Income from Continental		35,910
	Equity adjustment		11,265
12/31/x1	Income from Continental	5,700	
	Investment in Continental		4,500
	Equity adjustment		1,200

Calculation of equity adjustment for copyright amortization:		
Copyrights 1/1/x1 (EU 25,000 × $1.10)		$ 27,500
Copyrights 12/31/x1 (EU 20,000 × $1.15)		23,000
Decrease (credit to Investment in Continental)		4,500
Amortization (EU 5,000 × $1.14)		5,700
Equity adjustment		$ (1,200)

Case of functional currency = reporting currency

Exhibit 9-8 illustrates a remeasurement of Continental, SA, under the assumption that Continental's functional currency is the U.S. $, the reporting currency of the parent company. In this illustration, it is assumed that the ending inventory and other current assets were acquired during the last three months of the year when the exchange rate for the Euro averaged $1.145. The other operating expenses are assumed to consist of amortization of EU 8,000 of prepaid assets on hand at the date of acquisition, with the remaining balance of EU 10,000 of cash expenses incurred evenly over the year.

Remeasurement is nothing more than translation of the financial statement using the **temporal** method, an approach that preserves the historical cost basis of the subsidiary assets. In Exhibit 9-8, the monetary elements (cash, accounts receivable, and accounts payable) are translated using the current rate—the spot rate on the date of the financial statements. All non-monetary elements are translated using the appropriate historical rate—either the rate for the date the item arose or the rate on the date the subsidiary was acquired if later. The elements translated using historical rates in Exhibit 9-8 are Inventories, Other current assets, Land, Buildings, Equipment, Accumulated depreciation, Capital stock, and Retained earnings. Note Retained earnings is translated using historical rates only on the date of acquisition. All subsequent beginning of year retained earnings balances are obtained from the previous year's financial statements.[10] All income statement elements are translated at average rates except for cost of goods sold, depreciation, and other operating expenses, which

---

[10] Recall that retained earnings at the end of any year is beginning retained earnings from the previous translation + translated net income − translated dividends.

contain elements related to specific assets that were translated at historical rates. In Exhibit 9-8, depreciation expense is translated at the historical rates for the acquisition date of the subsidiary because the assets were on hand on that date. The cost of goods sold and other operating expense translations are illustrated at the bottom of Exhibit 9-8 based on the historical rates for the amounts that make up their totals. Sales revenue is translated at the average rate for the year 20x1.

EXHIBIT 9-7 US Int and Continental, SA
Worksheet for Consolidated Financial Statements

Statement of Income	US Int	Continental	Eliminations				Consolidated	
For the Year ended 12/31/x3								
Sales	$ 169,790	$ 124,260					$ 294,050	
Income from Continental	30,210		(1)	30,210			–	
Cost of sales	(75,000)	(55,290)					(130,290)	
Depreciation expense	(15,000)	(12,540)					(27,540)	
Operating expenses	(24,000)	(20,520)	(3)	5,700			(50,220)	
Net Income	86,000	35,910					86,000	
Retained earnings—1/1/x1	125,000	137,500	(2)	137,500			125,000	
Add: net income	86,000	35,910					86,000	A
Less: Dividends	(30,000)	(11,200)			(1)	11,200	(30,000)	
Retained earnings, Dec. 31	181,000	162,210					181,000	B
Balance sheet 12/31/x3								
Cash	42,500	17,250					59,750	
Accounts receivable	60,000	50,600					110,600	
Inventories	53,100	43,125					96,225	
Other current assets	10,000	13,800					23,800	
Land	10,000	23,000					33,000	
Buildings	40,000	172,500					212,500	
Accumulated depr—Blds	(22,000)	(23,000)					(45,000)	
Equipment	76,000	41,400					117,400	
Accumulated depr—Equip	(20,000)	(20,700)					(40,700)	
Investment in Continental	306,475				(1)	19,010	–	
					(2)	287,465		
Copyrights			(2)	28,700	(3)	5,700	23,000	
	556,075	317,975					590,575	
Accounts payable	62,610	34,500					97,110	
Long-term debt	100,000	–					100,000	
Common stock	200,000	110,000	(2)	110,000			200,000	
Retained earnings	181,000	162,210					181,000	B
Equity adjustment	12,465	11,265	(2)	11,265			12,465	
	$ 556,075	$ 317,975					$ 590,575	

The equity adjustments and elimination entries for the remeasurement are shown in Exhibit 9-9. These are done in the same way as for a domestic subsidiary. Because the functional currency of the subsidiary is the reporting currency, there are no complications in these entries related to the foreign currency. The consolidation worksheet is shown in Exhibit 9-10. It is also prepared in essentially the same manner as is the case for a domestic subsidiary.

EXHIBIT 9·8 Continental, SA
Remeasurement from Euros to U.S. dollars—12/31/x1

Debits	Euros EU	Translation Rate	Translated US $
Cash	€15,000	1.150	$ 17,250
Accounts receivable	44,000	1.150	50,600
Inventories	37,500	1.145	42,938
Other current assets	12,000	1.145	13,740
Land	20,000	1.100	22,000
Buildings	150,000	1.100	165,000
Equipment	36,000	1.100	39,600
Dividends	10,000	1.120	11,200
Cost of goods sold	48,500	(a)	54,103
Depreciation expense	11,000	1.100	12,100
Other operating expenses	18,000	(b)	20,250
	402,000		448,781
Credits			
Accounts payable	30,000	1.150	34,500
Accumulated depreciation—buildings	20,000	1.100	22,000
Accumulated depreciation—equipment	18,000	1.100	19,800
Capital stock	100,000	1.100	110,000
Retained earnings January 1	125,000	1.100	137,500
Sales Revenue	109,000	1.140	124,260
Remeasurement gain			721
	€402,000		$ 448,781

Remeasured Net Income of Continental, SA

Sales		$ 124,260	
Expenses:			
Cost of goods sold	$ 54,103		
Depreciation expense	12,100		
Other operating expenses	20,250	(86,453)	
Remeasurement gain		721	
Net Income		$ 38,528	

(a) Cost of goods sold			
Beginning inventory	25,000	1.100	$ 27,500
Purchases	61,000	1.140	69,540
Ending Inventory	(37,500)	1.145	(42,938)
Cost of goods sold	48,500		54,103

(b) Other operating expenses			
Amortization of beginning balances	8,000	1.100	8,800
Cash purchases during the year	10,000	1.145	11,450
			$ 20,250

EXHIBIT 9-9 Equity adjustments for Investment in Continental, SA
Remeasurement case

1/1/x1	Investment in Continental, SA	275,000	
	Cash		275,000
11/15/x1	Cash (or Investment in Euros)	11,200	
	Investment in Continental, SA		11,200
12/31/x1	Investment in Continental, SA	33,028	
	Income from Continental		33,028
	(Continental net income of $38,528 – $5,500 amorization)		
	Elimination entries		
12/31/x1	Income from Continental	33,028	
	Dividends—Continental		11,200
	Investment in Continental		21,828
	Common stock—Continental	110,000	
	Retained earnings—Continental	137,500	
	Copyrights	27,500	
	Investment in Continental		275,000
	Operating expenses	5,500	
	Copyrights		5,500
	($27,500 ÷ 5 years = $5,500)		

Managing foreign exchange risk associated with foreign investments

An investment in a foreign subsidiary carries risks associated with foreign exchange as well as the normal elements of risk related to any investment in another company. Assuming that the investment in the foreign subsidiary may be sold at some time in the future, its value at that time will be a function of its expected future profitability and the value of the foreign currency on that date. A parent company may wish to engage in hedging activities designed to mitigate the potential adverse consequences of a decline in the value of the foreign currency in which it has a substantial foreign investment. Since foreign investments are essentially long-term propositions, forward exchange contracts are not particularly well suited to hedge the risks associated with these investments. A more useful approach is to take out a loan in the foreign currency. This strategy offsets the foreign currency risk associated with the investment in the foreign subsidiary (an asset) with a long-term liability denominated in the foreign currency. Because the investment in the foreign subsidiary is generally for an indefinite term while the loan must be made for a specific term, this hedging strategy cannot normally be expected to cover all foreign exchange risks. However, a company may wish to pursue such a strategy under some conditions.

If the investment in the subsidiary is accounted for using the equity method and the subsidiary's financial statements are translated using the current rate method, the effects of changes in exchange rates are reflected in the parent's **equity adjustment** account as shown in Exhibit 9-6. A loan in a foreign currency on the books of the parent company will produce a foreign exchange loss if the value of the foreign currency rises and a foreign exchange gain if the value of the foreign exchange falls. **While this gain or loss is a realized gain or loss,** *FASB 52* requires that it also be reported as an equity adjustment because its purpose was to hedge the investment in the foreign subsidiary.

EXHIBIT 9-10 US Int and Continental, SA
Worksheet for Consolidated Financial Statements

Statement of Income	US Int	Continental	Eliminations				Consolidated	
For the Year ended 12/31/x3								
Sales	$ 169,790	$ 124,260					$ 294,050	
Income from Continental	33,028		(1)	33,028			–	
Cost of sales	(75,000)	(54,103)					(129,103)	
Depreciation expense	(15,000)	(12,100)					(27,100)	
Operating expenses	(24,000)	(20,250)	(3)	5,500			(49,750)	
Remeasurement gain		721					721	
Net Income	88,818	38,528					88,818	
Retained earnings—1/1/x1	125,000	137,500	(2)	137,500			125,000	
Add: net income	88,818	38,528					88,818	A
Less: Dividends	(30,000)	(11,200)			(1)	11,200	(30,000)	
Retained earnings, Dec. 31	183,818	164,828					183,818	B
Balance sheet 12/31/x3								
Cash	42,500	17,250					59,750	
Accounts receivable	60,000	50,600					110,600	
Inventories	53,100	42,938					96,038	
Other current assets	10,000	13,740					23,740	
Land	10,000	22,000					32,000	
Buildings	40,000	165,000					205,000	
Accumulated depr—Blds	(22,000)	(22,000)					(44,000)	
Equipment	76,000	39,600					115,600	
Accumulated depr—Equip	(20,000)	(19,800)					(39,800)	
Investment in Continental	296,828				(1)	21,828	–	
					(2)	275,000		
Copyrights			(2)	27,500	(3)	5,500	22,000	
	546,428	309,328					580,928	
Accounts payable	62,610	34,500					97,110	
Long-term debt	100,000	-					100,000	
Common stock	200,000	110,000	(2)	110,000			200,000	
Retained earnings	183,818	164,828					183,818	B
	$ 546,428	$ 309,328					$ 580,928	

For example, assume that the EU 250,000 investment in Continental, SA in Exhibit 9-6 was hedged on 1/1/x1 with an EU 250,000 loan due in five years. Further assume that the loan carries an interest rate of 6% with interest payable annually on December 31. On December 31, 20x1, the principle of this loan would be adjusted to the spot rate for the Euro and the interest would be paid. The exchange gain or loss on the liability, which would normally be included in income, is deferred as equity adjustment because the foreign exchange gain or loss on the investment is also deferred. The entries for this loan during the year 20x1 are illustrated in Exhibit 9-11. The equity adjustment on this loan results from two entries. Since interest expense is recorded at the average rate and the cash payment for interest is recorded at the spot rate at the end of the year, a $150 equity adjustment debit is recorded in the second entry. The third entry is an equity adjustment equal to the $12,500 exchange loss resulting from the increase in the spot rate for the Euro from $1.10 to $1.15 during the year 20x1.

EXHIBIT 9-11 Entries to hedge the investment in Continental with an EU 250,000 loan at 6%

1/1/x1	Cash	275,000	
	Notes payable		275,000
	(EU 250,000 × $1.10)		
12/31/x1	Interest expense	17,100	
	Equity adjustment	150	
	Cash		17,250
	(EU 250,000 × 6% × $1.14 = $17,100)		
	(EU 250,000 × 6% × $1.15 = $17,250)		
12/31/x1	Equity adjustment	12,500	
	Notes payable		12,500
	[EU 250,000 × ($1.15 − $1.10)]		

SUMMARY

The following learning objectives were stated at the beginning of the chapter:

- Explain the need for financial statement translation
- Demonstrate an understanding of the terminology used in translation
- Translate a foreign currency financial statement
- Remeasure a foreign currency financial statement
- Use the equity method to account for a foreign subsidiary
- Consolidate a foreign subsidiary
- Explain how to manage foreign exchange risk associated with foreign investments

Two factors made translation of foreign currency financial statements an important topic. Economic development in the post-World War II era greatly increased international business, increasing the amount of international trade and international investment. Abandonment of the international gold standard around the year 1971 meant that translation of the currency amounts in a foreign currency financial statement was no longer a straightforward process. The variation in exchange rates over time resulted in translation gains and losses, the size of which is affected by the particular translation method employed.

FASB 52 requires translation by the current rate method of foreign currency financial statements whose functional currency is the local currency. This procedure is relatively straightforward because historical exchange rates do not play a major role in the process. Current rate translation is complicated, however, by the FASB requirement to treat the translation gain or loss as an element of deferred income. The existence of deferred income and cost-book value differential (based on a foreign currency allocation schedule) also somewhat complicates both the parent company's equity adjustments and the consolidated statements worksheet.

If the functional currency of a foreign subsidiary is deemed to be the reporting currency, *FASB 52* requires translation using the so-called remeasurement approach. Because it requires historical exchange rates for historical cost elements, remeasurement is usually a more complex procedure than is current rate translation. The equity adjustment entries and the consolidation worksheet are virtually identical to a domestic subsidiary because the translation adjustment is included in income and the allocation schedule is prepared in the currency of the parent company.

Investment in a foreign company carries risks not normally encountered in investments in domestic companies. This risk is derived from the potential decline in value of the investment associated with depreciation in value of the foreign company's local currency vis-à-vis the currency of the parent company. A parent company may wish to hedge this investment by taking out a long-term loan denominated in the foreign currency. Under current accounting standards, the exchange gain or loss on the foreign currency loan is reported as an equity adjustment if the subsidiary financial statements are translated using the current rate method.

QUESTIONS

1. Explain why translation of the language in a financial statement is probably a more difficult task than translating a newspaper article.
2. Explain the meaning of the terms *foreign currency*, *local currency*, and *reporting currency*.
3. Define the term *functional currency*. Discuss the criteria that must be considered when determining the functional currency of a company.
4. Why is it unlikely that an unstable currency could be the currency of the primary economic environment of any company?
5. Define three concepts of exchange rates that are used in foreign currency translation.
6. Why was foreign currency translation a less important issue during the fixed exchange rate era than it is today?
7. Explain why temporal translation is called "remeasurement."
8. Discuss the issues, pro and con, for reporting translation gains or loss as an element of net income.
9. Explain how the ending retained earnings balance is calculated in a financial statement translation.
10. Explain the procedures for calculating equity adjustments for a foreign subsidiary when the current rate translation method is used.

EXERCISES

Exercise 9-1

(Multiple choice: select the best answer for each item.)

1. Which of the following is **not** a reason for translating a financial statement?
   a. To facilitate arrangement of a forward exchange contract
   b. To record equity adjustments for a foreign investee
   c. To consolidate a foreign subsidiary
   d. To comply with securities laws for listing of securities on a stock exchange
2. A convenience translation could **not** involve translation of
   a. language.
   b. accounting principles.
   c. currency.
   d. all of the above.

3. The currency of the local economy of a foreign subsidiary is called
   a. the foreign currency.
   b. the local currency.
   c. the functional currency.
   d. the historical currency.
4. In determining the functional currency of a foreign subsidiary, consideration should be given to
   a. where the subsidiary is selling its goods and services.
   b. the significance of intercompany transactions as compared with all business activity.
   c. the extent to which production inputs are purchased locally.
   d. all of the above.
5. Under the current rate method, which of the following accounts is translated using the current exchange rate on the financial statement date?
   a. Retained earnings
   b. Operating expenses
   c. Land
   d. Depreciation expense
6. Under the current rate method, which of the following assets is translated using a historical exchange rate?
   a. Capital stock
   b. Sales
   c. Allowance for bad debts
   d. Cost of goods sold
7. Under the current rate method, average exchange rates may usually be used for
   a. revenues and expenses.
   b. all expenses except depreciation and cost of goods sold.
   c. dividends.
   d. retained earnings.
8. Under remeasurement, which of the following assets is translated using historical exchange rates?
   a. Land
   b. Accumulated depreciation—buildings
   c. Capital stock
   d. All of the above
9. Under remeasurement, which of the following accounts would be translated at weighted average rates?
   a. Cash
   b. Cost of goods sold
   c. Sales revenue
   d. All of the above
10. Under remeasurement, which of the following assets wold usually be translated at a specific historical rate?
    a. Accounts payable
    b. Retained earnings
    c. Dividends
    d. Interest expense

Exercise 9-2   (Exchange rates for current-rate translation)

Hartford Company is a 90%-owned British subsidiary of All American Company, a U.S. Corporation. Hartford's functional currency is the British £. The acquisition occurred January 1, 20x0. All American is currently working to prepare consolidated financial statements for the year 20x1. Given the following exchange rates for the British £, indicate which will be used for the accounts of Hartford Company in the schedule below. If any item is not translated using the rates provided, indicate the answer is (f) and write a separate paragraph explaining how the U.S. dollar amount of that item is obtained.

(a) Spot rate 1/1/20x0
(b) Spot rate 1/1/20x1
(c) Spot rate 5/5/20x1
(d) Average rate for the year 20x1
(e) Spot rate 12/31/20x1
(f) Other (specify rate and appropriate date)

Item	Rate
1. Cash	
2. Accounts receivable	
3. Inventories	
4. Investments	
5. Land	
6. Building	
7. Accumulated depreciation—building	
8. Patents	
9. Goodwill	
10. Accounts payable	
11. Long-term debt	
12. Capital stock	
13. Retained earnings	

Exercise 9-3

(Acquisition of a foreign subsidiary)

Presidio Corporation acquired 100% of the outstanding common stock of Standifer Company (a British Corporation) on January 1, 20x1 for $675,000. On the date of the acquisition, Standifer had the following stockholders' equity balances:

Account	Balance
Capital stock	£ 40,000
Retained earnings	360,000
Total	£ 400,000

On January 1, 20x1, the spot rate for the £ was £ 1 = $ 1.50. Any excess of cost over book value was considered to be patents with a 10-year life. For the year ended December 31, 20x1, the weighted average exchange rate was £ 1 = $1.52.

Required:

1. Assume the functional currency of Standifer is the British £. Prepare an allocation schedule and compute patent amortization in U.S. dollars for the year 20x1.
2. Assume the functional currency of Standifer is the U.S. $. Prepare an allocation schedule and compute patent amortization for the year 20x2.

Exercise 9-4

(Selecting exchange rates for translation)

Using the appropriate letter corresponding to the exchange rates below, indicate how the accounts in the table would be converted to the reporting currency under (A) current rate translation and (B) remeasurement.
   a. Historical rate
   b. Weighted average rate
   c. Current rate
   d. Based on a calculation

	Current rate	Remeasurement
1. Cash		
2. Notes receivable		
3. Inventory		
4. Land		
5. Equipment		
6. Sales revenue		
7. Salaries expense		
8. Interest expense		
9. Depreciation expense		
10. Capital stock		
11. Retained earnings		

Exercise 9-5

(Internet exercise)

Go to the International Accounting Standards Board (IASB) Web site, www.iasb.org.uk. Find the summary of the business combinations standard—*IASB Standard No. 22*. Contrast the criteria for Uniting of Interests with the criteria for Pooling of Interests as defined in APB Opinion 17. How are these criteria different?

Exercise 9-6

(Internet exercise)

Go to the International Accounting Standards Board Web site, www.iasb.org.uk. Find the summary of *IASB Standard No. 21*, "The Effects of Changes in Foreign Exchange Rates." Contrast the requirements for translation of "foreign entities that are integral to the operations of the parent" and the requirements for "Other Foreign Entities" with the requirements of *FASB Statement 52*.

Exercise 9-7

(Internet exercise; classroom presentation)

Go to the International Accounting Standards Board Web site, www.iasb.org.uk. Find the list of member bodies. Locate a member in another country that has a URL link in English or another language that you read. (For example, there is a URL for the Ordre des Experts Comptables in France available in both English and French). Write a one-page report summarizing the information you find. Be prepared to make a five-minute presentation on your research.

Exercise 9-8

(Internet exercise)

Using the IASB Web site, find a URL for a Chartered Accountants or Certified Public Accountants Organization/Institute in a country located outside North America. For example, the Institute of Certified Public Accountants of Singapore has the URL: www.accountants.org.sg. Write a one-page report summarizing the requirements for membership in the organization/institute you find. Be prepared to make a five-minute presentation on your paper.

Exercise 9-9

(Understanding translation)

Remeasurement (temporal method translation) preserves the historical cost basis of accounting in financial statements, whereas translation (current rate method) does not preserve the historical cost basis. Assume that Passport Company, a German subsidiary of a U.S. corporation, has Equipment purchased on January 1, 1994 for 50,000 Marks. The exchange rate for the Mark on January 1, 19x4 was DM 1 = $.67. On the date of the most recent annual report, December 31, 20x2, the exchange rate for the Mark was DM 1 = $.52.

Required:

(a) Compute the U.S. $ value for the equipment as translated using both remeasurement and translation.

(b) Using the results you obtained in (a), explain how remeasurement preserves the historical cost basis whereas translation does not.

Exercise 9-10   (Understanding translation)

All foreign financial statement translation approaches will produce a translation gain or loss as long as more than one exchange rate is used in the translation process. The translation gain or loss results from the fact that the translated accounts will result in a trial balance where the total of the debit balance accounts are either greater or less than the total of the credit balance accounts. What potential dispositions are available for disclosure of the translation gain or loss? Discuss some arguments in favor of each.

PROBLEMS

Problem 9-1   (Translation and equity adjustments)

Pierpoint Company acquired a 90%-interest in Sandstone Company (a Canadian corporation) for U.S. $500,000 on January 1, 20x2 when Sandstone had the following stockholders' equity. Any differential is assumed to be trademarks with a 10-year life.

	Canadian $
Common stock	C$ 200,000
Retained earnings	400,000
Total	C$ 600,000

On the date of acquisition, the spot rate for the Canadian $ was C$ 1 = U.S. $ .80. The functional currency of Sandstone is the C$. At December 31, 20x2, Sandstone had the following C$ trial balance.

	Canadian $
Cash	C$ 210,000
Other current assets	350,000
Inventory	200,000
Investments (at market value)	230,000
Equipment—net	80,000
Depreciation expense	250,000
Other operating expenses	20,000
Dividends declared	30,000
	C$ 1,370,000
Sales	C$ 500,000
Common stock	400,000
Retained earnings	470,000
	C$ 1,370,000

Dividends were paid on May 15 and November 15 in the amount of C$ 15,000 on each date. Other relevant exchange rates during the year 20x1 are as follows:

	CS =
Spot rate on January 1, 20x2	U.S. $ .80
Average rate for the year 20x2	U.S. $ .76
Spot rate on December 31, 20x2	U.S. $ .74
Spot rate on May 15, 20x2	U.S. $ .78
Spot rate on November 15, 20x2	U.S. $ .75

Required:

(1) Translate the trial balance of Sandstone using the current rate method.
(2) Prepare all equity adjustments that Pierpoint Company would make on its books during the year 20x2 for its investment in Sandstone.
(3) Compute the balance in the account Investment in Sandstone for the year ended December 31, 20x2.

Problem 9-2 **(Translation and equity adjustments)**

Valentine Company acquired a 100%-interest in Sandini Company (an Italian Corporation) on January 1, 20x3 at a price of EU 300,000. On this date, Sandini had the following stockholders' equity:

	Euros (000's)
Capital stock	€200
Retained earnings	80
	€280

Any cost-book value differential is considered to be copyrights with a 10-year life. Plant assets were all acquired prior to 1/1/x3. The inventory on hand at the end of 20x3 was purchased during the fourth quarter of the year. Sandini's inventory on January 1, 20x3 was 20,000 Euros. Other current assets on Sandini's balance sheet consist of prepaid expenses that were incurred evenly throughout the year. Relevant exchange rates for the Euro during the year 20x3 are as follows:

	EU 1 = U.S. $
January 1	1.10
April 1	1.12
October 1	1.14
December 31	1.15
Weighted average for the 4th quarter	1.13
Weighted average for the year	1.125

At December 31, 20x3 Sandini had the following trial balance:

	000's of Euros
Cash	€40
Accounts receivable	70
Inventory	75
Other current assets	25
Land	50
Buildings	100
Equipment	200
Dividends	20
Cost of goods sold	150
Other operating expenses	50
	780

	000's of Euros (cont.)
Sales	300
Accumulated depreciation—Buildings	40
Accumulated depreciation—Equipment	80
Capital stock	200
Retained earnings	160
	€780

Dividends were paid April 1 and October 1 in the amount of EU 10,000 on each date. The functional currency of Sandini Company is the Euro. Other current assets consist of prepaid expenses incurred evenly throughout the year.

Required:

(1) Prepare a translation worksheet for the Sandini trial balance at December 31, 20x3.
(2) Record Valentine Company's equity adjustments for its Investment in Sandini Company for the year 20x3.
(3) Compute the balance in the account Investment in Sandini as of December 31, 20x3.

Problem 9-3   **(Remeasurement worksheet)**

Refer to the data for problem 9-2. Assume that the functional currency of Sandini Company is the U.S. dollar. Assume the inventory was acquired during the last quarter of the year. Also assume that the plant assets were all acquired prior to 1/1/x2. Sandini's inventory on January 1 was 20,000 Euros. Prepare a remeasurement worksheet.

Problem 9-4   **(Remeasurement worksheet)**

Southpark Corporation, a Canadian Subsidiary of Pathmaker Company (a U.S. Corporation) had a trial balance as shown below on December 31, 20x2. Southpark was acquired by Pathmaker on January 1, 19x9. There have been no changes in Southpark's contribution capital since that date.

	Canadian $
Cash	C$ 25,000
Accounts receivable	44,000
Inventories	35,000
Land	65,000
Buildings	70,000
Equipment	40,000
Dividends	10,000
Cost of goods sold	55,000
Depreciation expense	13,000
Other operating expenses	32,000
	389,000
Accounts payable	17,000
Long-term debt	48,000
Accumulated depreciation—buildings	27,000
Accumulated depreciation—equipment	30,000
Common stock	60,000
Retained earnings 1/1	102,000
Sales revenue	105,000
	C$389,000

Relevant exchange rate information is as follows:

	C$ 1 = U.S. $
Spot rate, January 1, 19x9	$.7540
Spot rate, July 1, 20x2 (dividend date)	.7430
Weighted average rate for 20x2	.7500
Spot rate January 1, 20x2	.7450
Spot rate December 31, 20x2	.7480
Weighted average rate for November–December, 20x2	.7470

Additional information:
1. The functional currency of Southpark is the U.S. dollar.
2. Retained earnings as translated in the December 31, 20x1 financial statements was U.S. $ 87,000.
3. On January 1, 20x2, Southpark acquired a building for C$ 30,000. All other plant and equipment was on hand on the date of acquisition.
4. Southpark uses the FIFO method of inventory valuation. Beginning inventory in C$ from the previous years' worksheet was C$ 30,000 and US$ 22,000. Purchases in C$ during the year 20x2 occurred evenly throughout the year and were C$ 60,000. Ending inventory of C$ 35,000 was acquired during the last two months of the year.
5. Depreciation rates were 10% straight-line for buildings and 15% straight-line for equipment.

Required:

Prepare a remeasurement worksheet for Southpark for the year ended December 31, 20x2.

Problem 9-5   (Translation worksheet)

Refer to the data for problem 9-4. Assume that the functional currency of Southpark is the Canadian $. Prepare a translation worksheet for the year ended December 31, 20x2.

Problem 9-6   (Internet project)

Do an Internet search on the name of a prominent foreign company (Daimler Chrysler, Matsushita, Michelin, Royal Dutch, Fiat, Nestle, Ciba-Geigy, Pernod-Ricard, Denso, Toyota, Thyssen, or another company suggested by your instructor). Try to find the company's home page. Respond to the following questions or discuss the issues in class:
1. Were you able to find the financial statements of the company? If not, why do you think this information is not available on the Internet?
2. What other information is available about the company on its Web site?
3. Find a set of financial statements for a foreign company. Characterize the nature of the financial statements —language(s), translations, accounting principles, currency. Did you find the information user-friendly?

Problem 9-7   (Internet project)

Find a foreign company annual report on the Internet whose financial statements are in English or another language you read. See problem 9-6 for examples of companies whose reports may be available. (Note: At the time this book was written, European company financial statement data was widely available on company home pages. Asian company data was more difficult to find.) Answer the following questions.
1. Is the annual report data available in more than one language? List these.

2. Refer to the English translation financial statements. Do the financial statements appear to be in U.S. accounting principles? Explain.
3. Find the footnotes to the financial statements. Is there a footnote that describes the principles of consolidation of the company's foreign subsidiaries? Characterize the readability of this footnote. How have subsidiaries been reported in the consolidated financial statements?
4. Refer to the consolidated statement of income. Describe the method of disclosing the financial effect of non-recurring (extraordinary items or similar event) items. Do these disclosures appear to be consistent with U.S. reporting standards?
5. Describe two items in the financial statements that appear to be unique to the company or to the country in which the company headquarters are located. Why are such items not found in the financial statements of U.S. corporations?

Problem 9-8

(Consolidation of a foreign subsidiary)

Paragon Company acquired a 100% interest in Groupe Pascal, S.A. (a French company) on January 1, 20x0 for a price of EU 300,000. On this date, Pascal had capital stock outstanding in the amount of EU 100,000 and retained earnings of EU 150,000. All Pascal assets and liabilities had book values approximately equal to fair market values except that excess of cost over book value is attributable to patents with a 10-year life. Relevant exchange rates for the acquisition and subsequent events are as follows:

	EU 1 = U.S. $
January 1, 20x0	$ 1.12
May 15, 20x0 (dividend date)	1.11
Weighted average for the year 20x0	1.13
December 31, 20x0	1.14

At the end of the year 20x0, Pascal had a trial balance as shown in the translation worksheet below. Following this schedule is a worksheet for consolidated financial statements for the two companies.

PROBLEM 9-8 (A) Groupe Pascal, SA
Translation from Euros to U.S. dollars—12/31/x0

Debits	Euros EU	Translation Rate	Translated U.S. $
Cash	€ 55,000	1.14	$ 62,700
Accounts receivable	52,000	1.14	59,850
Inventories	65,000	1.14	74,100
Other current assets	22,000	1.14	25,080
Land	50,000	1.14	57,000
Buildings	80,000	1.14	91,200
Equipment	100,000	1.14	114,000
Dividends	20,000	1.11	22,200
Cost of goods sold	147,500	1.13	166,675
Depreciation expense	20,000	1.13	22,600
Other operating expenses	45,000	1.13	50,850
	657,000		746,255
Credits			
Accounts payable	32,500	1.14	37,050
Accumulated depreciation—buildings	24,000	1.14	27,360
Accumulated depreciation—equipment	25,500	1.14	29,070
Capital stock	100,000	1.12	112,000

Retained earnings January 1	150,000	1.12	168,000
Sales Revenue	325,000	1.13	367,250
Equity adjustment			5,525
	€ 657,000		$ 746,255

Translated Net Income of Group Pascal, SA

Sales		$ 367,250
Expenses:		
Cost of goods sold	$ 166,675	
Depreciation expense	22,600	
Other operating expenses	50,850	240,125
Net Income		$ 127,125

PROBLEM 9-8 (B)

Statement of Income For the Year ended 12/31/x0	Paragon	Pascal	Consol
Sales	$ 205,000	$ 367,250	
Income from Pascal	121,475		
Cost of sales	(94,000)	(166,675)	
Depreciation expense	(21,000)	(22,600)	
Operating expenses	(31,000)	(50,850)	
Net Income	180,475	127,125	
Retained earnings—1/1/x0	315,000	168,000	
Add: net income	180,475	127,125	
Less: Dividends	(30,000)	(22,200)	
Retained earnings, Dec. 31	465,475	272,925	
Balance sheet 12/31/x0			
Cash	54,000	62,700	
Accounts receivable	66,000	59,850	
Inventories	123,000	74,100	
Other current assets	32,500	25,080	
Land	20,000	57,000	
Buildings	50,000	91,200	
Accumulated depr—Blds	(18,000)	(27,360)	
Equipment	77,000	114,000	
Accumulated depr—Equip	(19,000)	(29,070)	
Investment in Pascal	441,750		
Patents	—	—	
	827,250	427,500	
Accounts payable	87,300	37,050	
Long-term debt	188,000	–	
Common stock	80,000	112,000	
Retained earnings	465,475	272,925	
Equity adjustment	6,475	5,525	
	$ 827,250	$ 427,500	

Required:

(1) Prepare the four entries necessary on Paragon Company books to account for its investment in Groupe Pascal, S.A., during the year 20x0 assuming Paragon uses the equity
method of accounting. (Note these entries should produce a balance in the Investment in

Pascal account at the end of the year equal to the balance shown in the consolidated statements worksheet).

(2) Complete the worksheet for consolidated financial statements for the two companies.

Problem 9-9 (Consolidation of a foreign subsidiary)

Permian Company acquired a 100% interest in NWT Mining Company (a Canadian corporation) on January 1, 20x3 for a price of U.S. $496,800, at which time the spot rate for the Canadian dollar was C$ 1 = U.S. $.72. On this date, NWT mining had capital stock of C$ 300,000 and retained earnings of C$ 330,000. Any excess of cost over book value is assumed to be copyrights with a 10-year life. Relevant exchange rates for the year 20x3 are as follows:

	C$ 1 = U.S. $
January 1, 20x3	$ .72
July 15, 20x3 (dividend date)	.77
Weighted average for the year 20x3	.78
December 31, 20x3	.75

A translation worksheet and partially completed worksheet for consolidated financial statements are shown below. Permian company uses the equity method to account for its investment in NWT.

PROBLEM 9-9 (A) NWT Mining, Inc.
Translation from Canadian dollars to U.S. dollars—12/31/x3

Debits	Canadian Dollars	Translation Rate	Translated U.S. $
Cash	C$ 97,000	0.75	$ 72,750
Accounts receivable	125,000	0.75	93,750
Inventories	225,000	0.75	168,750
Other current assets	32,500	0.75	24,375
Land	80,000	0.75	60,000
Buildings	100,000	0.75	75,000
Equipment	340,000	0.75	255,000
Dividends	10,000	0.77	7,700
Cost of goods sold	455,000	0.78	354,900
Depreciation expense	35,000	0.78	27,300
Other operating expenses	80,000	0.78	62,400
	1,579,500		1,201,925
Credits			
Accounts payable	52,500	0.75	39,375
Long-term debt	57,000	0.75	42,750
Accumulated depreciation—buildings	80,000	0.75	60,000
Accumulated depreciation—equipment	156,000	0.75	117,000
Capital stock	300,000	0.72	216,000
Retained earnings January 1	330,000	0.72	237,600
Sales Revenue	604,000	0.78	471,120
Equity adjustment			18,080
	C$ 1,579,500		$ 1,201,925

Translated Net Income of NWT Mining

Sales		$ 471,120
Expenses:		
Cost of goods sold	$ 354,900	
Depreciation expense	27,300	
Other operating expenses	62,400	444,600
Net Income		$ 26,520

PROBLEM 9-9 (B)

Statement of Income For the Year ended 12/31/x3	Permian	NWT Mining
Sales	$ 844,000	$ 471,120
Income from NWT Mining	21,840	
Cost of sales	(345,000)	(354,900)
Depreciation expense	(90,000)	(27,300)
Operating expenses	(112,000)	(62,400)
Net Income	318,840	26,520
Retained earnings—1/1/x3	564,856	237,600
Add: net income	318,840	26,520
Less: Dividends	(60,000)	(7,700)
Retained earnings, Dec. 31	823,696	256,420
Balance sheet 12/31/x3		
Cash	263,456	72,750
Accounts receivable	244,000	93,750
Inventories	305,300	168,750
Other current assets	34,000	24,375
Land	60,000	60,000
Buildings	120,000	75,000
Accumulated depr—Blds	(35,000)	(60,000)
Equipment	235,000	255,000
Accumulated depr—Equip	(89,000)	(117,000)
Investment in NWT	531,000	
Copyrights		
	1,688,756	572,625
Accounts payable	25,000	39,375
Long-term debt	400,000	42,750
Common stock	400,000	216,000
Retained earnings	823,696	256,420
Equity adjustment	20,060	18,080
	$ 1,688,756	$ 572,625

Required:

(1) Prepare an allocation schedule for the acquisition in Canadian $.
(2) Prepare the equity adjustments for the year 20x3 on the books of the parent company.
(3) Prepare the worksheet for consolidated financial statements for the two companies.

Problem 9-10   **(Managing foreign exchange risk)**

Partridge Company has a $20 million investment in Giant Cola, Inc., a wholly owned subsidiary located in the country of Awnferania. Awnferania, a nation with a population of 60 million people, has a very unstable currency due to political instability and low economic growth. Until approximately 18 months ago, Partridge expected that the new government would undertake economic reforms designed to strengthen the free market system and promote economic growth. The subsidiary, Giant Cola, Inc. is a soft-drink maker, and Partridge management believed that growing economic prosperity in Awnferania would result in strong market growth for soft drinks. The local currency, the Af $, depreciated 25% relative to the U.S. dollar during the previous 12 months, a rate that is expected to continue for at least another year.

Required:

Discuss the economic issues affecting Partridge Company with respect to the above investment. In particular, discuss how the depreciating currency might or might not affect the value of the investment. Contrast the nature of an investment in a foreign subsidiary as compared with a monetary asset denominated in a foreign currency in your answer. Are there any additional steps that Partridge might take to minimize its foreign exchange risks?

Problem 9-11   **(Consolidation of a foreign subsidiary)**

An incomplete consolidated statements worksheet for Far-East, Inc. and its wholly owned subsidiary SPP, Inc., is shown below. The amounts for the subsidiary have already been remeasured into U.S. dollars—the functional currency of the subsidiary. Any excess of cost over book value is assumed to be goodwill with an indefinite life.

PROBLEM 9-11 Far-East, Inc. and Subsidiary

Statement of Income *For the Year ended 12/31/x1*	Far-East, Inc.	SPP, Inc.
Sales	$325,000	$ 134,500
Income from SPP	51,500	
Cost of sales	(98,000)	(55,000)
Depreciation expense	23,000	23,000
Operating expenses	(32,500)	(19,000)
Remeasurement gain		14,000
Net Income	223,000	51,500
Retained earnings—1/1/x1	110,000	125,000
Add: net income	223,000	51,500
Less: Dividends	(25,000)	(8,600)
Retained earnings, Dec. 31	308,000	167,900
Balance sheet 12/31/x1		
Cash	65,700	22,000
Accounts receivable	75,600	34,000
Inventories	113,400	34,500
Other current assets	10,000	12,000
Land	20,000	34,900
Buildings	30,000	125,000
Accumulated depr—Blds	(12,000)	(35,000)
Equipment	89,000	31,500
Accumulated depr—Equip	(31,000)	(4,000)
Investment in SPP	250,000	
Goodwill		
	610,700	254,900

Accounts payable	62,700	12,000
Long-term debt	40,000	30,000
Common stock	200,000	45,000
Retained earnings	308,000	167,900
	$ 610,700	$ 254,900

Required:

Prepare a worksheet for consolidated financial statements for Far-East, Inc., and subsidiary.

INDEX